SRI LANKA THE COOKBOOK

SRI LANKA
THE COOKBOOK

PRAKASH K SIVANATHAN
NIRANJALA M ELLAWALA
PHOTOGRAPHY BY KIM LIGHTBODY

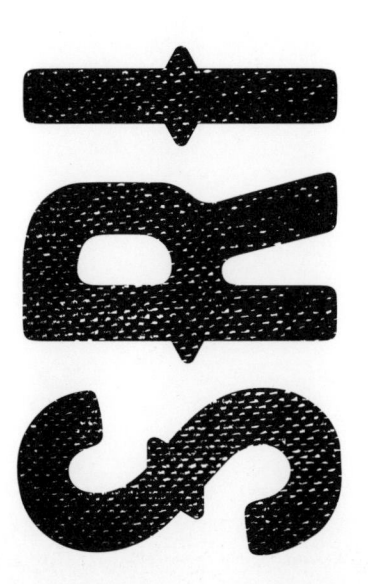

F FRANCES LINCOLN

7	INTRODUCTION
11	ABOUT THE AUTHORS
12	GLOSSARY
16	CURRY POWDERS
20	RECIPES
250	INDEX

KEY

● Tamil

● Sinhalese

 Vegetarian

 Fish

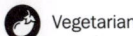 Meat

● Desserts

INTRODUCTION

Golden beaches fringed with palm trees, tea plantations on misty mountaintops, non-stop, traffic-packed cities, elephants, leopards, bananas, tuk-tuks and rainforests: Sri Lanka is the South Asian paradise of imagination, and so much more. It's intensely spiritual, deeply religious, tropical, ancient, booming; it's damaged by war and natural disaster but resilient, open to tourism but still traditional. It has been inhabited by native peoples since prehistoric times, but over the years its abundant natural resources and strategic position in the Indian Ocean has made it attractive to waves of colonisers.

The first Europeans, from Portugal, set foot on the island's shores in 1505, but for centuries before this it was frequented by merchants, mainly from Arabia, who came for exquisite spices and precious stones.

A period of Dutch control followed from 1658 to 1796, whereupon the British arrived and ruled what they called Ceylon until its independence in 1948. But Sri Lanka today shows influences from every era, from every group who lived in the country and fell for its bewitching charms. Now, in the twenty-first century, there is still a Muslim community who can claim lineage back to the Arab traders; many people in coastal areas in the south-west practise Catholicism and have Portuguese surnames; and the Dutch and British left fine colonial buildings. And the British introduced cricket, which was taken up with gusto by Sri Lankans and has become the national sport.

Today, Sri Lanka is dominated by two distinct groups: the majority Sinhalese, who are concentrated in the south, central and west of the island, and the Tamils, mostly found in the north and east. There are differences: separate languages (Sinhala has roots in north-east India, and Tamil can be traced back to southern India), unique traditions and cultures, and religion, whereby Sinhalese practise Buddhism and Tamils are mainly Hindus. The island also has smaller Christian and Muslim populations.

This mosaic of diversity has led to Sinhalese and Tamil styles of cooking developing their own identities. This, coupled with the tropical vegetables, vibrant spices and bounteous seafood, has given Sri Lankan cuisine a singular style, subtly different from that of its enormous neighbour to the north, India.

But this cultural split also led to the horrific civil war of 1983 to 2009, which pitted the government forces against Tamil Tiger insurgents, and also set Sinhalese against

Tamil, neighbour against neighbour, Sri Lankan against Sri Lankan. It cast a dark shadow over the island and is unfortunately still sometimes the first thing the world associates with the country. But since the end of the war in 2009, reparation efforts have been made and visitors are able to appreciate what really is a peaceful, united and beautiful island. Development continues apace, with new railways, infrastructure and hotels, but it remains a unique country, and one, most importantly, with incredible food.

Sri Lanka is a place where two separate peoples and cultures exist side-by-side, and as such Sinhalese and Tamil cooking each have their own characteristics, with both well represented in this book. They show influences of the southern and eastern states of India, but also have idiosyncratic traces of the foods of the countries that have colonised the island. The south is a green and lush land where cardamom, cloves and black pepper grow plentifully. 'Ceylon cinnamon' is acknowledged to be the best in the world. The Sinhalese, who mainly inhabit this region, use these spices more than Tamils. They are mostly a Buddhist people, so most (but not all) eat very little meat, meaning Sri Lanka (and this book!) is wonderful for vegetarians. Many Sinhalese follow the principles of Ayurveda: 'food is medicine, medicine is food', and believe plants and spices have powerful healing properties.

The north and east of the island has a shorter rainy season, more suited to crops of chilli, which is incorporated into the more fiery recipes of the Tamils, as you'll notice. Tamils say there are six tastes, 'arusuvai': sweet, sour, bitter, spicy, salty and astringent, and that every meal should be a harmonious balance of all. Tamils and Sinhalese are more likely to eat meat – chicken, usually, or goat. The cow is a sacred animal in Hinduism and so beef isn't seen often, although some cattle are kept by the Christian and Muslim communities.

But there is plenty of common ground: the humble coconut, in the form of its flesh, milk and oil, is used universally, as is rice, the staple carbohydrate, and lentils. Curry leaves are a vital part of many Sinhalese and Tamil dishes too. Vegetables grow so well in the warm, rainy climate that no day passes without a meal using juicy tomatoes, fragrant pineapples and jackfruit, or aubergines, beans and gourds. And the warm waters of the Indian Ocean provides the island with copious fish and shellfish, almost all wild – tuna, large trevally (jack fish), swordfish, kingfish, and prawns, squid and shrimp.

Sri Lankans tend to tuck into hearty breakfasts of string hoppers with curry and sambol relish, generous lunches and smaller, uncomplicated dinners in the evening. 'Short eats' are small takeaway snacks taken at any time of the day, and sold by shouting vendors in railway carriages and lively beachfronts; they include fish patties, crunchy lentil vadai and mince rolls. The classic Sri Lankan meal is 'rice and curry', a simple-sounding name that belies the thought and detail that goes into its preparation. It consists of a balance of several spiced, colourful curries, perhaps a dal, and some bread or rice, as well as accompaniments of sambol relish or pickle. It's a generous spread, and you could try it for a dinner party or special occasion, but for everyday cooking you'll find that two or even one of the dishes in this book make a memorable meal on their own.

ABOUT THE AUTHORS

My wife and I have lived in London for many years, but I was born a Tamil in the Jaffna peninsula in the north of Sri Lanka, and Niranjala is a Sinhalese from the south. Between us, we have a deep understanding and love of the unique styles of cooking that together make up our island's cuisine.

Niranjala was brought up in the hill country of Sri Lanka, in Ratnapura and Balangoda. Her father owned a tea factory and plantations, in a rural, rainy area famous for this crop. Her talent in cooking stems from her early childhood, when she would steal clay pots and ingredients from the kitchen with her sister and cook outside using a makeshift fire in a hidden spot in the garden. As a young girl she would watch her mother and the house maids make dishes with local produce, gradually learning their recipes.

At that time there were no restaurants, so cooking was done at home, although street hawkers could always be found selling their wares at markets, temples and festivals. Food was a way of life that brought together Sri Lankans of every ethnicity.

My mother and father were both excellent cooks too – unusual in an era when men were mostly banned from the kitchen! In 1974 I travelled to Paris to study, then on to London.

It was in England that cooking became a hobby and a necessity: the Sri Lankan community at the time was very small, there was no such thing as printed recipes from my homeland, and if I wanted the food I recognised I'd have to learn to cook it myself (although I remember Sri Lankan students flocking to the Ceylon High Commission in Bayswater, where they could eat for very cheap). When Niranjala joined me in London we would 'compete' to create the most delicious dishes from our own cultures, and so began a lifelong mutual delight in cooking.

After a few years we fulfilled a heartfelt dream and opened the Elephant Walk restaurant in London in 2004. It won the coveted Cobra Good Curry Guide Award in 2006 for the best Sri Lankan Restaurant in the UK and became much celebrated in a city where authentic Sri Lankan food was very hard to come by. Former Sri Lankan president Chandrika Kumaratunga even found time to stop by on a visit to London.

Niranjala and I retired from the restaurant in 2013, but our passion for the food of our country is as strong as ever, and we continue to pass on our knowledge to others through our Coconut Kitchens cookery school. We hope you enjoy exploring the food of Sri Lanka through this book, and you love it as much as we do!

GLOSSARY

Bitter gourd
Karawila in Sinhalese, pavakkai in Tamil, and also known as bitter melon. This extremely bitter vegetable looks a bit like a small cucumber but with a bumpy ridged skin. The dark green Sri Lankan variety is available from specialist stores, but any Asian grocery store will probably sell the paler green variety.

Breadfruit
Dhel in Sinhalese, eera pilakai in Tamil. About the size of small melons, breadfruit have a green, sometimes mottled, skin with slightly raised bumps. Breadfruit should be available in most specialist Asian grocers – choose a fruit that has a dull rather than bright green colour and that is not too soft.

Chana dal
Made from husked and split black chick peas, chana dal holds its shape better than yellow split peas but it is similar. You should be able to find it in any Asian grocery store and even many supermarkets.

Coconut
Coconuts are plentiful in Sri Lanka, so for an authentic flavour you should use fresh coconut if you can. You want the hard, brown-skinned variety (with or without hair if it's been trimmed). It should feel heavy (an indication that the flesh inside hasn't dried out). Crack it open by hitting it firmly around the middle with a pestle or a hammer, rotating it a little after each whack. Catch the coconut water when it pops open (and drink or discard as it's not used in recipes). Prise the two halves apart, and then scrape out the flesh using a coconut scraper.

Grated (shredded) coconut: Grate the flesh by hand with a grater or in a food processor – you should get about 250g (9oz/3¼ cups) per coconut. Or substitute with desiccated (shredded) coconut.

Coconut cream: This is the first extract of milk from a coconut, also called thick coconut milk. It is the same as canned coconut cream, and is really thick and creamy. To make it fresh, you put the grated (shredded) flesh of one coconut into a large bowl and top up with cold water – you'll need about 185ml (6 fl oz/¾ cup) of liquid. Stir well to combine. Take a handful of coconut flesh and squeeze it hard over the bowl. Put the coconut flesh back into the bowl and stir well again. Repeat with all the coconut flesh until you have a very thick and creamy liquid in the bowl. You can strain this off and use where a recipe calls for coconut cream. If you're going to go on to make coconut milk (below), return the coconut flesh back to the bowl to continue the extraction process.

Coconut milk: Coconut milk is the second extract of milk from a coconut, also called medium thick coconut milk. You can buy it canned as coconut milk, and it should be thinner than coconut cream. Use the same bowl and already squeezed coconut flesh (from the coconut cream, above). Add 300ml (12 fl oz/1½ cups) of water and repeat the squeezing and stirring process until you have a light, creamy coconut milk. Strain and use where a recipe calls for coconut milk.

Curry leaves
Available in Asian grocers. Try to use fresh if you can for their distinctive aromatic flavour.

Drumsticks
Murunga in Sinhalese, drumsticks are the long ridged seed pods of the *Moringa oleifera* tree. They have a slightly bitter flavour and are used in vegetable curries.

Goraka
Also known as Malabar tamarind, this is a small sour fruit, usually used in dried form. Sinhalese recipes often use a clove of goraka to give a tangy flavour and to thicken curries (where Tamil recipes would use tamarind). But if you can't find it you can just add lime juice to the dish at the end. One recipe calls for goraka paste, which you may find in Asian grocers or online, but this can easily be substituted with the more widely available tamarind paste (p14).

Gotu kola
Also known as pennywort, this leafy green herb with delicate fan-shaped leaves is a member of the parsley family. It is considered to have health benefits in Ayuverdic medicine. You may be able to buy this online, or you will probably need to find a specialist Sri Lankan grocery store.

Jaggery
Jaggery is an unrefined palm sugar, with kithul jaggery coming from the sap of the kithul palm and being the most highly prized. Sold in Asian grocers and some supermarkets. You want to buy jaggery in a block rather than a powder.

Jackfruit
A large elongated fruit, usually around 30cm (12 inches) long, with pronounced blunt spikes all over the green skin. Open up the jackfruit and you will see large bulbs inside (p128/9), which are used to cook Kiri Kos (p127). Asian grocers should have the fresh fruit, but if not they may have canned or frozen varieties. The jackfruit seeds are also used in Odiyal Kool (p226) and can be found sold in packets, but you can substitute with butter beans.

Kathurumurunga
Kathurumurunga is the Sinhalese name for the leaves of the *Sesbania grandiflora* tree, also known as agati or the hummingbird tree. The bunches have thick stalks with pairs of leaves all the way along. Available from specialist Sri Lankan stores.

Long beans
Also known as yard-long beans or snake beans, these are one of the longest beans in the world. Available from Asian grocers or specialist Sri Lankan stores.

Maldive fish
A very popular Sri Lankan ingredient, Maldive fish is actually skipjack tuna that has been boiled, smoked and dried. It is usually crushed and sprinkled into curries to give an authentic salty flavour. Available from specialist Sri Lankan stores, or substitute with dried prawns (shrimp).

Mung dal
Made from husked and split green mung beans or green gram. Available in Asian grocers and some supermarkets.

Oil
Coconut oil is the oil most traditionally used in Sri Lankan cooking, for all purposes. You can find it in most supermarkets, but Asian grocery stores will often have cheaper varieties – although make sure they are for cooking not haircare. Alternatively, use vegetable or sunflower oil.

Odiyal flour
Also known as palmyra flour, this comes from the dried roots of a palmyra palm tree. It is a starchy flour mainly used for thickening liquid, such as seafood soup, Odiyal Kool (p226).

Plantain
Belonging to the banana family, this green-skinned fruit is cooked as a vegetable. Available in Asian and West African grocers.

Rampe leaf
Also called pandan leaf, this is sold fresh in bunches or dried in most Asian grocers.

Try to use fresh if you can for the authentic flavour. It's a very common ingredient, used in many Sinhalese dishes to give a lovely aromatic fragrance, a bit like vanilla.

Rice flour
Made from very finely milled rice, this starchy, gluten-free flour is used to make dishes such as the Bamboo Pittu (p38), for which you'll also need a pittu maker, pictured below left.

Snake gourd
Pudalangai in Tamil and pathola in Sinhalese. These look like very long hard cucumbers, and are popular in vegetarian curries.

Tamarind
A common souring agent in Tamil curries, this tangy seed pod is most usually added to dishes in the form of tamarind water. To make tamarind water, you need to buy a block of dried tamarind pulp, available from Asian grocers. The standard tamarind water used in most recipes is a medium concentrate, for which you need to soak a piece of pulp about the size of a marble in 200ml (7 fl oz/generous ¾ cup) of warm water for about 10 minutes. Where 'thin concentrate' is specified, use about ¾ of a marble. Strain the tamarind water and use the back of a spoon to push as much of the softened pulp through the sieve as possible. Discard the fibrous pulp and seeds, and use the tamarind water in quantities directed. Alternatively, follow the individual packet instructions as concentrates vary.

Urid dal
Also called ulundu in Tamil. Made from husked and split black mung beans or black gram, this is a key ingredient in Tamil dishes such as Idli (p27), Thosai (p41) and Ulundu Vadai (p55). Available in Asian grocers.

Urid flour
Also udad flour. Made from husked and split black mung beans or black gram, this is a finely milled flour, commonly used in Appalam (p89).

THOOL

Roasted tamil curry powder

One of the bases of Sri Lankan cooking: a spice blend that is versatile enough to use in many recipes. Tamil food typically involves more chilli than Sinhalese food.

Makes 25–35 curry dishes

Method A
250g (9oz/4 cups) coriander seeds
50g (1¾oz/½ cup) cumin seeds
75g (2¾oz/¾ cup) fennel seeds
20g (¾oz/2 tbsp) fenugreek seeds
250g (9oz/6¾ cups) dried red chillies
20 fresh curry leaves
1 tsp ground turmeric
50g (1¾oz/6 tbsp) black peppercorns

Method B
20 fresh curry leaves
250g (9oz/2½ cups) ground coriander
50g (1¾oz/½ cup) ground cumin
75g (2¾oz/¾ cup) fennel powder
20g (¾oz/3 tbsp) ground fenugreek
250g (9oz/2½ cups) chilli powder
1 tsp ground turmeric
50g (1¾oz/½ cup) ground black pepper

Method A
In a dry frying pan (skillet) set over a low heat, dry-roast the coriander seeds until they are golden brown. Keep an eye on the seeds and make sure they don't burn, by shaking the pan forwards and backwards. Remove the roasted seeds and set aside.

Next, dry-roast the cumin, fennel and fenugreek seeds, in separate batches, until golden brown. Set aside.

Then, dry-roast the dried red chillies until beginning to colour, followed by the curry leaves until they start to go brown. Set them aside with the rest of the roasted ingredients.

While the pan is off the heat but still hot, add the turmeric and toss it about in the pan for a few seconds, until very lightly roasted. Add this to the other ingredients.

Put all the roasted ingredients and the black peppercorns into a spice grinder, or use a pestle and mortar, and grind them to a fine powder.

Method B
Dry-roast the curry leaves in a dry frying pan (skillet) over a low heat until beginning to colour. Remove from the heat and set aside.

Mix all the other ingredients together to form a blended powder.

Dry-roast this powder very lightly in a dry frying pan over a very low heat, for about a minute until the colour darkens slightly. Remove from the heat, stir and let it cool. Mix in the whole roasted curry leaves, before storing.

Be warned that there will be a very strong smell of chillies around the house and the mixture can burn very quickly.

Tip: You can store all these curry powders in an airtight container for up to 2 months.

THUNA PAHA

Sinhalese curry powder

The name translates as 'three or five', as this blend traditionally has three or five ingredients (although every cook in Sri Lanka has their own recipe). Unroasted curry powder is best with vegetable dishes.

Put all the ingredients into a spice grinder and grind into a fine powder. You may have to do this in batches, depending on the size of the grinder. Mix the blended powder well and keep it in an airtight container for 2 months.

Tip: When using any curry powder in a recipe, always measure it out with a dry spoon.

Makes 20–25 curry dishes

200g (7oz/3 cups) coriander seeds
100g (3½oz/1 cup) cumin seeds
50g (1¾oz/½ cup) fennel seeds
4 x 2.5cm (1-inch) cinnamon sticks
20 fresh curry leaves

BATHAPU THUNA PAHA

Roasted Sinhalese curry powder

This has more intense flavours than the unroasted version, which means it can stand up to the flavours of meat dishes. It's often sprinkled at the end of cooking to add a fragrant finish.

In a dry frying pan (skillet) set over a low heat, dry-roast the first four ingredients separately until golden brown. Shake the pan to avoid burning. Set aside in a medium bowl.

In the same pan, dry-roast the cinnamon sticks for about a minute. Add the rampe leaf and roast for about 30 seconds, and then add the curry leaves and roast together for another 30 seconds until beginning to colour. Add to the other roasted ingredients in the bowl.

Dry-roast the remaining ingredients together until beginning to colour, then add them to the other ingredients. Stir to combine.

Put all the ingredients into a spice grinder and grind to a fine powder. Do this in batches, depending on the size of the grinder. Mix the blend and store in an airtight container.

Makes 25–35 curry dishes

200g (7oz/3 cups) coriander seeds
100g (3½oz/1 cup) cumin seeds
50g (1¾oz/4 tbsp) uncooked white rice (basmati or patna)
2 tsp fennel seeds
3 x 2.5cm (1-inch) cinnamon sticks
10 x 2.5cm (1-inch) pieces of rampe (pandan) leaf
20 fresh curry leaves
7 dried red chillies
10 cardamom pods
10 cloves
30g (1oz/3 tbsp) black peppercorns

POL KIRI KANDA

Coconut milk congee

Congee is a rice-based dish that can be made sweet or savoury and is eaten at all times of the day; this is a filling, dairy-free breakfast that's a bit like a bolder version of porridge.

100g (3½oz/½ cup) brown rice
750ml (25 fl oz/generous 3 cups) water
2.5cm (1-inch) piece of ginger, peeled and sliced
2 garlic cloves, finely chopped
4 black peppercorns
½ tsp salt
250ml (9 fl oz/generous 1 cup) coconut milk

Serves 2-3

Put the rice into a medium saucepan and cover with water. Swirl the rice around to wash it, drain and repeat at least twice until the water is clear. Then, add the 750ml of water (to cover the rice by about 2.5cm/ 1 inch), and bring to the boil. Turn the heat down to medium, add the ginger, garlic, peppercorns and salt, and simmer uncovered for 12–15 minutes until cooked.

Add the coconut milk and cook for a further 3 minutes until beginning to thicken. There will still be plenty of liquid. Remove from the heat and leave to cool slightly.

Then, remove the peppercorns and ginger with a slotted spoon and pour the congee into a blender. Blitz until roughly blended (not puréed).

When you are ready to serve, pour the congee into a saucepan, taste for salt and warm it through.

- 200g (7oz) gotu kola (pennywort) (roughly half a bunch)
- 20 fresh curry leaves
- 2 garlic cloves
- 250ml (9oz/generous 1 cup) coconut milk
- 1 litre (35 fl oz/4¼ cups) water (250ml/9 fl oz/generous 1 cup for the gotu kola (pennywort), 750ml/25 fl oz/generous 3 cups for the rice)
- 100g (3½oz/½ cup) brown rice
- salt

Gotu kola congee

The leafy green herb gotu kola is said to be helpful in treating many ailments, including arthritis and skin complaints. Here, it's used in a nutritious breakfast drink, similar to a thick, soupy porridge.

Wash the gotu kola and roughly chop the leaves and stems. Wash and roughly chop the curry leaves as well.

Put the gotu kola, curry leaves, garlic, coconut milk and 250ml of the water into a blender. Blitz to purée, then strain the liquid into a medium bowl. Squeeze the pulp left in the sieve to extract the remainder of the liquid, then discard the pulp.

Put the rice in a medium saucepan and cover with water. Swirl the rice around to wash it, drain and repeat at least twice until the water is clear. Then, add the remaining 750ml of water and bring to the boil. Turn the heat down and simmer, uncovered, for 12–15 minutes until soft. There should be some liquid left in the pan. Remove from the heat and leave to cool slightly.

Then, put the rice into a blender and blitz until you have a smooth liquid. Pour the liquid congee into a medium saucepan, add the blended gotu kola and bring to the boil. Turn the heat down low and simmer for 5 minutes. Keep stirring frequently to prevent the liquid from curdling.

Season with salt and take off the heat. Serve hot.

Serves 4

GOTU KOLA KANDA

UPPUMA

Roasted semolina

In Tamil, 'uppu' means salt and 'ma' is flour, although there are a few more ingredients involved in this hearty and savoury breakfast dish. Think of it as something like couscous.

1 tbsp chana dal (split chick peas)
500g (1lb 2oz/2½ cups) semolina
2 tbsp oil
½ tsp mustard seeds
1 medium red onion, finely sliced
6 fresh curry leaves
¼ tsp cumin seeds
2.5cm (1-inch) piece of ginger, peeled and finely chopped
3 dried red chillies, broken
¼ tsp ground turmeric
150g (5½oz) carrots (about 2 medium), medium diced
150g (5½oz) cabbage or leeks, finely sliced
50g frozen peas, defrosted (optional)
½ tsp salt
400ml (14 fl oz/1⅔ cups) just boiled water
¼ tsp ghee

Serves 4

Rinse the chana dal and leave it to soak in cold water for at least 10 minutes. After soaking, drain it and dry-roast it in a large dry frying pan (skillet) on a low heat, until golden brown. Set aside. Put the semolina in the frying pan, and dry-roast until it starts to turn golden. Set aside.

Heat the oil in a large, lidded frying pan over a low heat, then add the mustard seeds. Let them cook for a few seconds until they pop, then add the onion and give it a stir or two. Add the curry leaves and cumin seeds and sauté for a few seconds. Then add the ginger and dried chillies and sauté until the onions are soft and turning golden.

Add the turmeric and the vegetables into the pan. Stir well and sprinkle with the salt. Cover the pan with the lid and cook for 2–3 minutes.

Add the boiled water, give it a good stir and bring to the boil. Boil for 2–3 minutes, then turn the heat down to the lowest setting, add the ghee and stir.

Start adding in the roasted semolina a little at a time, stirring all the while with the handle of a wooden spoon. Keep going until most of the liquid has been absorbed into the semolina, but it is still moist. This should take a minute or two, and you may not need to use all the semolina. Turn off the heat and give it a good stir with the handle again. Cover the pan with the lid and leave to rest for about 3 minutes. Add the roasted chana dal, mix well and it is ready to serve.

Tip: If you want to prepare Uppuma quickly, keep some semolina and chana dal already roasted in airtight containers.

100g (3½oz/½ cup) urid dal (split black gram)
400g (14oz/2 cups) uncooked white rice (basmati or patna)
250ml (9 fl oz/generous 1 cup) water (50ml/1¾ fl oz/scant ¼ cup for the urid dal and 200ml/7 fl oz/generous ¾ cup for the rice)
salt

Special utensil
idli steamer

A special steamer is essential for making these soft little pillows of rice and lentil. They're eaten at breakfast in Sri Lanka and across southern India, often with a spicy lentil and vegetable Sambar (pictured here, recipe on p81).

Preparation
Wash the urid dal and rice separately and soak them in water in two separate containers for at least 5 hours.

When soaked, drain and keep the urid dal and rice separate. Put the urid dal in a blender and liquidise, adding about 50ml of water little by little, until you have a thick, smooth paste. Set aside.

Repeat the process with the rice, adding the remaining water little by little, until you have a similar thick, smooth paste.

Mix both pastes together, stirring well, and season with salt. Leave this to ferment at room temperature for about 8 hours, ideally overnight.

Make the idli
Fill the base of the idli steamer with water and bring to the boil. Lightly oil the idli moulds with your fingers. Spoon the mixture into the moulds, place the tray on the base, cover with the lid and steam for 10–12 minutes. To check if the idli are cooked, gently press them with your fingertips. Your fingers should not stick to the rice.

Take the mould tray out of the steamer and the idlis are ready to serve.

Makes 12

IDLI

APPA

Plain hoppers

Hoppers – fermented savoury rice pancakes – are probably the number one street food in Sri Lanka: in fact, most households don't even make them because they're so readily available. A sambol is an essential accompaniment: try the Pol (p71), Seeni (p76) or Katta (p72) versions.

Makes 16

Tip the yeast into a small bowl. Add the sugar and water, give it a good stir and set aside for at least 15 minutes to activate. When the yeast is ready, put the flour in a medium bowl, sprinkle in the yeast mixture and stir well.

Pour half the coconut milk into the flour and mix well until you have a thick consistency. Add the rest of the coconut milk little by little, stirring as you go, until you have a thick but still runny batter. Leave the batter in a warm place for 30 minutes.

When you are ready to make the hoppers, add the salt to the batter and warm the hopper pan over a low heat. Using a ladle holding about 50ml (1¾ fl oz), give the prepared batter a good stir. Put one ladleful of batter into the middle of the hot pan, keeping the heat low throughout.

Swirl the pan around in a circular motion so that the batter spreads out and covers the base of the pan. Put the lid on and cook for 2–3 minutes until it is golden and crispy around the edges and soft but cooked in the middle. If you press the middle, your fingertips shouldn't stick.

Carefully remove the hopper with a spatula, and cook the rest. Serve warm.

7g (¼oz/2 tsp) dried yeast
3 tsp sugar (white or brown)
50ml (1¾ fl oz/scant ¼ cup) lukewarm water
400g (14oz/2½ cups) rice flour
800ml (28 fl oz/3⅓ cups) coconut milk
½ tsp salt

Special utensil
15cm (6-inch) non-stick wok or hopper pan with a lid. If you are not using a non-stick pan, then lightly oil the pan with a piece of cloth.

Egg hoppers
Follow the method for making plain hoppers. Ladle the batter into the pan, swirl it around as before, and then break an egg into the middle of the pan and season with salt and pepper. Cover with the lid and cook for about 2½–3½ minutes until the egg white is cooked and the yolk just runny.

Milk hoppers
Follow the method for making plain hoppers. Ladle the batter into the pan, swirl it around as before, and then add 2 tablespoons of thick coconut milk and sprinkle with ½ teaspoon of sugar. Cover with the lid and cook for 2–3 minutes as before.

Jaggery hoppers
Follow the method for making plain hoppers. Ladle the batter into the pan, swirl it around as before, and then sprinkle with 2 teaspoons of crushed jaggery. Cover with the lid and cook for 2–3 minutes as before.

INDIAPPA

String hoppers

These steamed noodle clusters are prepared with special moulds and mats as they have been for centuries. They're eaten everyday, often with curry at breakfast time. You also see them in Kerala, an area of India with a strong influence on Sri Lankan cooking.

500g (1lb 2oz/3¼ cups) string hopper flour (or roasted or steamed white or brown rice flour)
½ tsp salt
full kettle of just boiled water

Special utensils
1 x string hopper mould
16 x string hopper mats
steamer

Makes 16

Place the flour in a large bowl and sprinkle in the salt. Once your kettle has boiled, let the steam escape for 30 seconds or so, then slowly pour the water onto the flour, mixing with the handle of a thin wooden spoon as you go. Keep adding water until the flour begins to bind together.

At this point, stop adding water and see if you can bring the dough together into one big lump by kneading. If it doesn't come together, keep adding small amounts of water until it does. The dough should be soft and a non-sticky pliable consistency. As soon as it comes together into a ball, it is ready.

Fill the mould with the dough and lay eight string hopper mats on a work surface. Push the dough through the mould and onto the first mat, moving in a circular motion so that you cover the whole mat in strings. Repeat until all eight mats are covered.

Carefully arrange the mats in a circle in the steamer, with one mat sat partially on top of another so that the hoppers don't get squashed. Cover and steam for 7–8 minutes until cooked, and not sticky to the touch. Remove the steamer from the pan before taking out the mats. Slide the string hoppers off the mat and pile them up ready to serve.

Repeat the process and serve warm when they are all ready.

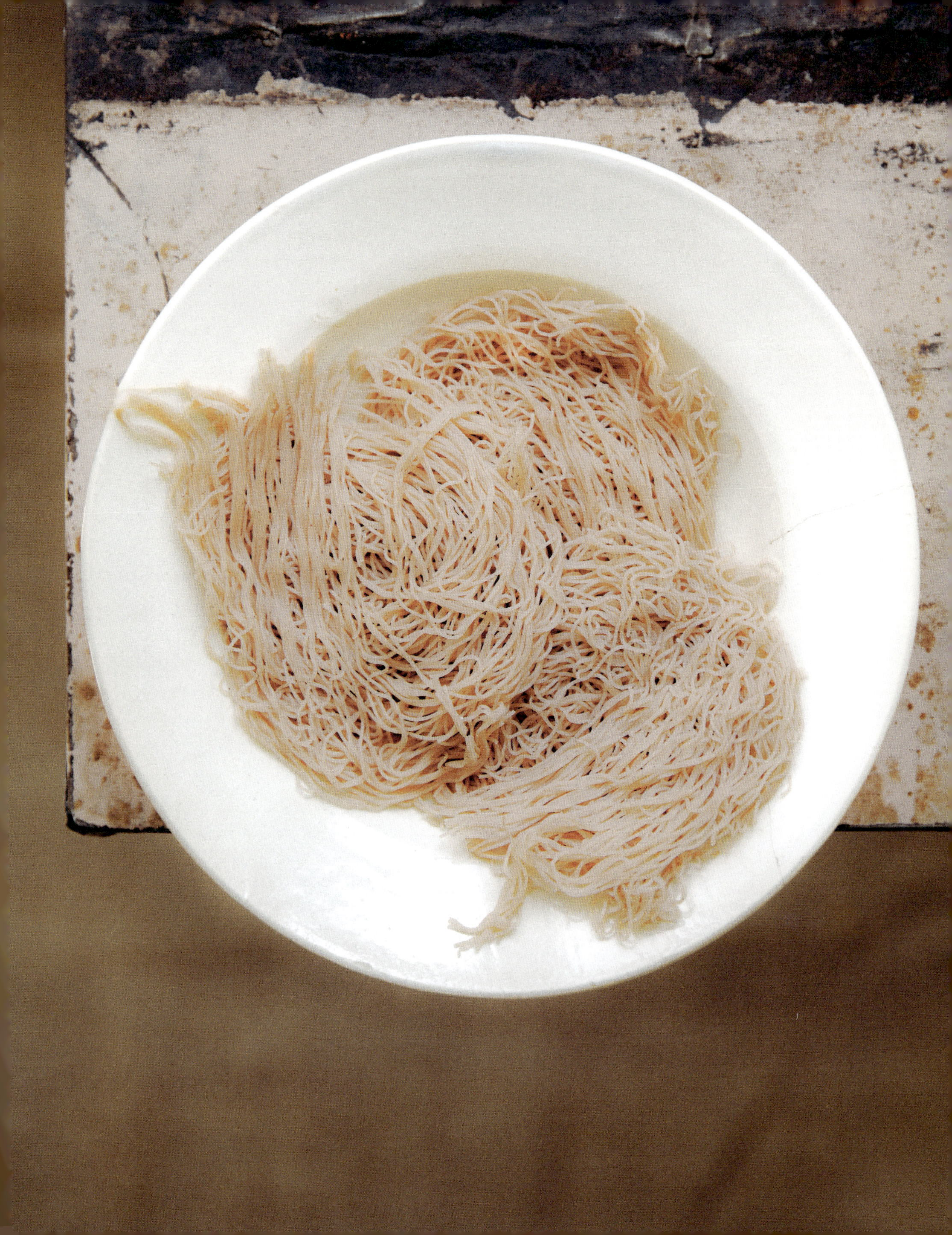

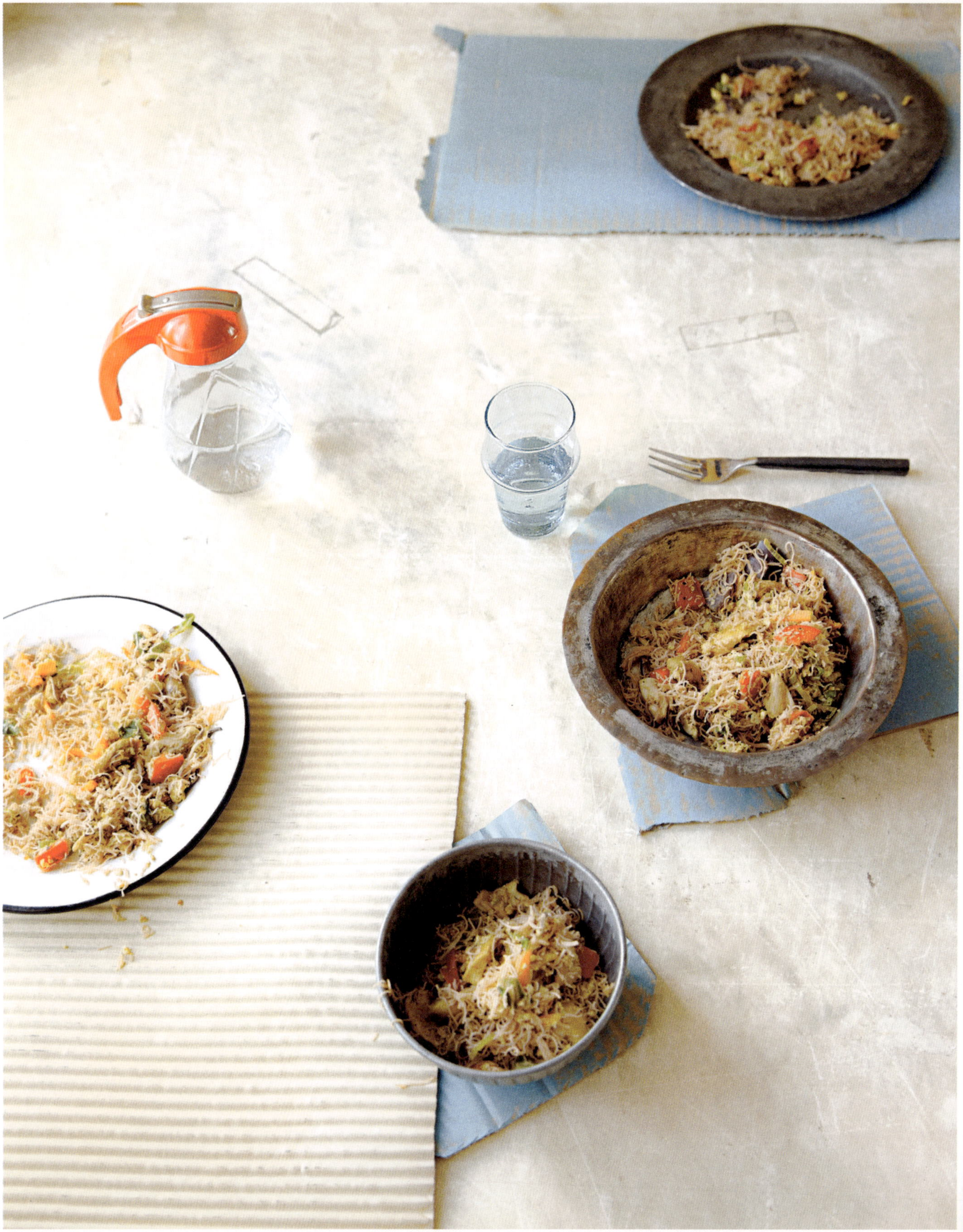

INDIAPPA KOTHU

String hopper stir-fry

'Kothu' translates as 'chopped' in Tamil, and the vegetables, meat and hoppers in this vibrant dinner dish are cut up to be cooked quickly. It's ample enough to be a meal on its own.

16 string hoppers (Indiappa recipe on p34)
2 tbsp oil
7 fresh curry leaves
2 green chillies, deseeded and roughly chopped
1 medium red onion, roughly chopped
¼ tsp ground turmeric
150g (5½oz) carrots (about 2 medium), medium diced
1 tbsp frozen peas, defrosted (optional)
150g (5½oz) cabbage or leeks or both, finely sliced
½ red (bell) pepper, cut into 1cm (½-inch) pieces
salt
2 eggs
250g (9oz) mutton or chicken curry (Elumas on p201, Kukul Mas Mirisata on p193 or Koli Kari on p197) with only a little sauce

Gently loosen the string hoppers with your fingers until they look more like noodles.

Heat the oil in a medium wok or frying pan (skillet) over a low heat. Add the curry leaves and green chillies and stir-fry for a few seconds. Add the onions and sauté until they are just soft, about a minute or so, then add the turmeric.

Turn the heat up to high, add the vegetables, and stir-fry for a couple of minutes. Season with salt.

Reduce the heat to medium and push the stir-fried vegetables to one side of the pan. Add a little extra oil to the pan if it is looking dry, then break in the eggs. Add a pinch of salt and scramble the eggs. When they are ready, mix them into the vegetables and turn the heat back up to high.

Tip in the string hoppers a little at a time, stirring them into the mixture. Use your wooden spoon to break them up into smaller pieces as you go.

Finally, add the cooked mutton or chicken curry (with only a little sauce) into the string hopper mix and stir well. Cook for 2 minutes on high to warm through completely. Serve hot.

Variation: For a vegetarian version, simply leave out the mutton or chicken curry.

Serves 4

500g (1lb 2oz/3¼ cups) roasted red rice flour
1 tsp salt
250ml (9 fl oz /generous 1 cup) cold water
150g (5½oz/2 cups) freshly grated or desiccated (shredded) coconut

Special utensil
Bamboo pittu steamer (picture on p14)

Steamed coconut and red rice flour rolls

A Tamil breakfast staple: steamed, layered tubes of coconut and rice flour pearls. The 'bamboo' comes from the fact it is traditionally made in bamboo stalks. Hindu legend has it that the god Lord Shiva came to earth disguised as a man, and carried earth on his head for an old lady in exchange for this modest but tasty dish. Try with the Lunu Dehi Sambola (pictured left, recipe p80) and Katta Sambol (pictured centre, recipe p72).

BAMBOO PITTU

Put the flour in a large bowl, add the salt and mix it together with your fingers.

Sprinkle a little bit of water at a time onto the flour. Using your fingertips, lightly mix the flour and water together in a circular motion. The mixture will begin to bind together into little lumps.

When it is just lumping together, tip in half the coconut and continue the process of adding water and lightly mixing. The little lumps will firm up and turn into small pearl-sized balls about ½cm (¼ inch) wide on the top of the mixture. Remove these balls as they form, and set aside. Keep mixing lightly with your fingertips until all the dough has turned into these pittu balls.

Fill the bottom of the bamboo pittu steamer with water and put it on a high heat to boil. Place the small disc with holes into the bottom of the tube. Put 1 heaped tablespoon of coconut into the tube, followed by spoonfuls of raw pittu balls until about halfway up the tube, and then another tablespoon of coconut. Repeat these steps, finishing with the coconut.

Place the tube on the steamer and steam until the steam comes out of the top of the tube, roughly 8–10 minutes. At this stage put the lid on the tube and steam for a further 3–4 minutes.

Lift the tube off the steamer bottom and, using the handle of a long wooden spoon inserted into the small hole in the bottom of the tube, push the steamed pittu onto a serving dish (with a lid). Cover so the pittu does not dry out while you make the rest.

Repeat this process until all the raw pittu are steamed. Serve warm.

Note: If you are using a normal steamer, lay a clean tea towel (dish cloth) over the holes at the bottom of the steamer and place half the raw pittu on top. Steam until the steam pushes through the pittu.

Serves 4

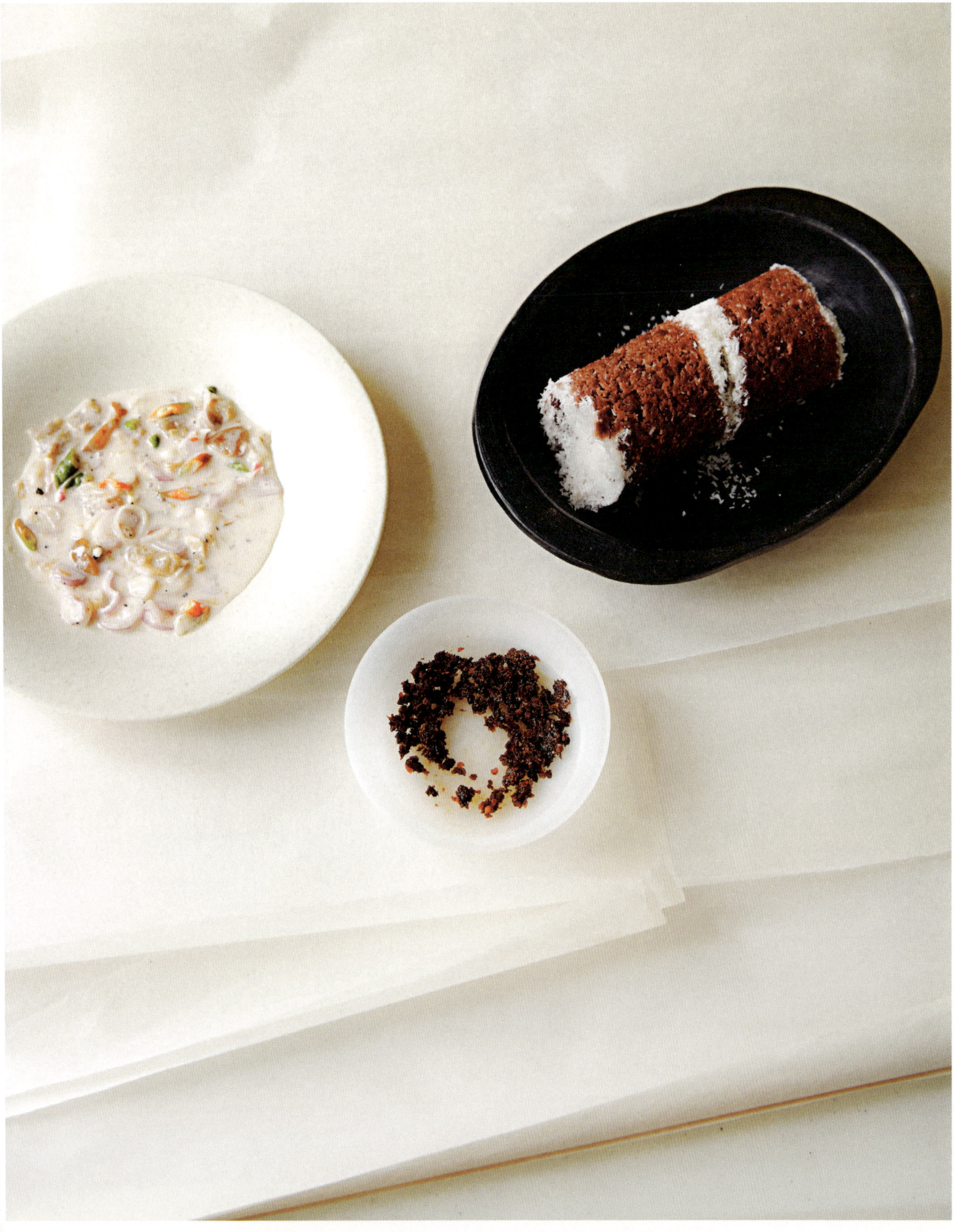

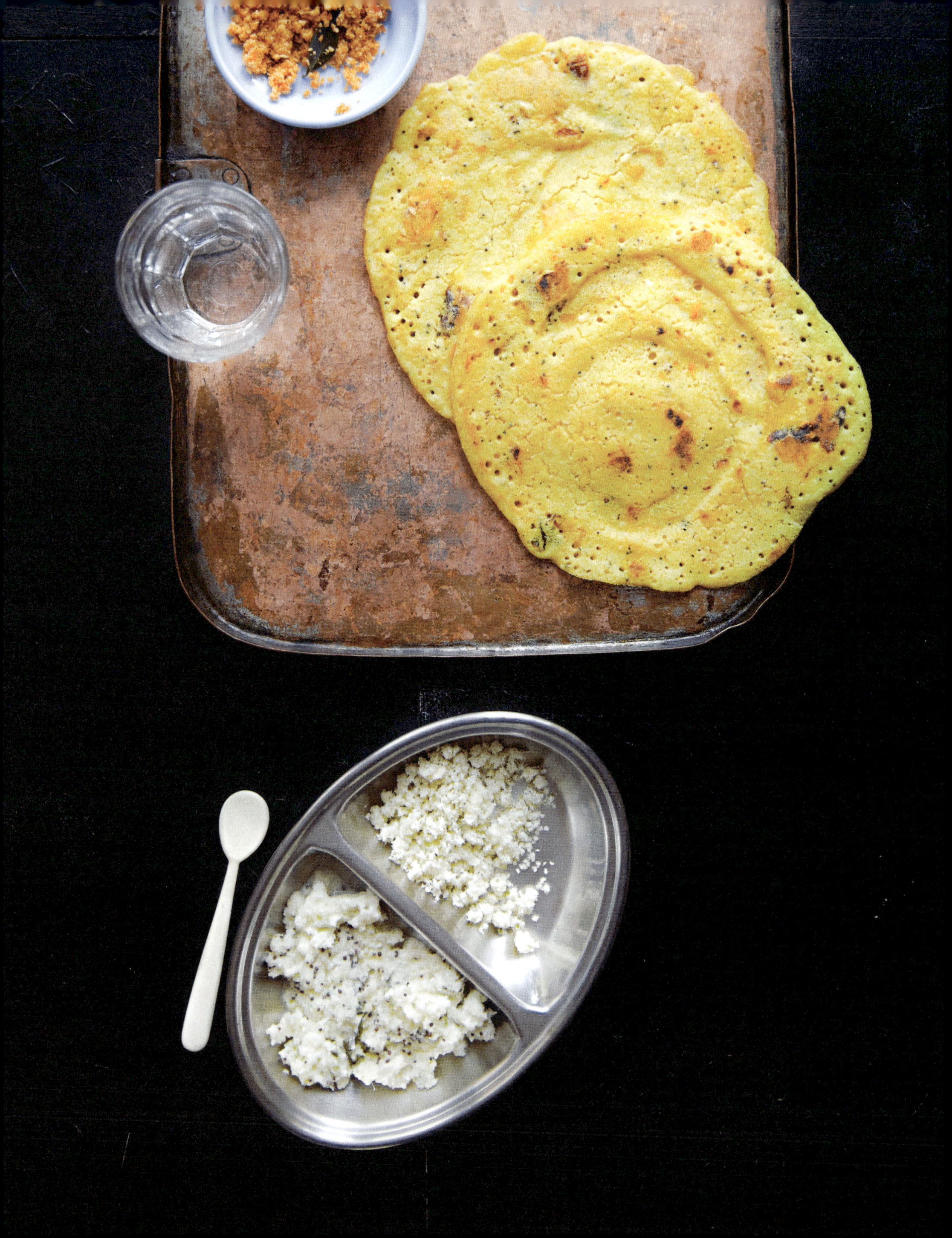

THOSAI

Savoury pancakes
A slightly thicker take on the Indian fermented dosa. Here they're paired with Pol Sambol (p71) and Pachai Sambal (p80); fill them with Masala Thosai (p45).

200g (7oz/1 cup) urid dal (split black gram)
400g (14oz/2 cups) uncooked white rice (basmati or patna)
2 tsp fenugreek seeds
250ml (9 fl oz/generous 1 cup) water
1 tbsp oil
¼ tsp mustard seeds
¼ medium onion, finely chopped
2 fresh curry leaves
3 dried red chillies, broken
¼ tsp cumin seeds
salt

Makes 12

Preparation
Wash the urid dal, rice and fenugreek seeds separately and put them in three separate containers. Cover with water and soak for at least 5 hours.

When soaked, drain the three containers. Put the urid dal and fenugreek seeds in a blender and liquidise, adding about 80ml of water little by little, until you have a thick, smooth paste. It should be flowing but not runny. Set aside.

Repeat the process with the rice, adding the remaining water little by little, until you have a similar thick, smooth paste.

Mix both pastes together, stirring well, and season with salt. Leave to ferment at room temperature for about 8 hours, ideally overnight.

Make the thosai
Heat the oil in a small frying pan (skillet) on a low heat, then add the mustard seeds. Let them cook for a few seconds until they pop, then add the onion and curry leaves and sauté until the onions begin to soften. Then, add the dried chillies and cumin seeds and sauté until the onions are golden brown. Remove from the heat and when it is cool, add it to the thosai batter, stirring it in well.

Grease the flat griddle or frying pan with oil using a piece of cloth, and put it on a low to medium heat.

Put a ladleful of batter into the middle of the pan and, using the back of the ladle, spread it out from the centre in a circular motion, until the batter makes a circle about 17.5cm (7 inches) in diameter (almost like how you make pancakes). Add a little additional batter to complete the circle if necessary.

Keep an eye on the heat and make sure the thosai doesn't burn on the bottom. Cook for about 3 minutes, then use a spatula to lift the thosai and check the colour on the bottom. When it is golden brown, flip the thosai over and let it cook for another 2 minutes until the other side is also golden.

Pile them up and continue cooking. Serve warm when they are all ready. It is best eaten with Sambar (p81), Pol Sambol (p71) or Pachai Sambal (p80).

Variation: thin and crispy paper thosai
While the thosai is cooking on its first side, gently use a spatula to scrape off the excess batter on the top, without making holes in the thosai. Sprinkle a little oil on top of the thosai. When the bottom is golden brown, after about 2 minutes, flip it over and cook for another minute or two until the other side is also golden. Roll the paper thosai up loosely and serve.

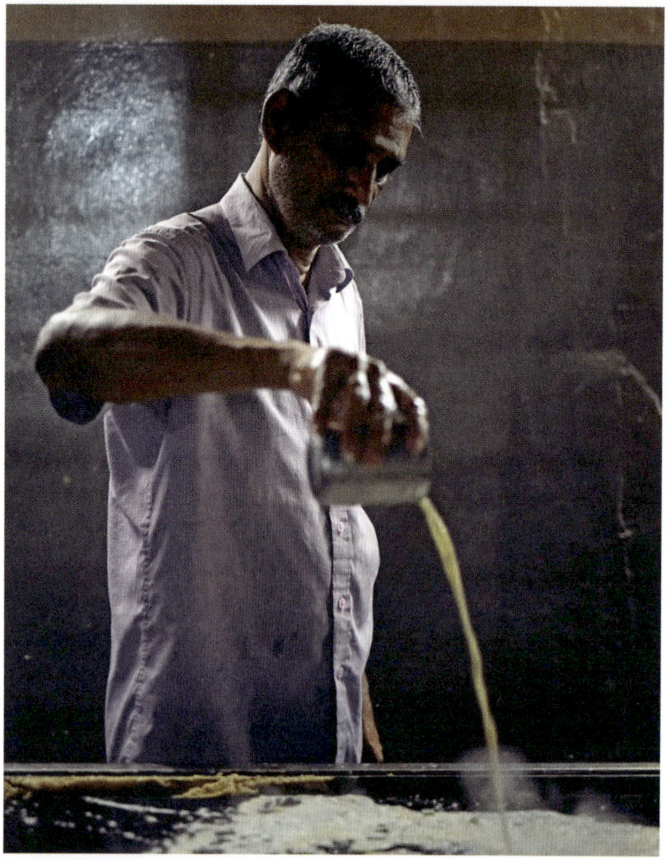
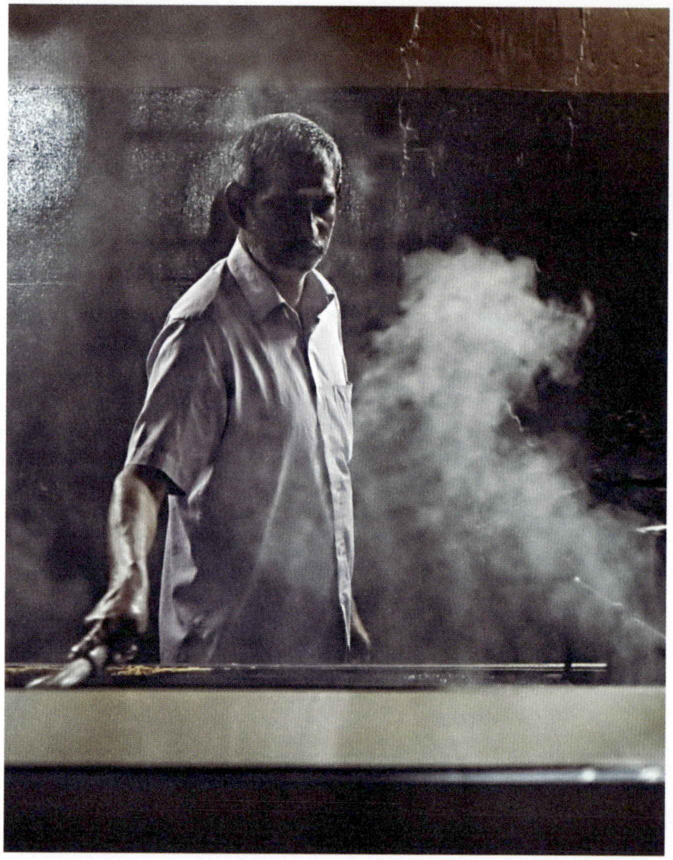
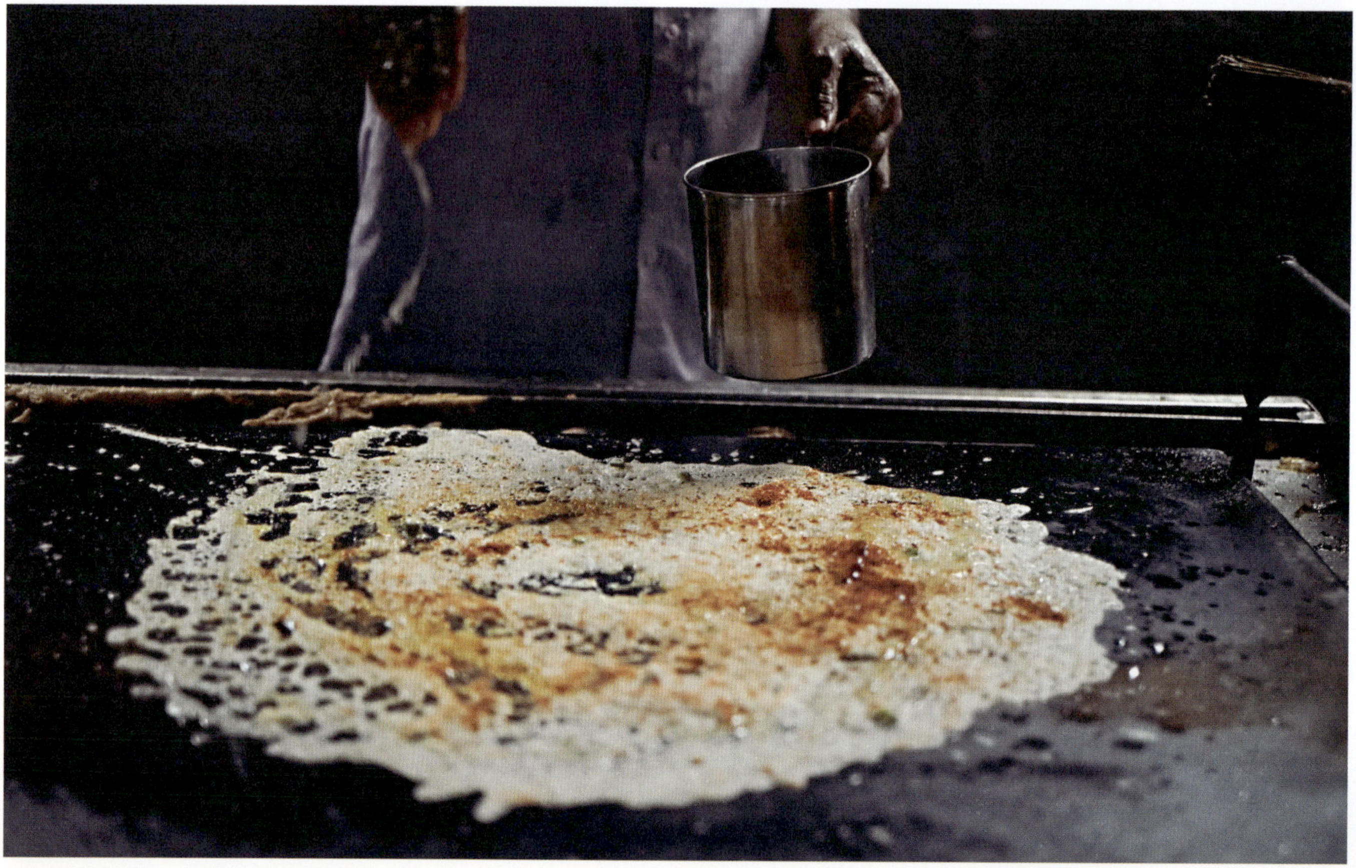

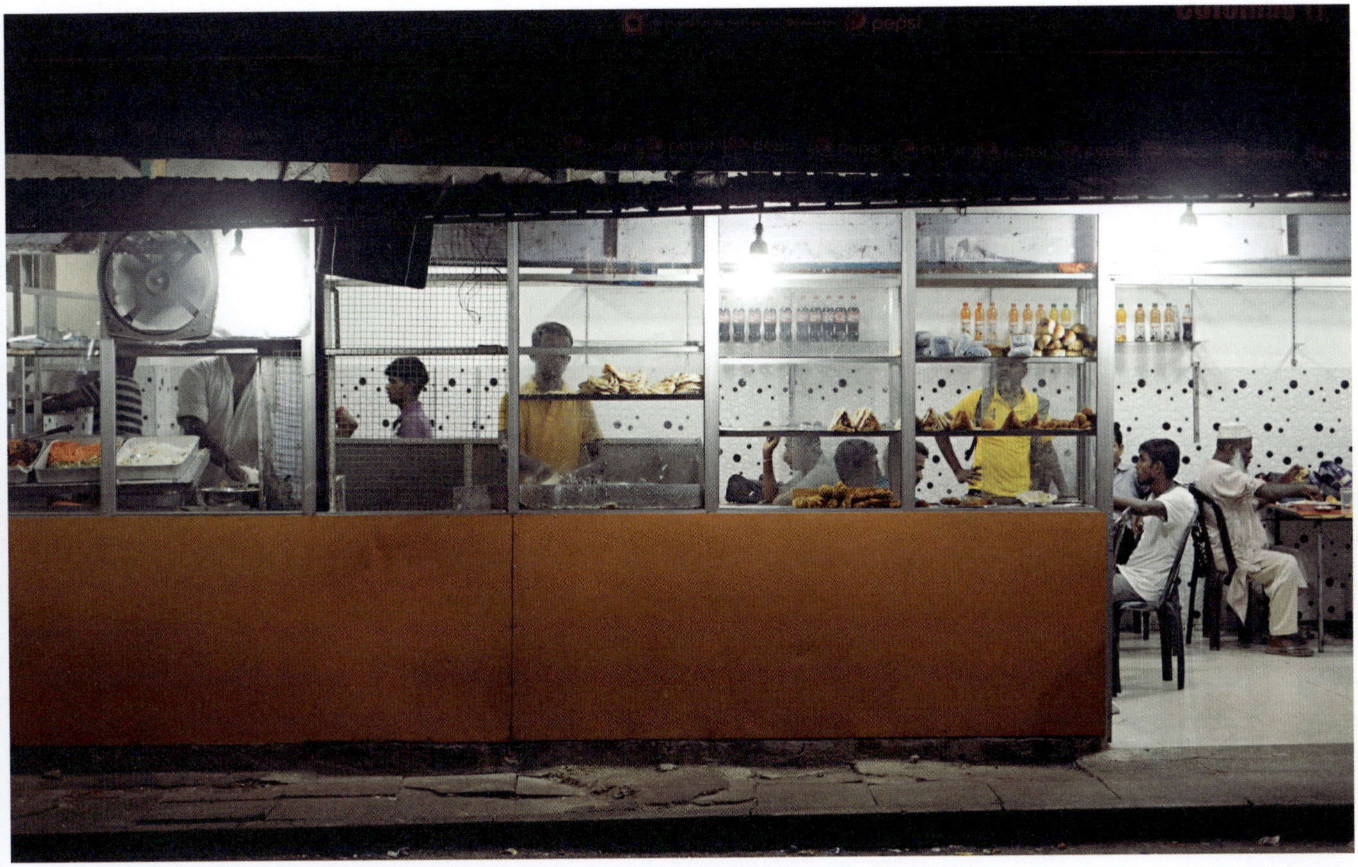
pepsi

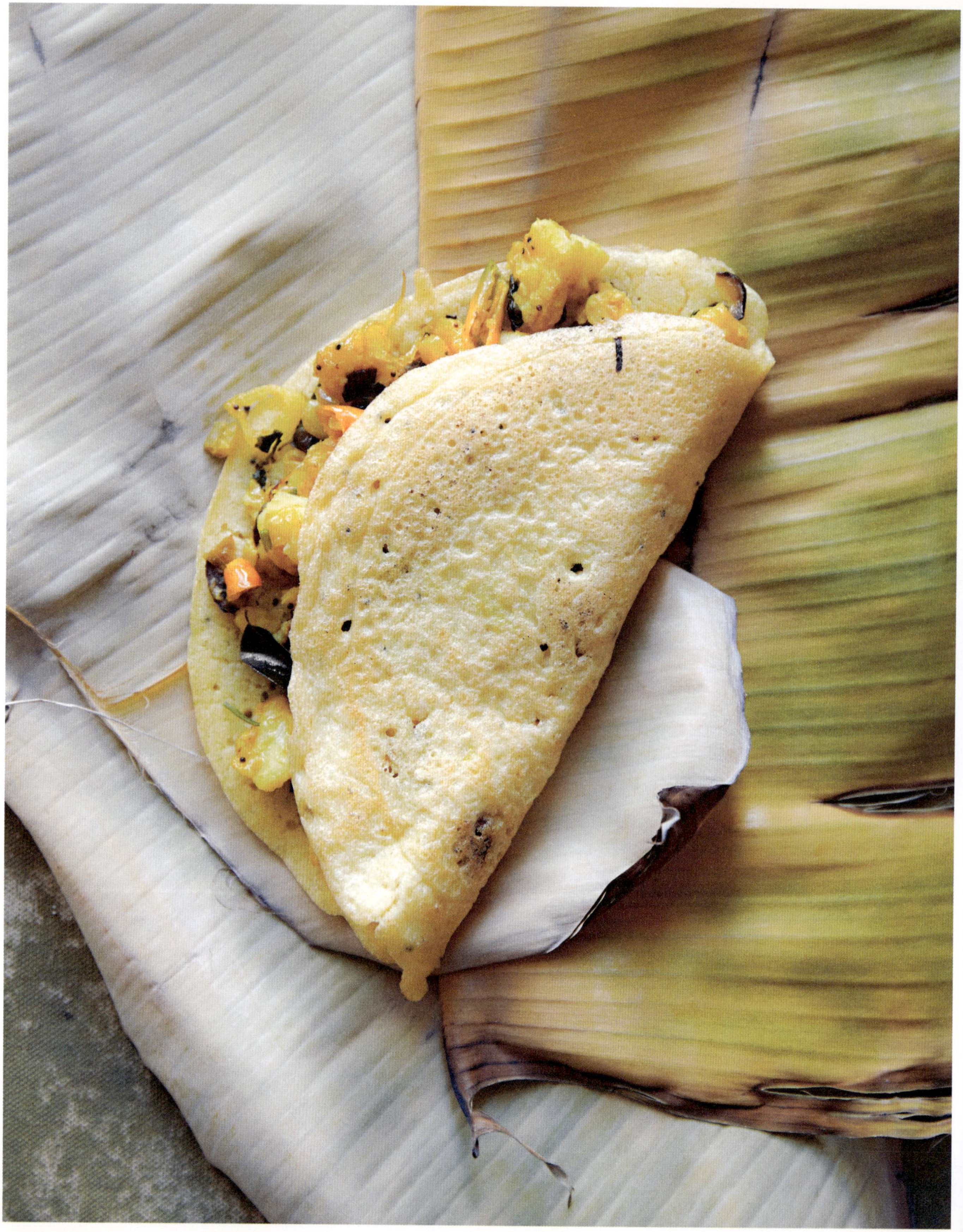

50g (1¾oz/¼ cup) chana dal (split chick peas)
300g (10½oz) potatoes
2 tbsp oil
1 tsp mustard seeds
7 fresh curry leaves
1 medium onion, finely sliced
2 green chillies, finely chopped with seeds in
2.5cm (1-inch) piece of ginger, peeled and finely chopped
½ tsp ground turmeric
1 tsp butter or ghee
1 tsp salt
1 x Thosai (recipe on p41)

Potato masala pancakes
Thosai (p41) are the perfect container for this chilli-laced, satisfying filling. This dish is easy to make at home on a griddle or frying pan.

Make the masala
Wash the chana dal and then put it in a bowl, cover with water and soak for 10 minutes.

Wash the potatoes and boil them with skins on for about 15 minutes until cooked. Take them off the heat and leave to cool. Then, peel off the skins and gently mash them, leaving plenty of small chunks.

Heat the oil in a medium frying pan (skillet) over a low heat, then add the mustard seeds. Let them cook for a few seconds until they pop, then add the curry leaves and the drained chana dal and sauté until the chick peas turn golden.

Add the onion, green chillies and ginger and sauté until the onion is soft and golden brown. Add the turmeric and give it a quick stir.

Add the butter and salt and mix it in well. Then, tip the potato into the pan, give it a good stir and cook for a minute or two. Taste for salt and take the pan off the heat.

Fill the thosai
Make the thosai as on p41. After flipping to the second side, place about 2 tablespoons of filling on one half of the thosai, about 2.5cm (1 inch) from the edge, and fold the other half of the thosai over the filling. Cook for 2–3 minutes until the filling is completely warmed through. Serve hot.

Variation: Paper thin masala thosai
Make the thin and crispy thosai on p41 but, before flipping over, place the filling in a line along the middle up to 2.5cm (1 inch) from the edges. Fold one half over the top of the filling and tuck it underneath. Bring the other half over and roll it loosely on top. Cook for another minute and serve.

Makes 12

MASALA THOSAI

MUTTON ROLLS

200g (7oz) potatoes
3 tbsp oil, plus 500ml (17 fl oz/generous 2 cups) for deep-frying
1 large red onion, finely chopped
5 garlic cloves, crushed to a paste
7.5cm (3-inch) piece of ginger, peeled and very finely chopped
3 green chillies, deseeded and finely chopped
200g (7oz) minced (ground) mutton or lamb
1 tsp ground turmeric
1 tsp chilli powder
2 tsp salt
1 tbsp white wine vinegar
1 tbsp brown sauce
1 tsp ground black pepper
1 tsp ground cardamom
12 spring roll wrappers
250g (9oz/4 cups) breadcrumbs

For the batter
200g (7oz/1½ cups) plain (all-purpose) flour
1 tsp ground black pepper
½ tsp ground turmeric
½ tsp salt
300ml (10½ fl oz/1¼ cups) water

Makes 12

Prepare the mutton filling
Wash the potatoes and boil them with skins on for about 15 minutes until cooked. Take them off the heat and leave to cool. Then, peel off the skins and mash them well.

While the potatoes are cooking, heat the oil in a large, lidded saucepan over a low heat. Sauté the onions, garlic, ginger and green chillies until the onions are soft and golden.

Add the mutton, stir well and fry for 10 minutes. Add the turmeric, chilli powder, salt and vinegar and stir well to coat the meat with spices. Cover and cook for a further 15 minutes.

Add the brown sauce, pepper and cardamom, give it a stir and take it off the heat. Add the mashed potatoes, mix it all together well, and taste for salt.

Make the batter
Mix all the ingredients except the water in a medium bowl. Then, add the water little by little, until you have a slightly runny batter.

Make the rolls
Remove the spring roll wrappers from the packet and cover them with a wet cloth so they don't dry out.

Lay one wrapper on a worktop or board in a diamond shape. Place a tablespoon of the filling about 1cm (½ inch) from the top of the diamond.

Spread the filling out horizontally into a sausage shape across the top of the diamond, leaving roughly the same space at each side.

Start folding the pastry sheet from the top of the diamond, pulling the top corner over the mince mix and tucking it under the mixture. Next fold the two side corners in and roll the parcel downwards, tightly but gently.

Continue rolling towards the bottom, and when you reach the end dip a fingertip into the batter and use it to seal the the roll. Repeat until all the rolls are made.

Spread the breadcrumbs on a plate. Dip one roll at a time into the batter and then roll them in the breadcrumbs, making sure they are fully covered. Be careful to avoid batter dripping into the breadcrumbs. Repeat until all the rolls are crumbed.

Bring the 500ml of oil in a deep saucepan to boiling point, then reduce the heat to medium. Slide the mutton rolls into the pan in batches of five or six and deep-fry for about 4 minutes until golden brown, gently turning them as they cook. Remove with a slotted spoon and lay them on kitchen towel to absorb the excess oil.

Serve with tomato sauce, brown sauce or chilli sauce.

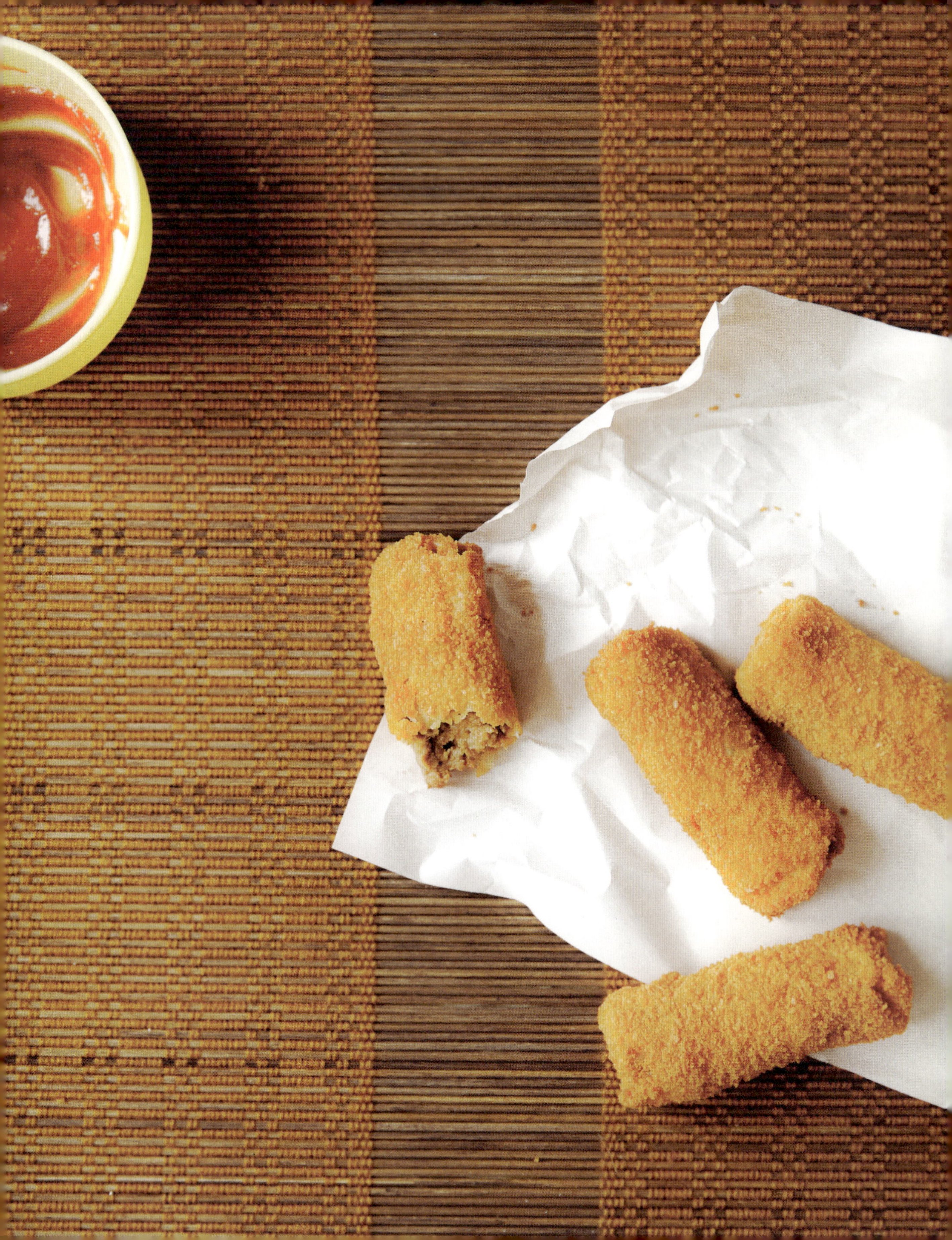

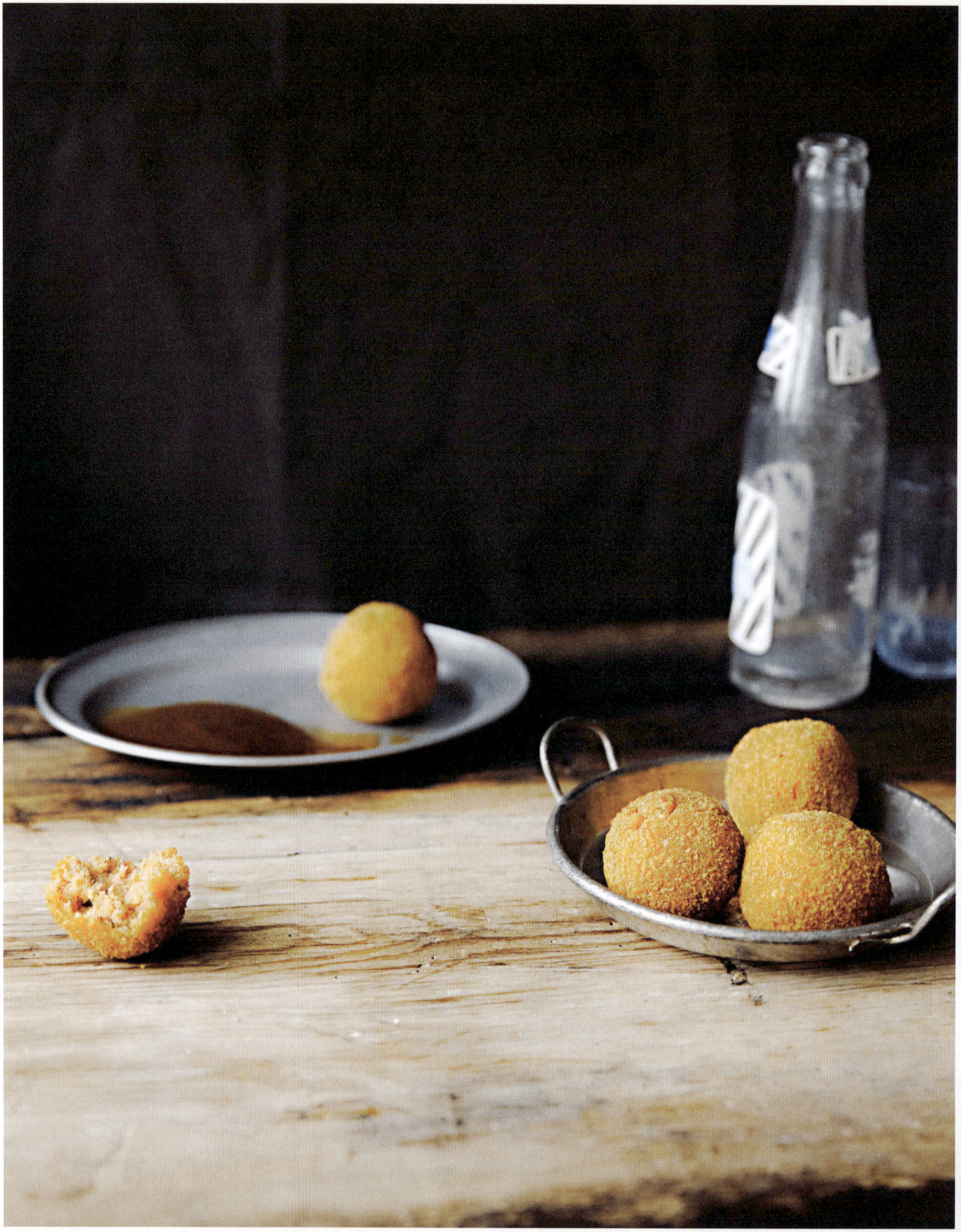

200g (7oz) potatoes
4 tbsp oil, plus 500ml
   (17 fl oz/generous 2 cups)
   for deep-frying
1 large onion, finely chopped
4 garlic cloves,
   finely chopped
5cm (2-inch) piece of ginger,
   peeled and finely chopped
2 green chillies, deseeded
   and finely chopped
225g (8oz) fresh tuna
   (steamed and flaked) or
   canned tuna (drained
   weight, broken into chunks)
2 tbsp tomato sauce
   (ketchup)
1 tsp chilli powder
1 tsp ground cardamom
1 tsp ground black pepper
½ tsp salt
juice of ½ lime
200g (7oz/3⅓ cups)
   breadcrumbs

For the batter
200g (7oz/1½ cups) plain
   (all-purpose) flour
¼ tsp ground turmeric
1 tsp coarsely ground
   black pepper
½ tsp salt
300ml (10½ fl oz/
   1¼ cups) water

Tuna features regularly in Sri Lankan cooking, both fresh and tinned: here it is in fragrant little croquettes that are served at social events.

Make the cutlets
Wash the potatoes and boil them with skins on for about 15 minutes until cooked. Take them off the heat and leave to cool. Then, peel off the skins and mash them well.

While the potatoes are cooking, heat the oil in a deep frying pan (skillet) over a low heat. Sauté the onions, garlic, ginger and green chillies until the onions are soft and turning golden.

Add the tuna, tomato sauce and chilli powder, stir well and cook for 2 minutes. Remove from the heat, add the cardamom, pepper, salt and lime juice and give it a stir. Taste for salt and lime.

Finally, add the potatoes and mix together well. Using your hands, make 12 lime-size balls and set aside.

Make the batter
Mix all the ingredients except the water in a medium bowl. Then, add the water little by little until you have a slightly runny batter.

Fry the cutlets
Spread the breadcrumbs on a plate. Dip two or three balls at a time into the batter and then roll them in the breadcrumbs, making sure they are fully covered. Repeat until all the balls are crumbed.

Bring the 500ml (17 fl oz/2 generous cups) of oil to boiling point in a deep saucepan, then reduce the heat to medium. Slide the cutlets into the pan in batches of five or six and deep-fry for about 3 minutes until golden brown, gently turning them as they cook. Remove with a slotted spoon and lay on kitchen towel to absorb excess oil.

Serve with tomato sauce, brown sauce or chilli sauce.

Makes 12

TUNA CUTLETS

FISH PATTIES

These resemble pasties or dumplings, and are an incredibly popular snack. There's a Portuguese influence at play: compare them to the very similar empanada.

For the filling
250g (9oz) potatoes
3 tbsp oil, plus 500ml (17 fl oz/generous 2 cups) for deep-frying
1 medium onion, finely chopped
3 garlic cloves, finely chopped
2.5cm (1-inch) piece of ginger, peeled and finely chopped
1 tsp ground turmeric
½ tsp ground cumin
¼ tsp ground cinnamon
¼ tsp ground cloves
1 tsp ground black pepper
300g (10½oz) fresh tuna (steamed and flaked) or canned tuna (drained weight, broken into chunks)
1 tbsp dill, finely chopped
2 tsp salt
juice of ½ lime

For the pastry
300g (10½oz/2⅓ cups) plain (all-purpose) flour
½ tsp salt
3 tbsp butter
1 egg yolk
60ml (2 fl oz/¼ cup) coconut milk

Makes 12

Make the filling
Wash the potatoes and boil them with skins on for about 15 minutes until cooked. Take them off the heat and leave to cool. Then, peel off the skins and finely chop.

Heat the oil in a medium saucepan over a low heat and sauté the onions, garlic and ginger, until the onions are soft and turning golden.

Add the turmeric, cumin, cinnamon and ground cloves and pepper and stir well. Add the fish and dill, and cook for 3 minutes, stirring frequently.

Add the potato and salt and mix well. Cook for another 2 minutes, stirring frequently. Squeeze in the lime and take the pan off the heat.

Make the pastry
Mix the flour and salt together in a large bowl. Add the butter and rub it into the flour mixture until it turns into crumbs. Beat the egg yolk and mix it into the crumbs. Then gradually pour in the coconut milk while kneading the mixture into a soft, pliable dough. You may need to add a little extra flour or water to get the right consistency.

Wrap the dough in clingfilm (plastic wrap) and chill in the fridge for 30 minutes.

Break the dough in half and roll it out on a lightly floured surface until it is about ½cm (¼ inch) thin. Use a pastry cutter to make six circles about 5–6cm (2–2½ inches) in diameter.

Put 1 tablespoon of the fish mixture on one of the pastry circles. Lightly beat the egg whites, then dip your finger in it and apply it along the edge of the pastry circle. Fold the pastry over to make a half-moon shape and gently press together to seal.

Using a fork, press along the edge of the half circle so that the patty is well sealed, then put it on a tray. Repeat this process with the second batch of dough.

Bring the 500ml (17 fl oz/2 generous cups) of oil to boiling point in a deep saucepan, then reduce the heat to medium. Slide the patties into the pan in batches of five or six and deep-fry for about 3 minutes until golden brown, turning them as they cook. Remove with a slotted spoon and lay on kitchen towel to absorb the excess oil.

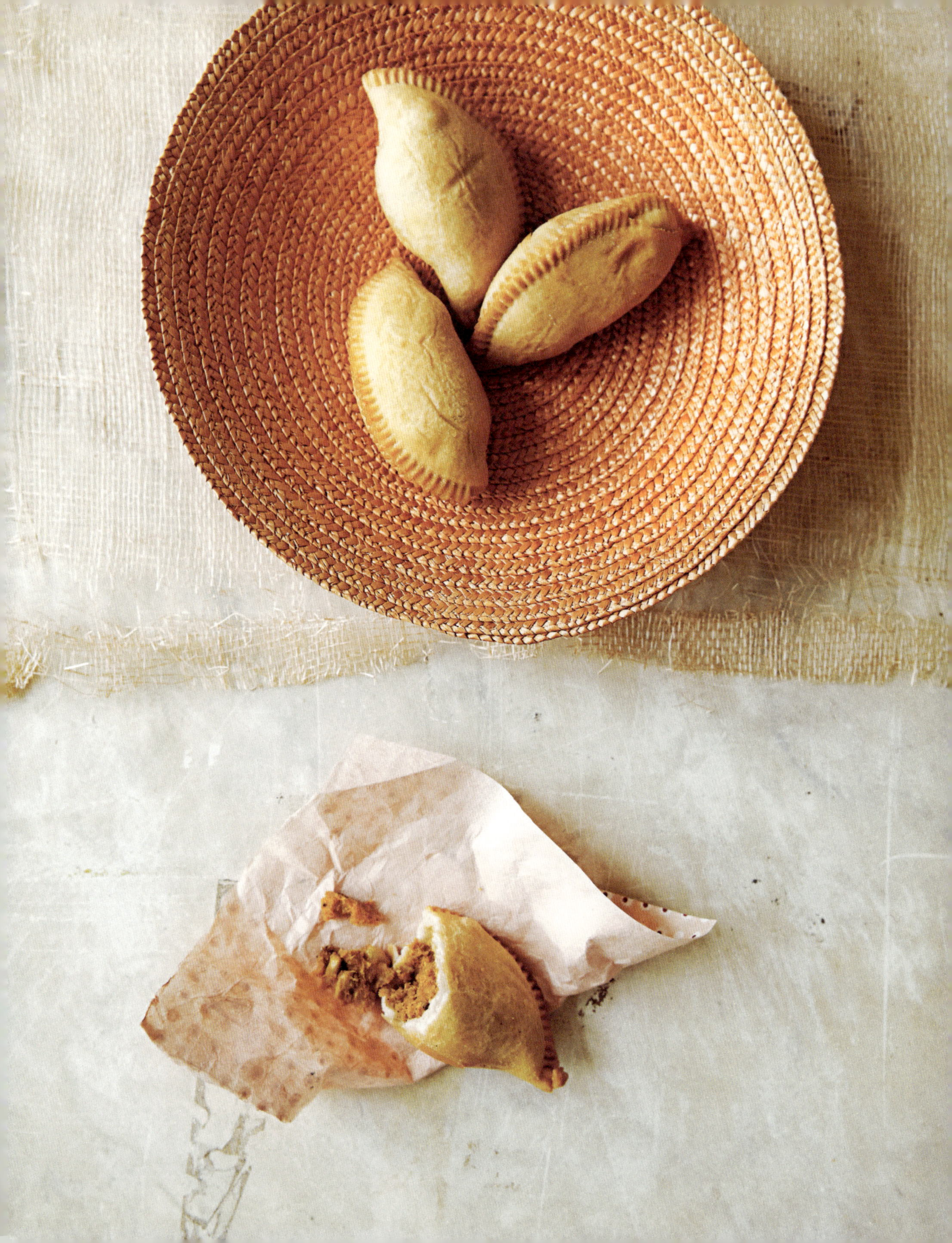

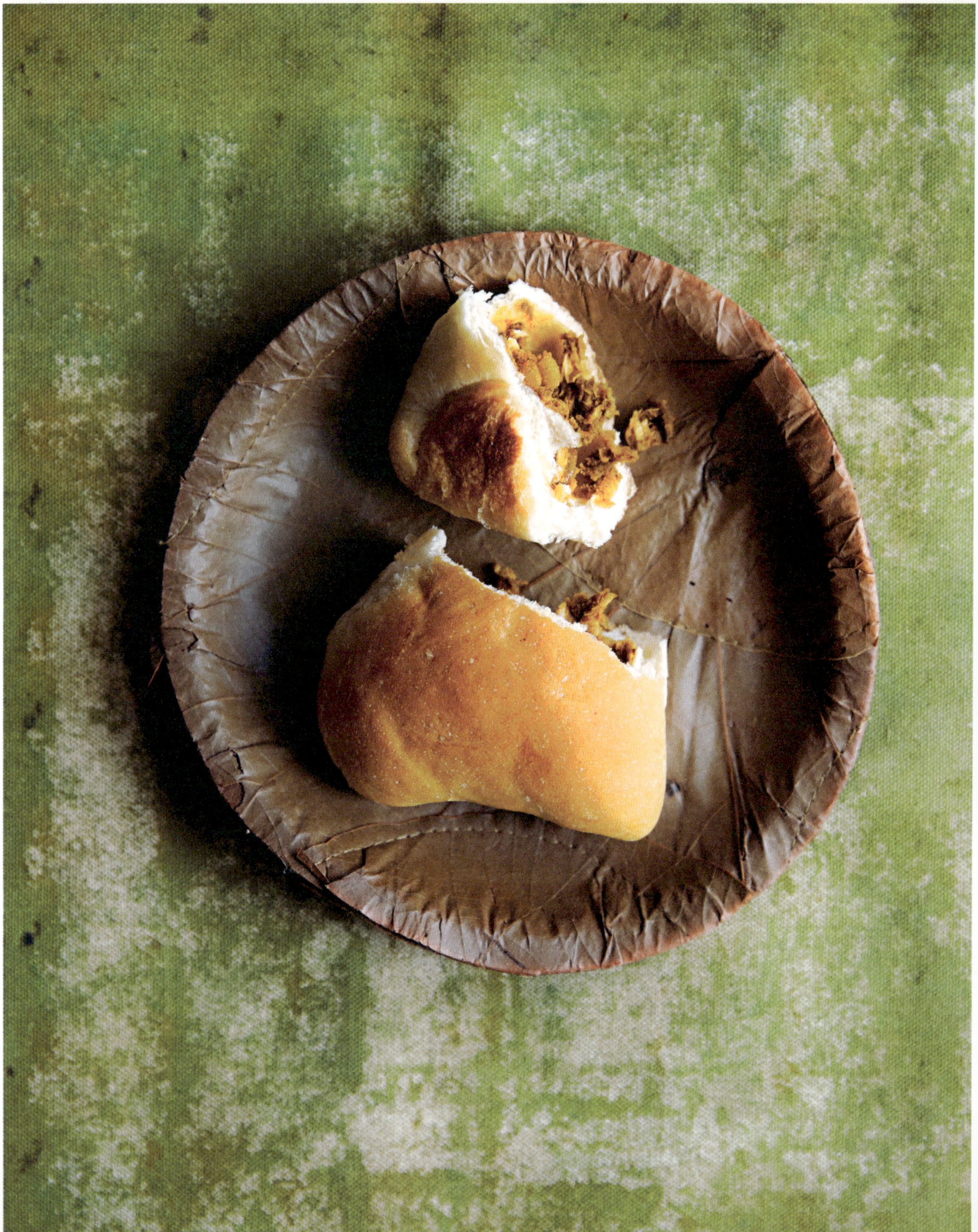

MAALU PANG

Fish buns
A classic 'short eat' (takeaway snack).

For the bun dough
7g (¼oz/2 tsp) dried yeast
1 tsp sugar (white or brown)
350ml (12 fl oz/1½ cups) lukewarm water (50ml/1¼ fl oz/¼ cup for the yeast, 300ml/10½ fl oz/1¼ cups for the dough)
400g (14oz/3 cups) plain (all-purpose) flour
½ tsp salt
1 egg, beaten, for 'egg wash'

For filling
300g (10½oz) potatoes
3 tbsp oil
1 medium onion, finely chopped
3 garlic cloves, finely chopped
2.5cm (1-inch) piece of ginger, peeled and finely chopped
1 tsp ground coriander
½ tsp ground cumin
¼ tsp ground cinnamon
1 tsp ground turmeric
½ tsp chillli powder
¼ tsp ground cloves
2 tsp ground black pepper
2 tsp salt
300g (10½oz) firm fish like tuna (fresh or canned) or flaky white fish like haddock

Makes 8

Make the dough
Place the yeast in a small bowl. Add the sugar and 50ml of lukewarm water and leave to activate the yeast for 15 minutes.

Put the flour, salt and activated yeast into a large mixing bowl. Start adding the 300ml of lukewarm water, little by little, mixing it together with your hands as you go. Keep adding water until it all begins to bind together. You may need to add a little more flour or water to make a soft, pliable dough. Then, knead it well for about 10 minutes into a ball shape. Wrap the dough in clingfilm (plastic wrap) and set aside to rest for at least 30 minutes.

The dough will have risen slightly. Sprinkle a little flour on a work surface and knead the dough again a few times.

Make the filling
Wash the potatoes and boil them with skins on for about 15 minutes until cooked. Take them off the heat and leave to cool. Then, peel off the skins and roughly mash.

Heat the oil in a medium saucepan over a low heat and sauté the onions, garlic and ginger, until the onions are soft and golden.

Add the coriander, cumin, cinnamon, turmeric, chilli powder, ground cloves, pepper and salt, and stir well.

Add the fish and potato and cook for 2 minutes, stirring frequently. Take the pan off the heat.

Make the buns
Preheat the oven to 150°C (300°F/Gas Mark 2) and line a baking sheet with baking (parchment) paper.

Taking a handful of dough at a time, shape it into 12 lemon-sized balls. Set them aside.

Sprinkle some flour on the work surface, lay one dough ball at a time down and, using the palm of your hand and your fingers, flatten the ball into a triangle shape about ½cm (¼ inch) thick.

Put 2 tablespoons of the filling in the middle of the triangle and fold the three edges of the dough in over the filling, to make a smaller triangle and press firmly to seal. Place the filled buns on the prepared baking sheet one by one.

When all the buns are filled, use a pastry brush to brush the top of the dough with the beaten egg.

Bake for 40 minutes until golden. Serve immediately.

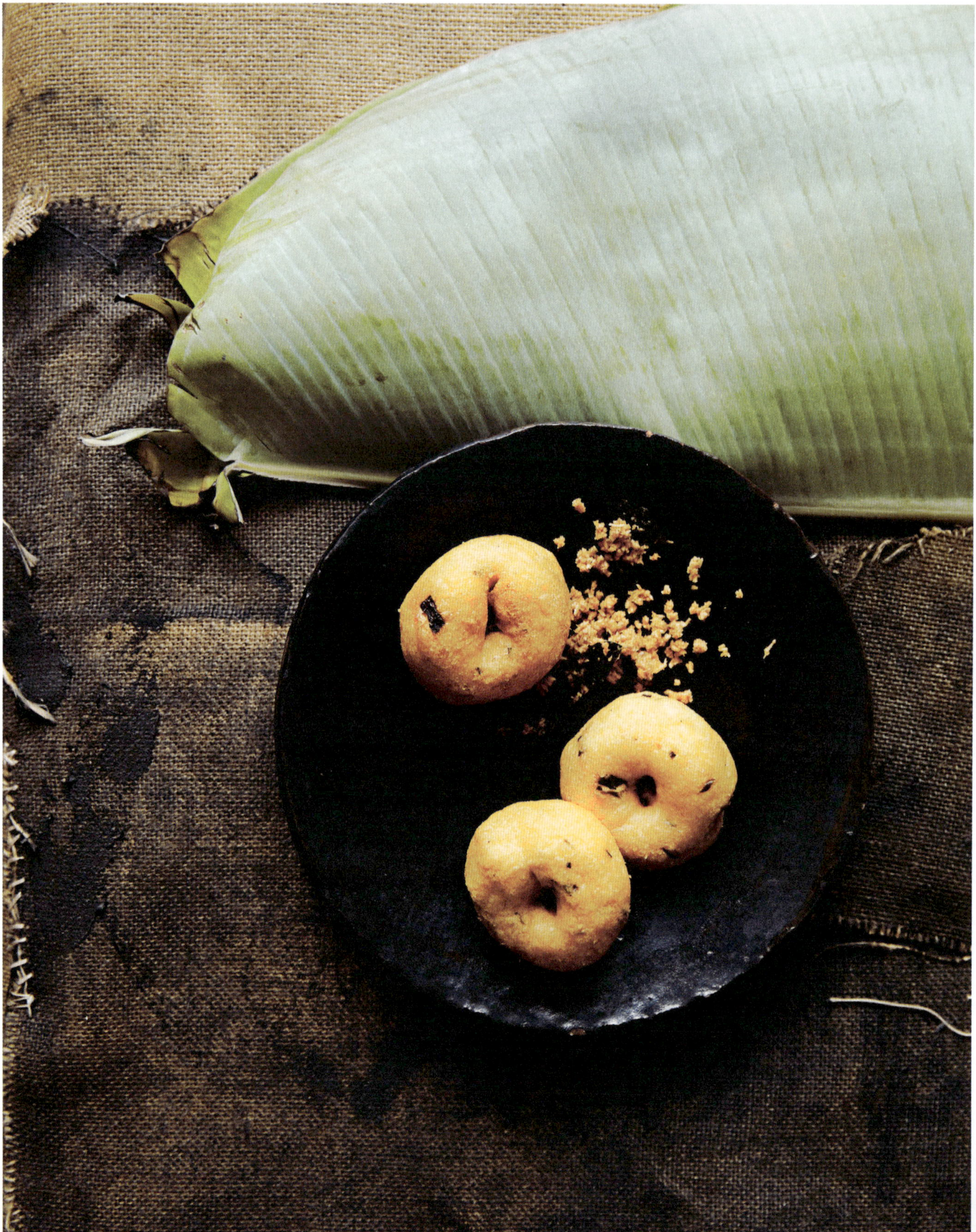

300g (10½oz/1½ cups) urid dal (split black gram)
150ml (5 fl oz/scant ⅔ cup) water
1 medium red onion, finely chopped
5cm (2-inch) piece of ginger, peeled and finely chopped
3 green chillies, finely chopped with seeds in
1 tsp cumin seeds, crushed
4 fresh curry leaves, finely chopped
½ tsp salt
500ml (17 fl oz/generous 2 cups) oil

Black gram doughnuts

'Vadai, vadai, vadai' is a common cry of hawkers on trains and at markets: these deep-fried snacks are ideal for eating on the go.

Wash the urid dal and put in a bowl. Cover with water and soak for at least 1 hour. Drain and put it in a blender and liquidise, adding the water little by little, until you have a thick, smooth paste. Mix in the onion, ginger, chillies, cumin seeds, curry leaves and salt.

Grease your palms with a little oil and shape the mixture into 12 large lemon-sized balls. Set them aside.

Bring the oil to boiling point in a deep saucepan, then reduce the heat to medium. When the oil is hot, take one ball at a time and flatten it between your palms into a 2.5cm (1-inch) thick disc. Make a hole in the middle with your index finger and slide it into the hot oil. Deep-fry in batches of four or five.

Turn the vadai from time to time so they cook evenly, and keep an eye on the heat. You want the outside to turn golden brown on both sides and the inside to be cooked through. This should take about 7–8 minutes.

Remove the vadai with a slotted spoon and lay them on kitchen towel to absorb the excess oil. Eat while still hot and crispy, served with Pol Sambal (pictured here, recipe on p71) or Seeni Sambol (p76).

Makes 12

ULUNDU VADAI

PARIPPU VADAI

Deep-fried chana dal

Similar to Ulundu Vadai (p55), this disc-shaped short eat gets a crunchy, nutty texture from the chana dal. Serve with Pachai Sambal (p80).

Makes 12

300g (10½oz/1⅓ cups) chana dal (split chick peas)
150ml (5 fl oz/scant ⅔ cup) water
1 medium red onion, finely chopped
5cm (2-inch) piece of ginger, peeled and finely chopped
3 green chillies, finely chopped
1 tsp cumin seeds, crushed
4 fresh curry leaves, finely chopped
½ tsp salt
500ml (17 fl oz/generous 2 cups) oil, for deep-frying

Wash the chana dal well and put it in a bowl. Cover with water and soak for at least 1 hour. Drain and reserve 2 teaspoons of the chick peas, then put the rest in a blender. Liquidise, adding the water little by little, until you have a thick, smooth paste. Mix in the onion, ginger, chillies, cumin seeds, curry leaves and salt.

Stir in the reserved chick peas and mix well. Grease your palms with a little oil and shape the mixture into 12 large lemon-sized balls. Set them aside.

Bring the oil to boiling point in a deep saucepan, then reduce the heat to medium. Take one ball at a time and flatten it between your palms into a 1.5cm (½-inch) thick disc, then slide it into the hot oil. Deep-fry in batches of four or five.

Turn the vadai from time to time so they cook evenly, and keep an eye on the heat. You want the outside to turn golden brown on both sides and the inside to be cooked through. This should take about 7–8 minutes.

Remove the vadai with a slotted spoon and lay them on kitchen towel to absorb the excess oil. Eat while still hot and crispy.

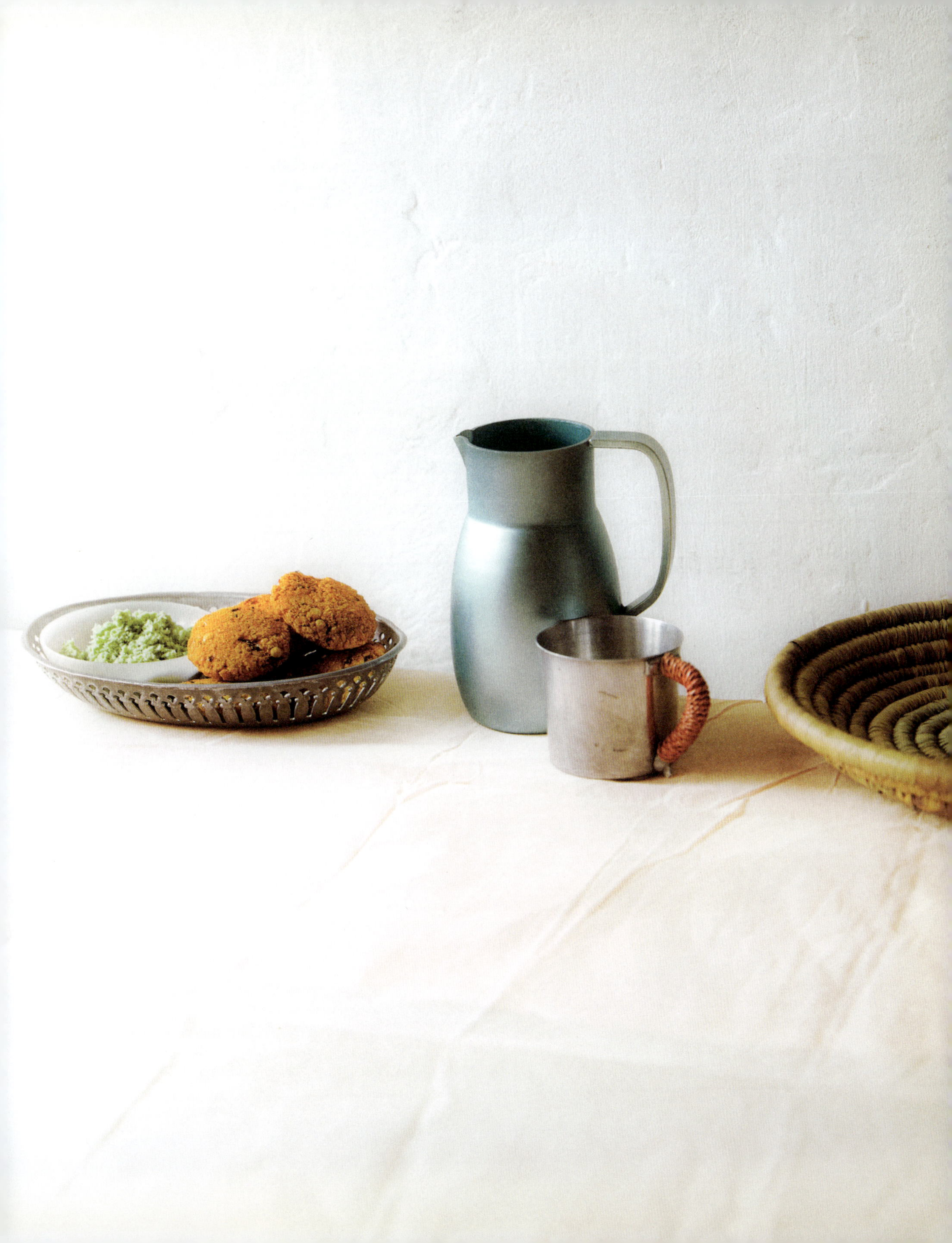

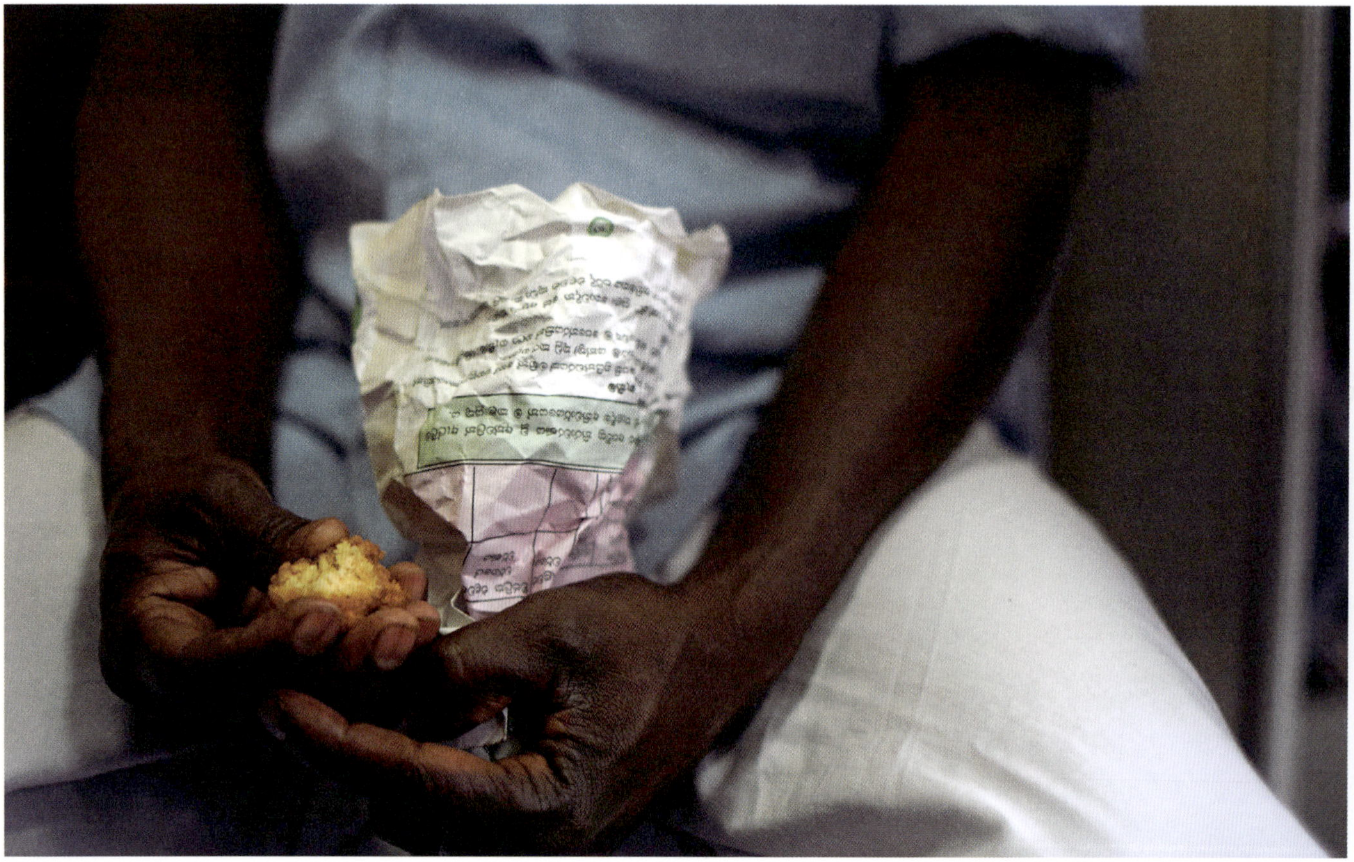

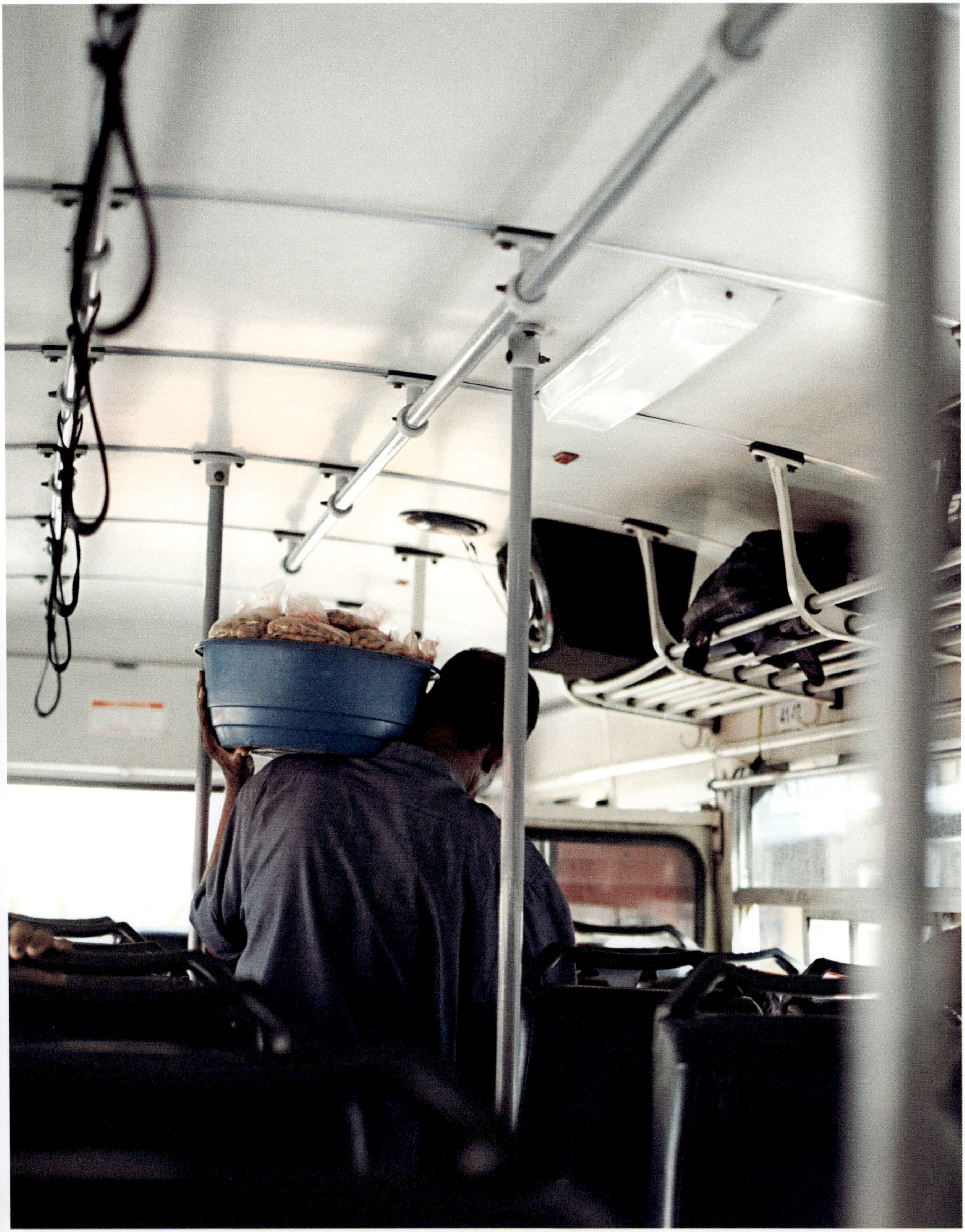

POL ROTTI

Coconut flatbread

Coconut adds sweetness and texture to flatbreads spiked with green chilli. They're quick to make and go wonderfully with a sambol or a hot curry. Don't worry if you've never made bread before – they are very easy.

600g (1lb 5oz/5⅓ cups) self-raising (self-rising) flour
100g desiccated (shredded) coconut
½ medium onion, finely chopped
3 green chillies, deseeded and finely chopped
1 tsp salt
2 tbsp oil (plus 1 tbsp for greasing palms)
250ml (9 fl oz/generous 1 cup) water

Makes 8

Put all the ingredients except the water in a large bowl. Mix the ingredients together by hand, adding the water little by little as you go. Gradually bring everything together, kneading the dough until it forms a ball. Set aside to rest for 15 minutes.

Grease your palms and fingers with oil and divide the dough into eight equal portions, then shape these portions into balls. One at a time on a plate, flatten the dough balls into 1.5cm (½-inch) thick discs.

Heat up a dry flat griddle or frying pan (skillet) on a medium heat, then cook one or two rotti at a time, for about 5 minutes on each side, until golden. Remove from the pan and pile them up as you continue cooking the rest of the rotti.

Serve warm with Lunu Sambol (p75), Seeni Sambol (p76), Kukul Mas Mirisata (p193), Koli Kari (p197) or Elumas (p201).

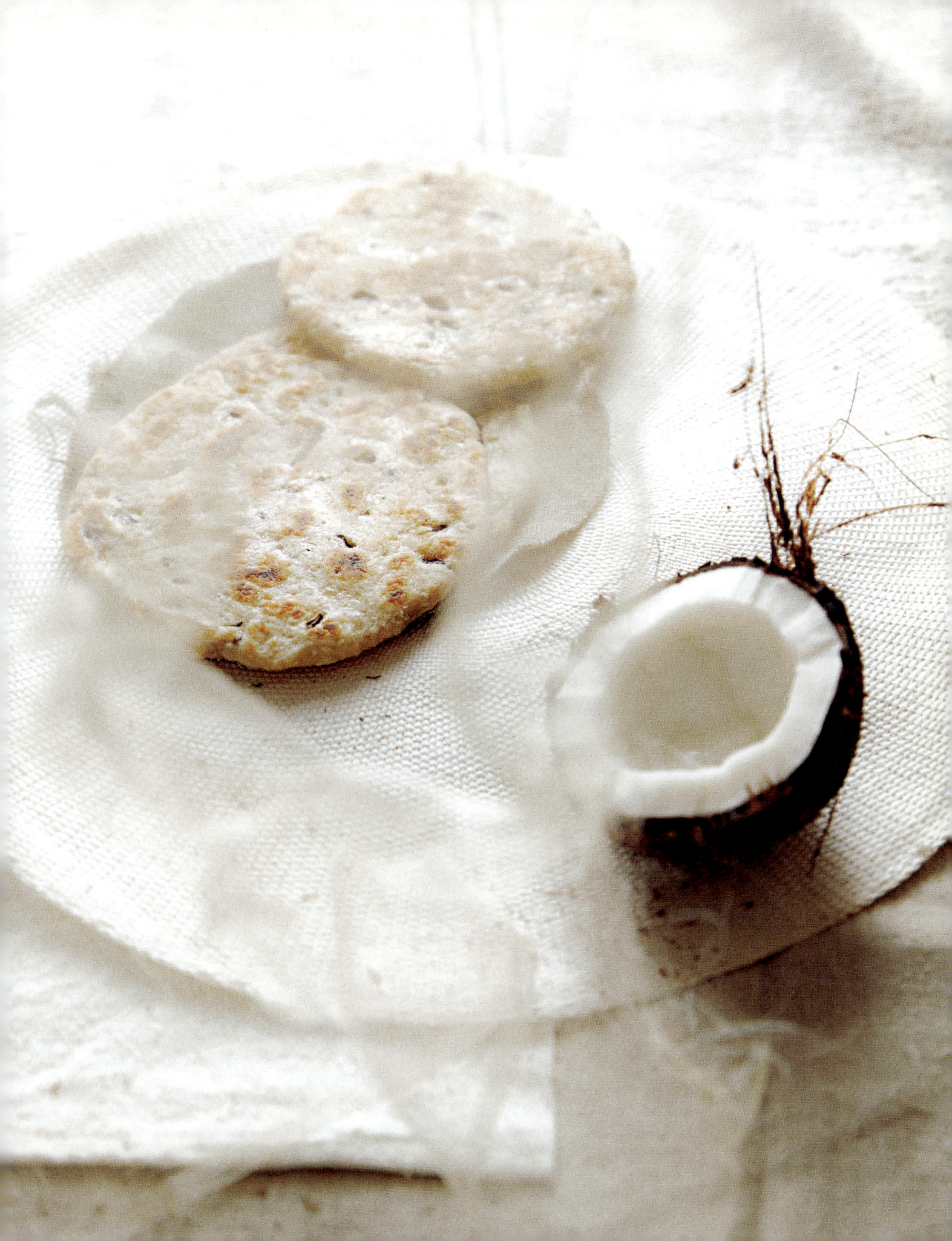

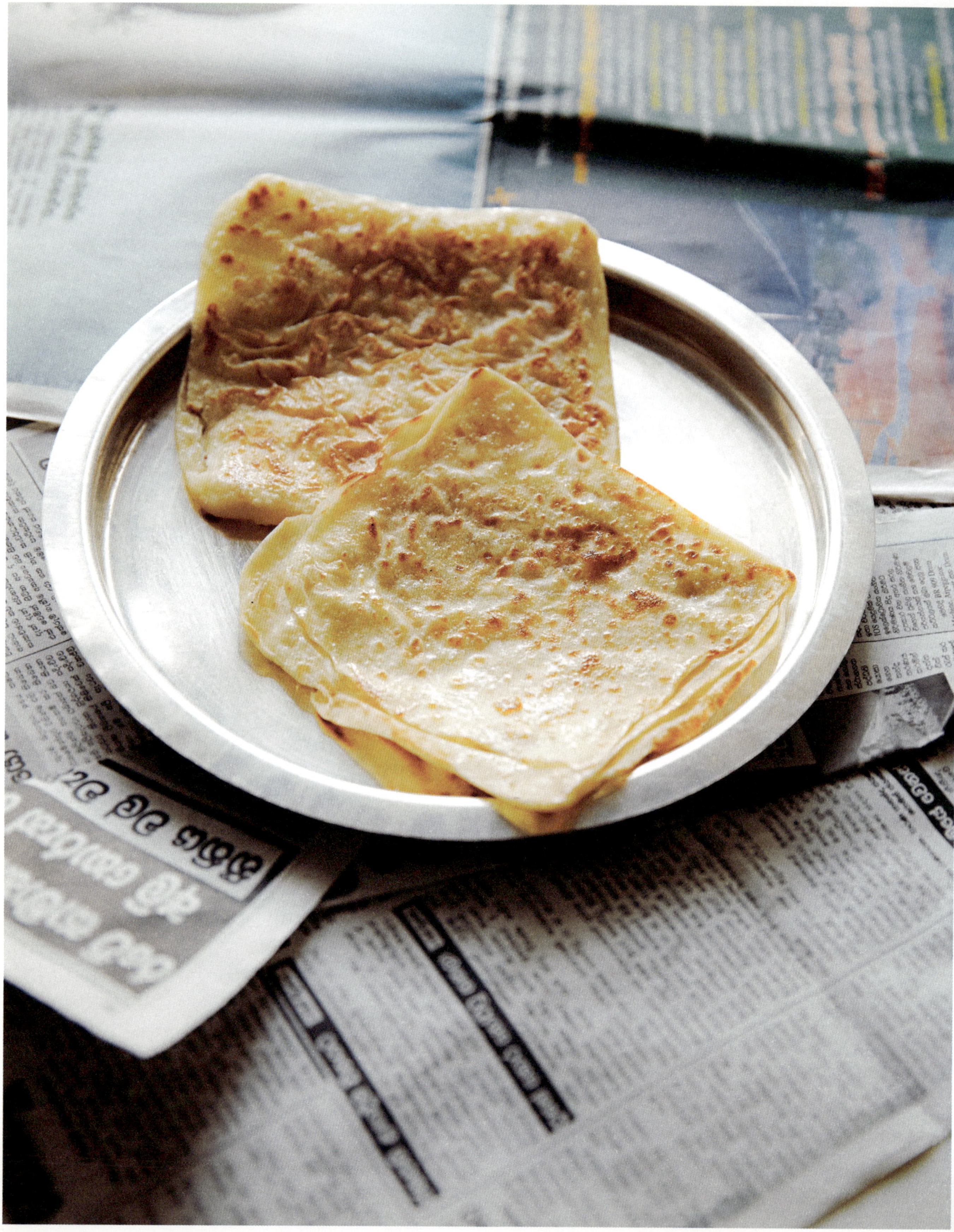

VEECHU ROTTI

Thin flatbread

'Veechu' translates as 'thrown' in Tamil, referring to the hand motion used to form this simple bread. They were introduced to the island by early Arab traders and resemble Middle Eastern khobz flatbreads.

5 tbsp oil (3 tbsp for the dough and 2 tbsp for frying)
500g (1lb 2oz/4 cups) plain (all-purpose) flour
1 tsp salt
200ml (7 fl oz/generous ¾ cup) water

First, heat 3 tbsp of oil in a small saucepan over a medium heat until nearly sizzling.

Put the flour and salt in a large bowl and pour in the hot oil. Mix it in well with the handle of a wooden spoon. Add water little by little, stirring all the time, until it all begins to bind together. Then, start kneading the dough.

At first, the dough will stick to your hands but as you continue kneading it will lose its stickiness and and become a firm, round ball. Knead well for about 10 minutes. Cover it with a wet cloth and set aside for at least an hour.

Taking a handful of dough at a time, shape it into 12 large lemon-sized balls. Set them aside.

Heat up a flat griddle pan or frying pan (skillet) on a medium heat. While it is heating, place one dough ball on a work surface and start to flatten it into a large, very thin circle, using a rolling pin or your palm.

To stretch the dough out very thin, experienced veechu rotti makers hold two corners of the flattened dough between their thumbs and index fingers, and roll it in a circular motion through the air, moving their hands around the circle as they go.

Lay the stretched-out dough on a work surface and fold in each side to make a 15cm (6-inch) square.

Spread 2 tbsp of oil on the now hot pan and fry the folded rotti one at a time. Cook for 2–3 minutes until golden brown on the bottom, then turn over and repeat on the other side. Pile them up as you continue cooking the rest.

Serve warm with any curry or Pol Sambol (p71) or Seeni Sambol (p76).

Makes 12

KOTHU ROTTI

Flatbread stir-fry

The staccato clacking of cleavers on a hotplate heralds a street stall making this iconic dish. It uses Veechu Rotti (p63) along with vegetables, chicken or meat.

Serves 4

8 Veechu Rotti (recipe on p63)
2 tbsp oil
7 fresh curry leaves
2 green chillies, deseeded and roughly chopped
1 medium red onion, roughly chopped
½ tsp ground turmeric
150g (5½oz) carrots (about 2 medium), medium diced
1 tbsp frozen peas, defrosted (optional)
150g (5½oz) cabbage or leeks or both, finely sliced
salt
2 eggs
250g (9oz) mutton or chicken curry (Elumas on p201, Kukul Mas Mirisata on p193 or Koli Kari on p197) with about 50ml (1¾ fl oz scant ¼ cup) sauce

Chop the rotti into pieces roughly 1.5cm (½ inch) square either by hand or using a food processor. If you're doing it by hand, cut the rotti into thin strips and then take a handful and cut these crossways into small pieces. Set aside.

Heat the oil in a medium wok or frying pan (skillet) over a low heat. Add the curry leaves and green chillies, and sauté for a few seconds. Add the onions and sauté until they are just soft, about a minute or so, then add the turmeric.

Turn the heat up to high, add the vegetables and stir-fry for a couple of minutes. Season with salt.

Reduce the heat to medium and push the stir-fried vegetables to one side of the pan. Add a little extra oil to the pan if it is looking dry, then break in the eggs. Add a pinch of salt and scramble the eggs. When they are ready, mix them into the vegetables and turn the heat back up to high.

Tip in the chopped rotti a little at a time, stirring them into the mixture as you go. Finally, add the cooked chicken or mutton curry and sauce into the rotti mix and stir well. Cook for 2 minutes on high to warm through completely. Serve hot.

Variation: For a vegetarian version, simply leave out the mutton or chicken curry.

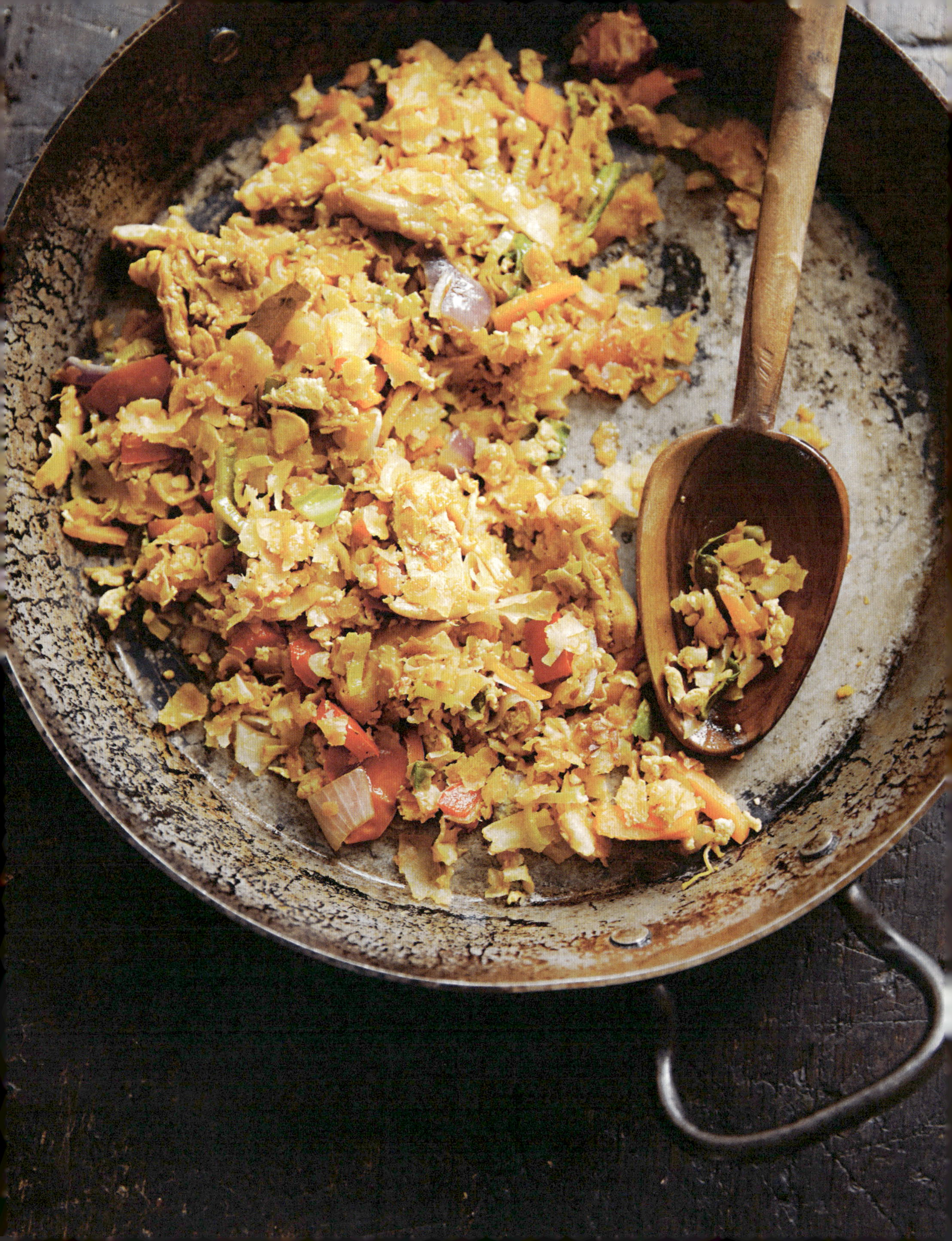

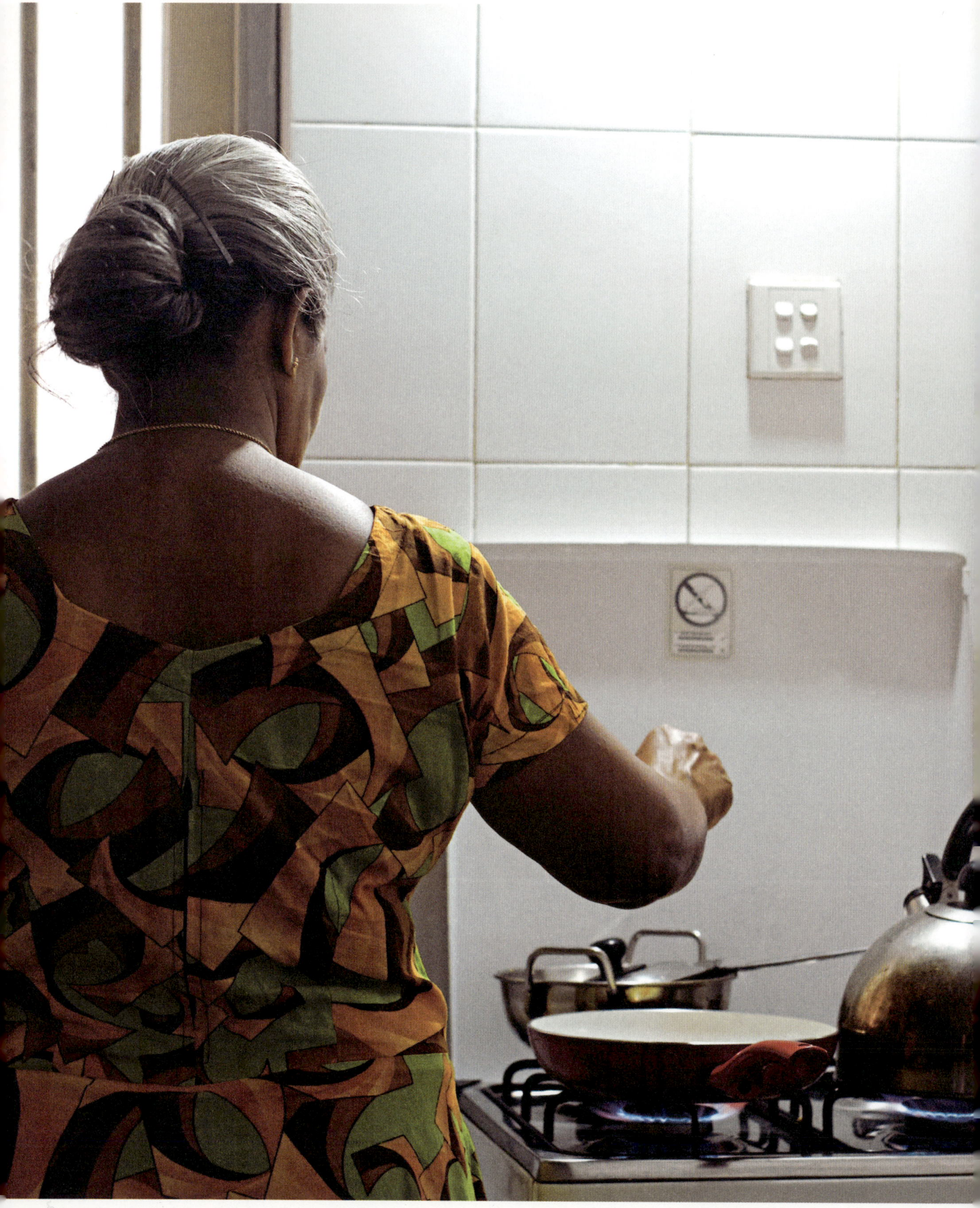

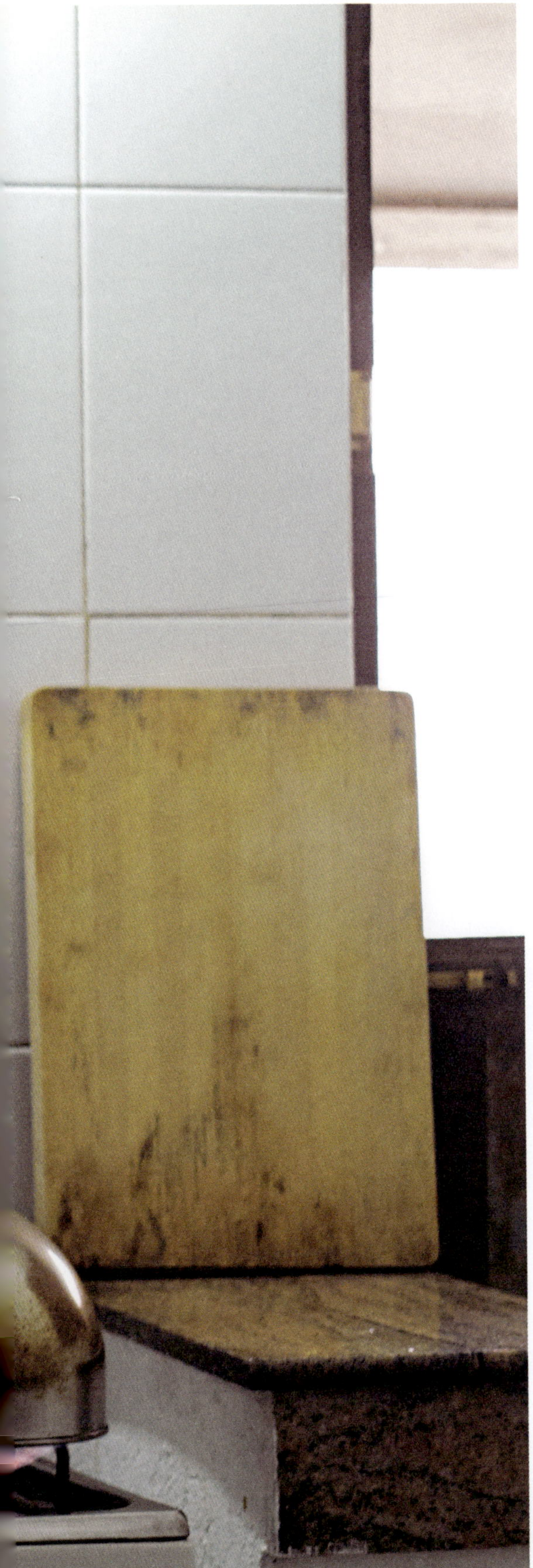
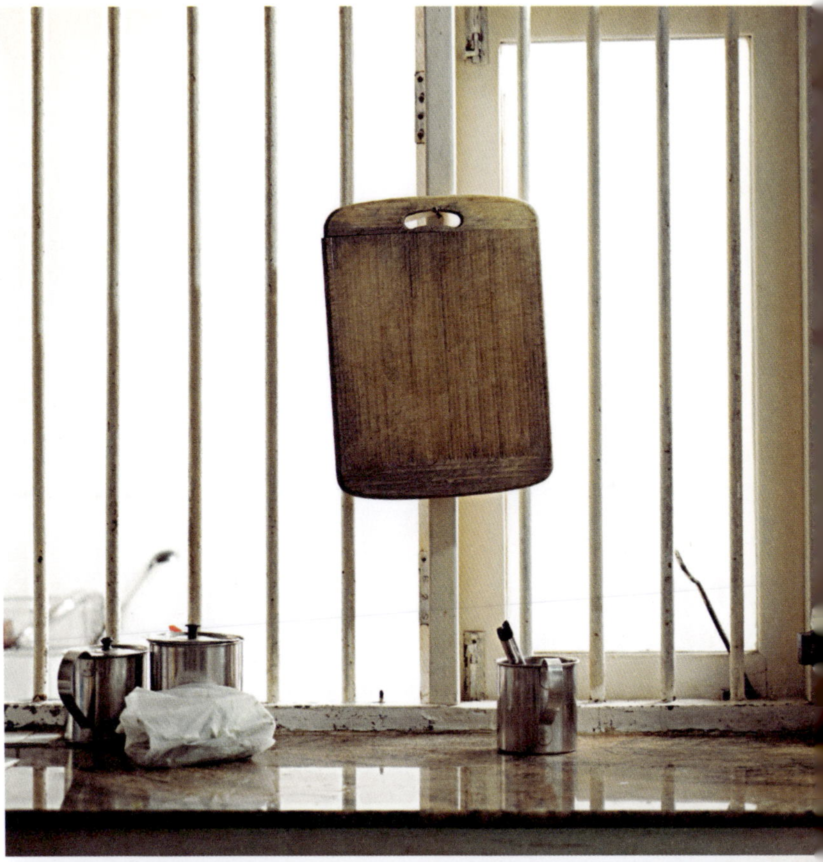
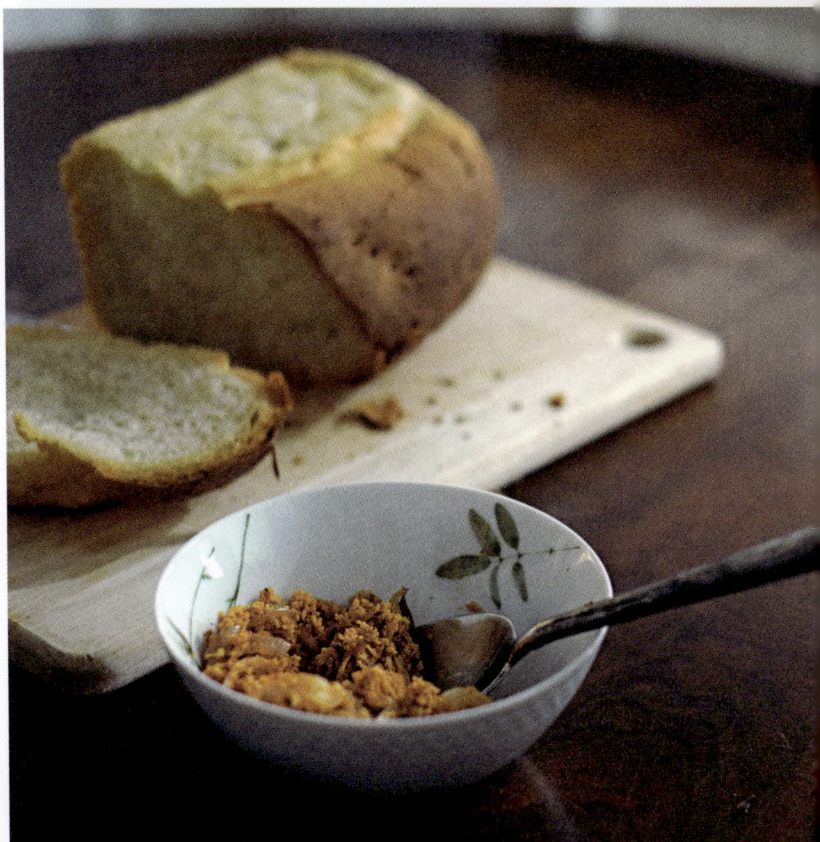

KIRIBATH

Coconut milk rice

It's a humble combination of two everyday ingredients, but Kiribath has enormous significance in Sri Lanka – it's cooked by the Sinhalese to mark new year in April, and on other special occasions that celebrate new beginnings.

500g (1lb 2oz/2⅓ cups) white rice (basmati or patna)
1 litre (35 fl oz/4¼ cups) water
2 tsp salt
400ml (14 fl oz/1⅔ cups) coconut milk
butter, for greasing

Serves 4

Put the rice into a medium, lidded saucepan and cover with water. Swirl the rice around to wash it, drain and repeat at least twice until the water is clear. Then, add the 1 litre (35 fl oz/4¼ cups) of water and bring to the boil. Reduce the heat to medium, half-cover with the lid, and cook until all the water is absorbed, about 18–20 minutes. Then, add the salt and coconut milk and stir into the rice.

Cook uncovered over a low to medium heat until all the milk is absorbed, about 5–10 minutes depending on the rice you use. If the rice is not cooked, add extra boiling water and cook over a very low heat until soft. Take the rice off the heat and set aside for a couple of minutes to cool very slightly.

Transfer the moist rice to a platter, and then smooth and flatten it until it is about 5cm (2 inches) tall and the same shape as the platter. You can either use a spatula, or you can put your hand inside a sandwich bag and use that to shape the rice. Put a little buttter on the spatula or the sandwich bag for a smooth effect.

Leave the rice to rest for 1–2 minutes, then cut it into diamond shapes or squares while slightly warm so that the pieces do not break.

Serve with Pol Sambol (pictured here, recipe on p71), Katta Sambol (p72) or Ambul Thial (p161).

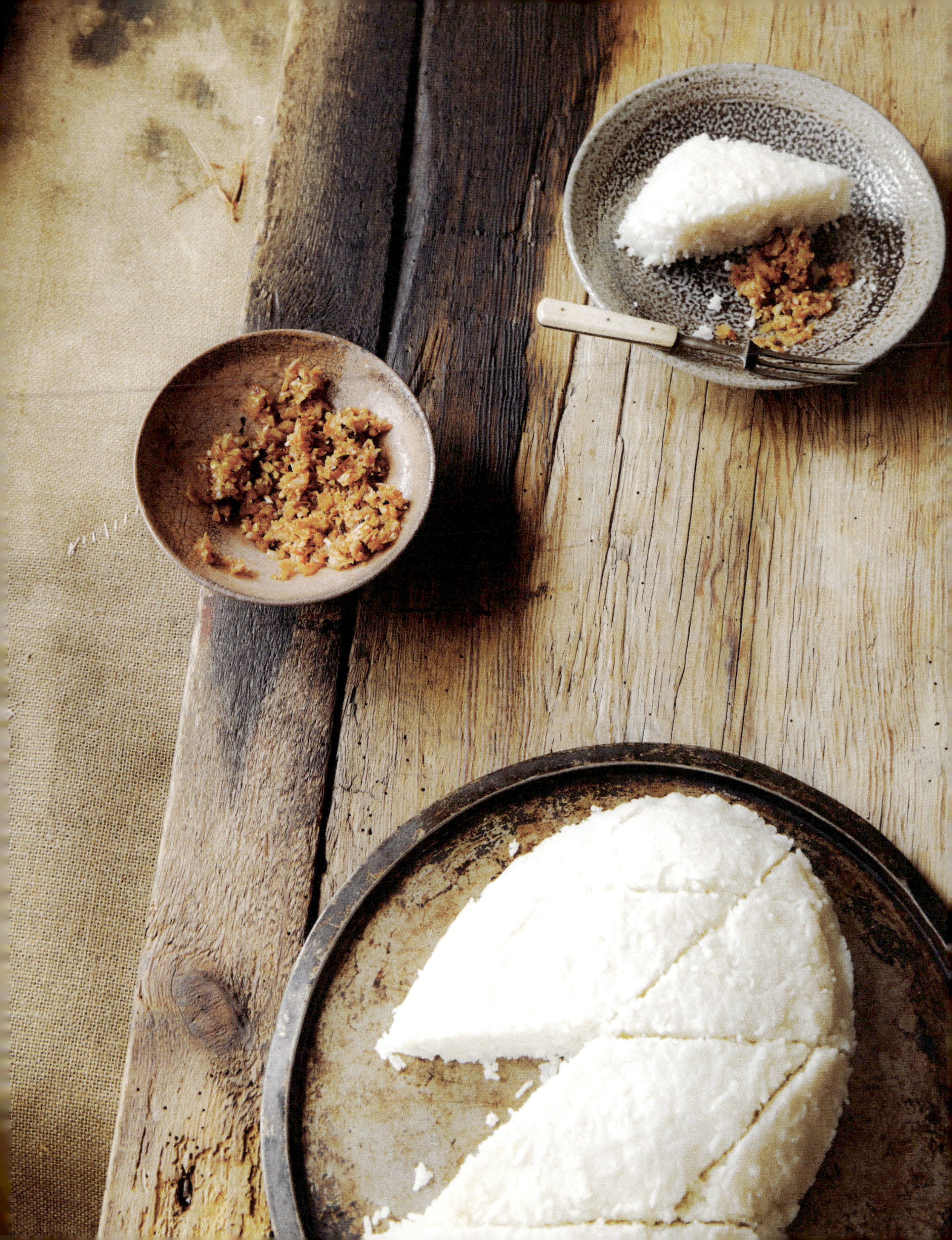

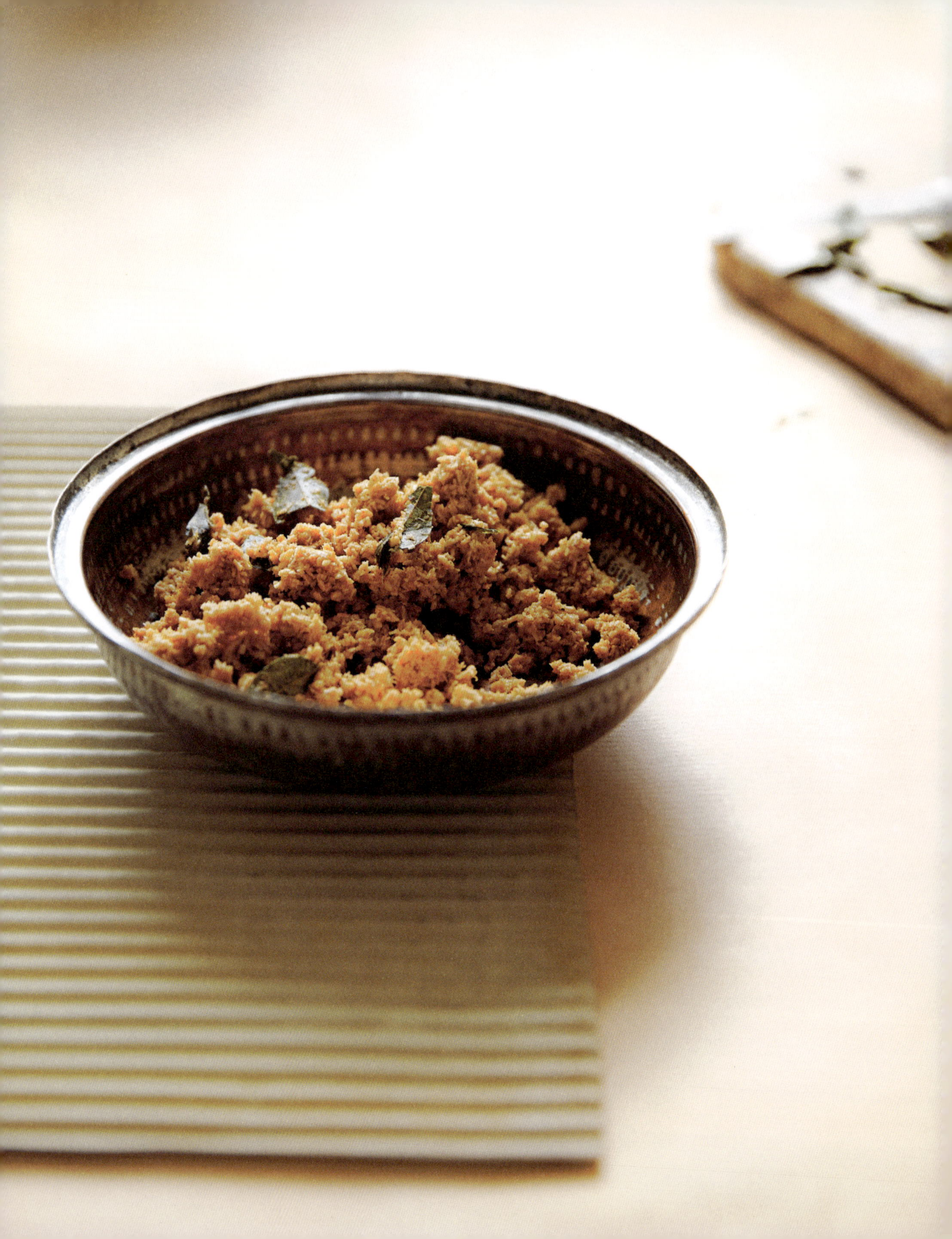

POL SAMBOL

Coconut relish

Coconut palms grow in abundance on the island, and the fruits find their way into just about every meal in some form. Pol Sambol (like all sambols) is a versatile, vivid relish, given an intense hit of flavour from Maldive fish: smoked, sun-dried tuna, flaked and used sparingly.

1 small onion, roughly chopped
1 garlic clove, halved
1 medium tomato, cut into quarters
5 black peppercorns
1 green chilli, deseeded
¾ tsp chilli powder
5 fresh curry leaves
200g (7oz/2½ cups) freshly grated or desiccated (shredded) coconut
1 tsp Maldive fish, crushed (optional)
juice of ½ lime
salt

Place the onion, garlic, tomato, black peppercorns, green chilli, chilli powder and curry leaves in a food processor and blitz until you have a fine paste.

Place the paste in a medium bowl and add the coconut, Maldive fish (if using) and mix well by hand. Then add the lime juice and salt to taste, mixing well. A few crushed curry leaves can be used as a garnish. *Pictured left.*

Serves 4

PULLI CHATHAM

Lemon rice

2 tbsp chana dal (split chick peas)
2 tbsp oil
½ tsp mustard seeds
½ tsp cumin seeds
12 fresh curry leaves
2 dried red chillies, broken
2 green chillies, split lengthways with seeds
½ tsp ground turmeric
salt
100ml (3½ fl oz/7 tbsp) lemon juice

For the rice
400g (14oz/1¾ cups) white rice (basmati or patna)
500ml (17 fl oz/generous 2 cups) water
2 tsp oil
½ tsp salt

First, soak the chana dal in water for 15 minutes.

Meanwhile, cook the rice. Put the rice into a medium, lidded saucepan and cover with water. Swirl the rice around to wash it, drain and repeat at least twice until the water is clear. Then, add the 500ml of water, so it covers the rice by about 5cm (2 inches), plus the oil and the salt, and bring to the boil, stirring a couple of times.

Turn the heat down to medium and cook, uncovered, until the water level reaches the rice. Then, cover with the lid and reduce the heat to low. Leave to cook for 7–8 minutes, then turn off the heat and leave the lid on.

Next, make the tempered mix. Heat the oil in a medium saucepan over a low heat, then add the mustard seeds. Let them cook for a few seconds until they pop, then add the cumin seeds, curry leaves, dried chillies and green chillies and stir-fry for a minute. Add the turmeric and the drained chana dal, and stir-fry for about a minute, until the chick peas turn golden.

Turn the heat down, add half the cooked rice, a pinch of salt and half the lemon juice and give it a gentle stir.

Tip in the other half of the rice, add another pinch of salt and the remaining lemon juice, and gently mix it altogether. Remove the pan from the heat and serve.

Serves 4

3 medium carrots,
    grated (shredded)
1 medium red onion,
    finely sliced
1 green chilli, deseeded
    and finely chopped
1 medium tomato,
    finely chopped
2 tbsp freshly grated or
    desiccated (shredded)
    coconut
1 tsp ground black
    pepper
1 tsp Maldive fish
    (optional)
juice of ½ lime
½ tsp salt

CARROT SAMBOL

Spicy carrot relish

Put the grated (shredded) carrot into a bowl. Add the onion, green chilli, tomato, coconut, pepper, Maldive fish (if using), lime juice and salt. Mix it all together well. Taste for salt and lime and serve. *Pictured right.*

Variation: For Beetroot (Beet) Sambol, follow the method for Carrot Sambol, but use beetroot instead of carrot and exclude the coconut.

Serves 4

100g (3½oz)
    Maldive fish
3 tbsp chilli flakes
juice of ½ lime
½ tsp salt
2 large onions,
    finely chopped

KATTA SAMBOL

Hot and sour fish relish

Put the Maldive fish, chilli flakes, lime juice and salt into a pestle and mortar or food processor. Pound or blitz until the ingredients are roughly combined.

Add the onions and gently pound or blitz them into the mix until you have a coarse paste. Taste for salt and lime and serve. *Pictured on p39.*

Serves 4

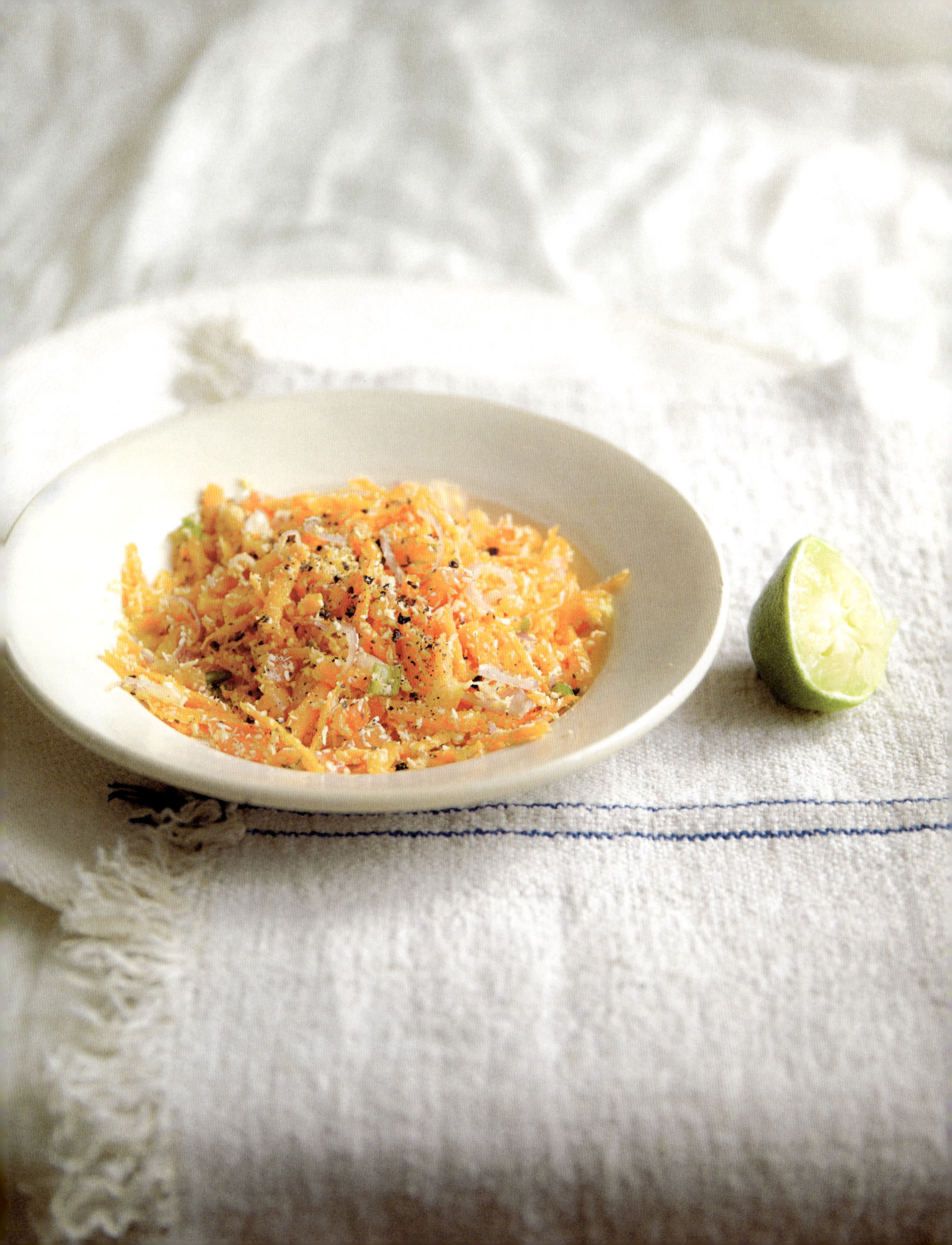

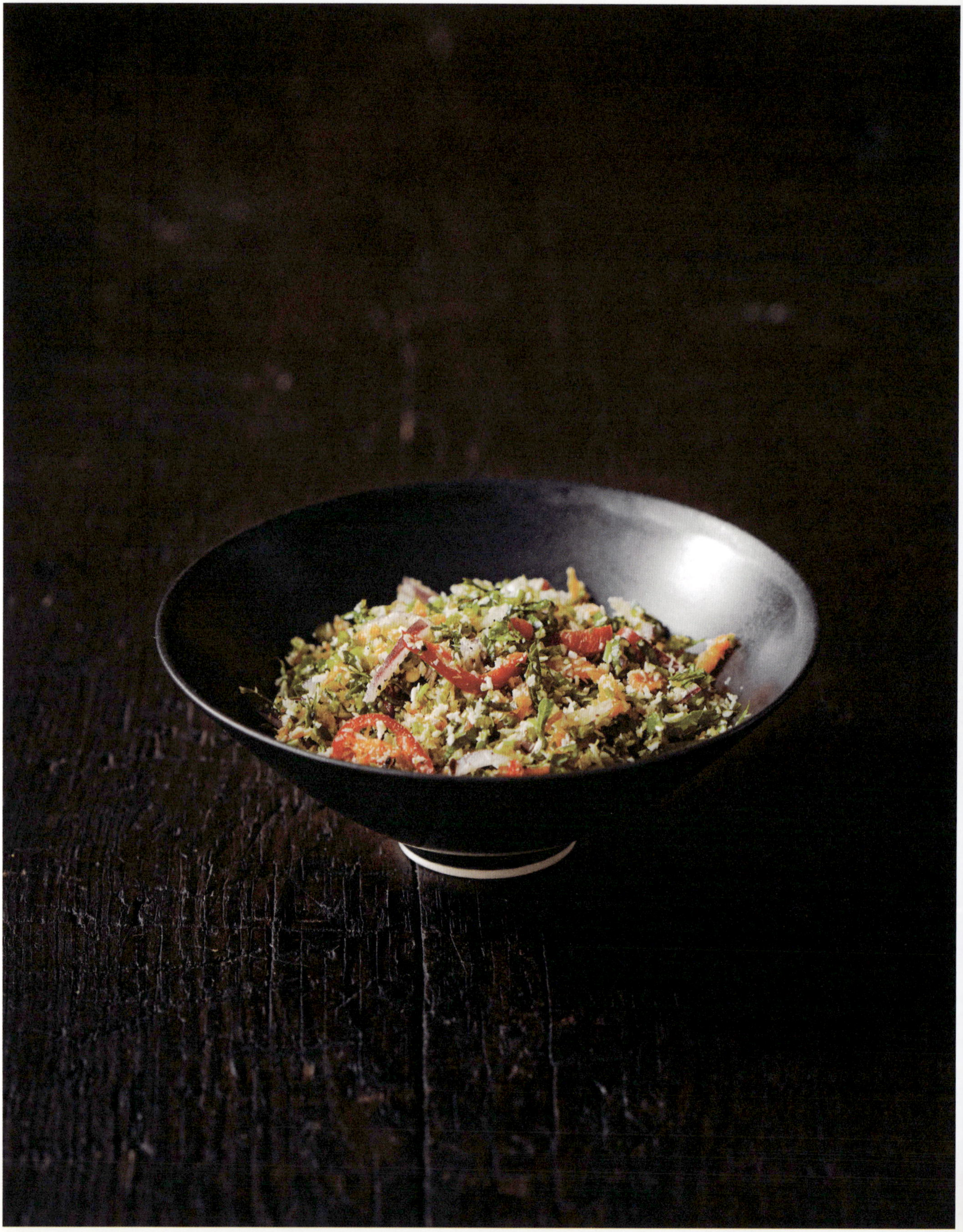

GOTU KOLA SAMBOL

250g (9oz) gotu kola (pennywort) (1 bunch)
3 tbsp freshly grated or desiccated (shredded) coconut
½ medium red onion, finely chopped
1 green or red chilli, deseeded and finely chopped (optional)
½ medium tomato, finely chopped
1 tsp Maldive fish, crushed (optional)
½ tsp ground black pepper
juice of ½ lime
½ tsp salt

Cut off half the length of the stems of the gotu kola bunch and set aside. You can use these to make Gotu Kola Kanda (p23).

Discard any spoilt leaves and wash the gotu kola thoroughly. Taking a handful of the washed leaves with stems at a time, cut the gotu kola very finely. Put it in a medium bowl.

Add the coconut, onion, green chilli, tomato, Maldive fish (if using), pepper, lime juice and salt. Mix well and serve. *Pictured left.*

Green herb salad

Serves 4

LUNU SAMBOL

2 large onions, finely sliced
1 tbsp chilli powder
juice of ½ lime
½ tsp salt

Put all the ingredients into a bowl, mix them together by hand, and serve.

Onion relish
This is a very simple and always effective accompaniment to rice and curry.

Serves 4

3 tbsp oil
500g (1lb 2oz) onion (about 4 medium), medium diced
4 garlic cloves, finely chopped
1.5cm (½-inch) ginger, peeled and finely chopped
12 fresh curry leaves
2 tbsp chilli flakes
2 tbsp cardamom pods, crushed
2.5cm (1-inch) cinnamon stick, broken into two
3 x 2.5cm (1-inch) pieces of rampe (pandan) leaf
4 cloves
¼ lemongrass stalk
200ml (7 fl oz/generous ¾ cup) tamarind water
200ml (7 fl oz/generous ¾ cup) coconut milk
1 tbsp sugar (white or brown)
juice of ½ lime

Sweet and sour onion relish
A fiery cooked sambol with a more involved method than others, which gives it a unique sweet, hot and sour taste. This goes very well with Kiribath (p68) or Veechu Rotti (p63).

Heat the oil in a medium, lidded frying pan (skillet) over a medium heat and sauté the onions until soft and golden brown. If the oil is quickly absorbed by the onions, add a few more tablespoons of oil. Take the pan off the heat and remove the onions using a slotted spoon, gently squeezing any excess oil back into the pan.

Put the pan back on a low heat and heat the oil again. Add a little extra oil to the pan if it is looking dry, then add the garlic, ginger, curry leaves, chilli flakes, cardamom pods, cinnamon, rampe leaf, cloves and lemongrass and sauté for about 5 minutes.

Add the sautéed onions back into the pan and mix well. Add the tamarind water and coconut milk, and give it a good stir. Half-cover the pan with the lid and simmer on a low heat for 5–6 minutes until the liquid has reduced by half.

Then, add the sugar and lime juice. Mix well and simmer until the gravy dries out, about 2 minutes. Keep an eye on it to make sure that the onions do not burn in the bottom.

Serves 6

SEENI SAMBOL

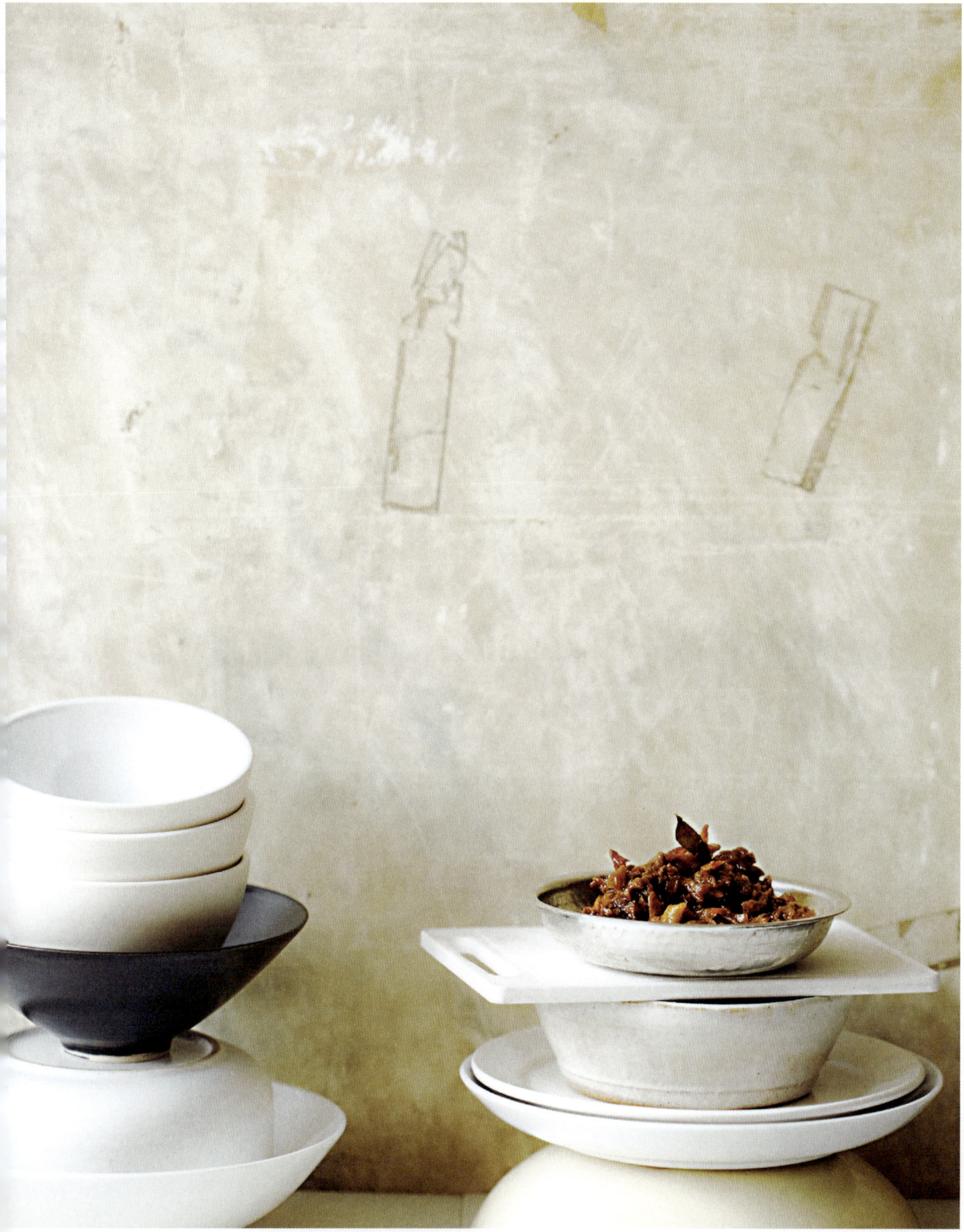

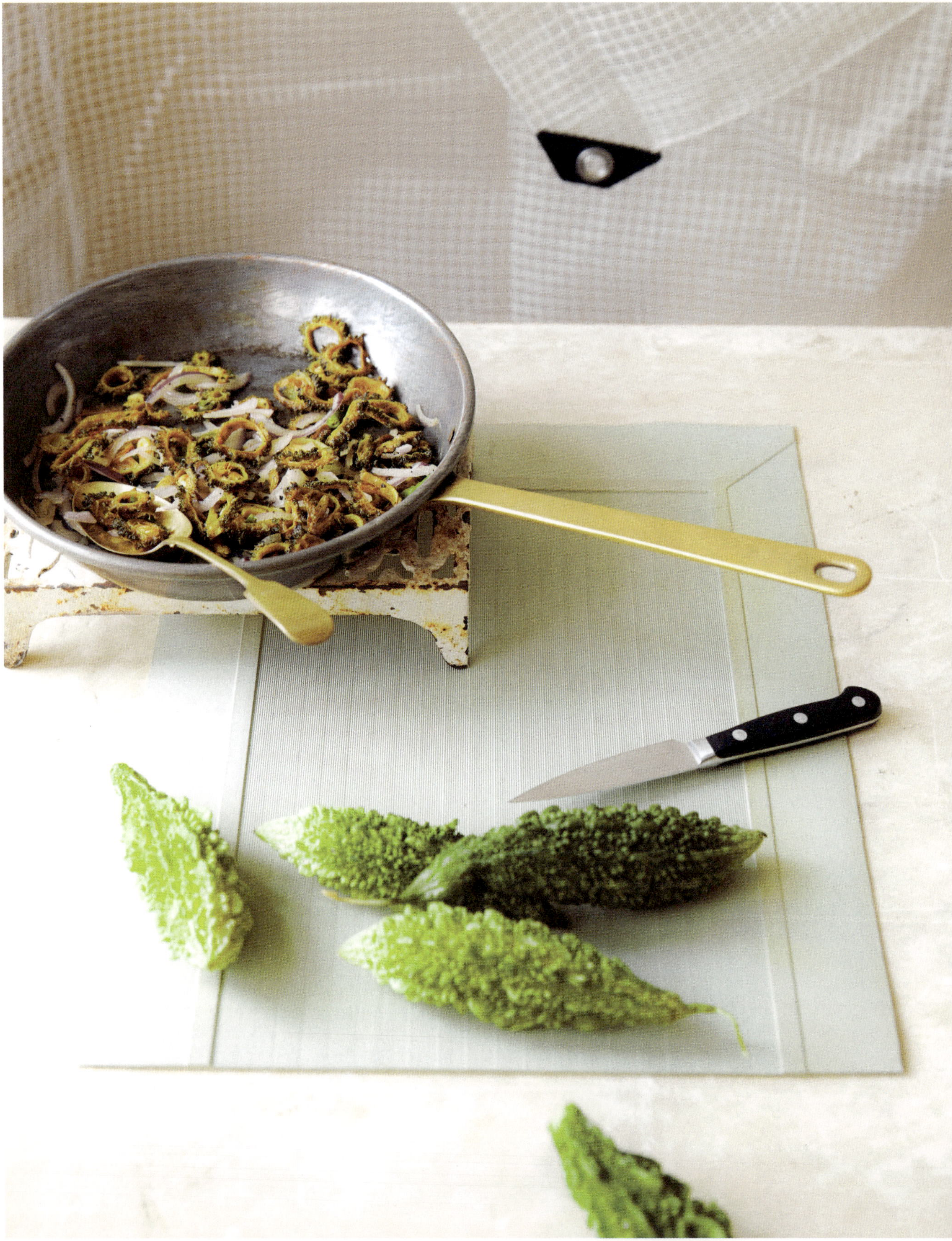

400g (14oz) bitter gourd (about 3 medium gourds)
½ tsp ground turmeric
½ tsp salt, plus a pinch for soaking
500ml (17 fl oz/generous 2 cups) oil, for deep-frying
1 medium red onion, finely sliced
2 green chillies, deseeded and sliced
¼ tsp ground black pepper
juice of ½ lime

Warm bitter gourd relish
In Ayurvedic medicine karawila has many health properties, and is believed to be beneficial for those with psoriasis and eczema. But it's also delicious, with an intriguing bitterness that's tempered here by lime and salt.

Wash the bitter gourd, top and tail it and cut it into thin round slices. Remove the fibres and seeds from the centre.

Fill a medium saucepan with cold water and add a large pinch of salt. Tip the gourd slices into the salt water, swirl them around, then take out a handful of slices at a time, squeezing out the water and putting them in a large flat dish as you go. This helps to reduce the bitterness of the vegetable.

Sprinkle the gourd with the turmeric and ½ teaspoon of salt.

Bring the oil to boiling point in a deep saucepan, then reduce the heat to medium. Deep-fry the gourd slices in small batches for 3–4 minutes until they turn golden brown, turning them as they cook. Remove from the pan with a slotted spoon and put them in a medium bowl.

When they have cooled down slightly, add the raw onions, green chillies and pepper, and give it a good mix with your hands. Squeeze in the lime juice, stir and taste for salt. It is ready to serve.

Variation: This dish also works well with tomato. Add a finely chopped small tomato into the mix with the onions and chillies if you wish.

Serves 4

KARAWILA SAMBOL

2 quarters of pickled lime (Oorukai recipe on p85), finely chopped
½ medium onion, finely chopped
3 green chillies, deseeded and finely sliced
½ tsp ground black pepper
100ml (3½ fl oz/7 tbsp) coconut cream
salt

LUNU DEHI SAMBOLA

Pickled lime with coconut milk
A hot and tart relish happy on the side of any rice and curry.
(Pictured on p84.)

Combine all the ingredients together and mix well. Taste for salt and serve.

Serves 4

---

1 small onion, roughly chopped
4 green chillies, deseeded (seeds in if you would like it hot)
2.5cm (1-inch) piece of ginger, peeled and roughly chopped
5 fresh curry leaves
200g (7oz/2½ cups) freshly grated or desiccated (shredded) coconut
juice of ½ lime
salt

PACHAI SAMBAL

Chilli coconut relish
(Pictured on p56.)

Place all the ingredients except the coconut, lime and salt in a food processor or spice grinder. Blitz until you have a fine paste.

Place the paste in a medium bowl, add the coconut and mix it together well, using your fingers. Add lime juice and salt to taste.

Serves 4

SAMBAR

Lentil and vegetable side
'Sambar' means 'mix' in Tamil. There are many recipes for sambar – but at minimum it needs two types of veg, and lentils. Tamarind is also essential, as is the spice blend. (Pictured on p27.)

Serves 4

Make the Sambar Podi spice blend
In a dry frying pan (skillet) over a low heat, dry-roast the urid dal and chana dal until they turn golden, taking care not to burn them. Tip them into a dry bowl. In the same pan, dry-roast the coriander and fenugreek seeds for a minute, and add the chillies and peppercorns and dry-roast for another minute. Add the cumin seeds, curry leaves (if using) and coconut, and dry-roast until the coconut begins to turn brown.

Mix the spices with the roasted pulses. When cool, grind them into a fine powder in a spice grinder. Add the asafoetida and mix well. You can store it in an airtight container for about 6 weeks.

Make the Sambar
Wash the red lentils in a medium, lidded saucepan, changing the water a few times until it is clear. Then, add the measured water, so it comes 2.5cm (1 inch) above the lentils, add half of the garlic, the green chilli and turmeric and bring to the boil. Reduce the heat to medium, half-cover with the lid and cook for 15 minutes until the lentils are soft. Do not drain.

Meanwhile, heat the oil in a medium saucepan on a low heat and add the mustard seeds. When they begin to pop, add the curry leaves, cumin seeds and dried chillies, followed by the onions, and sauté for 30 seconds, then add the remaining garlic and sauté until the onions are soft and turning golden.

Tip in all the vegetables and sauté until the aubergine (eggplant) goes a little soft. Add the tamarind water, the Sambar Podi spice blend and the salt. Mix well and bring to the boil. Lower the heat and half-cover with the lid, and cook until the pumpkin is soft, about 10–12 minutes.

Add the cooked lentils and give it a good stir. Taste for salt, half-cover with the lid and cook for a further 5 minutes to warm the lentils through. Taste for salt once again, remove from the heat and serve hot.

- 150g (5½oz/¾ cup) red lentils
- 300ml (10½ fl oz/1¼ cups) water
- 4 garlic cloves, finely chopped
- 1 green chilli, slit lengthways with seeds in
- ½ tsp ground turmeric
- 2 tbsp oil
- ½ tsp mustard seeds
- 5 fresh curry leaves
- ½ tsp cumin seeds
- 2 dried red chillies, broken
- ½ medium onion, finely chopped
- 100g (3½oz) pumpkin (about ½ small), cut into 1cm (½-inch) chunks
- 100g (3½oz) aubergine (eggplant), cut into 1cm (½-inch) chunks
- 8 x 2.5cm (1-inch) drumsticks, with outer green skin removed (optional)
- 100g (3½oz) carrots (about 1 large), medium diced
- 200ml (7 fl oz/generous ¾ cup) tamarind water (medium strength)
- 2 tsp Sambar Podi spice blend (see below)
- 1 tsp salt

For the Sambar Podi spice blend
- 100g (3½oz/½ cup) urid dal (split black gram)
- 100g (3½oz/scant ½ cup) chana dal (split chick peas)
- 100g (3½oz/1½ cups) coriander seeds
- ¼ tsp fenugreek seeds
- 7 dried red chillies
- ½ tsp black peppercorns
- 1 tbsp cumin seeds
- 11 fresh curry leaves (optional)
- 2 tbsp freshly grated or desiccated (shredded) coconut
- ½ tsp asafoetida powder

WAMBATU MOJU

Pickled aubergine and shallots
A very lightly pickled side dish to add zip to simple rice dishes, pittu and String Hoppers (p34).

400g (14oz) aubergine (eggplant) (about 1 large or 2 small)
500ml (17 fl oz/generous 2 cups) oil, for frying aubergine, plus 1 tbsp for frying spices
400g (14oz) small shallots
6 green chillies, slit lengthways and deseeded
100ml (3½ fl oz/7 tbsp) red wine vinegar
1 tbsp ground turmeric
2 tbsp chilli flakes
2 tbsp ground mustard seeds
½ tsp cardamom pods, crushed
1 tbsp sugar (white or brown)
½ tsp salt
6 fresh curry leaves
2.5cm (1-inch) piece of rampe (pandan) leaf
4 garlic cloves, finely chopped
2.5cm (1-inch) piece of ginger, peeled and finely chopped

Serves 4

Wash the aubergine (eggplant) and cut it into three equal chunks about 4cm (1½ inches) long. Put the pieces of aubergine flat side down on a chopping board and cut into slices about 1.5cm (½ inch) thick. Hold the slices together in one chunk, turn it round 90 degrees and cut the same slices again. You will get thick sticks.

Put the oil in a deep saucepan and bring it to the boil. It is important that the oil is at boiling point, to avoid the aubergine absorbing the oil. Deep-fry the aubergine sticks in two or three batches, until golden brown, for about 5 minutes. The aubergine must fry, rather than boil, so do not put too many sticks in the pan at once.

Remove the sticks with a slotted spoon and lay them on kitchen towel to absorb any excess oil.

Deep-fry the shallots for about 2 minutes until turning golden. Remove with a slotted spoon and lay them on kitchen towel.

Deep-fry the green chillies for 30 seconds. Remove with a slotted spoon and lay them on kitchen towel.

Put the vinegar, turmeric, chilli flakes, ground mustard seeds, cardamom pods, sugar and salt into a small bowl and mix well. Set aside.

Heat 1 tablespoon of oil in a deep frying pan (skillet) over a low heat. Add the curry leaves, rampe leaf, garlic and ginger and sauté for 2 minutes, stirring frequently. Add the vinegar mixture and cook gently for 2–3 minutes.

Take off the heat and add the fried aubergine, shallots and chillies. Mix well and taste for salt.

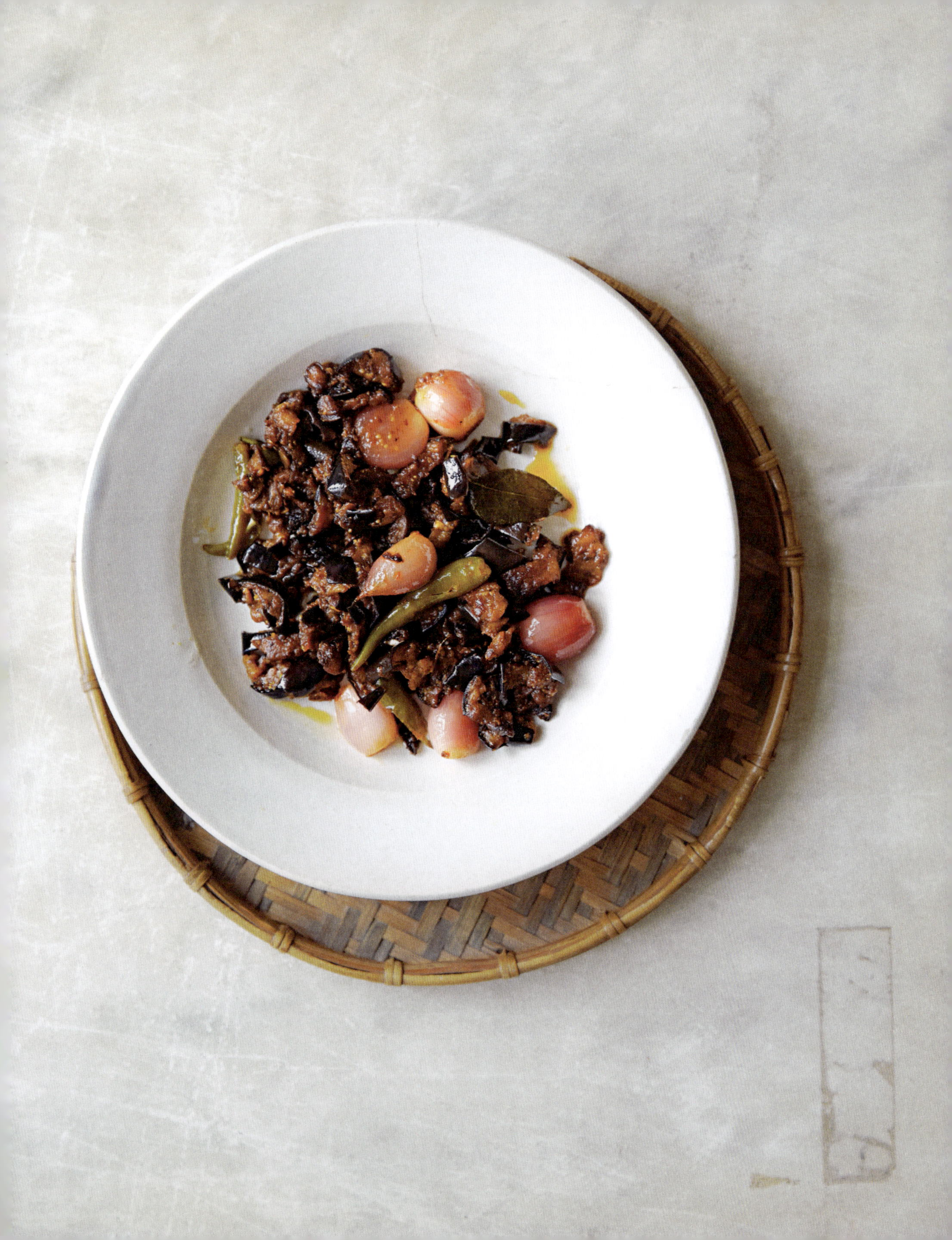

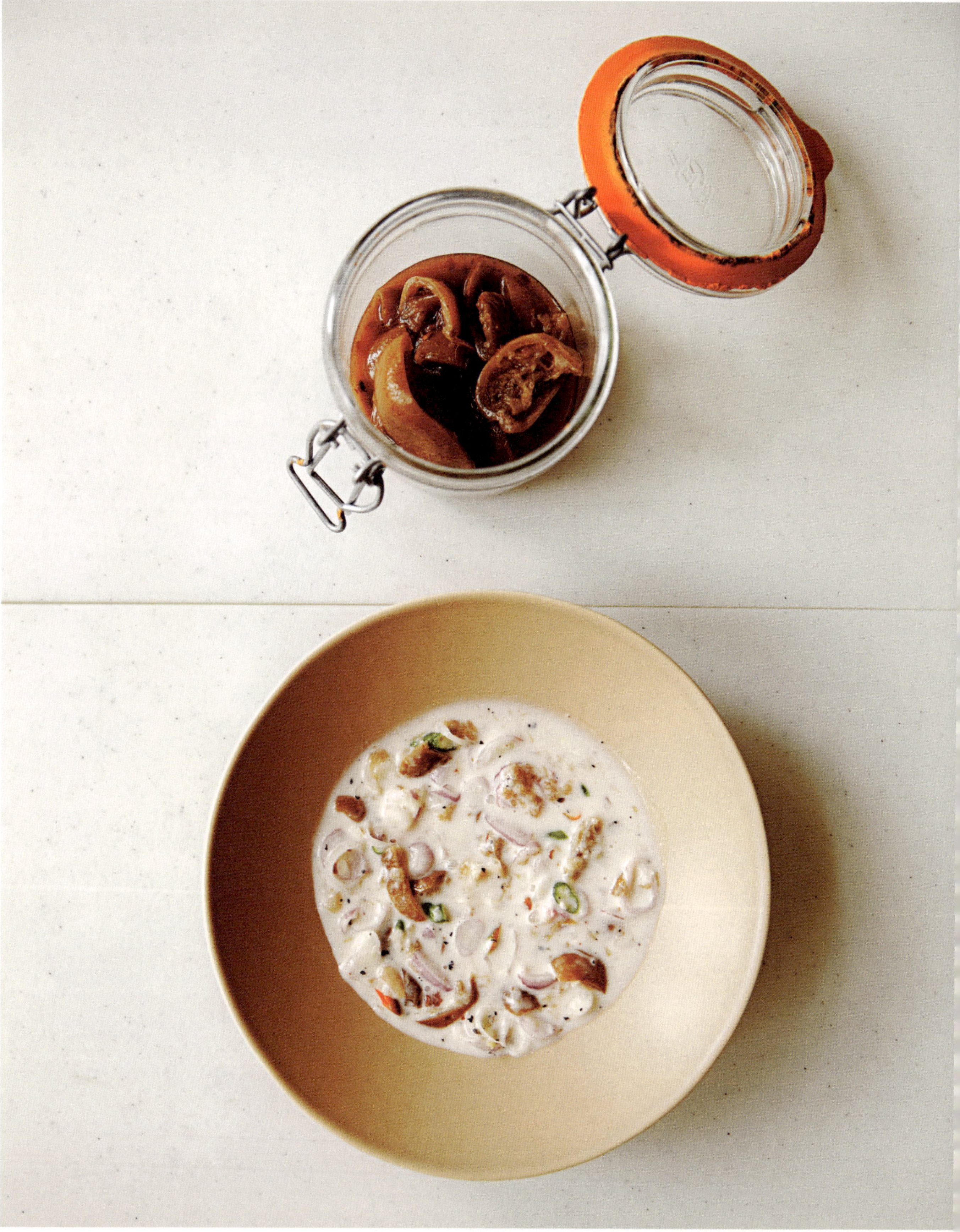

- 8 medium limes with soft skins
- 2 tbsp rock salt, finely crushed (or cooking salt)
- 10 green chillies
- 2 whole dried red chillies
- 1 tbsp fenugreek seeds
- 1 tbsp cumin seeds
- 1.5cm (½-inch) piece of turmeric root or ¼ tsp ground turmeric
- 100ml (3½ fl oz/7 tbsp) lime juice (about 3 or 4 limes)

Lime pickle

An excellent accompaniment to a vegetarian meal. Make enough to fill a couple of jam jars – if they're airtight it will keep for up to six months. You can use it to make the coconut milk relish Lunu Dehi Sambola (pictured here, recipe on p80).

Cut the limes into quarters without slicing all the way down to the bottom so the lime quarters stay connected together. Lightly cover the inside edges with the salt and put them in a non-metal container or a large glass bottle with a non-corrosive lid.

Make a small slit lengthways down each green chilli, leaving the seeds and stems intact, and add them to the salted lime. Mix well and put the lid on. Leave to marinate for 3 days.

After 3 days marinating, take the limes out of the container and lay them out in a large shallow dish to dry. Put them uncovered in the sun until they are very dry. This may take 2 or 3 days in the sunshine.

When the limes are ready, gently dry-roast the dried chillies, fenugreek and cumin seeds and the turmeric if using the root in a dry frying pan (skillet) until they begin to colour. Take them off the heat and leave to cool. Put them in a spice grinder and grind to a powder. If using ground turmeric, add it now and stir to combine.

Mix the lime juice with this prepared spice powder and pour it all over the limes. Mix well and store the lime pickle in a sterilised airtight jar.

Makes 300g/10½oz

OORUKAI

ACHCHARU

Date and shallot pickle
In Sri Lanka, many vegetables are turned into zingy pickles, from the common carrot to the exotic ambarella sour plum. Here, the sweet, soft dates are a beautiful match for the sharp shallots, creating a spicy side dish that will enliven even the simplest platefuls.

5 garlic cloves, peeled
7.5cm (3-inch) piece of ginger, peeled and roughly chopped
2 tbsp mustard seeds
2 tbsp chilli powder
250g (9oz/1⅔ cups) dates (200g/7oz deseeded and halved and 50g/2oz finely chopped)
1 tsp salt
250ml (9 fl oz/generous 1 cup) red wine vinegar
2 tbsp sugar (white or brown)
250g (9oz) small shallots
3 medium carrots, cut into thin strips
200g (7oz) green chillies, slit lengthways with seeds in

Makes 300g/10½oz

Put the garlic, ginger, mustard seeds, chilli powder, 50g chopped dates, salt and 125ml of vinegar in a food processor. Blitz until you have a thick paste and set aside.

Put the remaining vinegar in a deep stainless steel saucepan, add the sugar and bring to the boil.

Add the shallots and cook for 2 minutes, then remove with a slotted spoon and set aside. Add the carrots and cook for 3 minutes, then remove. Add the chillies and cook them for 2 minutes, then remove. Finally, add the dates and cook for 2 minutes, then remove.

Add the paste to the reduced vinegar and bring to the boil. Add all the cooked vegetables, mix well, then take off the heat and let it cool.

When cool, place the pickle in a sterilised airtight jar and refrigerate. It will keep for 2 months.

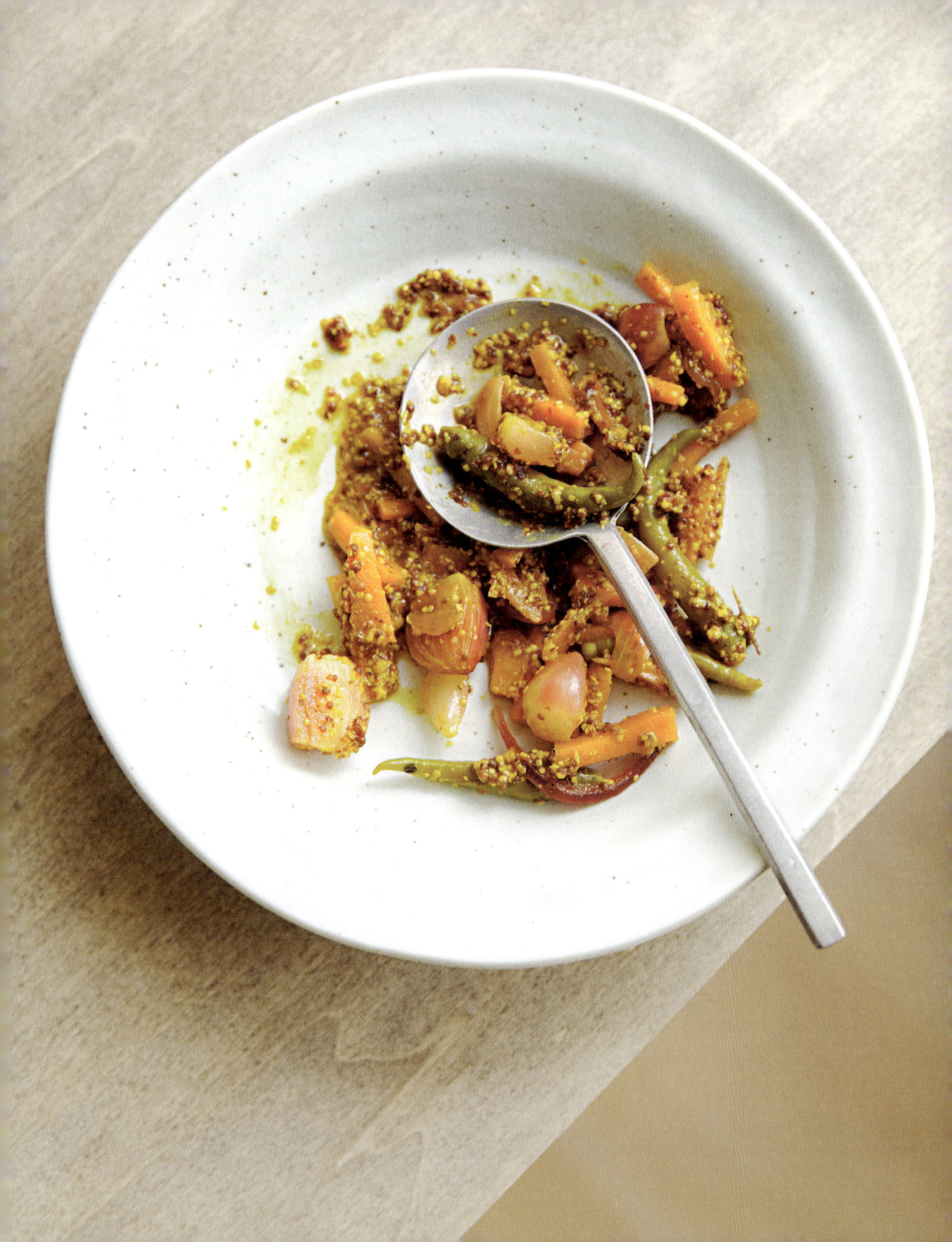

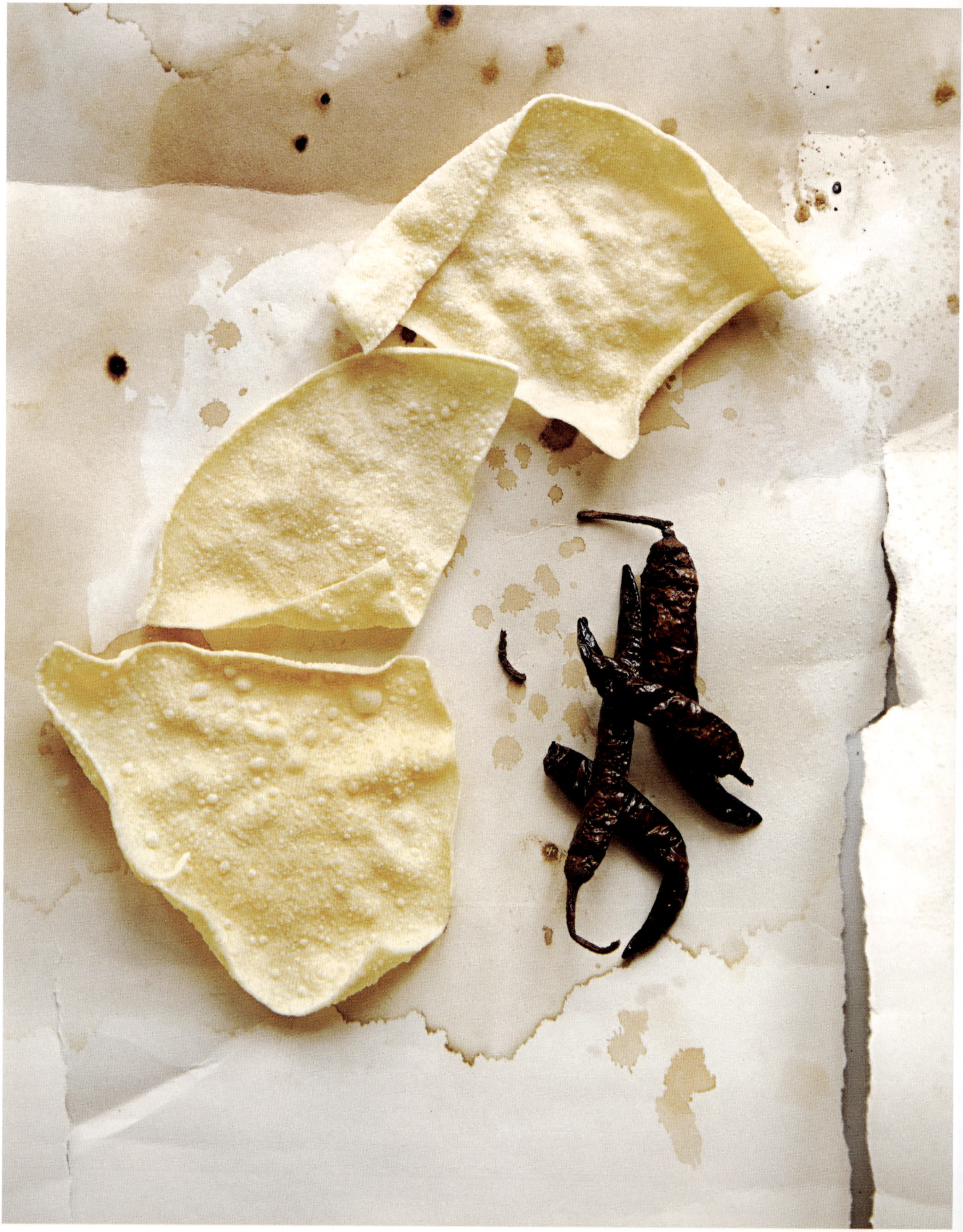

APPALAM

Papadums
Traditionally, the dough for these thin crisps is dried under direct sunlight. At home, however, you can do it in a normal oven on a low heat with the door partially open – a very successful method.

100g (3½oz/¾ cup) urid flour (black gram flour)
100g (3½oz/¾ cup) white rice flour
½ tsp salt
200ml (7 fl oz/generous ¾ cup) water
300ml (10½ fl oz/ 1¼ cups) oil

Makes 8

Mix the two flours in a medium bowl with the salt. Start adding the water little by little, stirring all the time with your hands until it begins to bind together. Then, start kneading the dough.

At first, the dough will stick to your hands but as you continue kneading it will lose its stickiness and become a firm, round ball. Knead well for about 10 minutes until you have a stiff dough. Cover it with a wet cloth and set aside for 15–20 minutes.

Meanwhile, preheat the oven to its lowest possible setting, and line two baking sheets with baking (parchment) paper.

When the dough is ready, shape it into 8 lemon-sized balls. Roll each ball out into a 12cm (5-inch) diameter circle, about 2mm (⅛ inch) thin, laying them on the prepared trays as you go.

Put the trays in the oven, leaving the oven door partially open, and gently dry the appalam. It should take about 15–20 minutes until they feel firm and dry, almost rubbery.

Store the appalam in an airtight container until you are ready to fry them.

Frying the appalam
Heat the oil in a small but deep frying pan (skillet) over a medium heat. Take three appalam and break them into quarters by folding them in half down the middle and then in half again.

When the oil is nearly at boiling point, reduce the heat to very low and slide two quarters in at a time. Keep the appalam immersed in oil with a long slotted spoon for 3–4 seconds until just beginning to colour. The appalam will expand.

Turn the appalam over, then take them straight out and lay them on kitchen towel to absorb the excess oil. Serve as soon as they are all cooked.

MORR MILAGAI

Curd chillies

There's really nothing else like this side dish – dried, salted, marinated, sun-dried chillies, given a subtle tangy kick from the yogurt. They'll keep well in an airtight bottle for a couple of months.

500g (1lb 2oz) green chillies
500g (1lb 2oz/2 cups) yogurt
3 tbsp salt

Makes 300g/10½oz

Make a small slit lengthways down each chilli, leaving the seeds and stems intact.

Mix the yogurt and salt together well in a non-metal container or large glass bottle with a non-corrosive lid.

Add the chillies to the pot and give them a good stir so that the yogurt coats every chilli inside and out. Put the lid on and leave to marinate for 3 days.

After 3 days marinating, take the chillies out of the container, squeezing the excess liquid back in as you go. Lay them out in a large shallow dish and put this uncovered in the sun to dry the chillies during the daytime.

At night, put the chillies back into the container and mix well with the yogurt. Then, put them back out to dry in the sun in the morning.

Repeat this process until all the liquid in the container has been used up and the chillies are brown and dried without being crunchy. Store in a sterilised airtight container.

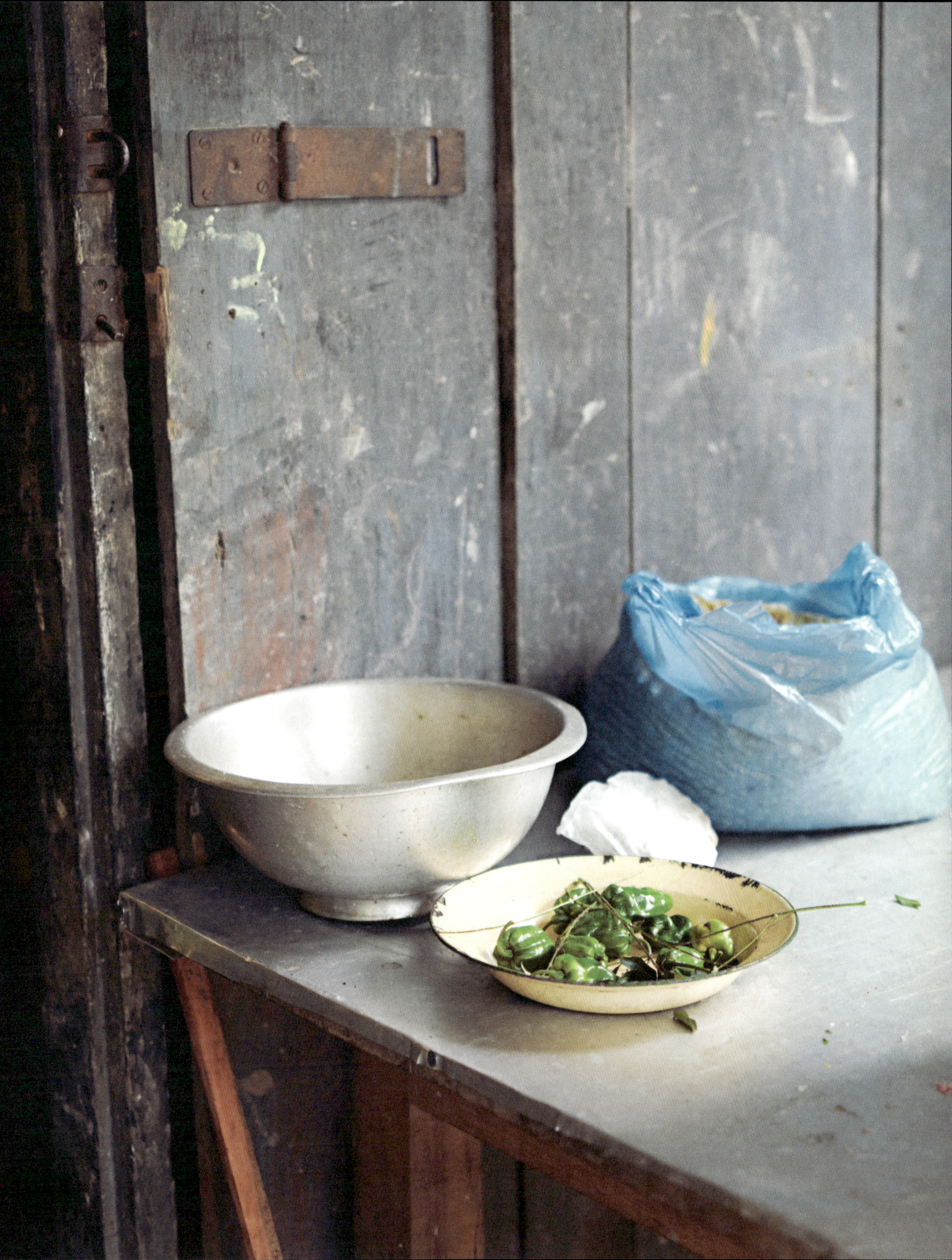

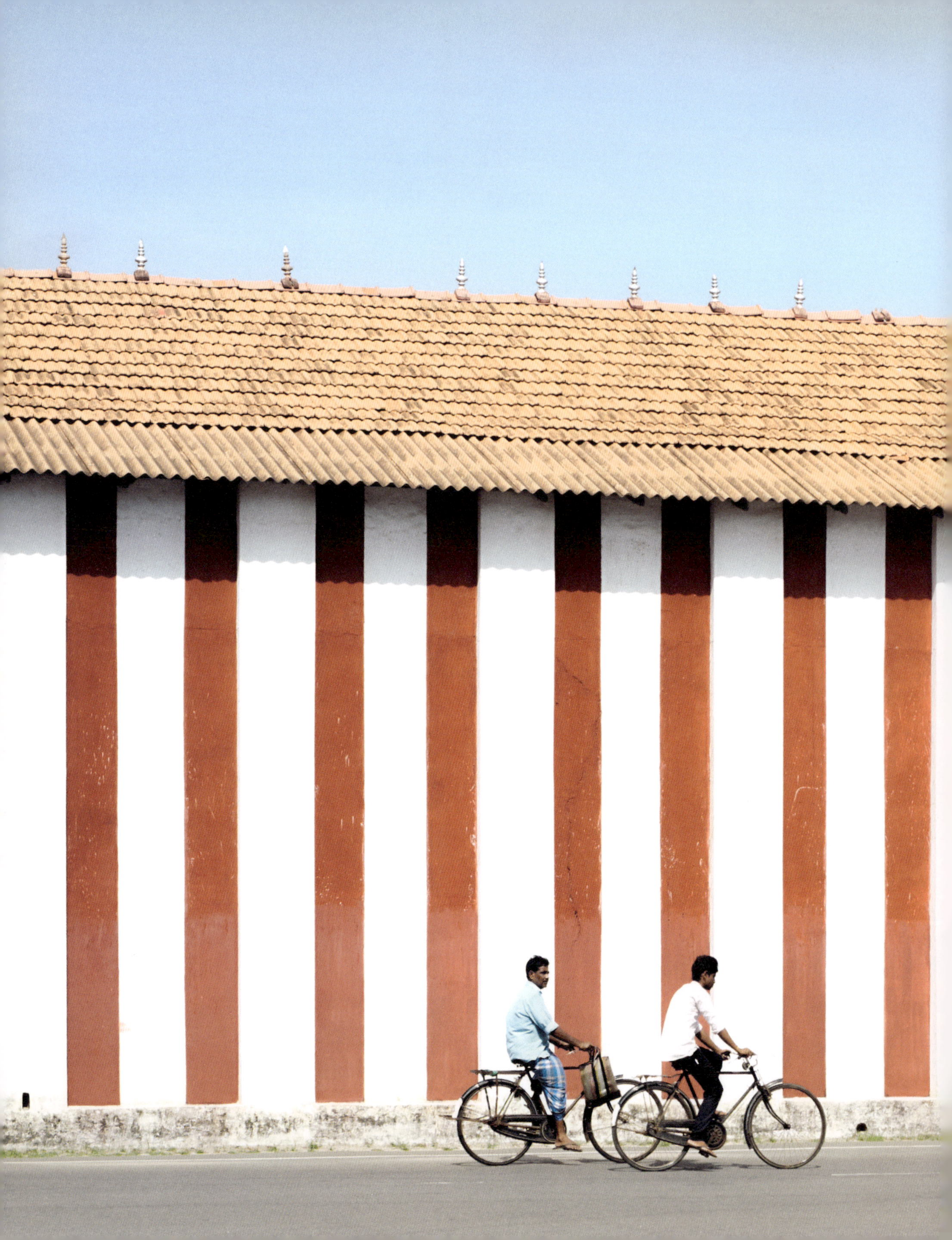

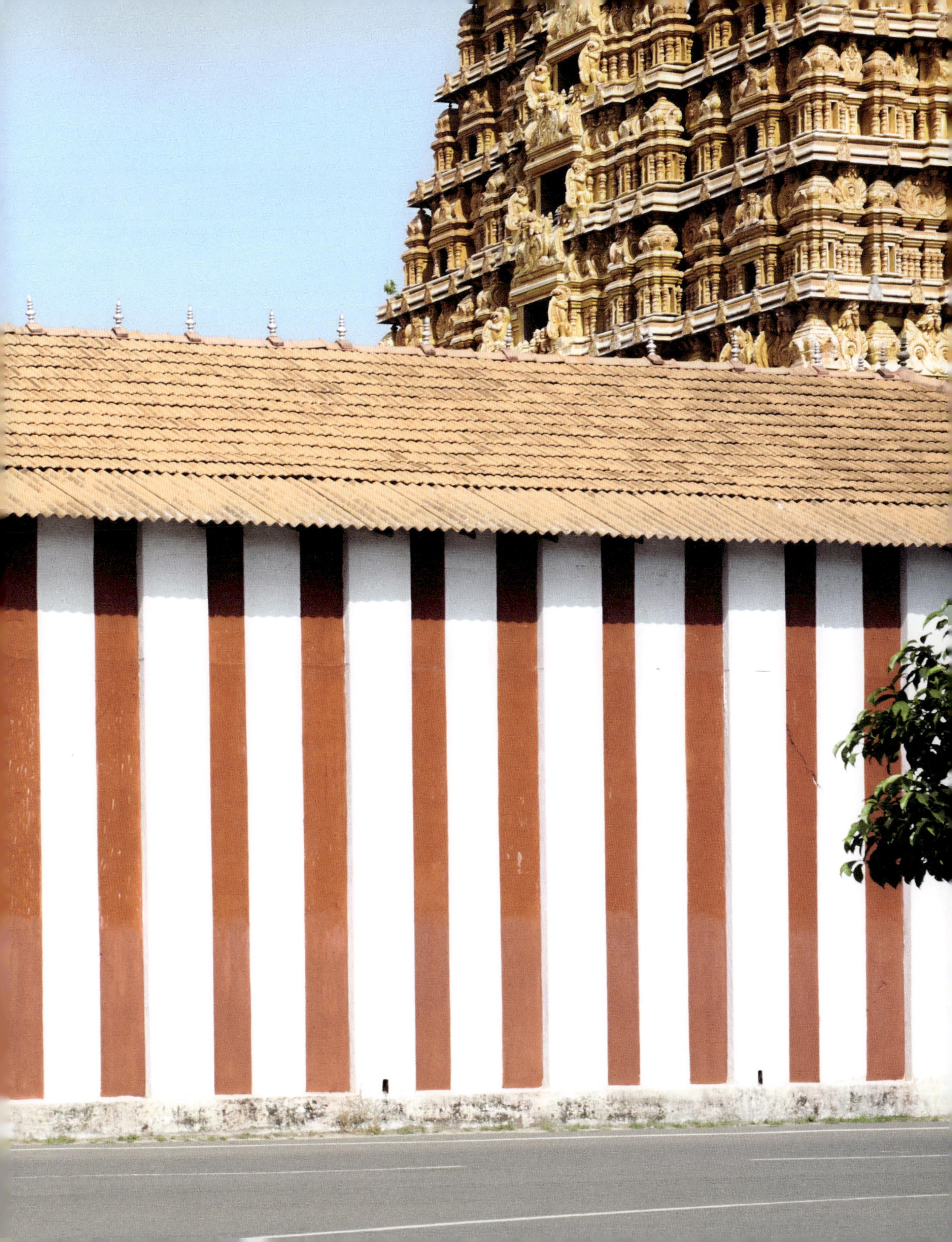

1 tbsp oil
½ tsp cumin seeds
½ garlic clove,
    finely chopped
1 small onion,
    finely chopped
2.5cm (1-inch) piece
    of rampe (pandan) leaf
    or 1 bay leaf
5 fresh curry leaves
½ tsp fenugreek seeds
200ml (7 fl oz/generous
    ¾ cup) water
1 green chilli,
    deseeded and sliced
2.5cm (1-inch)
    cinnamon stick
5 black peppercorns,
    crushed
1 tsp ground turmeric
1 tsp Maldive fish,
    crushed (optional)
1 tsp salt
200g (7oz/2½ cups)
    freshly grated or
    desiccated coconut
juice of ¼ lime

POL MALLUNG

Spiced coconut salad

Mallung, or mallum, is a 'dry' side dish, often of green vegetables mixed with coconut and spice. This is a plain version, and on the following pages are variations with cauliflower and kale.

Heat the oil in a medium frying pan (skillet) over a low heat, then add the cumin seeds. Cook for a few seconds until they begin to sizzle, add the garlic, onion, rampe leaf, curry leaves and fenugreek seeds, and sauté for a minute or so, stirring occasionally. Add the water to the pan, followed by the green chilli, cinnamon, peppercorns, turmeric, Maldive fish (if using) and salt, and give it a good stir. Bring to the boil and then lower the heat, cover the pan and simmer for about 10 minutes until most of the water has gone.

Add the coconut and mix well, cover the pan and cook for about 3 minutes over a low heat until the coconut is warmed through and softened. Remove from the heat, add the lime juice, mix well and taste for salt. Serve at room temperature. *Pictured right.*

Serves 4

200g (7oz/1 cup) red lentils
400ml (7 fl oz/generous
    ¾ cup) water
3 tbsp oil
1 tsp mustard seeds
2 dried red chillies, broken
6 fresh curry leaves, torn
    into halves
3 garlic cloves,
    finely chopped
2 green chillies,
    deseeded and sliced
1 large onion, finely sliced
½ tsp ground turmeric
100g (3½oz/1 cups)
    freshly grated or desiccated
    (shredded) coconut
juice of ½ lime
1 tsp salt

PARIPPU MALLUNG

Lentil mallung

Filling lentils make this a healthy and lively side dish, although one that's substantial enough to pair with rice for a quick meal.

Put the lentils into a medium saucepan and cover with water to wash them. Drain and repeat. Add the 400ml (7 fl oz/generous 3/4 cup) of water, so it covers the lentils by about 5cm (2 inches), and bring to the boil. Scoop the froth or scum off the top. Reduce the heat and simmer for 12-14 minutes, until cooked. Drain any remaining water and set the lentils aside.

Heat the oil in a separate medium saucepan, then add the mustard seeds. Let them cook for a few seconds until they pop, then add the red chillies and curry leaves and stir-fry for about 30 seconds. Add the garlic, green chillies and onion, and sauté until the onions are soft and turning golden. Add the turmeric, stir once or twice, then add the coconut. Give it a good stir and cook for 2 minutes. Tip in the lentils, add the lime juice and salt, and cook for 2 more minutes, stirring with a fork as it cooks.

Serves 4

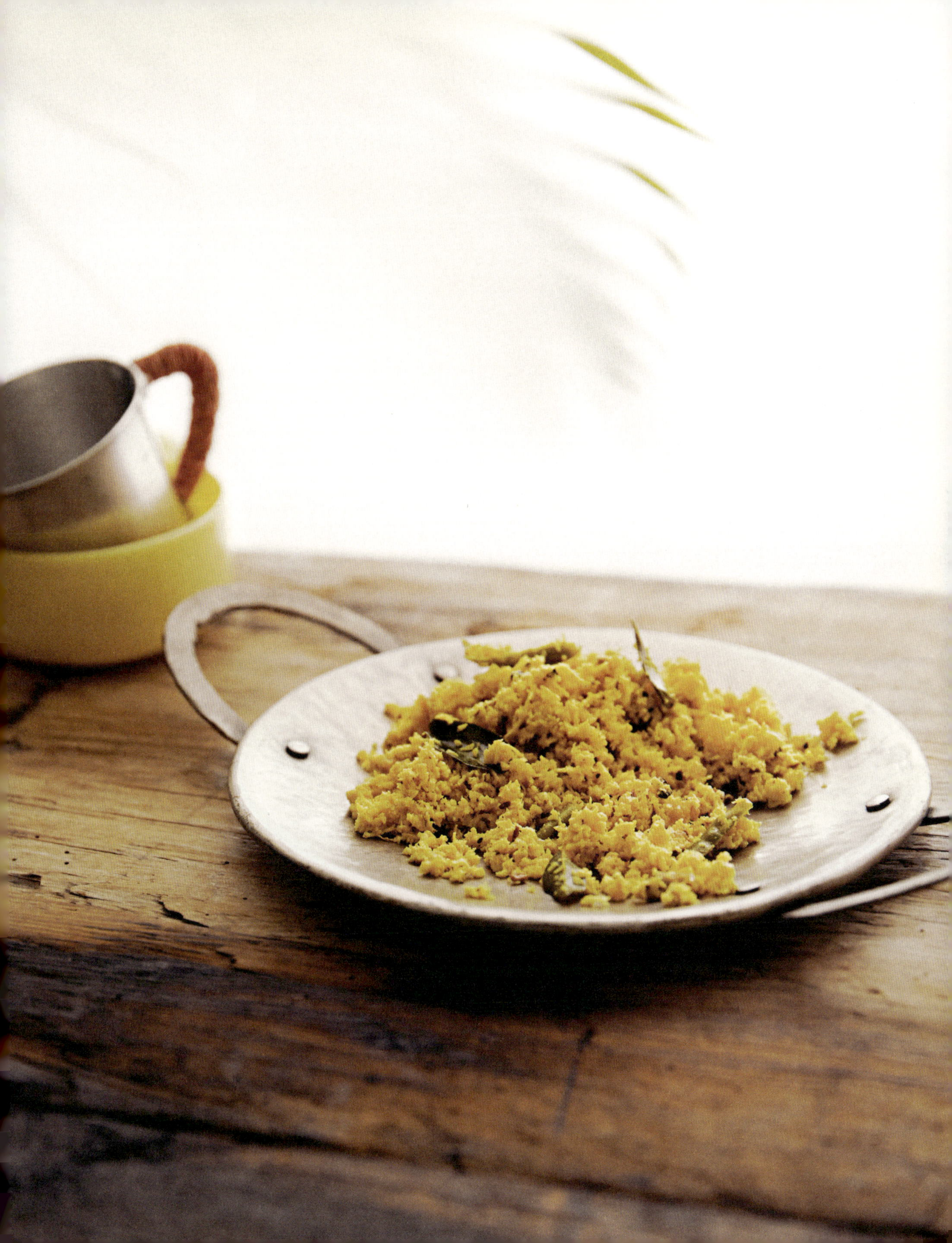

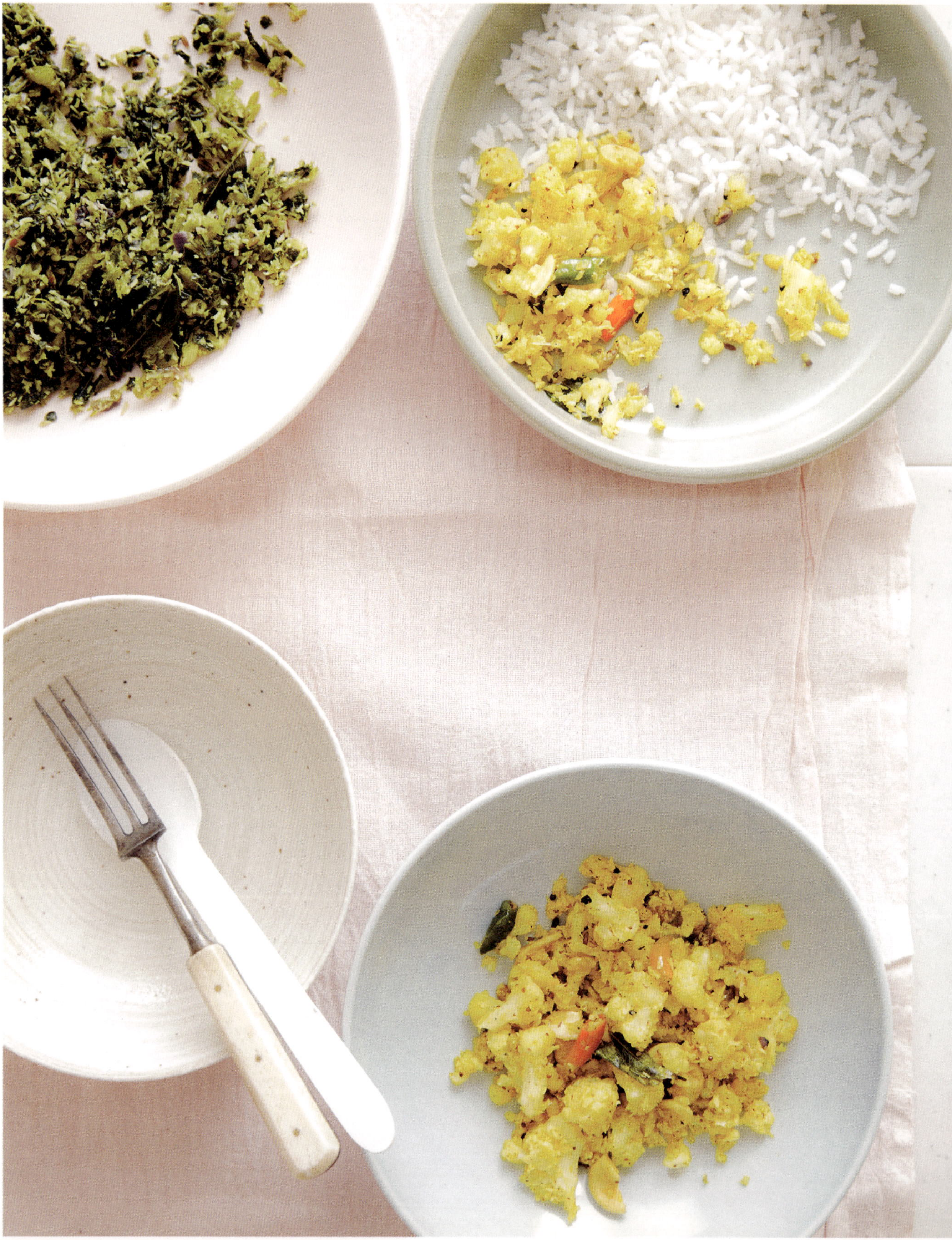

CAULIFLOWER MALLUNG

10 cashew nuts
1 small cauliflower, broken into florets
2 tbsp oil
½ tsp cumin seeds
8 fresh curry leaves, broken into pieces
1 medium onion, finely chopped
3 garlic cloves, finely chopped
2 green chillies, slit lengthways and deseeded
100ml (3½ fl oz/ 7 tbsp) water
1½ tsp ground turmeric
1 tbsp mustard seeds, crushed
5 tbsp freshly grated or desiccated (shredded) coconut
juice of ½ lime
salt

Put the cashew nuts in a small saucepan, cover with water and bring to the boil. Cook for 3 minutes to soften. Cool, roughly chop, set aside.

Steam the cauliflower for 5–6 minutes, until still crunchy. When cool, chop it into small 1–2cm (½–1 inch) pieces.

Heat the oil in a medium frying pan (skillet) over a low heat. Add the cumin seeds, curry leaves, onion, garlic and green chillies, and sauté until the onions are soft and golden.

Add the water, turmeric, crushed mustard seeds and coconut. Turn the heat down, and keep stirring for 2–3 minutes until the coconut is warmed through and softened.

Add the chopped cashew nuts and cauliflower. Stir well and take it off the heat. Add the lime juice and salt to taste. Serve at room temperature.

Serves 4

KALE MALLUNG

400g (14oz) kale
1½ tsp chilli flakes
1 tsp ground cumin
1 tsp ground turmeric
½ tsp salt
2 tbsp oil
1 tsp cumin seeds
7 fresh curry leaves
1 medium red onion, finely chopped
3 garlic cloves, finely chopped
2 tbsp freshly grated or desiccated (shredded) coconut
juice of ½ lime

In a food processor, finely chop the kale.

In a medium bowl, mix the chopped kale, chilli flakes, ground cumin and turmeric, and salt. Set aside.

Heat the oil in a large, lidded frying pan (skillet) or wok over a low heat. Add the cumin seeds, curry leaves, onion and garlic, and sauté until the onions are soft and golden.

Add the kale mixture to the pan and give it a good stir so it is well mixed in. Cover and cook for 6 minutes over a medium heat, keeping an eye on it so it does not burn.

Add the coconut and cook for 2 minutes, stirring frequently, until it is warmed through and softened. Remove from the heat.

Add the lime juice, mix well and taste for salt. Serve at room temperature.

Serves 4

250g (9oz) bunch of kathurumurunga
2 tbsp oil
4 fresh curry leaves
2 green chillies, slit lengthways with seeds in
1 large onion, finely chopped
2 garlic cloves, finely chopped
½ tsp chilli flakes
½ tsp salt
¼ tsp ground tumeric
1 tsp ground cumin
3 tbsp freshly grated or desiccated (shredded) coconut

Stir-fried greens
Kathurumurunga, sometimes known as the hummingbird tree, is a small tree with edible flowers and green leaves that taste slightly lemony with a hint of bitterness. In Ayurveda it is used to treat sinus problems and fever. A nice green cabbage or kale, finely chopped, can be substituted.

Hold the bottom end of one kathurumurunga stem with your thumb and index finger. Start pulling the leaves off with your other thumb and index finger, working your way up the stem in a scooping motion. Repeat for all the stems, collecting all the leaves together in a medium bowl of water. Give them a good wash, then drain.

Finely chop the leaves, a handful at a time, and set them aside.

Heat the oil in a medium, lidded frying pan (skillet) over a low heat. Add the curry leaves, chillies, onion and garlic, and sauté for about 2 minutes, stirring occasionally.

Add the chilli flakes and salt and give it a quick stir. Add the ground turmeric and cumin, give it another stir, and then tip in the kathurumurunga leaves.

Stir well, turn the heat up to medium, cover with the lid and cook for about 5 minutes, stirring now and then.

Add the coconut and stir well. Fry for another 3 minutes, continuously stirring, then remove from the heat. Taste for salt. Serve at room temperature.

Serves 4

KATHURUMURUNGA MALLUNG

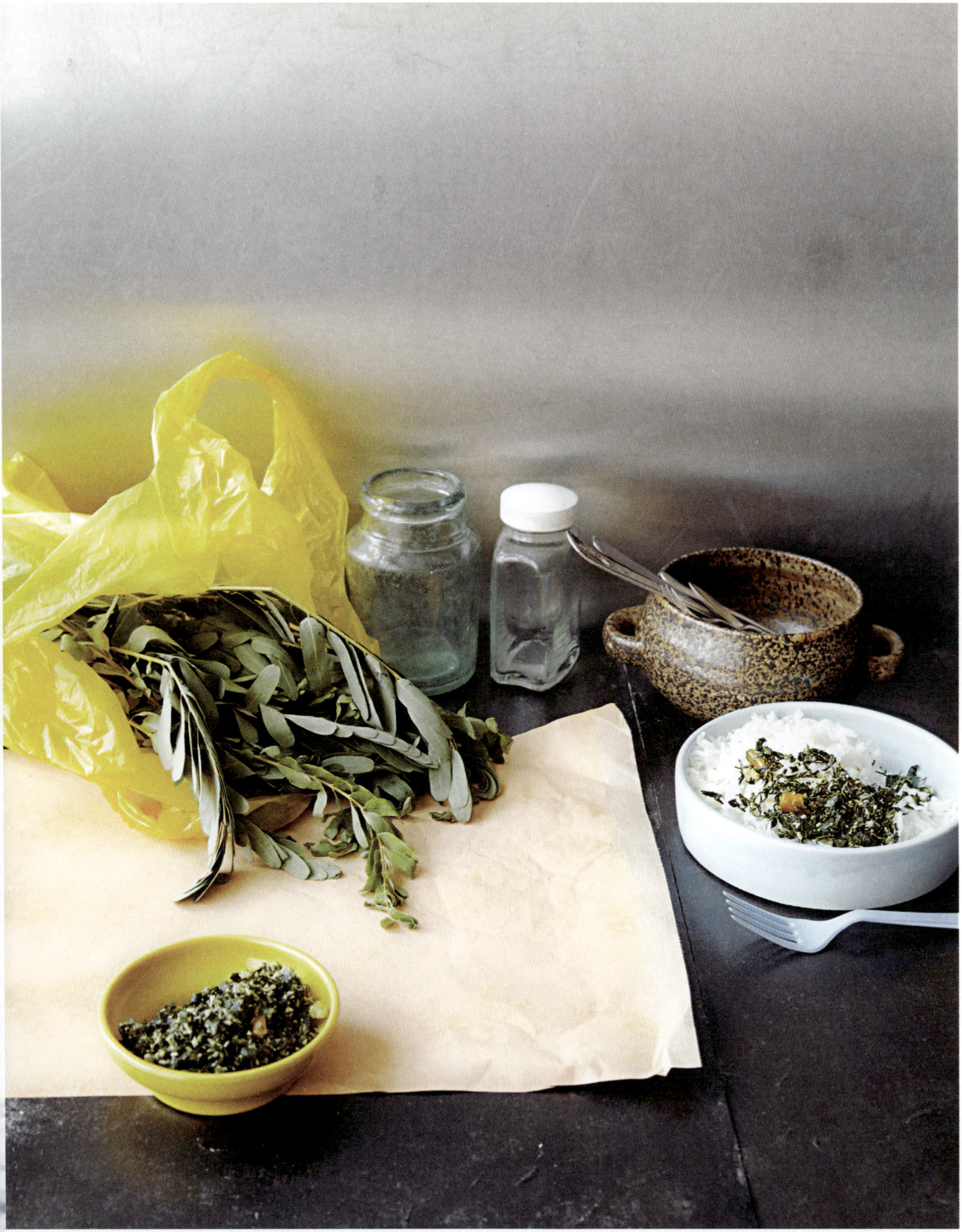

WATTAKKA KALU POL

*Pumpkin and coconut milk curry
With its classical Sri Lankan spicing, this perfect vegetarian dish adds sweetness and colour to the table. Typically, Sinhalese cooks crush mustard seeds rather than cooking with them whole.*

250g (9oz) chunk of pumpkin (about ⅛ medium)
2 tbsp oil
½ tsp fenugreek seeds
5 fresh curry leaves
2.5cm (1-inch) piece of rampe (pandan) leaf
1 green chilli, slit lengthways and deseeded
1 onion, medium diced
3 garlic cloves, finely chopped
2.5cm (1-inch) piece of ginger, peeled and finely chopped
½ tsp salt
½ tsp ground turmeric
¼ tsp chilli powder
375ml (13 fl oz/1½ cups) water
1½ tsp mustard seeds
½ tsp black peppercorns
2 tbsp freshly grated coconut or desiccated (shredded) coconut, dry-roasted
125ml (4 fl oz/½ cup) coconut milk
1 tbsp uncooked white rice

Serves 4, as a side dish

Peel the pumpkin. Remove the seeds and stringy fibres using a spoon and give it a wash. Cut it into 2.5cm (1-inch) chunks.

Heat the oil in a medium saucepan over a low heat. Add the fenugreek seeds, curry leaves, rampe leaf, green chilli, onions, garlic and ginger, and sauté until the onions are soft and turning golden.

Add the pumpkin, salt, turmeric, chilli powder and water (to just cover the pumpkin), and bring to the boil. Reduce the heat to medium and cook until the pumpkin begins to soften a little, about 12–15 minutes. Give it a stir every now and then.

Meanwhile, blitz the mustard seeds and peppercorns in a food processor, then add the coconut and continue until you have a coarse paste. Set aside. Then, dry-roast the rice in a small dry frying pan over a low heat until turning golden. Leave to cool, then blitz the rice in a spice grinder until you have a fine powder.

When the pumpkin is just beginning to soften, add the paste, the coconut milk and the powdered rice into the curry and mix together well. Simmer for another 6–7 minutes until the pumpkin is soft.

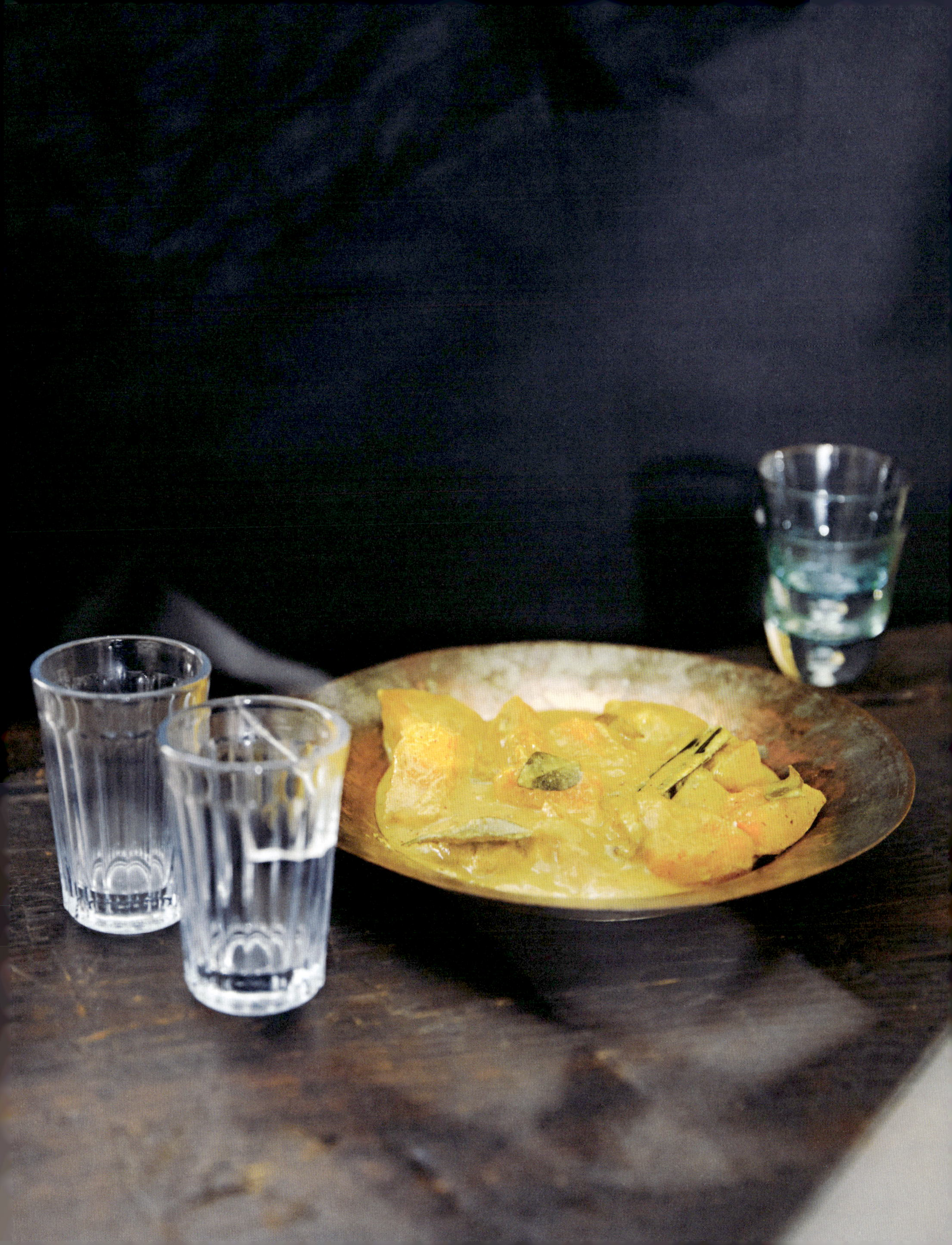

BATHALA

Sweet potato

The sweet potato isn't native to Sri Lanka, but is an example of one of the vegetables introduced to the island by Europeans and adopted enthusiastically by the locals, along with beetroot and cabbage.

Serves 4, as a side dish

Scrape the skin off the sweet potatoes, wash them well and chop them into 2.5cm (1-inch) chunks. Boil the sweet potatoes for 10-12 minutes until cooked. Drain them and set aside.

Heat the oil in a medium saucepan on a low heat, then add the cumin seeds and mustard seeds. Let them cook for a few seconds until they pop, then add the garlic, ginger, curry leaves and onions. Sauté until the onions are soft and turning golden.

Add the chilli flakes and turmeric and stir for 1 minute, then add the coconut and salt and a little lime juice, and give it a good stir.

Tip in the boiled sweet potato and mix well. Taste for lime and salt, and serve.

300g (10½oz) sweet potatoes
4 tbsp oil
½ tsp cumin seeds
1 tsp mustard seeds
4 garlic cloves, finely chopped
2.5cm (1-inch) piece of ginger, peeled and finely chopped
7 fresh curry leaves
2 medium onions, finely chopped
2 tsp chilli flakes
½ tsp ground turmeric
100g (3½oz/1 cups) freshly grated or desiccated (shredded) coconut
1 tsp salt
juice of ½ lime

2 whole garlic bulbs
2 tbsp oil
½ tsp cumin seeds
½ tsp mustard seeds
1 medium onion,
  finely chopped
6 fresh curry leaves
½ tsp ground turmeric
1 green chilli, deseeded
  and sliced
1 tsp Maldive fish,
  crushed (optional)
200ml (7 fl oz/generous
  ¾ cup) water
1 tsp Bathapu Thuna Paha
  (curry powder on p17)
½ tsp chilli powder
2 tbsp freshly grated
  or desiccated (shredded)
  coconut
200ml (7 fl oz/generous
  ¾ cup) coconut milk
juice of ½ lime
salt

Garlic curry
We often think of garlic as merely an addition to a curry, but it is technically a vegetable and can be a primary ingredient. Needless to say, it's one for garlic lovers and is as assertively flavoured as you'd expect!

Gently break the garlic bulbs into individual cloves. Peel and wash the cloves and set aside.

Heat the oil in a medium, lidded frying pan (skillet) over a low heat. Add the cumin seeds, mustard seeds, onion and curry leaves, and stir-fry for 2 minutes.

Turn the heat up to medium. Add the garlic cloves, turmeric, green chillies, Maldive fish and water, and cover and cook for 5 minutes.

Put the curry powder, chilli powder, grated coconut and coconut milk into a blender. Liquidise until well combined, and add it to the curry.

Simmer for a further 5 minutes or so, until the sauce thickens slightly. Squeeze in the lime juice, season with salt, and serve.

Serves 4, as a side dish

SUDU LUNU KARI

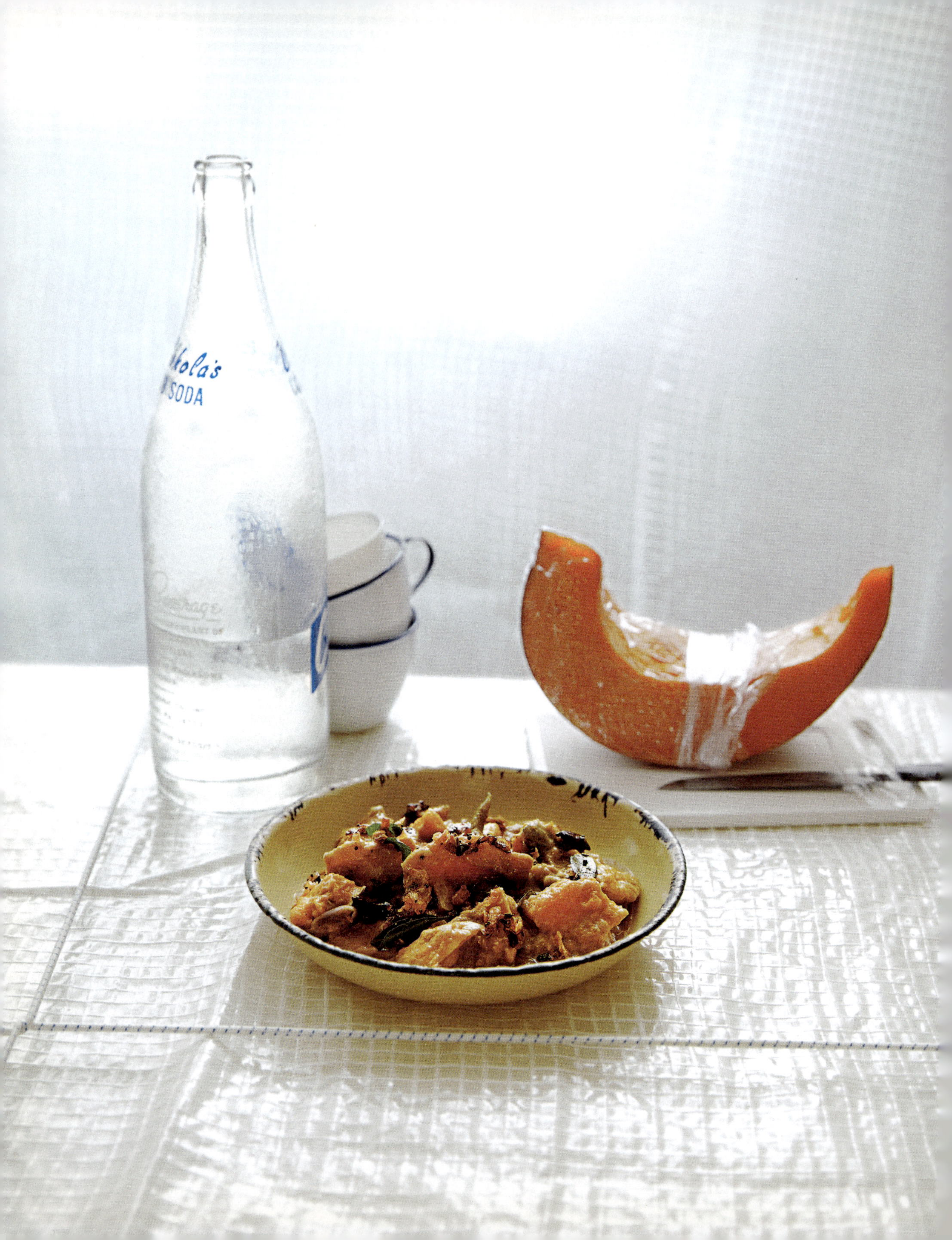
SODA

POOSANIKAI KARI

Pumpkin curry

Tamil cooking often involves tempering, a technique seen in this recipe – the late addition of a quick-fried sprinkle of spices and onion, which gives a burst of fresh flavour to the finished dish.

400g (14oz) chunk of pumpkin (about ¼ small one)
300ml (10½ fl oz/ 1¼ cups) water
1 green chilli, slit lengthways with seeds in
½ medium onion, finely chopped
6 garlic cloves, finely chopped
½ tsp ground turmeric
1 tsp ground cumin
1 tsp ground coriander
½ tsp salt
100ml (3½ fl oz/7 tbsp) coconut milk

For the tempering
2 tbsp oil
½ tsp mustard seeds
6 fresh curry leaves
¼ tsp cumin seeds
1 dried red chilli, broken
½ medium onion, finely chopped

Serves 4, as a side dish

Peel and halve the pumpkin. Remove the seeds and stringy fibres using a spoon and give it a wash. Cut it into 2.5cm (1-inch) chunks and put them in a medium saucepan.

Add the water (to cover the pumpkin) and the green chilli, onion, garlic, spice powders and salt, and bring to the boil. Reduce the heat to medium and cook until the pumpkin begins to soften a little, about 12–15 minutes. Give it a stir every now and then.

Add the coconut milk at this stage and cook for a further 6–7 minutes, until the pumpkin is soft. Taste for salt and remove from the heat. The curry should be nice and thick, not too dry or runny.

Now temper the spices. Heat the oil in a medium frying pan (skillet) over a low heat, then add the mustard seeds. Let them cook for a few seconds until they pop, then add the curry leaves, cumin seeds and dried chilli and give it a stir or two. Add the chopped onions and sauté until they are brown and almost crispy.

Tip the tempered mix into the cooked pumpkin and give it a good stir. Leave for a couple of minutes to infuse, and then serve.

VENDIKAI PAAL KARI

Okra and coconut milk curry
The highly nutritious vendikai, also known as okra, or more fancifully lady fingers, grows across the world from South Asia to the Mediterranean and the USA. This Tamil recipe is an ideal introduction if you've never cooked with them yourself.

400g (14oz) okra
1 tbsp oil
½ tsp mustard seeds
4 fresh curry leaves
2 green chillies, slit lengthways with seeds in
1 medium red onion, finely sliced
½ tsp ground turmeric
½ tsp salt
200ml (7 fl oz/generous ¾ cup) coconut milk
juice of ½ lime

Serves 4, as a side dish

Wash the okra before chopping them, so the cut pieces don't get slimy. Then, chop off the hard stem at the bottom of the vegetable and the top 1cm (½ inch). Cut them into pieces about 2.5cm (1 inch) long and set aside.

Heat the oil in a medium saucepan over a low heat, then add the mustard seeds. Let them cook for a few seconds until they pop, then add the curry leaves and green chillies and give it a stir or two. Add the onion, and sauté until it is soft and golden brown.

Add the turmeric and give it a stir, then tip in the okra and sauté for about 5 minutes. Add the salt and coconut milk and stir gently. Cover and simmer for a further 5 minutes until the okra are cooked but still slightly crunchy, then taste for salt and remove from the heat.

Squeeze in most of the lime juice, give it a gentle stir and serve.

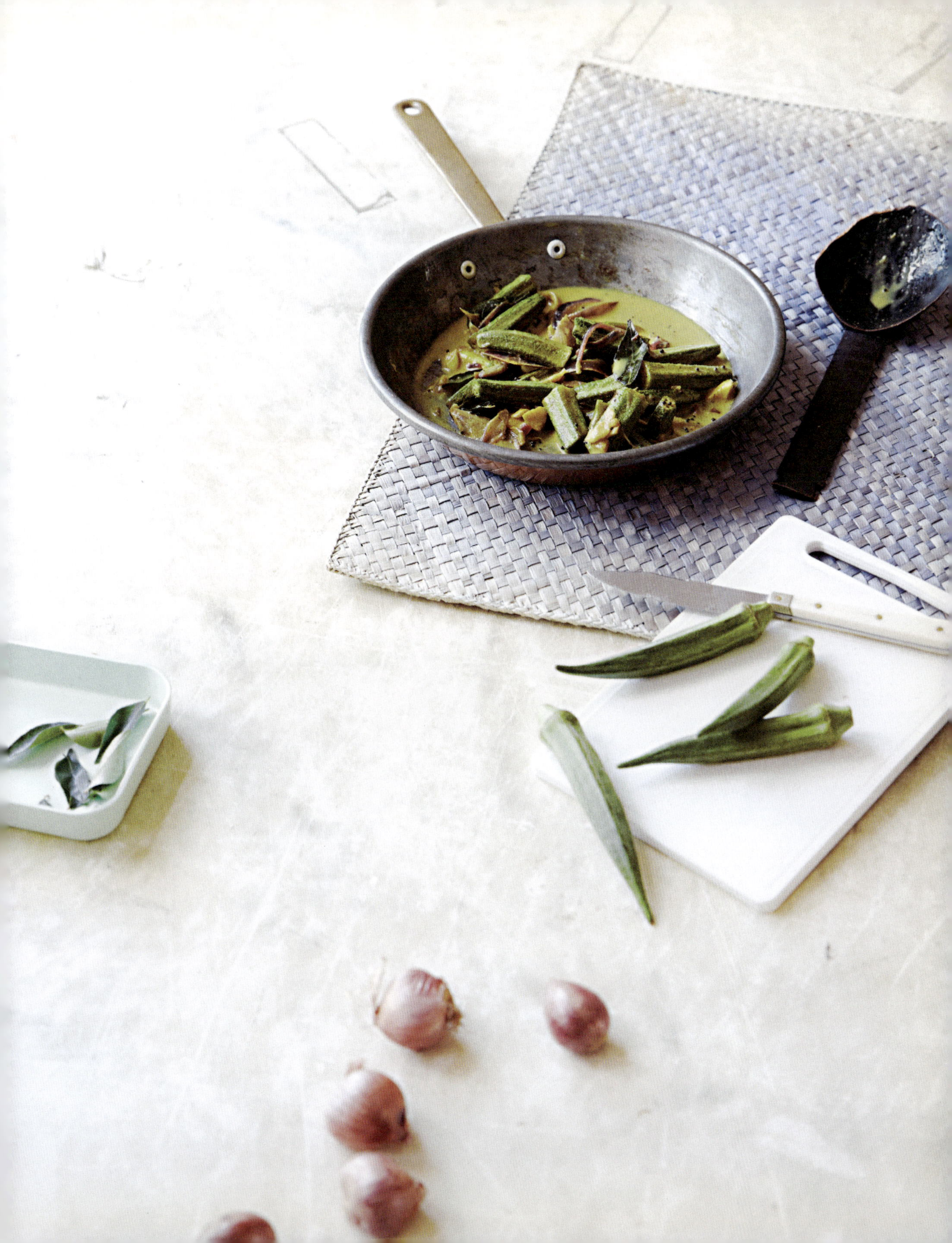

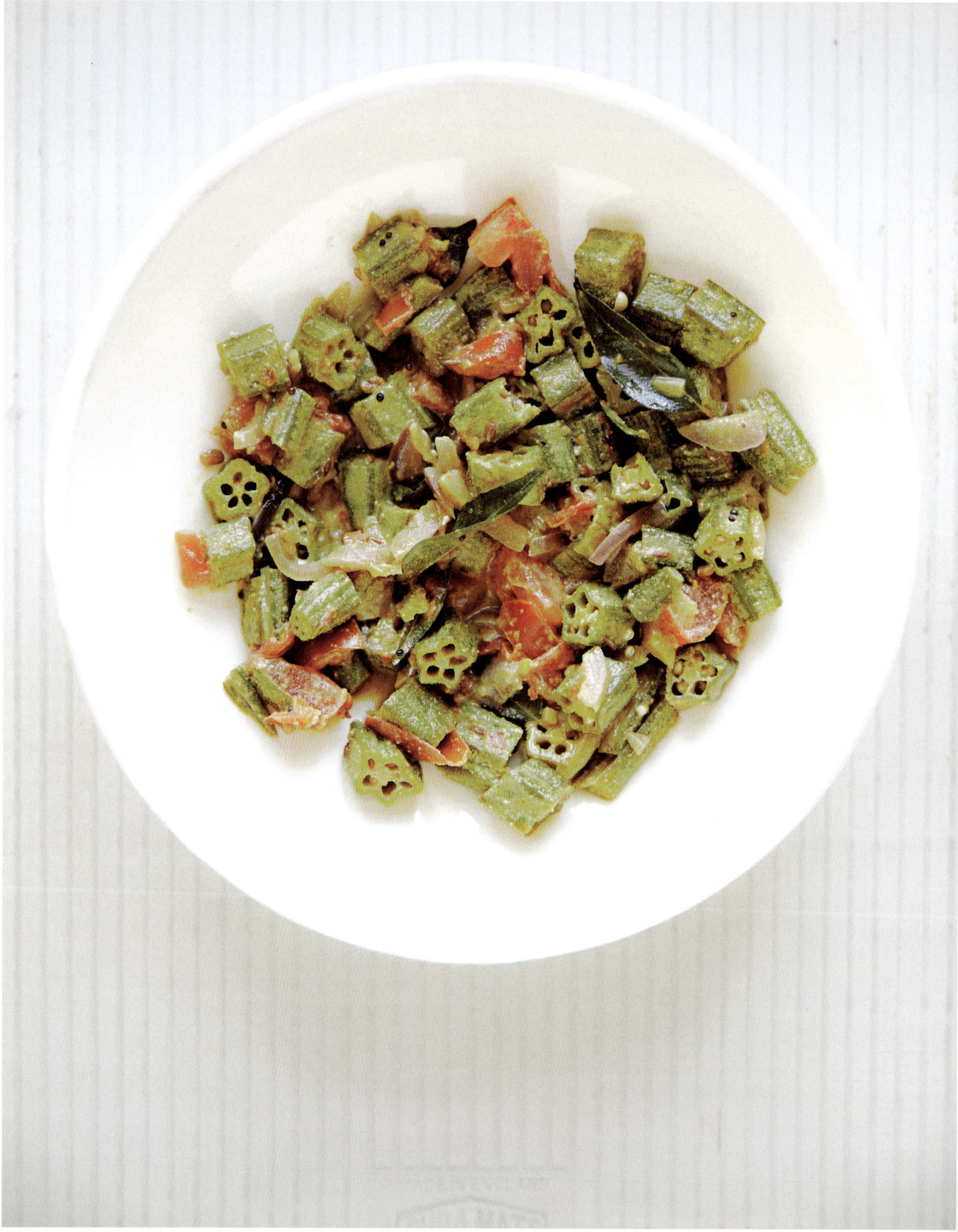

BANDAKKA KARI

Spiced okra curry

Here's a delightfully fragrant Sinhalese recipe. Tamils don't use tomatoes in their okra dishes (p106), whereas Sinhalese do: one of the many nuanced differences between the two cuisines.

400g (14oz) okra
½ tsp ground turmeric
1 tsp ground cumin
¼ tsp ground coriander
½ tsp chilli powder
1 tsp salt
2 tbsp oil
½ tsp cumin seeds
½ tsp fenugreek seeds
½ tsp mustard seeds
8 fresh curry leaves
3 garlic cloves, finely chopped
2.5cm (1-inch) piece of ginger, peeled and finely chopped
2 green chillies, deseeded and roughly sliced
1 medium red onion, finely chopped
2.5cm (1-inch) cinnamon stick
1 medium tomato, medium diced
100ml (3½ fl oz/ 7 tbsp) water
125ml (4 fl oz/½ cup) coconut milk
juice of ½ lime

Wash the okra before chopping them, so the cut pieces don't get slimy. Then, chop off the hard stem at the bottom of the vegetable and the top 1.5cm (½ inch). Cut them into pieces about 1.5cm (½ inch) long and put them in a medium bowl.

Add the turmeric, cumin, coriander, chilli powder and salt, and set aside.

Heat the oil in a medium, lidded saucepan over a low heat. Add the cumin seeds, fenugreek seeds, mustard seeds and curry leaves, and stir-fry for 1 minute. Take care not to burn the seeds.

Add the garlic, ginger, chillies, onion and cinnamon stick, and sauté until the onions are soft and turning golden.

Add the okra, chopped tomato and water, cover the pan with the lid, and cook on a low to medium heat for 5 minutes.

Add the coconut milk and simmer for a further 8 minutes or so, uncovered, stirring occasionally, until the okra is soft and the coconut milk is almost all absorbed. Remove from the heat and add the lime juice. Taste for salt and lime, then serve.

Serves 4, as a side dish

VALAKKAI PAAL KARI

3 plantain
200ml (7 fl oz/generous ¾ cup) water
2 green chillies, slit lengthways with seeds in
¼ medium onion, finely chopped
4 fresh curry leaves
½ tsp ground turmeric
½ tsp salt
200ml (7 fl oz/generous ¾ cup) coconut milk
juice of ¼ lime

For the tempering
1 tbsp oil
½ tsp mustard seeds
4 fresh curry leaves
1 dried red chilli, broken
¼ medium onion, finely chopped

Plantain and coconut milk curry
This tropical fruit curry is made with ash plantain, an astringent Sri Lankan variety with far less sugar content than some others. Green cooking bananas would suit this recipe well too. They're tastier when unripe, so use them soon after buying.

Fill a medium saucepan with water. Peel the plantain and cut them into 1cm (½-inch) slices, dropping them in the water to avoid discoloration and to remove the slight bitter taste. Drain the plantain and rinse once or twice. Then, pour the 200ml of water into the saucepan (to just cover the plantain), add the green chillies, chopped onion, curry leaves, turmeric and salt, and bring to the boil. Lower the heat and simmer gently for 6–7 minutes. Add the coconut milk, cover and cook until the plantain is soft, almost mushy, another 4–5 minutes. Taste for salt and remove from the heat.

Now temper the spices. Heat the oil in a frying pan (skillet) over a low heat, add the mustard seeds. Cook for a few seconds until they pop, then add the curry leaves and chilli. Add the onions and sauté until almost crispy. Pour the mix into the cooked plantain and stir. Squeeze in the lime, mix well. *Pictured right.*

Serves 4, as a side dish

VENDAYA KULAMBU

3 tbsp oil
1 tbsp fenugreek seeds
½ tsp mustard seeds
4 fresh curry leaves
2 green chillies, slit lengthways with seeds in
1 medium onion, finely chopped
6 garlic cloves, peeled
¼ tsp ground turmeric
½ tsp ground coriander
½ tsp ground cumin
200ml (7 fl oz/generous ¾ cup) tamarind water
100ml (3½ fl oz/7 tbsp) water
1 tsp chilli powder
½ tsp salt
100ml (3½ fl oz/7 tbsp) coconut milk

Fenugreek sauce
Fenugreek (methi) seeds lend their characteristic tangy bitterness to this side dish, which is perfect for soaking up with rotti or rice.

Heat the oil in a medium, lidded saucepan over a low heat. Add the fenugreek seeds and stir-fry until brown, less than a minute. Try not to burn the seeds as this would make the sauce bitter. Remove the seeds with a slotted spoon and set aside.

Put the same pan with a little oil back on the heat, and add the mustard seeds. Let them cook for a few seconds until they pop, add the curry leaves and green chillies and stir. Add the onion and garlic, sauté until the onions are soft and golden. Add the fried fenugreek seeds, turmeric, coriander and cumin and give it a stir. Add the tamarind water and water, the chilli powder and salt and give it a stir. Half-cover the pan with the lid and simmer for about 10 minutes until the liquid begins to reduce. Then add the coconut milk and simmer for a further 5–6 minutes until the sauce has thickened. Taste for salt, take it off the heat. Serve warm.

Serves 4

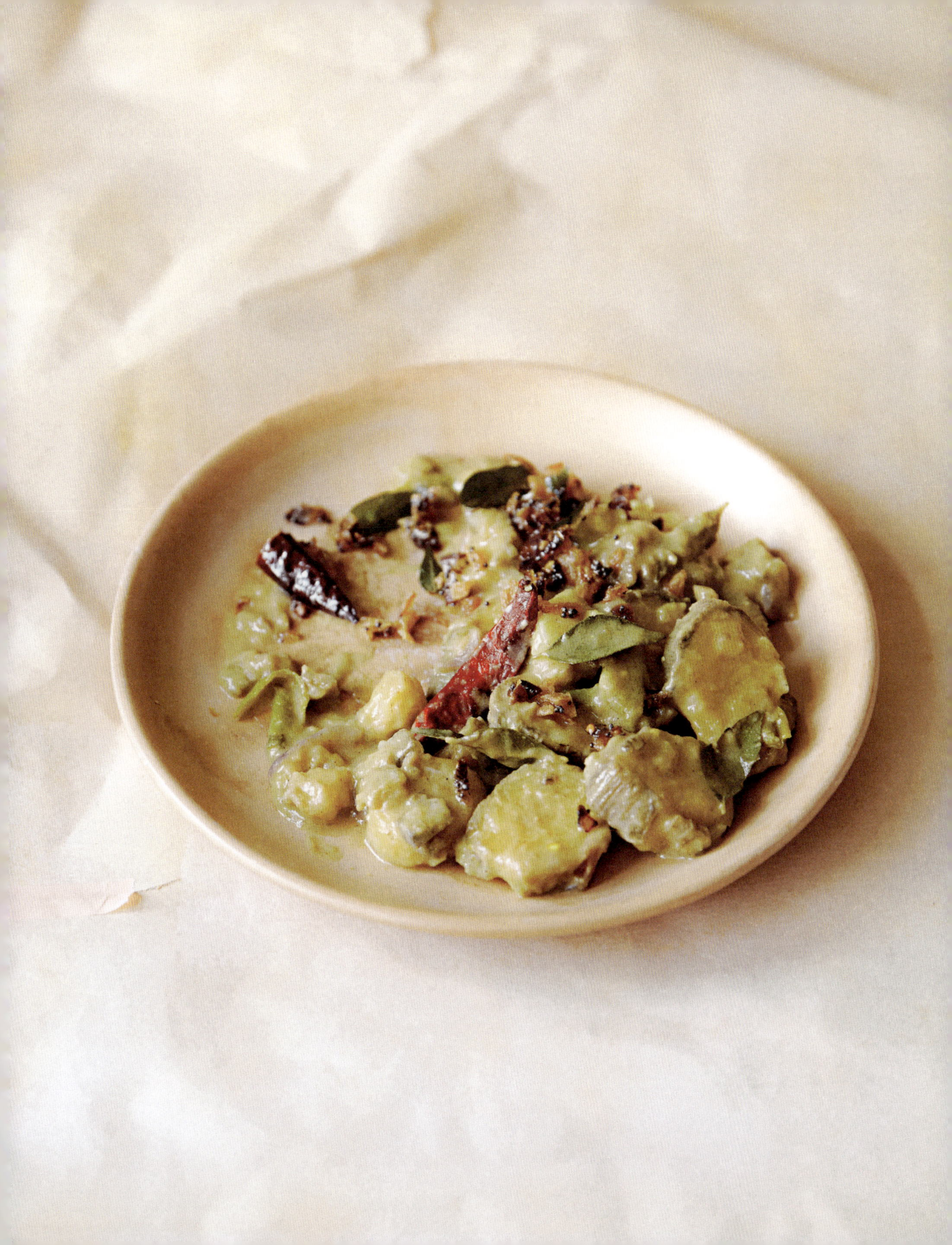

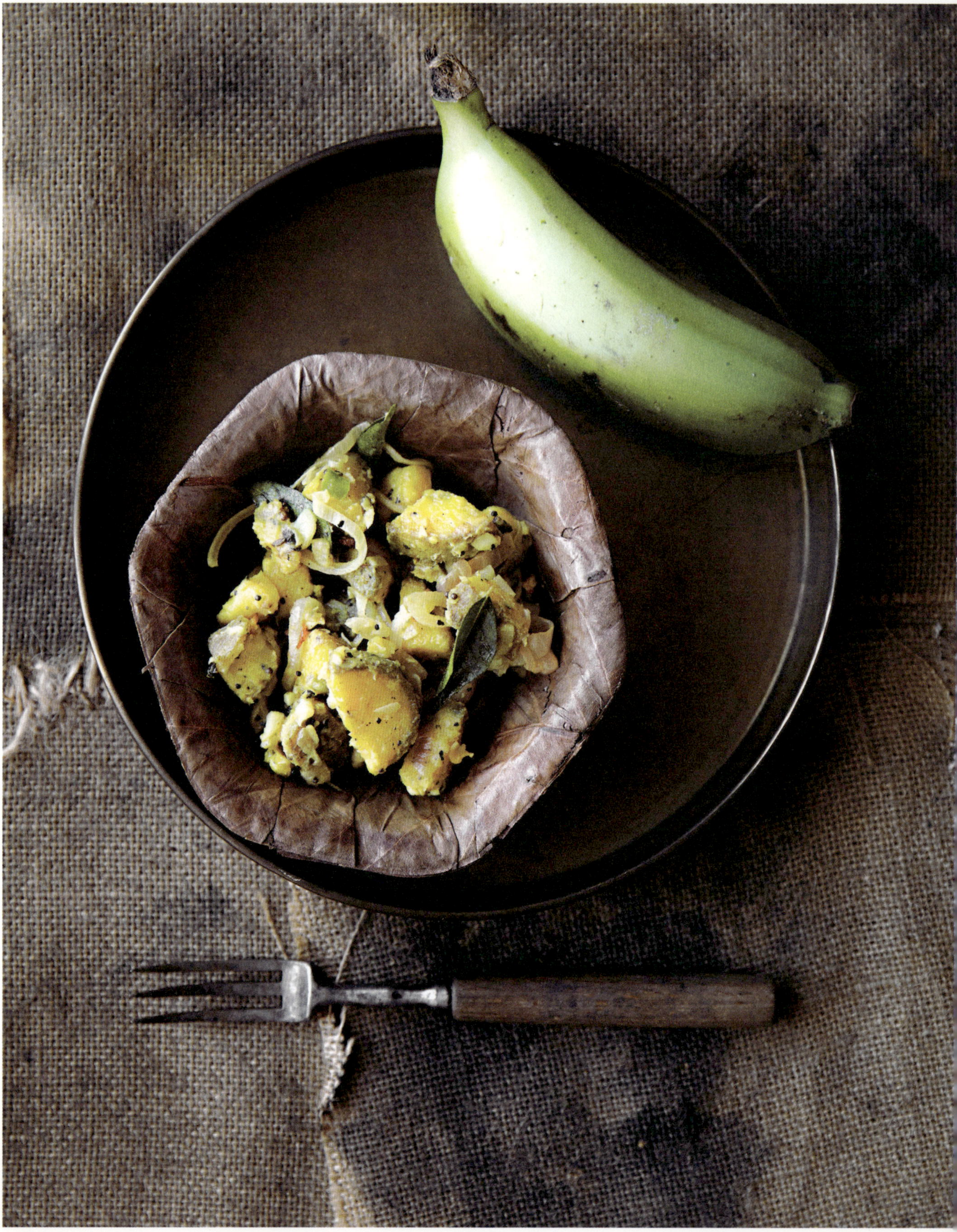

Stir-fried plantain

Plantains grow in just about every garden in Sri Lanka – and they're a favourite with wild monkeys too, who love any sort of banana. I remember as a young boy visiting a temple in Thirukonamalai, in the north-east of the island, where a monkey who was living there stole my banana snack right from my hand. This is a pleasingly uncomplicated recipe spiced generously with black pepper, harking back to the days before chilli was introduced to the island.

3 plantain
300ml (10½ fl oz/ 1¼ cups) water
3 tbsp butter
6 fresh curry leaves (optional)
2 green chillies, deseeded and finely sliced
1 medium onion, finely sliced
3 garlic cloves, finely chopped
2 tsp coarsely ground black pepper
¾ tsp salt
juice of ½ lime

Fill a medium, lidded saucepan with water. Peel the plantain and halve them lengthways, then cut them into 1.5cm (½-inch) half-moon slices, dropping them in the water as you go to avoid discoloration and to remove the slight bitter taste.

Drain the plantain and rinse once or twice. Then, pour the 300ml of water into the saucepan (to just cover the plantain) and bring to the boil. Reduce the heat, cover and simmer for 12 minutes until the plantain is soft. Be careful not to overcook or they will become very mushy, drain the water and set aside.

Heat the butter in a medium frying pan (skillet) over a low heat. Add the curry leaves (if using), chillies, onion and garlic, and sauté until the onions are soft and turning golden.

Tip the plantain into the spices, sprinkle with pepper, mix well and take off the heat. Add the salt and lime juice and give it a good stir. Taste for salt and lime before serving.

Serves 4, as a side dish

ALU KESEL BADUMA

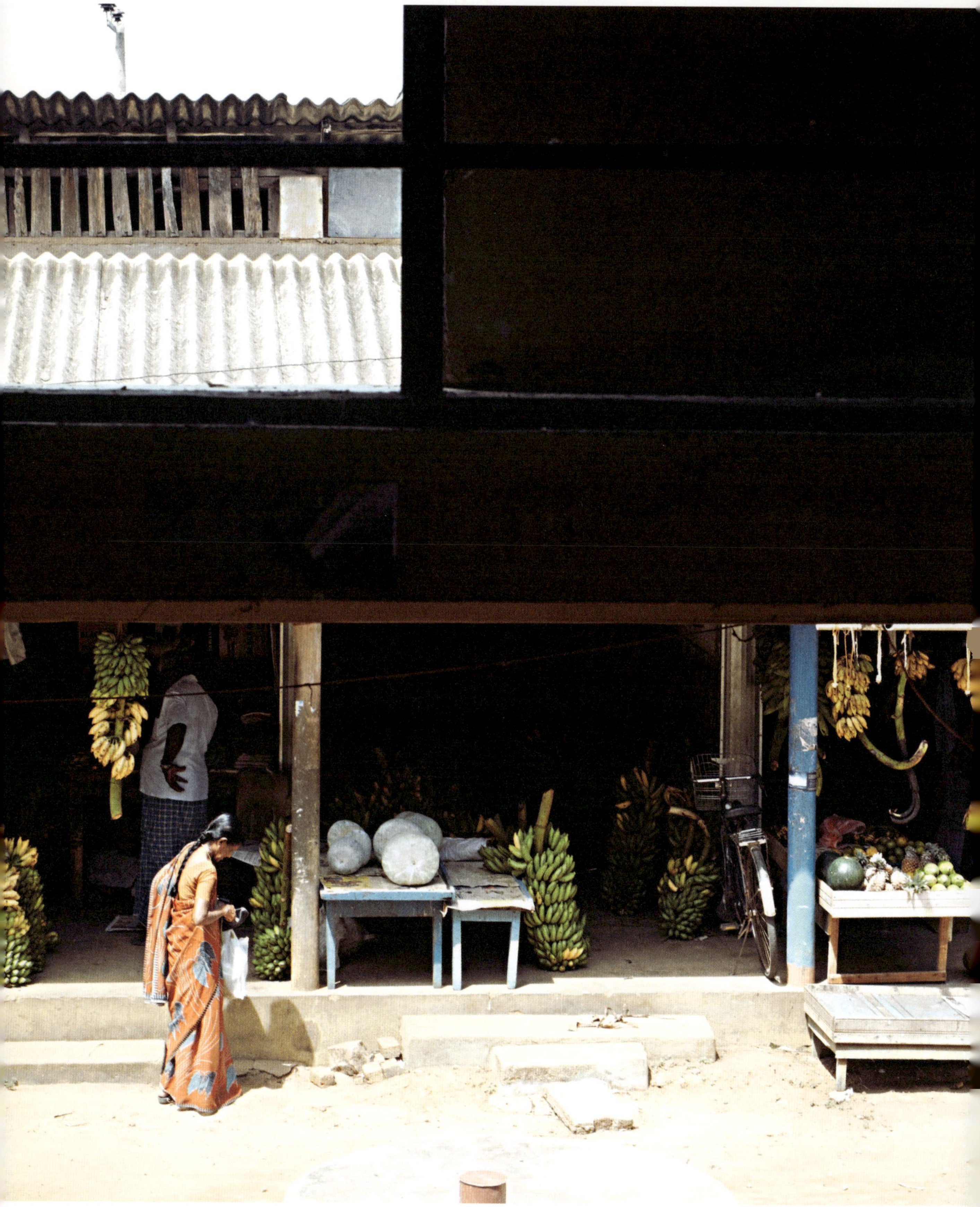

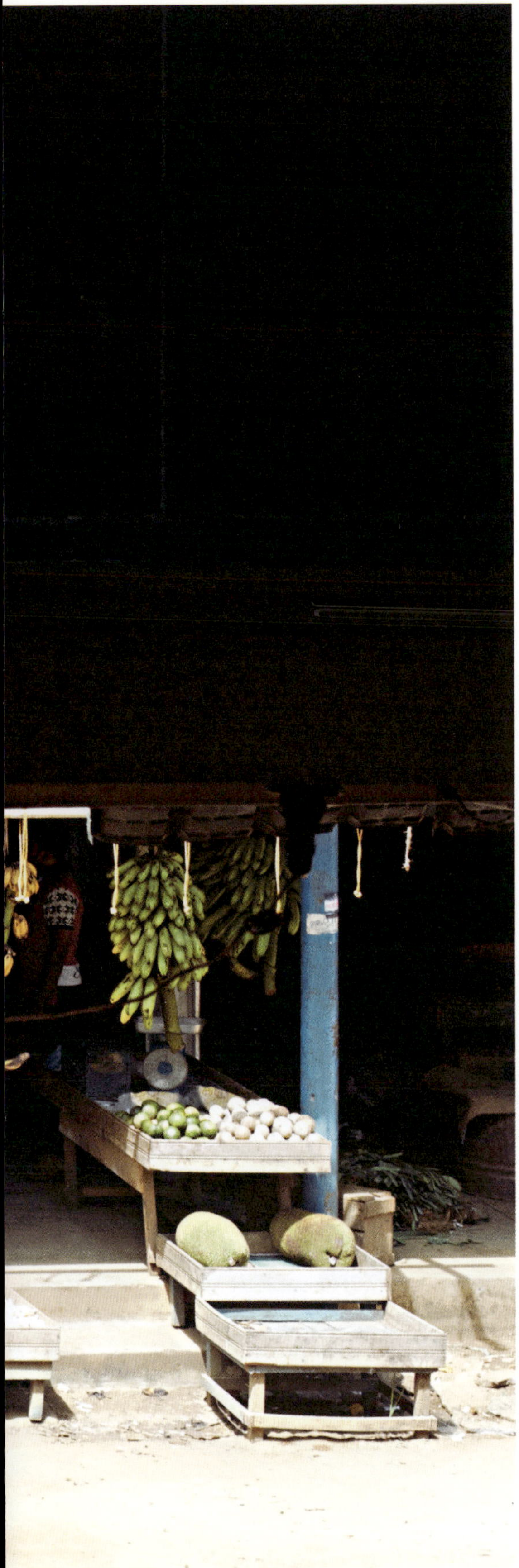

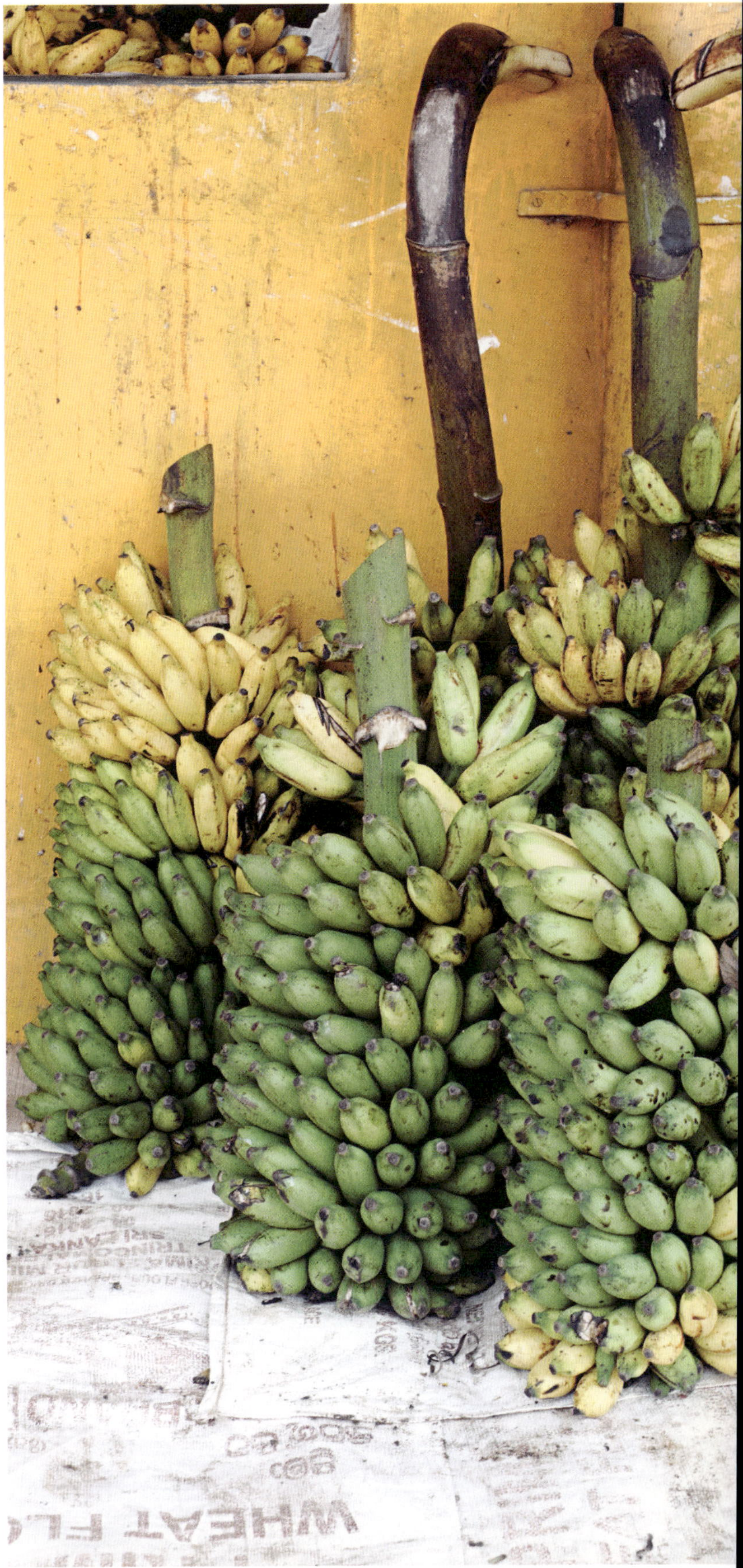

PUDALANGAI VARAI

Stir-fried snake gourd
It's clear why the long, thin snake gourd (pictured on p121) got its name from the way it dangles eerily from its vines. It tastes very distinctive and is quite firm. You'll be able to buy it at Asian supermarkets.

2 tbsp mung dal
  (split green mung bean)
400g (14oz) snake gourd
1 tbsp oil
½ tsp mustard seeds
6 fresh curry leaves
¼ tsp cumin seeds
2 green chillies,
  slit lengthways with
  seeds in
2 dried red chillies, broken
1 medium red onion,
  finely sliced
½ tsp ground turmeric
½ tsp salt
200ml (7 fl oz/generous
  ¾ cup) water
150g (5½oz/2 cups)
  freshly grated or desiccated
  (shredded) coconut

Serves 4, as a side dish

Wash the mung dal in a medium, lidded saucepan and rinse a couple of times. When the mung dal is clean, cover it with water and leave to soak while you prepare everything else.

Wash the snake gourd and cut it into manageable lengths, about 15cm (6 inches) long. Slice the pieces in half lengthwise, scoop out the seeds and fibres, and cut them into ½cm (¼-inch) half-moon slices.

Heat the oil in a medium saucepan over a low heat, then add the mustard seeds. Let them cook for a few seconds until they pop, then add the curry leaves and cumin seeds and give it a stir or two. Add the green and red chillies and give it a stir, then add the onions and sauté until they are soft and golden brown.

Drain the mung dal and add it, along with the turmeric, and give it a stir or two. Finally, add the snake gourd and salt and mix it all together.

Add the water (to cover the vegetables), cover the pan with the lid and bring to the boil. Reduce the heat and simmer for 10–12 minutes until the snake gourd is cooked but still slightly crunchy and the water has evaporated.

Finally, add the coconut, mix well and stir-fry for about 2 minutes. Taste for salt, remove from the heat and serve.

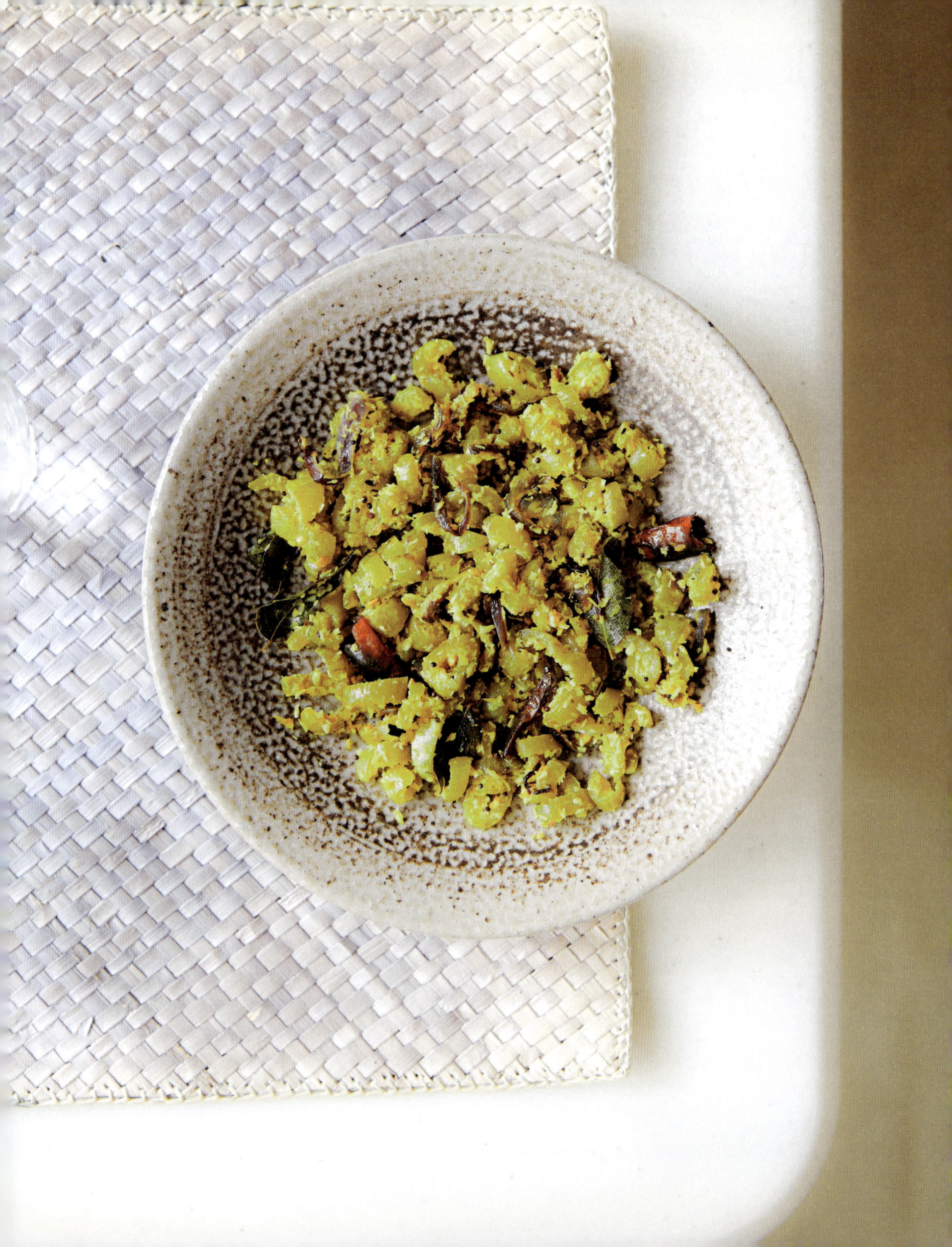

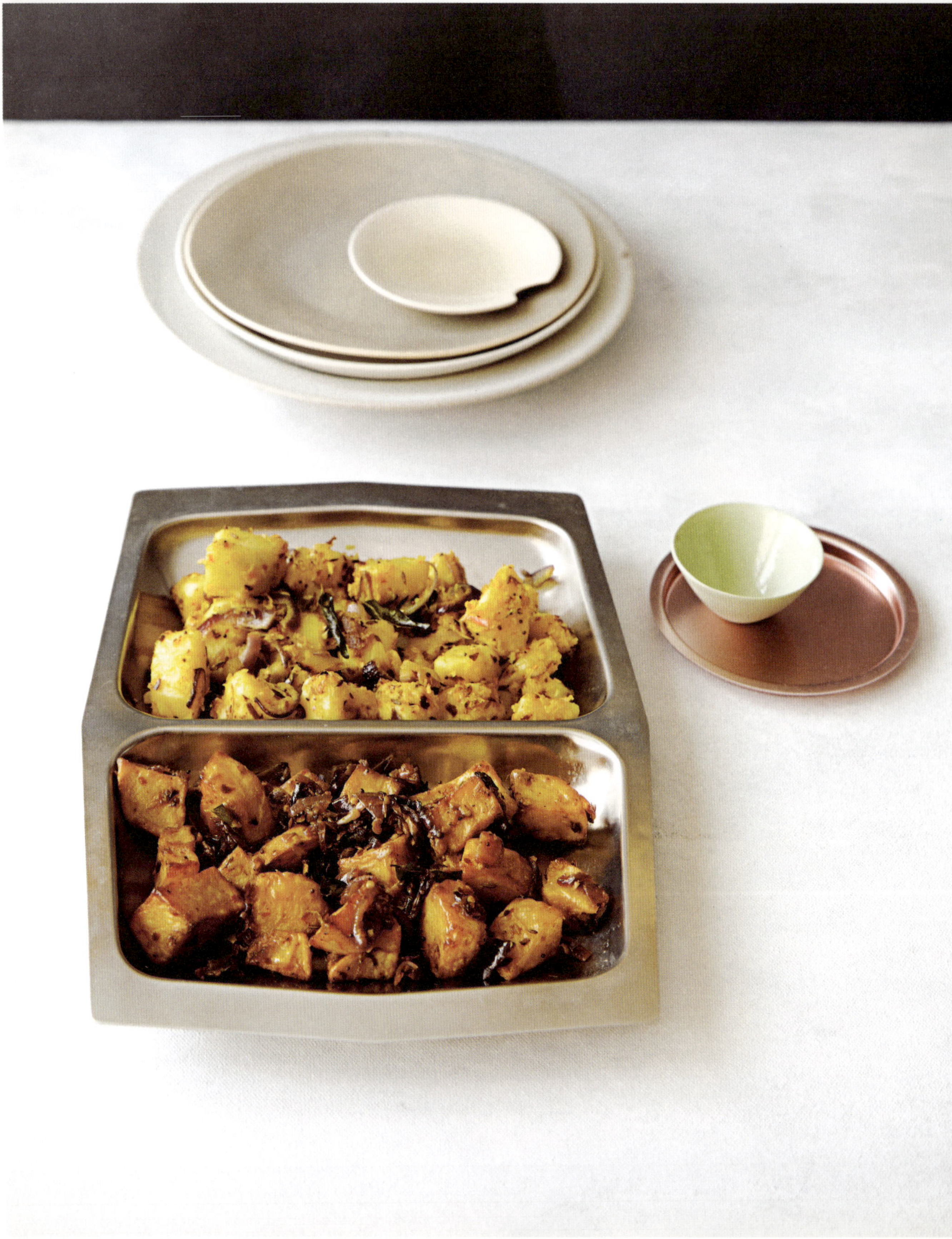

ALA THEL DALA

Devilled potatoes

Devilling is an old British technique of spicing that became popular in Sri Lanka following colonisation. This take on it is more locally appropriate, using ginger and chilli instead of English mustard, but is no less enticing.

400g potatoes
3 tbsp oil
1 tsp mustard seeds
½ tsp cumin seeds
10 fresh curry leaves
2.5cm (1-inch) piece of rampe (pandan) leaf
5 garlic cloves, finely chopped
2.5cm (1-inch) piece of ginger, peeled and finely chopped
1 green chilli, deseeded and roughly chopped
2 medium red onions, finely sliced
1 tsp ground turmeric
1½ tbsp chilli flakes
juice of ½ lime
1 tsp salt

Serves 4, as a side dish

Wash the potatoes and boil them with skins on for about 15 minutes until cooked. Take them off the heat and leave to cool. Then, peel off the skins and cut them into approximately 1.5cm (½-inch) cubes.

Heat the oil in a deep frying pan (skillet) on a low heat. Add the mustard seeds and let them cook for a few minutes until they pop. Next add the cumin, curry leaves, rampe leaf, garlic, ginger and green chillies and stir-fry for 30 seconds. Then add the onions and sauté until they are soft and golden brown.

Add the turmeric and chillies and stir-fry the mixture again for 1 minute, then add the potatoes. Season with lime juice and salt and stir-fry for a further 2–3 minutes. Serve hot.

Variation: This recipe also works well with deep-fried potato cubes (pictured in the front half of the dish). Simply fry the potatoes instead of boiling.

PATHOLA MALUWA

Snake gourd curry

Snake gourd is perhaps the longest vegetable in the world – it can grow to a metre and a half – and this subcontinental ingredient has a texture similar to squash when cooked, along with a gentle flavour that gets along perfectly with the layered spices in this curry.

300g (10½oz) snake gourd
2 tbsp oil
1 tsp cumin seeds
7 fresh curry leaves
2 garlic cloves, finely chopped
½ medium onion, medium diced
2.5cm (1-inch) cinnamon stick, broken into two
2.5cm (1-inch) piece of rampe (pandan) leaf
1 green chilli, slit lengthways and deseeded
½ tsp fenugreek seeds
125ml (4 fl oz/½ cup) water
¼ tsp ground turmeric
1 tsp Thuna Paha (curry powder on p17)
½ tsp salt
250ml (9 fl oz/generous 1 cup) coconut milk
juice of ½ lime

Serves 4, as a side dish

Wash the snake gourd and cut it into manageable lengths, about 15cm (6 inches) long. Lightly scrape the skin off. Slice each piece in half lengthwise, scoop out the seeds and fibres, and cut them into ½cm (¼-inch) half-moon slices. Set aside.

Heat the oil in a medium, lidded saucepan over a low heat, then add the cumin seeds. Let them cook for a few seconds until they pop, then add the curry leaves, garlic, onions, cinnamon, rampe leaf, green chilli and fenugreek seeds. Sauté until the onions are soft and turning golden. Add the snake gourd and stir-fry for 1–2 minutes.

Add the water, turmeric, curry powder and salt, cover and bring to the boil. Turn the heat down to medium and cook for about 10 minutes.

Add the coconut milk and cook for another 6–7 minutes, stirring frequently, until the snake gourd is cooked but still slightly crunchy. There should be plenty of liquid left in the pan. Remove from the heat and add the lime juice, to taste, and extra salt if required.

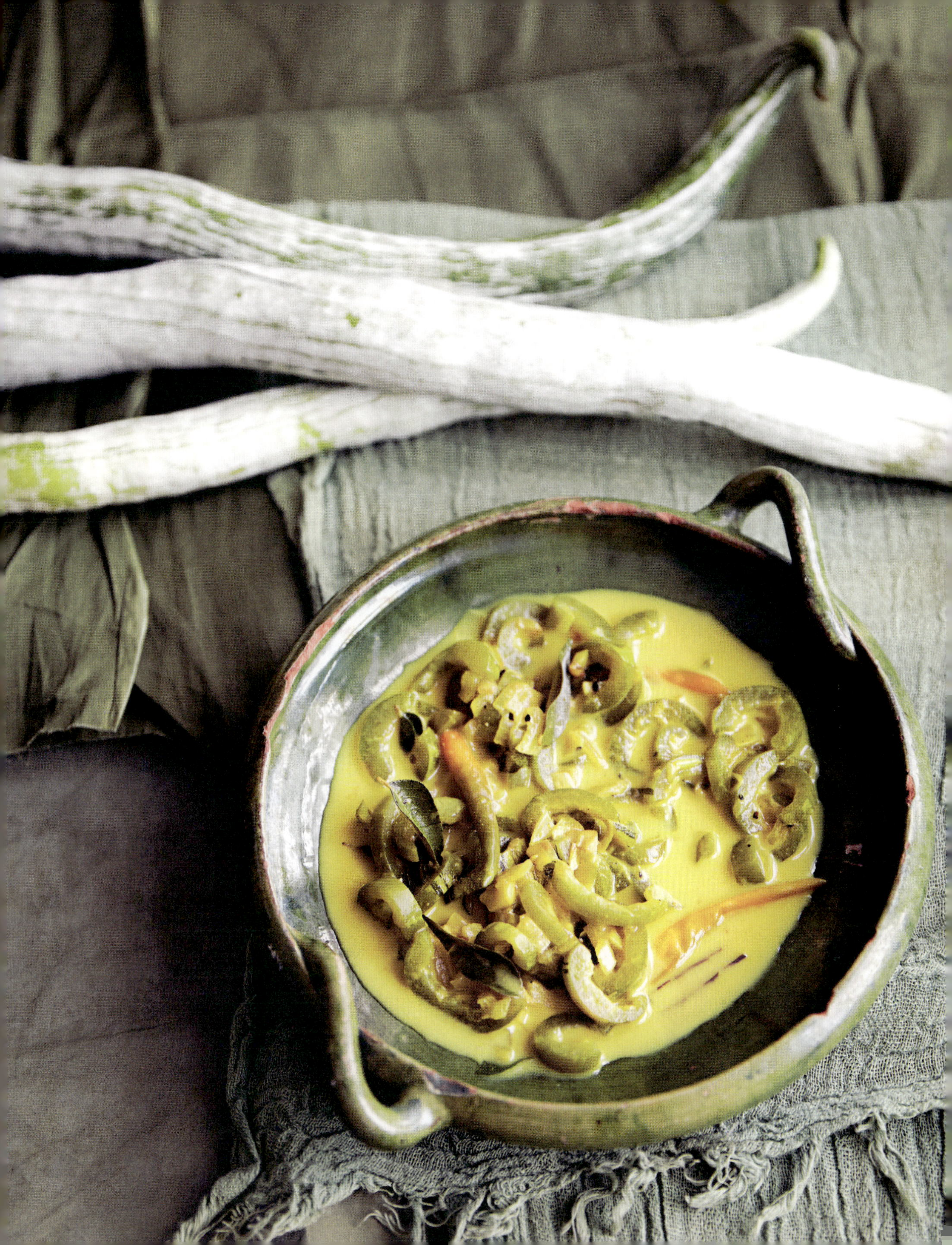

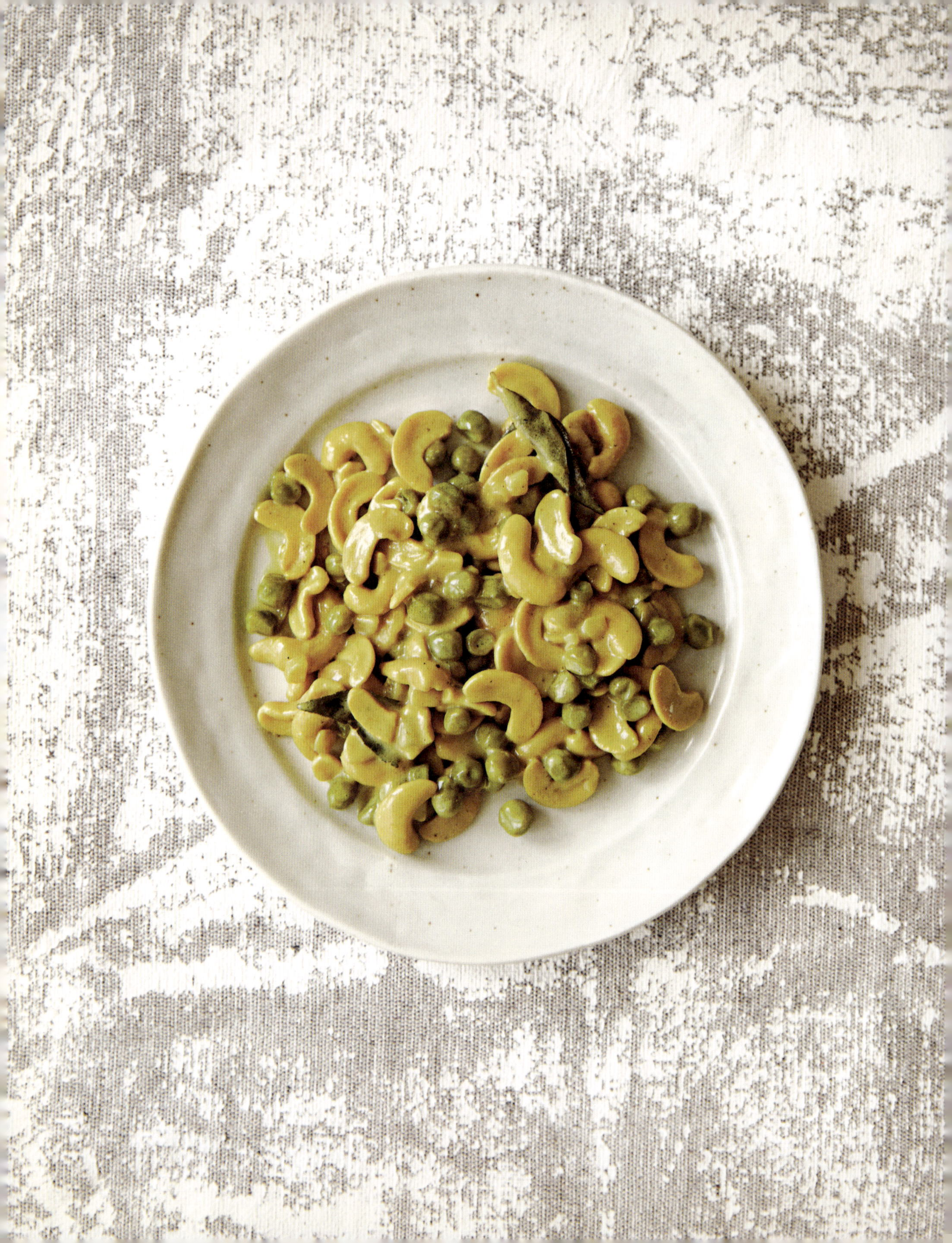

KAJU KARI

Cashew nut curry

Cashew nuts are the main ingredient in this creamy, mild curry: they're expensive, and as such kaju kari is most often served at celebrations. Fresh cashews are unique, in that the nut grows outside the fruit. The fruit is an acquired taste but is often pickled on the island.

300g (10½oz/2¼ cups) cashew nuts, halved
300ml (10½ fl oz/1¼ cups) water
1 medium onion, finely chopped
2 garlic cloves, finely chopped
8 fresh curry leaves
1.5cm (½-inch) piece of ginger, peeled and very finely chopped
2 green chillies, split lengthways and deseeded
2.5cm (1-inch) cinnamon stick
½ tsp ground cumin
½ tsp ground turmeric
½ tsp fenugreek seeds
250ml (9 fl oz/generous 1 cup) coconut milk
½ tsp salt
100g (3½oz/⅔ cup) frozen peas, defrosted (optional)
juice of ½ lime

For the tempering
2 tbsp butter or oil
½ medium onion, finely chopped
5 fresh curry leaves
½ tsp ground cumin
½ tsp ground turmeric
½ tsp coarsely ground black pepper
¼ tsp ground cardamom

Serves 4, as a side dish

First, fill a medium saucepan with water and soak the cashew nuts for 1 hour, then drain.

Pour the 300ml of water into the saucepan with the cashew nuts, then add the onions, garlic, curry leaves, ginger, chillies cinnamon, cumin, turmeric and fenugreek seeds, and bring to the boil. Reduce the heat to medium and cook for 20 minutes until the nuts are soft.

Add the coconut milk and salt and simmer for about 10 minutes until the milk has thickened. Give it a stir every now and then to stop the milk from curdling. If you are using peas, add them to the curry after 5 minutes.

Now temper the onions. Heat the oil or butter in a medium frying pan (skillet) on a low heat, and sauté the onions and curry leaves until the onions are soft and turning golden. Tip them into the curry and sprinkle over the cumin, turmeric, pepper and cardamom. Stir well.

Take off the heat and add the lime juice, to taste, and extra salt if required.

MAALU MIRIS

Stuffed peppers

In Sri Lanka this dish is most often made with long, thin banana peppers, but bell peppers are lovely here too. Serve with a creamy dal to balance its sharpness.

Serves 4, as a side dish

Wash the potatoes and boil them with skins on for about 15 minutes until cooked. Take them off the heat and leave to cool. Then, peel off the skins and roughly mash.

Wash the (bell) peppers. Leaving the stem in place, make a slit down the length of each one, from the top 1.5cm (½ inch) from the bottom and remove the seeds.

First make the filling. Heat the oil in a medium saucepan over a low heat. Add the onion, garlic, ginger and curry leaves, and sauté for a couple of minutes. Add the mashed potato, Maldive fish, salt, pepper and vinegar and give it a good stir. Remove from the heat and leave to cool.

When the mixture is cool enough to handle, place the peppers on a work surface. Working one at a time, spoon the mixture inside and pile it along one half of the pepper. Close up the other half like a lid, and tie a piece of cotton thread tightly around the middle to keep it secure. Repeat for all the peppers.

Now make the sauce. Heat the oil in a large saucepan over a low heat. Add all the ingredients up to and including the salt, and sauté until the onions are soft and turning golden. Add the tomato and water and bring to the boil. Cook over a medium heat for about 7 minutes until reduced by half.

Add the coconut milk, turmeric and cumin and give it a good stir. Gently put the stuffed peppers into the pan and simmer for 5 minutes. Carefully turn the peppers over with a long spoon and simmer for a further 3–4 minutes until slightly soft and the sauce is thickened.

Remove from the heat and add the lime juice. Give the pan a gentle shake so the gravy is evenly mixed, and serve.

4 green (bell) peppers

For the filling
150g potatoes
1 tbsp oil
½ medium onion, finely chopped
2 garlic cloves, finely chopped
1.5cm (½-inch) piece of ginger, peeled and finely chopped
5 fresh curry leaves, finely chopped
1 tsp Maldive fish
½ tsp salt
1 tsp ground black pepper
½ tsp vinegar (white or red)

For the sauce
1 tbsp oil
½ medium onion, finely chopped
½ tsp fenugreek seeds
½ tsp cumin seeds
5 fresh curry leaves
3 garlic cloves, finely chopped
1.5cm (½-inch) piece of ginger, peeled and finely chopped
2.5cm (1-inch) piece of rampe (pandan) leaf
2.5cm (1-inch) cinnamon stick, broken into two
1 green chilli, slit lengthways and deseeded
1 tsp salt
1 tomato, finely chopped
350ml (12 fl oz/ 1½ cups) water
250ml (9 fl oz/generous 1 cup) coconut milk
¾ tsp ground turmeric
1 tsp ground cumin
juice of ½ lime

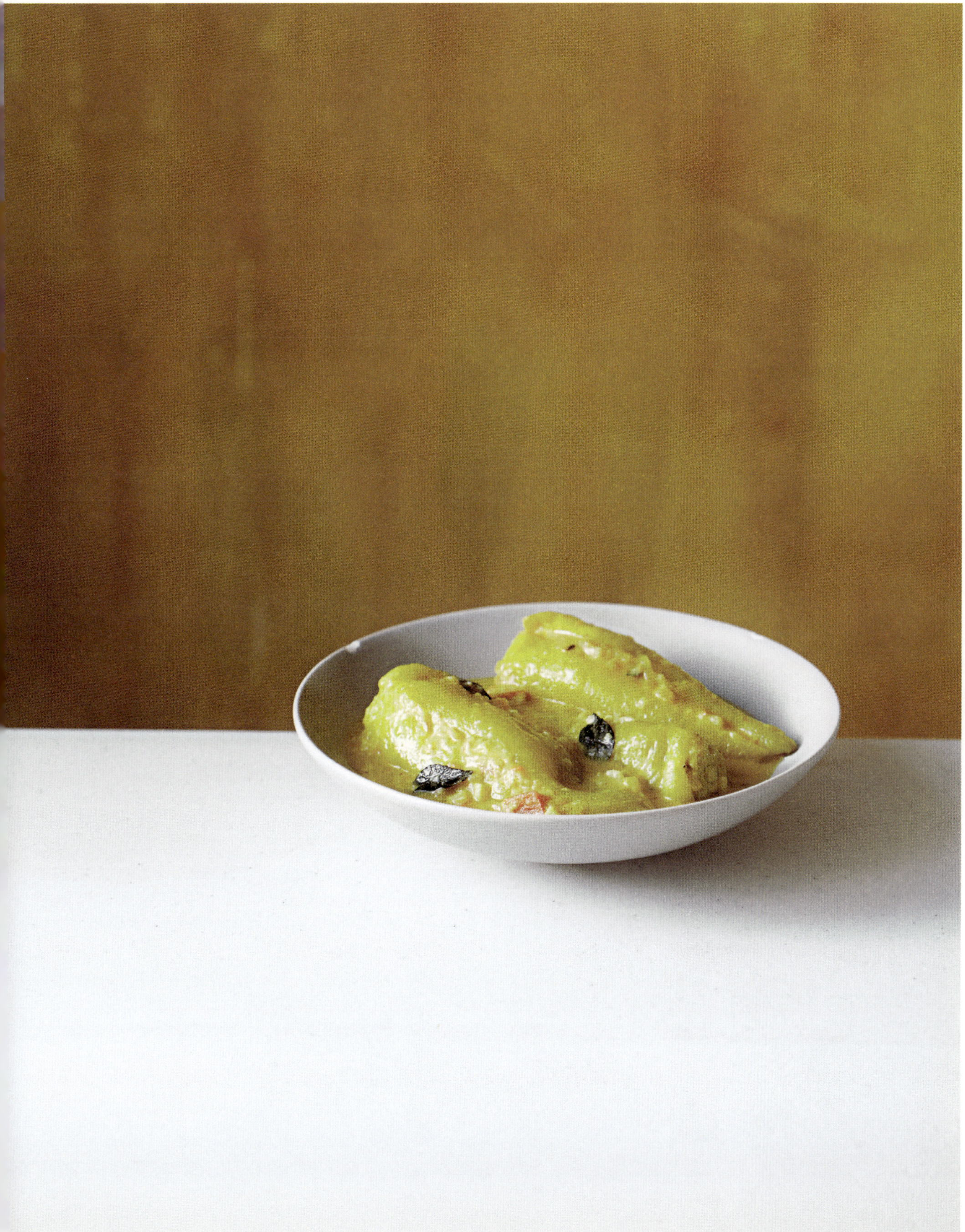

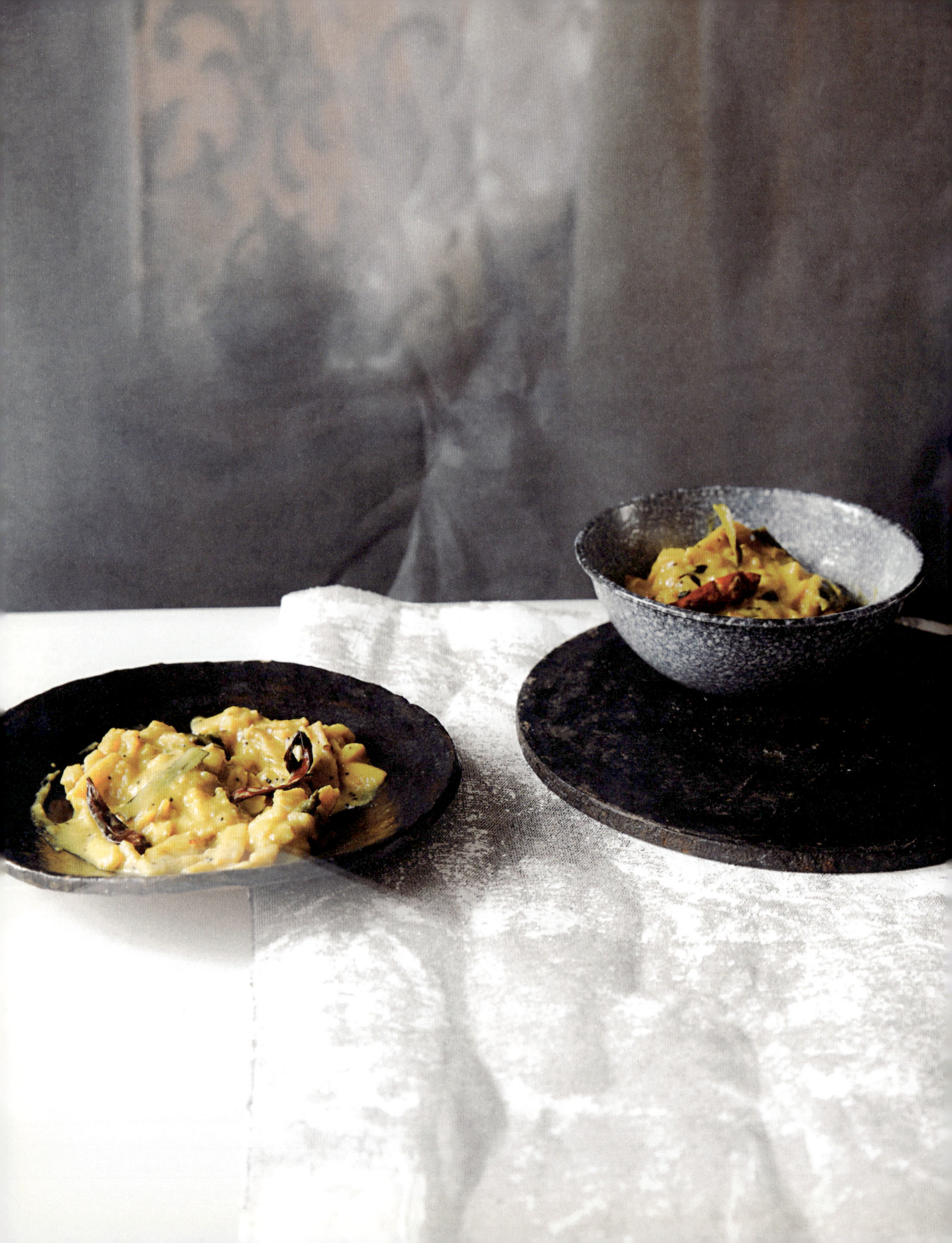

KIRI KOS

Jackfruit curry

The bulbous, knobbly jackfruit is used at all stages of ripeness in Sri Lankan cooking: when young it has a creamy, tropical-fruit taste and firm texture.

Serves 4, as a side dish

400g (14oz) fresh jackfruit bulbs (or see *Note*)
250ml (9 fl oz/generous 1 cup) water
1 medium onion, finely chopped
¾ tsp ground turmeric
1 tsp ground cumin
6 black peppercorns
4 garlic cloves, finely chopped
1 green chilli, slit lengthways and deseeded
5 fresh curry leaves
2.5cm (1-inch) piece of rampe (pandan) leaf
½ tsp salt
200ml (7 fl oz/generous ¾ cup) coconut milk

For the tempering
1 tbsp oil
½ tsp mustard seeds
½ tsp fenugreek seeds
5 fresh curry leaves
2 dried red chillies
½ tbsp finely chopped onion
½ tbsp Bathapu Thuna Paha (curry powder on p17)

Wash and cut the jackfruit bulbs in half and put them in medium saucepan. Add the water and all the other ingredients except the salt and coconut milk.

Bring to the boil, then lower the heat and simmer for about 15 minutes until slightly thickened. Add the salt and stir well.

Pour in the coconut milk and simmer for a further 10 minutes until thick and almost all the liquid is absorbed.

Meanwhile, temper the spices. Heat the oil in a small frying pan (skillet) over a low heat. Add the mustard seeds, fenugreek seeds, curry leaves, chillies and chopped onions, and sauté until the onions are brown and almost crispy. When the curry is ready, add the tempered mix and give it a good stir.

Take the curry off the heat and sprinkle with the curry powder. Cover and leave for about 3 minutes to infuse, taste for salt and serve.

Note: If you can't find fresh jackfruit, you can use frozen (defrosted) or canned. For canned, cook for about 7 minutes instead of 15.

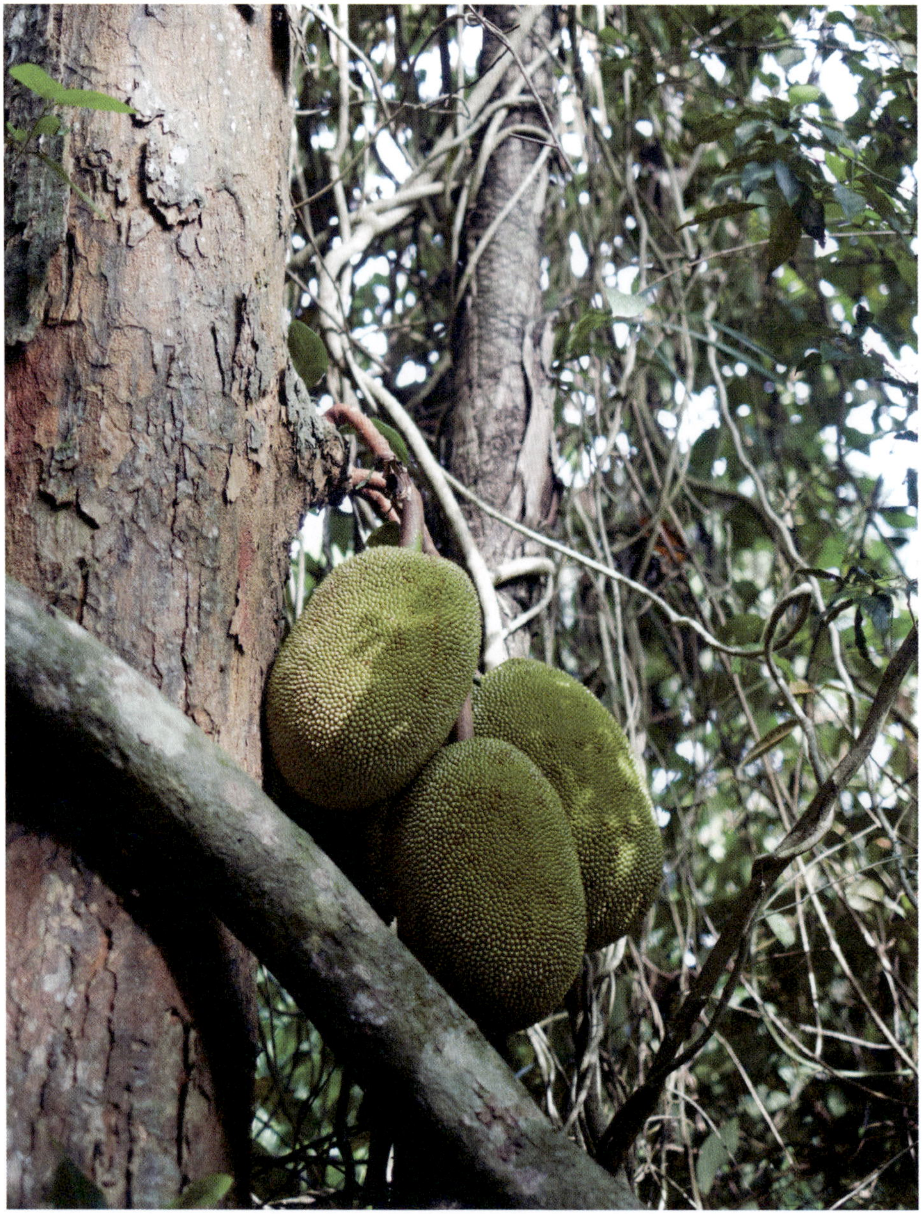

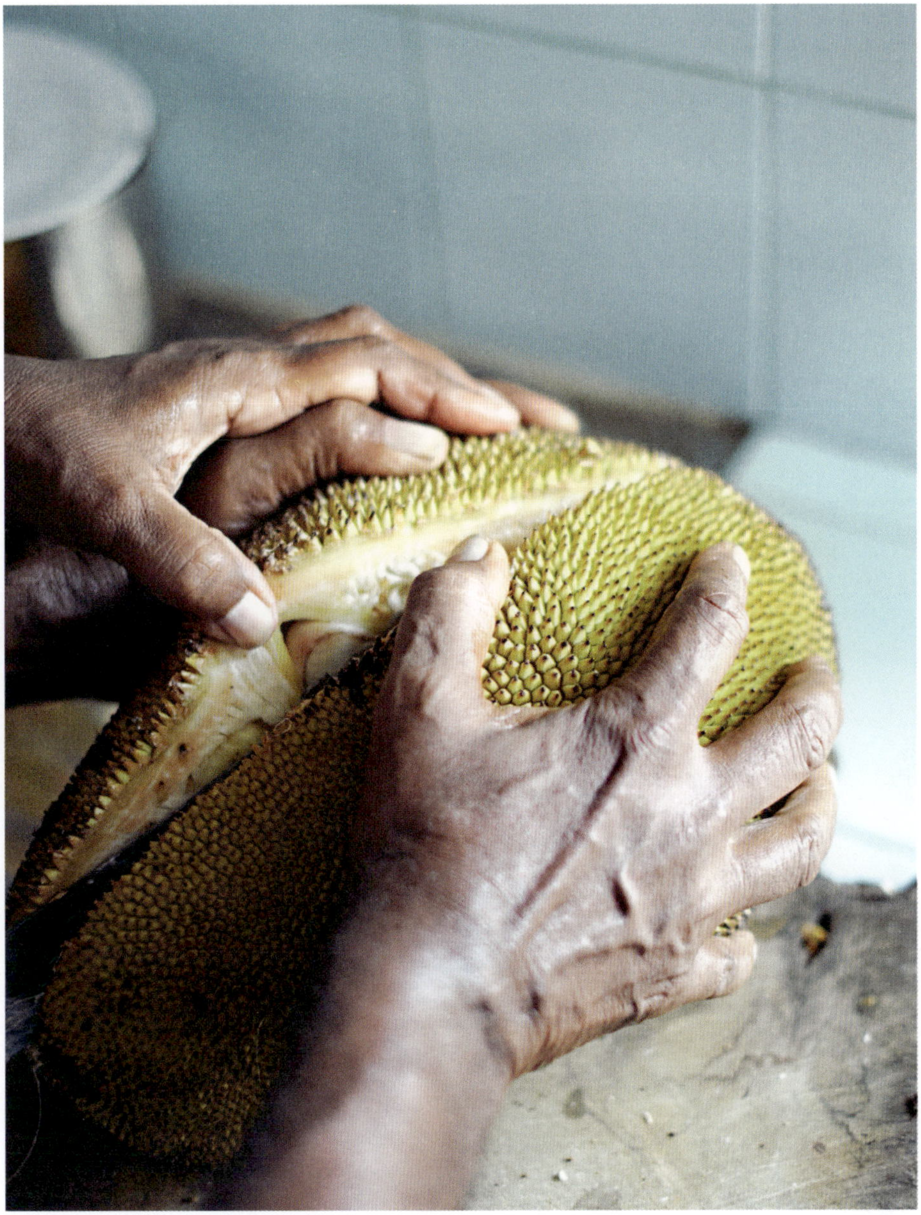

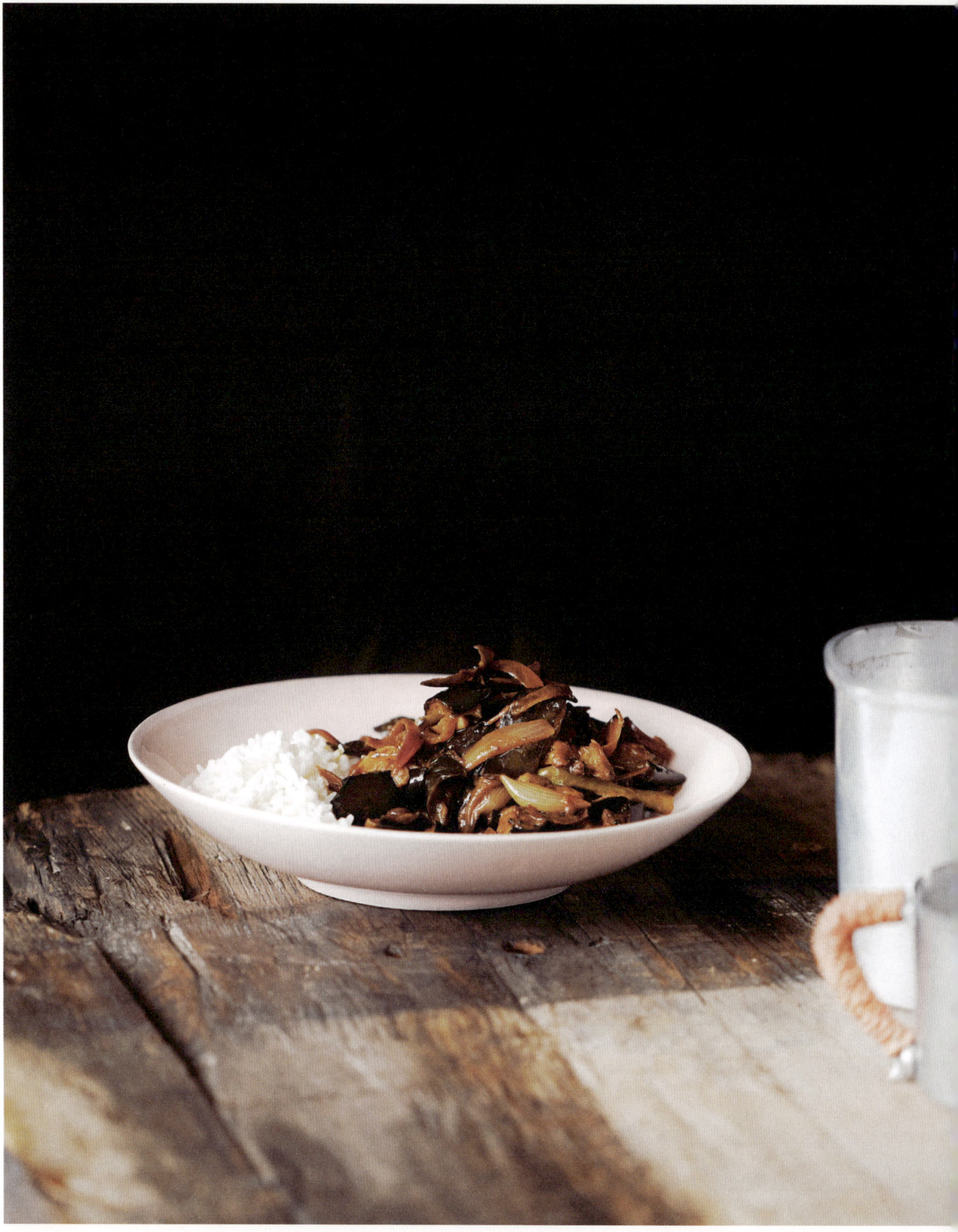

- 400g (14oz) aubergine (eggplant) (about 1 large)
- 4 tbsp oil
- ½ tsp mustard seeds
- 6 fresh curry leaves
- ¼ tsp cumin seeds
- ½ tsp fenugreek seeds
- 2 green chillies, slit lengthways with seeds in
- 1 medium onion, sliced
- 6 garlic cloves, cut into quarters
- 300ml (7 fl oz/generous ¾ cup) tamarind water
- ½ tsp ground turmeric
- 1 tsp ground cumin
- 1 tsp ground coriander
- ½ tsp chilli powder
- ½ tsp sugar (optional)
- ½ tsp salt
- 100ml (3½ fl oz/7 tbsp) coconut milk

Aubergine and tamarind curry

Aubergine is the most versatile vegetable in the kitchen. Here it takes centre stage paired with tart tamarind, a regular element of Tamil cooking. Without fail this is served at a Hindu wedding, along with dal.

KATHIRIKAI PIRATTAL

Fill a medium saucepan with water. Wash and cut the aubergine (eggplant) into 2.5cm (1-inch) chunks. Drop them in the water as you go to avoid discoloration and to remove the slight bitter taste.

Heat the oil in a medium saucepan over a low heat. Squeeze the water out of the cut aubergine pieces with your hands and place them into the pan. Sauté until it begins to soften and turn brown. When cooked, take the pan off the heat. Remove the aubergine pieces, gently squeezing any excess oil back into the pan with a spoon as you go, and set them aside.

Place the pan back on the heat, add a little extra oil to the pan if it is looking dry, then add the mustard seeds. Let them cook for a few seconds until they pop, then add the curry leaves and cumin seeds and give it a stir or two. Next, add the fenugreek seeds and stir-fry for a minute or so, then the green chillies and give it another stir. Add the onions, stir-fry for 30 seconds, and finally add the garlic, then sauté until the onions are soft and turning golden.

Then, add the tamarind water and all the spice powders, sugar (if using) and salt. Mix well and bring to the boil. Reduce the heat and simmer for about 10 minutes, until the curry starts to thicken. Add the coconut milk and a little extra water if it's too dry, and cook for about 5 minutes until the curry thickens.

Tip in the aubergine and mix it together on a low heat. Taste for salt and remove from the heat. Leave to rest for about 3 minutes before serving.

Tip: Instead of sautéing the aubergine, you could bake it in the oven (180°C/350°F/Gas Mark 4) for 30 minutes until soft.

Serves 4, as a side dish

THALANA BATTU

Round aubergine curry

An aromatic, mellow curry with 'Thai' or small, round aubergines. They're firmer than the larger ones – they make a difference to the texture of the dish, so seek them out if you can.

Serves 4, as a side dish

Put a handful of aubergines (eggplants) with stems into a plastic food bag and seal or put a knot in it. Place it on a hard surface and gently smash ('thalanda') the aubergines using a mallet or rolling pin, until they break up a bit and the seeds inside are loosened.

Tip the slightly smashed aubergines into a bowl of water, and repeat with them all. Remove the seeds by sliding your thumb in between the outer layer of flesh and the inner ball of seeds and gently pushing the seeds out in one go. Rinse well and set the aubergine aside in fresh water to avoid discoloration.

Heat the oil in a medium, lidded saucepan over a low heat, then add the cumin seeds. Let them cook for a few seconds until they pop, then add the curry leaves, garlic, onion, cinnamon, rampe leaf, green chilli and fenugreek seeds, and stir. Sauté until the onions are soft and turning golden. Add the aubergine and stir-fry for 1–2 minutes.

Add the coconut milk, water, turmeric, curry powder and salt, cover and cook over a medium heat for 10–12 minutes until the aubergine is slightly soft.

Add the coconut cream and cook for a further 6–7 minutes, stirring frequently, until the aubergine is cooked. You should have plenty of thick sauce. Remove from the heat, add the lime juice, to taste, and extra salt if required.

- 300g (9oz) round aubergine (eggplant) (about 1, small)
- 1 tbsp oil
- ½ tsp cumin seeds
- 7 fresh curry leaves
- 3 garlic cloves, finely chopped
- 1 medium onion, roughly chopped
- 2.5cm (1-inch) cinnamon stick, broken into two
- 2.5cm (1-inch) piece of rampe (pandan) leaf
- 1 green chilli, slit lengthways and deseeded
- ½ tsp fenugreek seeds
- 250ml (7 fl oz/generous ¾ cup) coconut milk
- 125ml (4 fl oz/½ cup) water
- ½ tsp ground turmeric
- 1 tsp Thuna Paha (curry powder on p17)
- 1 tsp salt
- 100ml (4 fl oz/½ cup) coconut cream
- juice of ½ lime

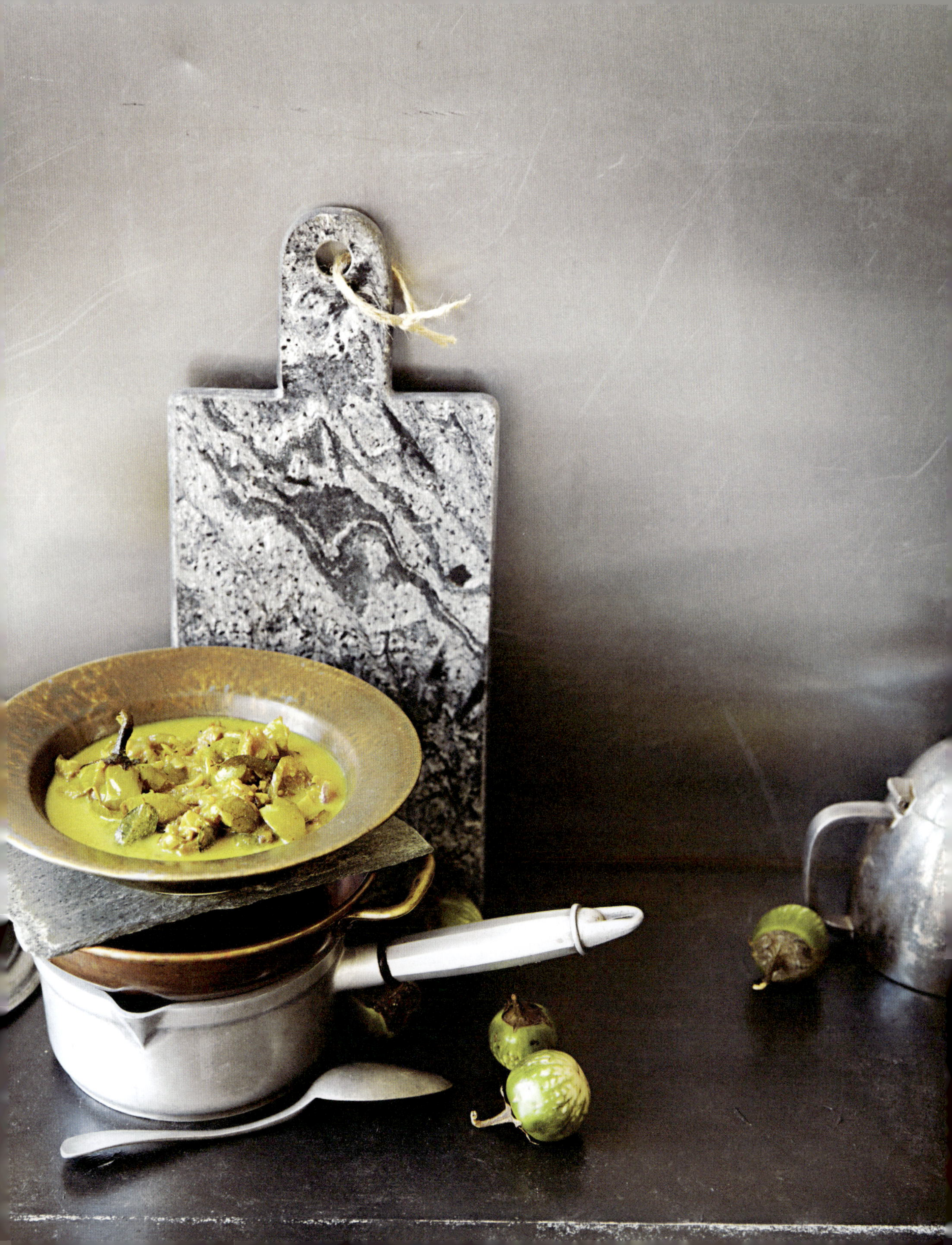

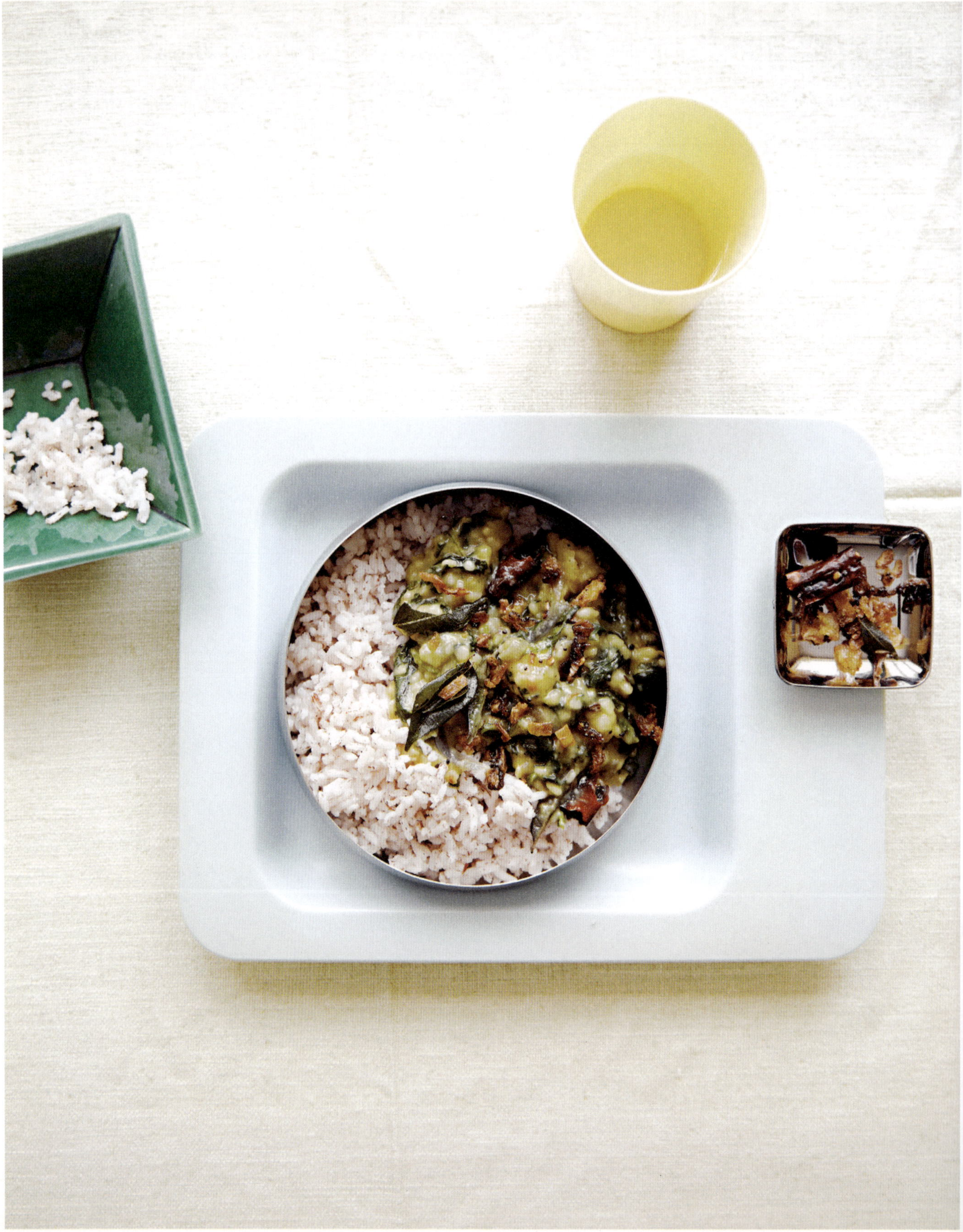

300g (10½oz/1½ cups) mung dal (split green mung bean)
300ml (10½ fl oz/ 1¼ cups) water
½ medium onion, finely chopped
2 garlic cloves, finely chopped
¼ tsp cumin seeds
½ tsp ground turmeric
4 fresh curry leaves
100g (3½oz) spinach, roughly chopped
1 tsp salt
1 tsp butter or ghee (optional)

For the tempering
1 tbsp oil
½ tsp mustard seeds
¼ tsp cumin seeds
2 dried red chillies, broken
4 fresh curry leaves
½ medium onion, finely chopped
2 garlic cloves, finely chopped

Dal and spinach curry
Dry-roasting the mung dal before cooking gives this protein-packed dish a deeply nutty flavour. For those in Sri Lanka who eat no meat, lentils are a basic and daily source of protein.

Lightly dry-roast the mung dal in a medium saucepan over a low heat, until golden. Leave to cool, then wash the mung dal in a pan of cold water by rubbing it between your hands. Drain and repeat three or four times until the water is nearly clear.

Then, add the 300ml of water, so it covers the mung dal by about 2.5cm (1 inch), and bring to the boil. Scoop the froth or scum off the top of the water. You may have to do this a few times.

Reduce the heat to low, add the onion, garlic, cumin seeds, turmeric and curry leaves. Give it a good stir, cover and cook for 10–12 minutes until beginning to soften, then add the spinach.

When the mung dal is soft, after about 6–7 minutes, add the salt and butter or ghee (if using) and mix well.

Now temper the spices. Heat the oil in a small fying pan over a low heat, then add the mustard seeds. Let them cook for a few seconds until they pop, then add the cumin seeds and chillies and give it a stir or two. Add the curry leaves, give it a stir, and then add the onion and garlic. Sauté until the onion is brown and slightly crispy.

Tip the tempered mix into the mung dal and give it a good stir, then serve.

Serves 4

PAYARU KEERAI

- 400g (14oz) bitter gourd
- 1 tsp salt
- 1 tsp ground turmeric
- 300ml (10½ fl oz/ 1¼ cups) water
- 2 tbsp oil
- ½ tsp mustard seeds
- 6 fresh curry leaves
- ½ tsp cumin seeds
- 2 green chillies, slit lengthways with seeds in
- 1 medium onion, sliced
- 6 garlic cloves, chopped
- 2 medium tomatoes, medium diced
- 1 tsp ground cumin
- 1 tsp ground coriander
- ½ tsp chilli powder
- ½ tsp sugar (white or brown)
- 100ml (3½ fl oz/ 7 tbsp) coconut milk (medium thick)

Bitter gourd curry

As the name suggests, this curry is indeed mildly bitter – but certainly not unpleasantly so. The soaking helps reduce the bitterness too, but this flavour is an essential part of Sri Lankan cuisine.

Wash the bitter gourd, top and tail it and slit it down the middle lengthwise. Scoop out the fibres and seeds from the centre using a teaspoon. Cut into lengths about 4cm (1½ inches) by 1cm (½ inch).

Fill a medium saucepan with water and add the salt and the turmeric. Soak the bitter gourd in this water for about 10 minutes. This helps reduce the bitterness of the vegetable. Throw away the water and rinse the bitter gourd a couple of times to get rid of the saltiness.

Then, add the 300ml of water to the pan, so it covers the bitter gourd, bring to the boil and cook for 5 minutes. Drain and set aside.

Heat the oil in a medium saucepan over a low heat, then add the mustard seeds. Let them cook for a few seconds until they pop, then add the curry leaves and cumin seeds and give it a stir or two. Next, add the green chillies and give it another stir, then the onions and stir-fry for 30 seconds. Finally, add the garlic and sauté until the onions are soft and turning golden.

Add the tomatoes, mix well, then cover and cook until the tomato is soft and almost puréed.

Add all the spice powders and sugar and season with salt, mix well. Add the bitter gourd and the coconut milk and mix it all together, then cover and cook for about 6–7 minutes until the gourd is soft with a slight bite to it. Taste for salt and remove from the heat. Let it rest for about 3 minutes before serving.

Serves 4, as a side dish

PAVAKKAI KARI

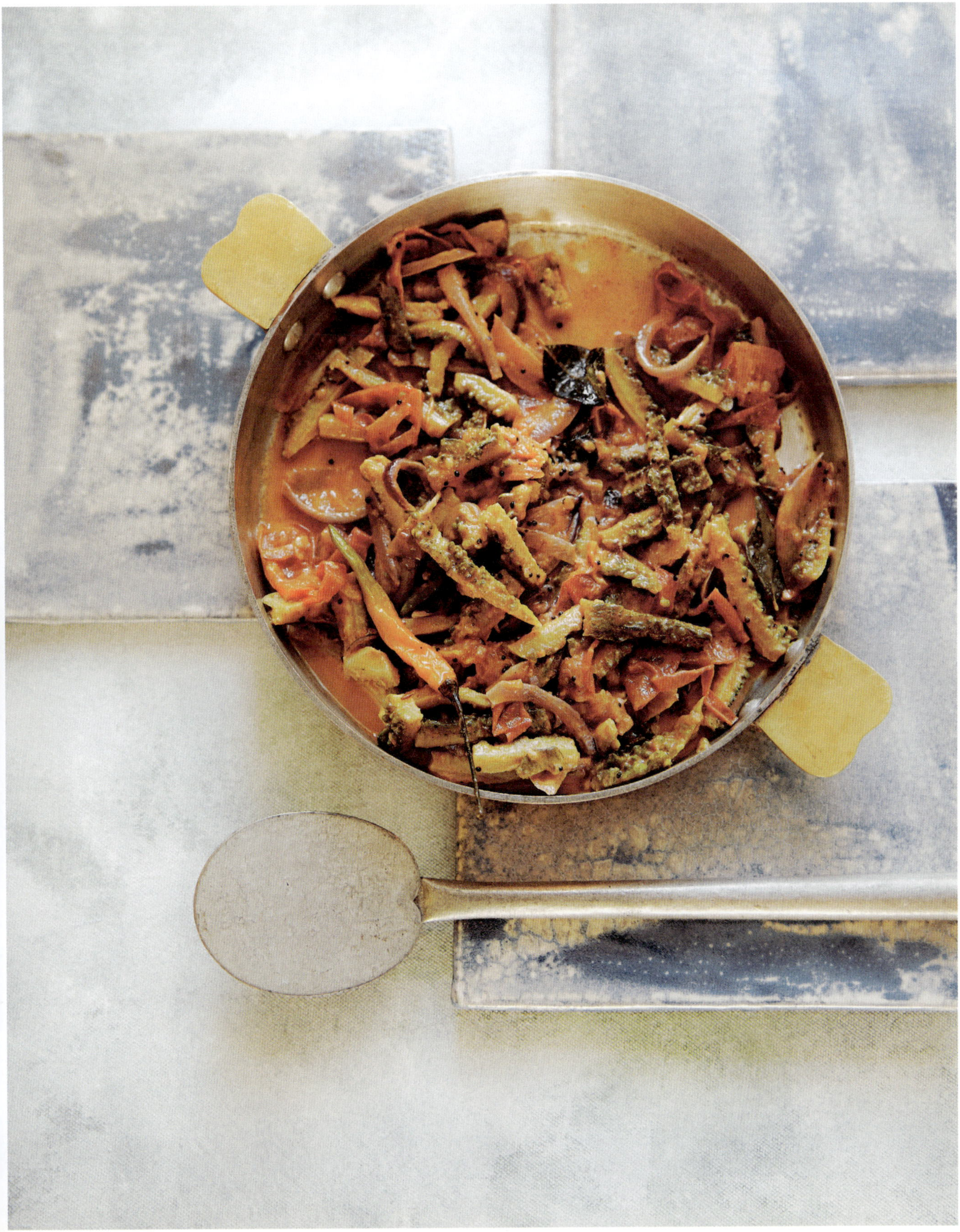

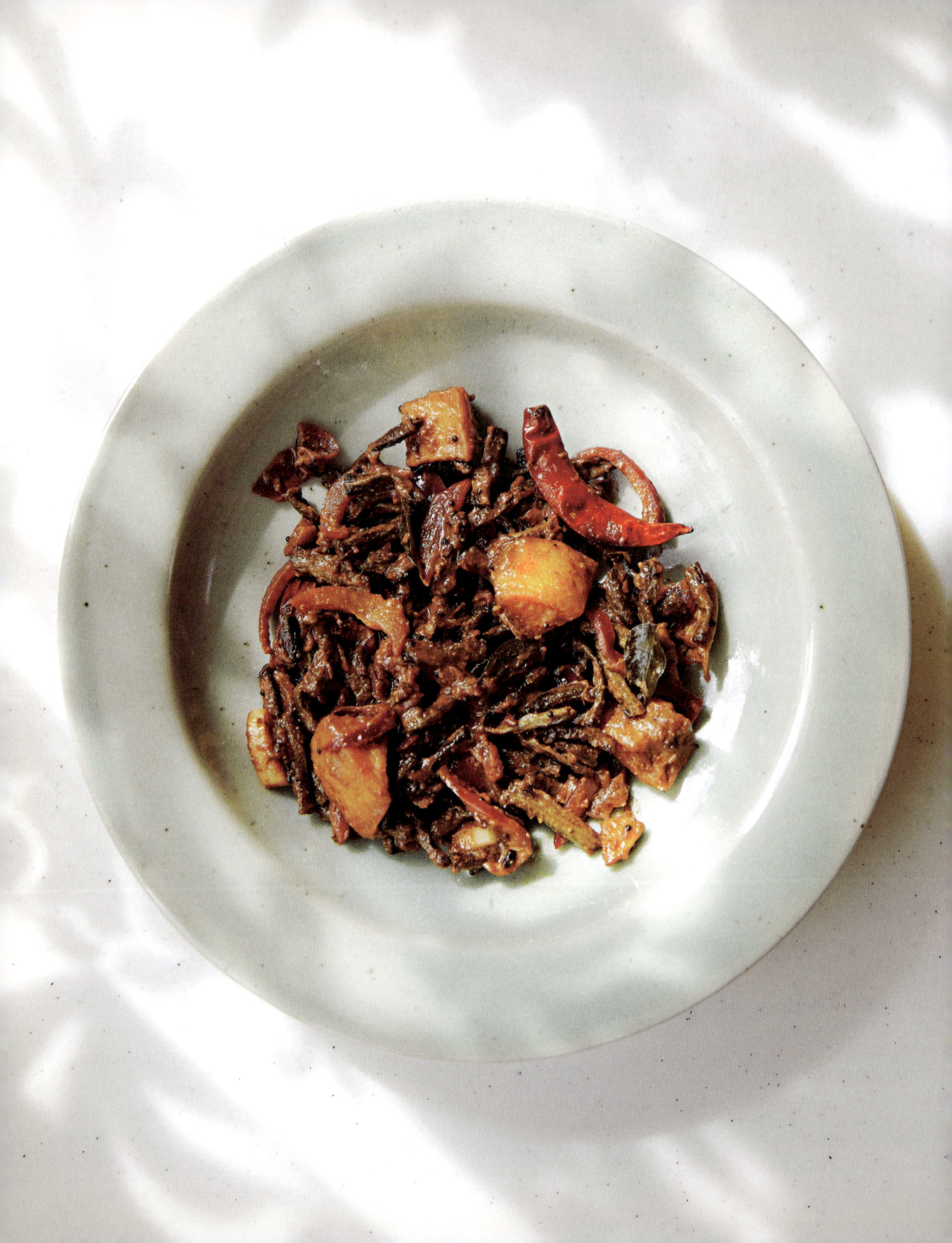

PAITHANGAI PIRATTAL

Long bean curry

The long bean is an Asian legume, similar to but longer and thinner than the European runner bean. This recipe works with all such pods, although runner and broad beans should be thinly sliced.

Serves 4, as a side dish

400g (14oz) long beans
2 tbsp oil
½ tsp mustard seeds
6 fresh curry leaves
½ tsp cumin seeds
¼ tsp fenugreek seeds
2 green chillies,
    slit lengthways
    with seeds in
1 medium onion, sliced
6 garlic cloves,
    cut into quarters
250ml (7 fl oz/generous
    ¾ cup) tamarind water
½ tsp ground turmeric
1 tsp ground cumin
1 tsp ground coriander
½ tsp chilli powder
½ tsp sugar
    (white or brown)
½ tsp salt
100ml (3½ fl oz/7 tbsp)
    coconut milk
    (medium thick)

Snap each long bean by hand right at the top, then pull the top down along one side of the bean to remove the long string fibre. Then, snap the bottom off the bean and pull this along the other side of the bean to remove the fibre from the other side as well.

Again by hand, snap the beans into 2.5cm (1-inch) long lengths, making sure that no stringy fibre is left at the sides of the bean.

Heat the oil in a medium saucepan over a low heat, then add the mustard seeds. Let them cook for a few seconds until they pop, then add the curry leaves and cumin seeds and give it a stir or two. Next, add the fenugreek seeds and stir-fry for a minute or so, then the green chillies and give it another stir. Add the onions, stir-fry for 30 seconds, and finally add the garlic, then sauté until the onions are soft and turning golden. Tip in the prepared beans and sauté gently until the beans begin to soften, about 7–8 minutes.

Add the tamarind water and all the spice powders, sugar and salt, mix well and bring to the boil. Reduce the heat and simmer for about 10 minutes, until the curry starts to thicken. Add the coconut milk and a little extra water if it's too dry, and cook for about 5 minutes until almost all the liquid is absorbed and the beans are very soft.

Taste for salt and remove from the heat. Leave it to rest for about 3 minutes before serving.

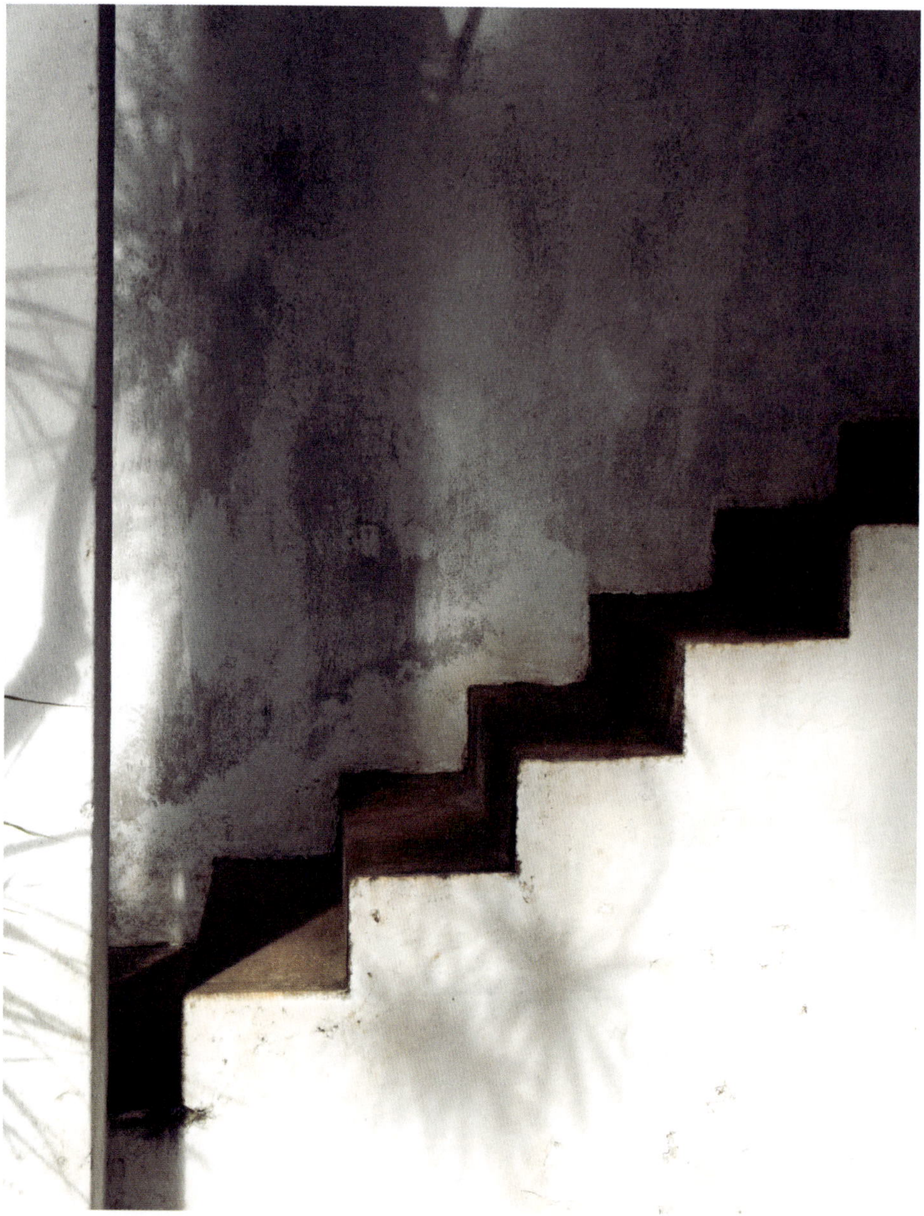

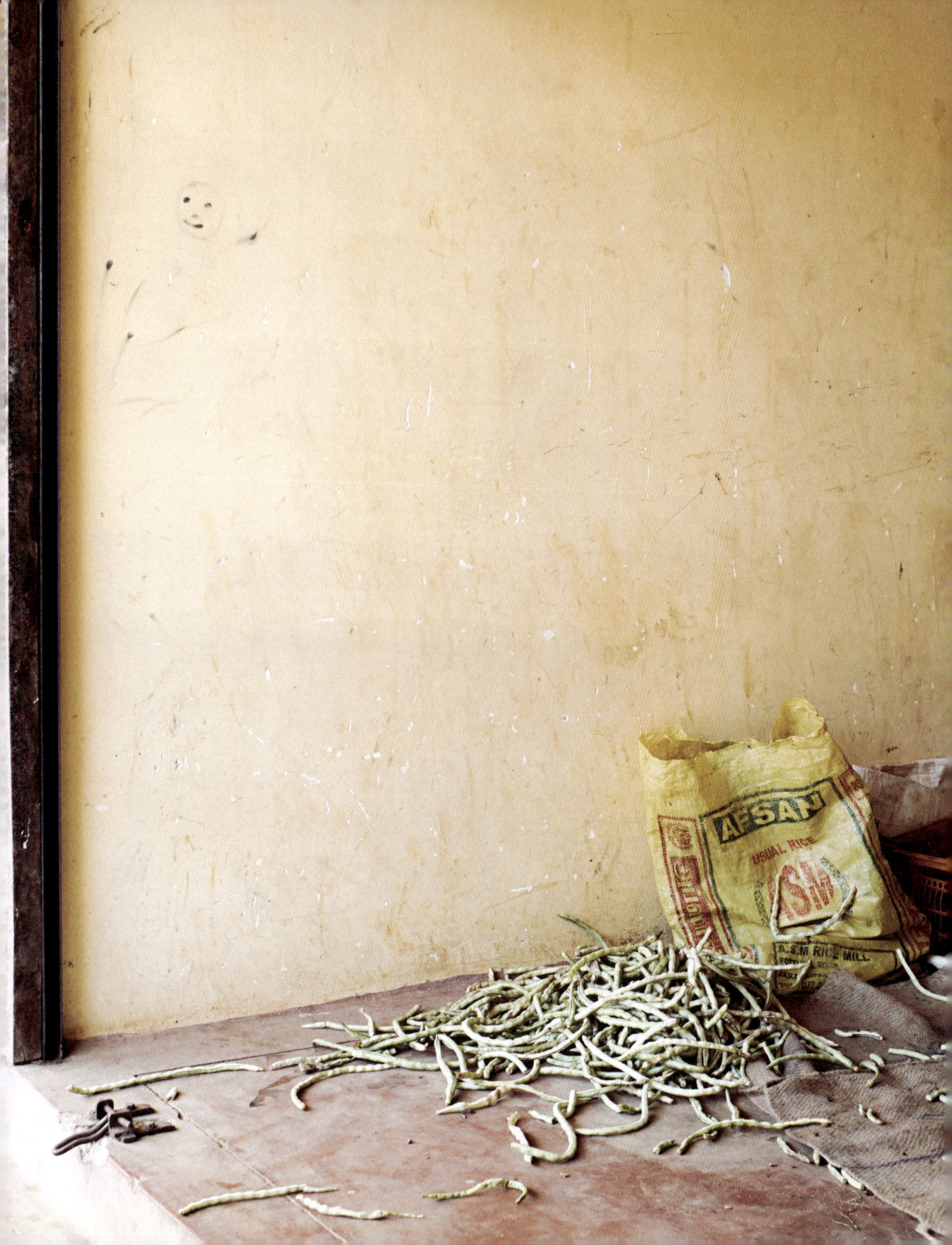
AFSAN
USUAL RICE
ASM
A.S.M RICE MILL

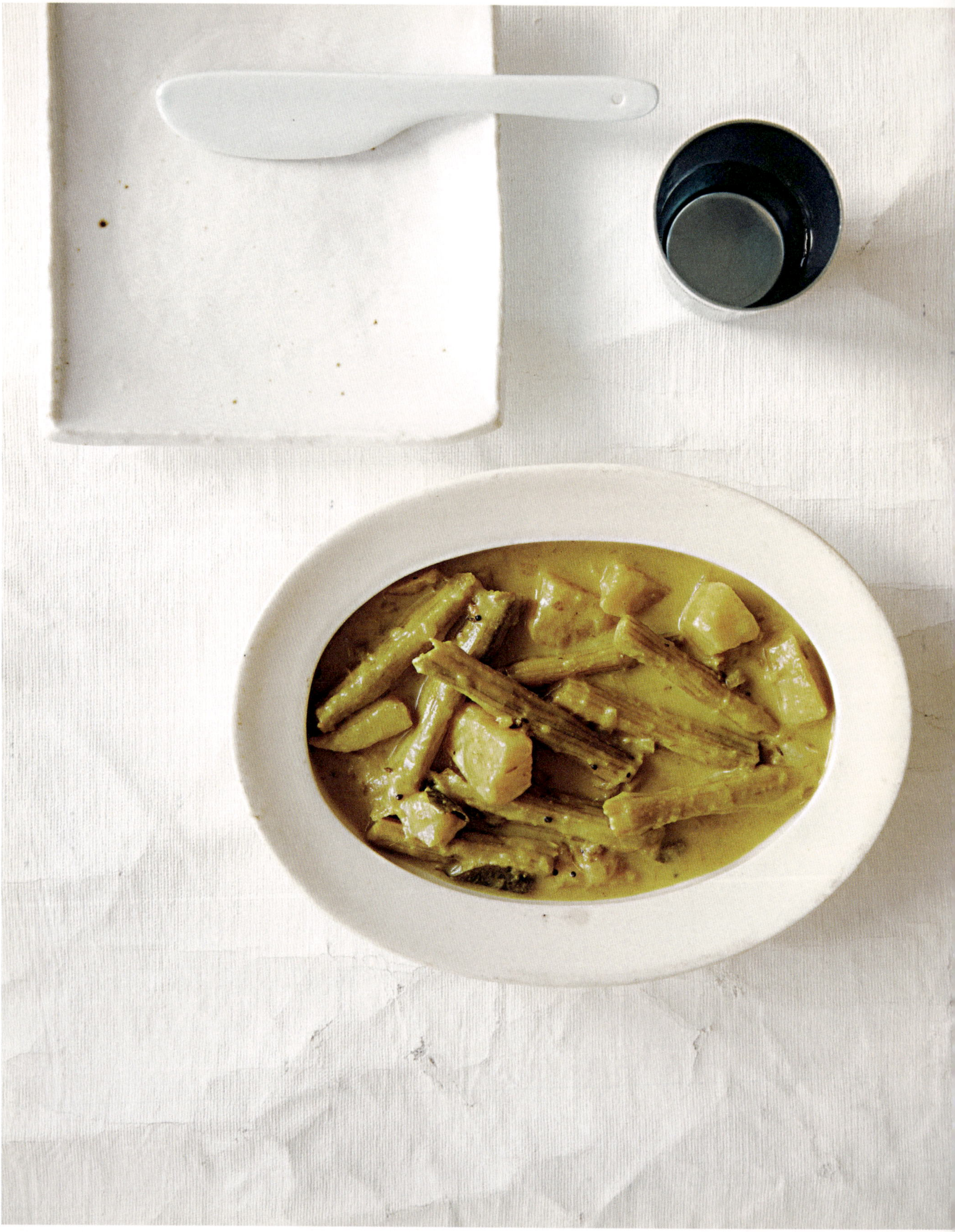

- 400g (14oz) drumsticks
- 200g potatoes, peeled and chopped into 1.5cm (½-inch) chunks
- ½ medium onion, finely chopped
- 3 garlic cloves, finely chopped
- 2 green chillies, slit lengthways and deseeded
- 6 fresh curry leaves
- 2.5cm (1-inch) piece of rampe (pandan) leaf
- 2.5cm (1-inch) cinnamon stick, broken into two
- ½ tsp fenugreek seeds
- 1 tsp Thuna Paha (curry powder on p17)
- ½ tsp ground turmeric
- 2 tsp Maldive fish, crushed (optional)
- ½ tsp salt
- 200ml (7 fl oz/generous ¾ cup) water
- 200ml (7 fl oz/generous ¾ cup) coconut milk
- juice of ½ lime

Drumstick tree curry
Drumsticks are the fruit of the murungu tree; they taste somewhat like asparagus and are loaded with an almost miraculous amount of nutrition, including protein, several vitamins and potassium.

First, prepare the drumsticks. You need to remove the thin layer of green fibres on top of the hard skin. You do this at the same time as cutting the long drumsticks into smaller lengths.

With a small knife, make a cut right at the bottom of a drumstick, cutting almost but not completely through to the other side. Then, hold the blade of the knife and the fibre together between your thumb and index finger and pull it down the drumstick, removing the fibre as you go.

After about 5cm (2 inches), make another cut almost through to the other side and pull the strings away. If there is any green skin left on the cut piece, peel it off using the knife. Continue like this until the drumsticks are all cut, putting the pieces into a bowl of water as you go. Give them a good wash.

Put all the ingredients up to and including the water in a medium saucepan, cover and bring to the boil. Reduce the heat and simmer for 12–15 minutes until the drumsticks are soft. Give it a good stir once or twice while cooking.

Add the coconut milk and bring to the boil. Cook for a minute or two and remove from the heat. Squeeze in the lime juice, give it a stir, taste for salt and serve.

Serves 4, as a side dish

MURUNGA HODI

KIRI HODI

Coconut milk broth

Is it a soup? A sauce? A broth? It's a bit of all three. Kiri Hodi is usually described as 'gravy' in Sri Lanka, but whatever you call it, it's a deeply comforting and simply spiced bowlful, perfect with String Hoppers (p34) for breakfast.

Serves 6

Heat the oil in a medium saucepan over a low heat, and sauté the onions, garlic and curry leaves, until the onions are soft and turning golden.

Add all the rest of the ingredients up to and including the water, and bring to the boil. Cook on a medium heat for 10 minutes.

Add the coconut milk and simmer on a low heat, stirring frequently, for a further 6-7 minutes until slightly thickened.

Remove from the heat, add the lime juice and salt to taste, and keep stirring for 1 minute. Serve hot.

2 tbsp oil
1 medium onion, finely chopped
3 garlic cloves, finely chopped
8 fresh curry leaves
1 green chilli, deseeded and sliced
1 tsp fenugreek seeds
1 tsp ground turmeric
2.5cm (1-inch) cinnamon stick
2.5cm (1-inch) piece of rampe (pandan) leaf
1 goraka clove (Malabar tamarind) (optional)
½ tsp Maldive fish (optional)
1 medium tomato, medium diced (optional)
200ml (7 fl oz/generous ¾ cup) water
250ml (9 fl oz/generous 1 cup) coconut milk
juice of ½ lime
1 tsp salt

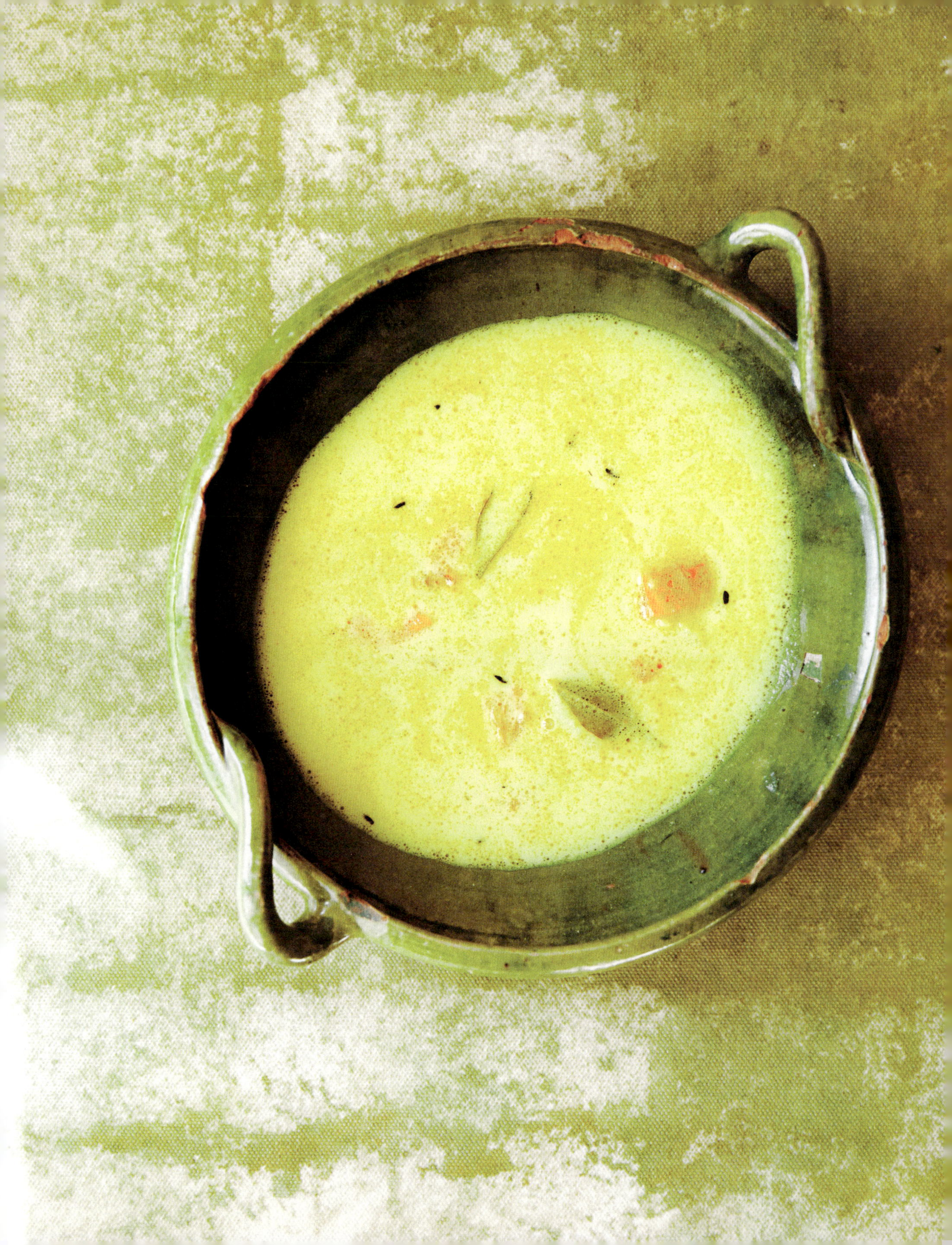

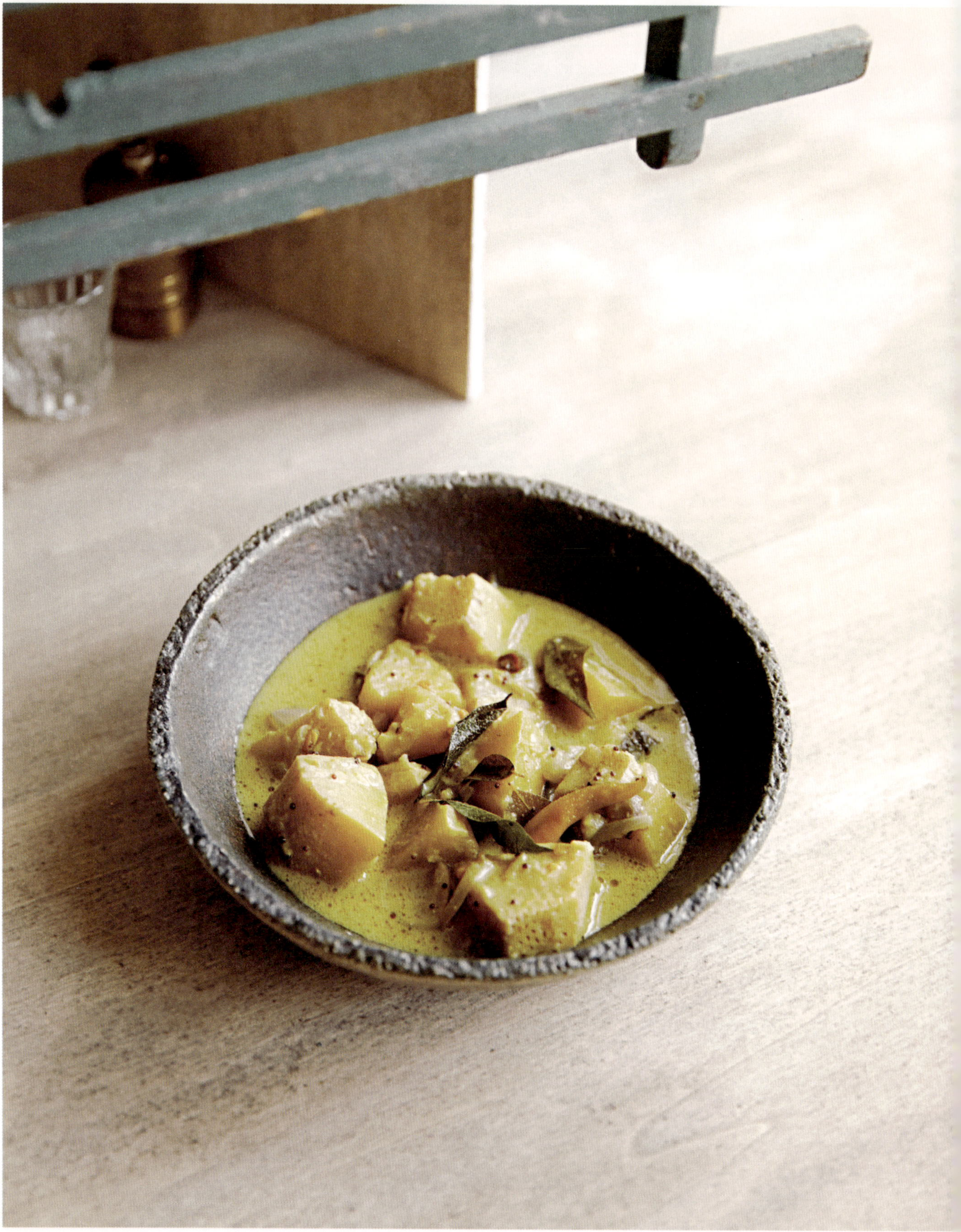

400g breadfruit (1lb 2oz)
    (about ½ a fruit)
2 tbsp oil
½ tsp cumin seeds
1 medium onion,
    finely sliced
3 garlic cloves,
    finely chopped
8 fresh curry leaves
2.5cm (1-inch) piece of
    rampe (pandan) leaf
1 green chilli,
    sliced with seeds
300ml (10½ fl oz/
    1¼ cups) water
1 tsp ground turmeric
¼ tsp ground coriander
½ tsp ground cumin
1 tsp salt
250ml (9 fl oz/generous
    1 cup) coconut milk
¼ tsp Bathapu Thuna Paha
    (curry powder on p17)

Breadfruit curry
Breadfruit (dhel) isn't a clever name – when cooked, its texture and colour is indeed similar to baked bread, and it also shares with bread an unassuming character. That makes it ideal to soak up all the savoury, subtle notes in this hearty curry.

Cut the breadfruit through the middle lengthways. Then cut each half into two pieces again lengthways. Cut off the hard green skin and remove the slightly spongy centre of the fruit. Chop them into 2.5cm (1-inch) chunks, putting them in a bowl of water as you go. Give them a good wash and leave in the water.

Heat the oil in a medium, lidded saucepan over a low heat. Add the cumin seeds, onion, garlic, curry leaves, rampe leaf and chilli, and sauté until the onions are soft and golden.

Drain the breadfruit and tip it into the mix, give it a stir or two, and add the water to just cover the fruit. Add the turmeric, coriander, cumin and salt, cover with the lid and bring to the boil. Reduce the heat and simmer for about 12 minutes until the breadfruit is slightly soft. Then, add the coconut milk and cook for a further 5–6 minutes until it is completely soft.

Sprinkle with the roasted curry powder and remove from the heat. Taste for salt, and serve.

Serves 4, as a side dish

DHEL

MUTTAI KULAMBU

Egg curry

Try this everyday curry in place of your usual meat curry for a vibrant brunch, lunch or dinner.

4 hard-boiled eggs
1½ tbsp oil
½ tsp mustard seeds
½ medium onion, finely chopped
6 fresh curry leaves
6 garlic cloves, cut into quarters
2 green chillies, chopped
½ tsp fenugreek seeds
¼ tsp cumin seeds
¼ tsp ground turmeric
200ml (7 fl oz/generous ¾ cup) coconut milk
400ml (14 fl oz/ 1⅔ cups) water
1 tbsp Thool (curry powder on p16)
¼ tsp salt

Serves 4

Shell the boiled eggs, cut them in half lengthways and set aside.

Heat the oil in a medium, lidded saucepan over a low heat, then add the mustard seeds. Let them cook for a few seconds until they pop, then add the onion and curry leaves and stir-fry for a few seconds. Add the garlic, chillies, fenugreek and cumin seeds, and sauté until the onions are soft and turning golden.

Add the turmeric and give it a stir. Add the coconut milk, water, curry powder and salt, and mix well. Bring to the boil, then reduce the heat, half-cover the pan with the lid and simmer for 8–10 minutes until the sauce has thickened.

Gently slide in the halved eggs, then half-cover with the lid again and simmer for a further 5 minutes. Taste for salt, then remove from the heat and serve.

Variation: Make an omelette mix by beating 4 eggs with ½ teaspoon of chilli powder, ½ teaspoon of ground cumin, ¼ teaspoon of ground turmeric and a pinch of salt. Set aside. Heat 1 tablespoon of oil in a frying pan (skillet), then sauté 2 tablespoons of chopped onion until soft and golden brown. Add the beaten egg mix and make an omelette. Once cooked, cut into 2.5cm (1-inch) chunks and add them to the curry instead of the boiled eggs.

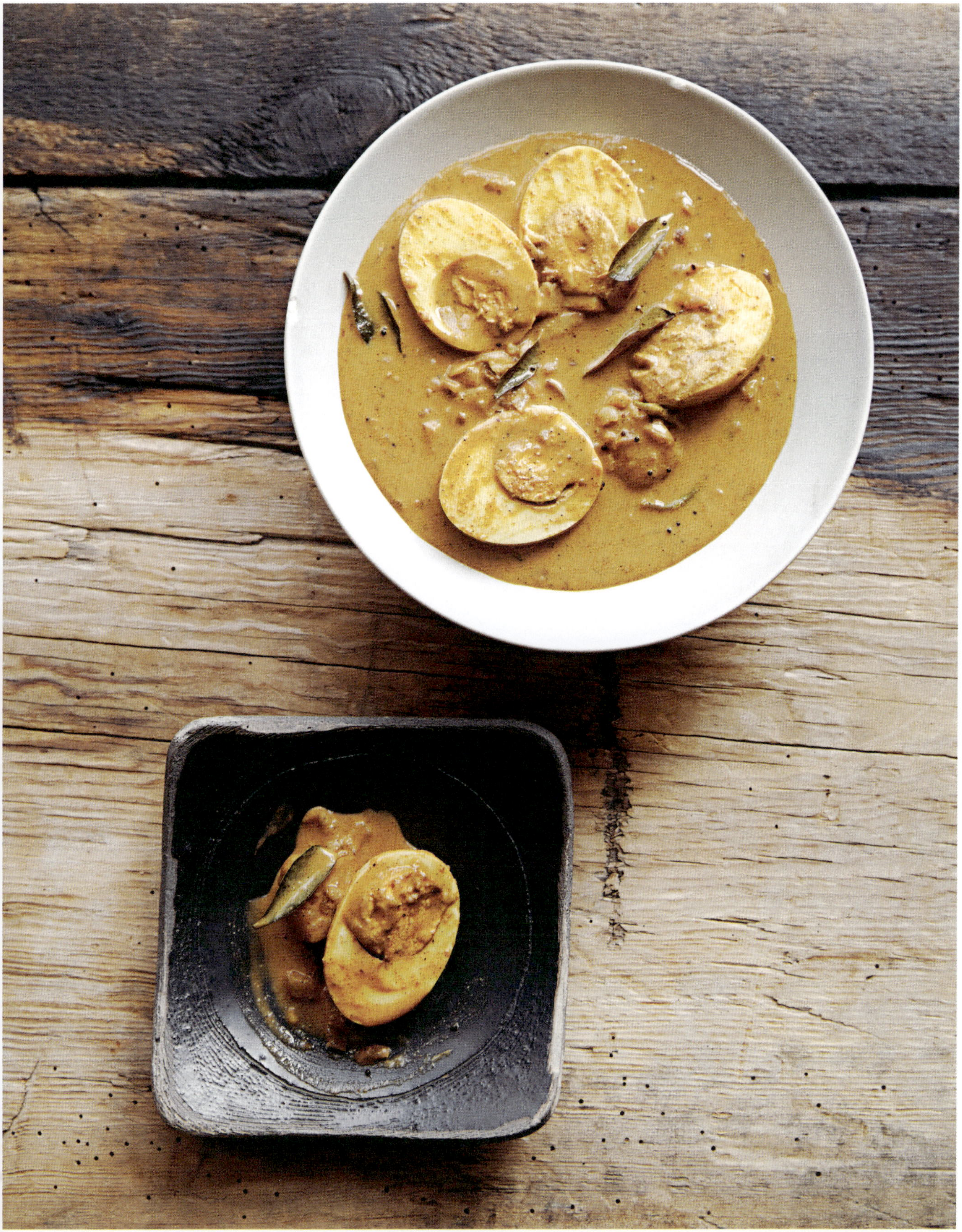

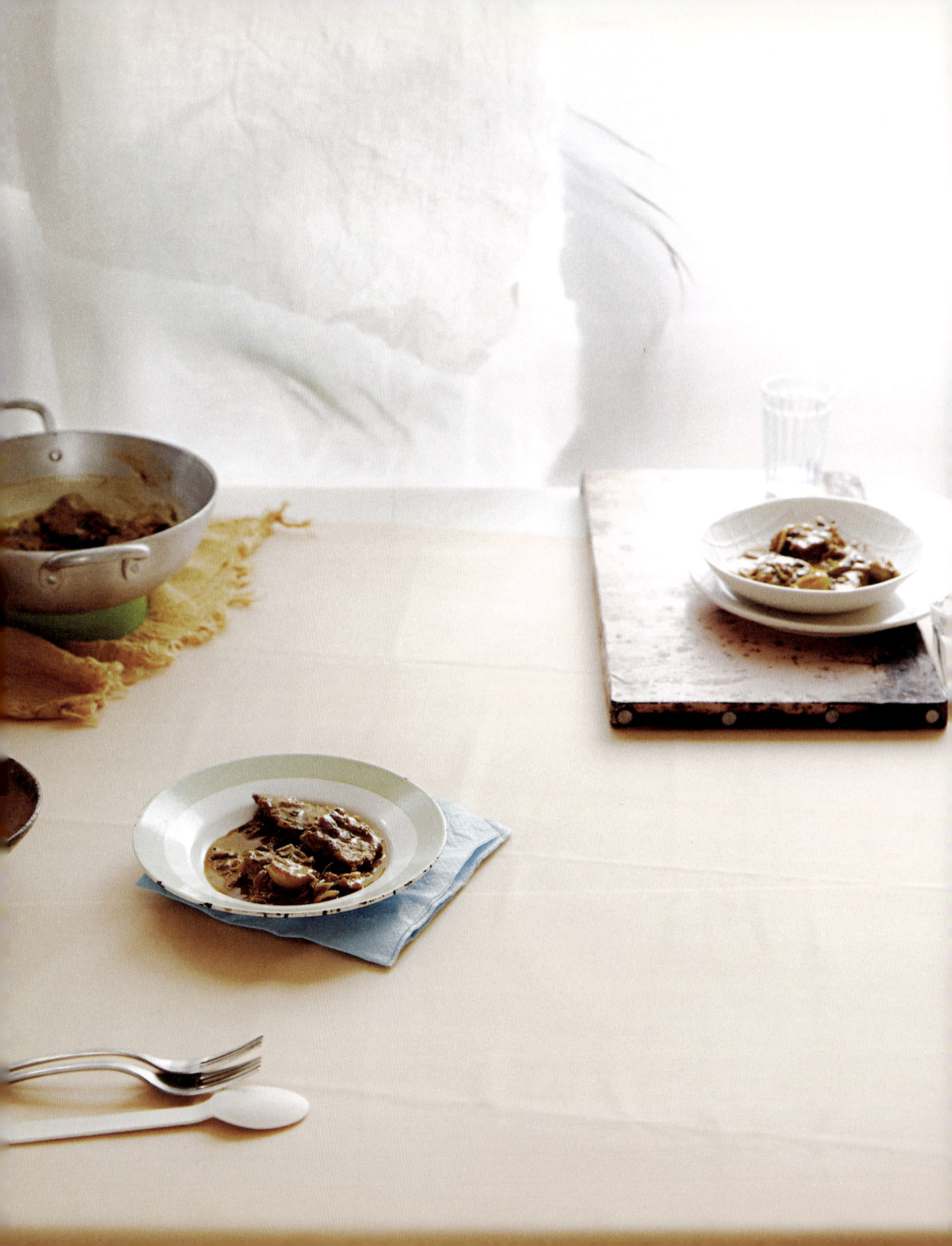

BITHARA MIRIS HODI

Omelette curry
More elaborate than a standard omelette, for sure, but a hot, spicy and full-flavoured meal at any time of day.

Serves 2

For the omelette
4 eggs
¼ tsp ground turmeric
1 tbsp plain (all-purpose) flour
½ tsp baking powder
½ tsp salt
juice of ¼ lemon
1 tbsp oil
6 fresh curry leaves, finely chopped
3 green chillies, deseeded and finely sliced
1 medium onion, finely chopped

For the sauce
1 tbsp oil
8 fresh curry leaves
½ tsp fenugreek seeds
½ tsp cumin seeds
½ medium onion, sliced
2 garlic cloves, finely chopped
200ml (7 fl oz/generous ¾ cup) water
½ tsp chilli powder
1 tsp Thuna Paha (curry powder on p17)
½ tsp ground turmeric
1 tsp salt
300ml (10½ fl oz/ 1¼ cups) coconut milk
¼ tsp Bathapu Thuna Paha (curry powder on p17)
juice of ¼ lime

Start by making the omelette. In a medium bowl, beat the eggs with the turmeric, until the eggs have loosened. Add the flour, baking powder, salt and lemon juice, and beat again.

Heat the oil in a medium frying pan (skillet) over a low heat. Add the curry leaves and green chillies and give it a stir or two. Then, tip in the onions and sauté until they are soft and golden brown.

Beat the prepared eggs again and pour the mixture evenly into the frying pan and let it cook on a low heat. When the bottom browns, flip it over and cook the other side until brown too. Remove from the heat and place the omelette on a plate.

Now make the sauce. Heat the oil in a medium saucepan over a low heat. Add the curry leaves, fenugreek and cumin seeds, and give it a stir or two. Next, add the onions and garlic, and sauté until the onions are soft and turning golden.

Pour in the water and add the chilli powder, Thuna Paha curry powder, turmeric and salt, then bring to the boil. Reduce the heat and simmer for 5 minutes, add the coconut milk and simmer for another 6–7 minutes until the sauce is thick.

Chop the omelette into 2.5cm (1-inch) pieces and tip it into the curry. Cook for another 2 minutes, sprinkle with the Bathapu Thuna Paha curry powder and take it off the heat. Leave to rest for about 2 minutes, add the lime juice, taste for salt, and serve.

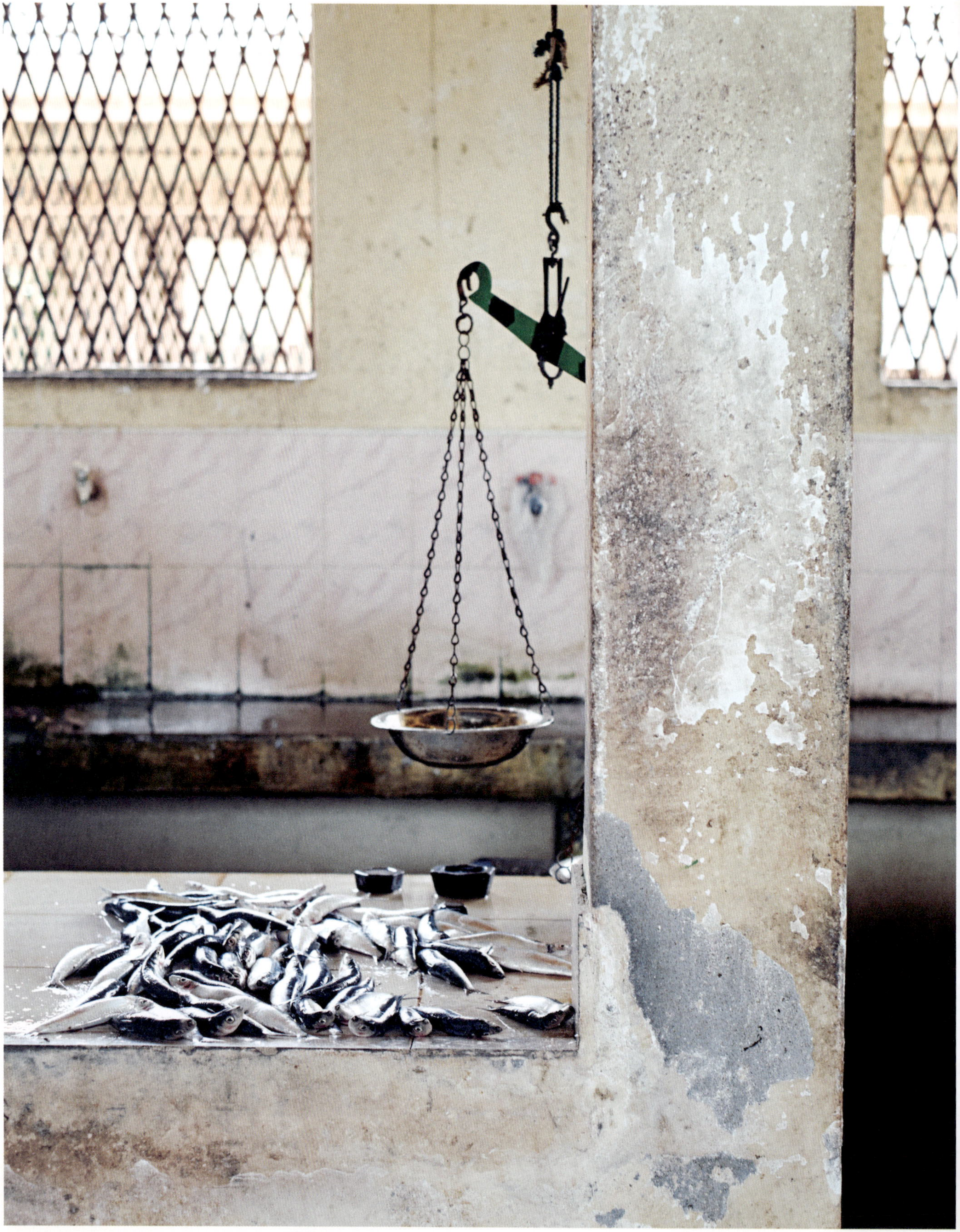

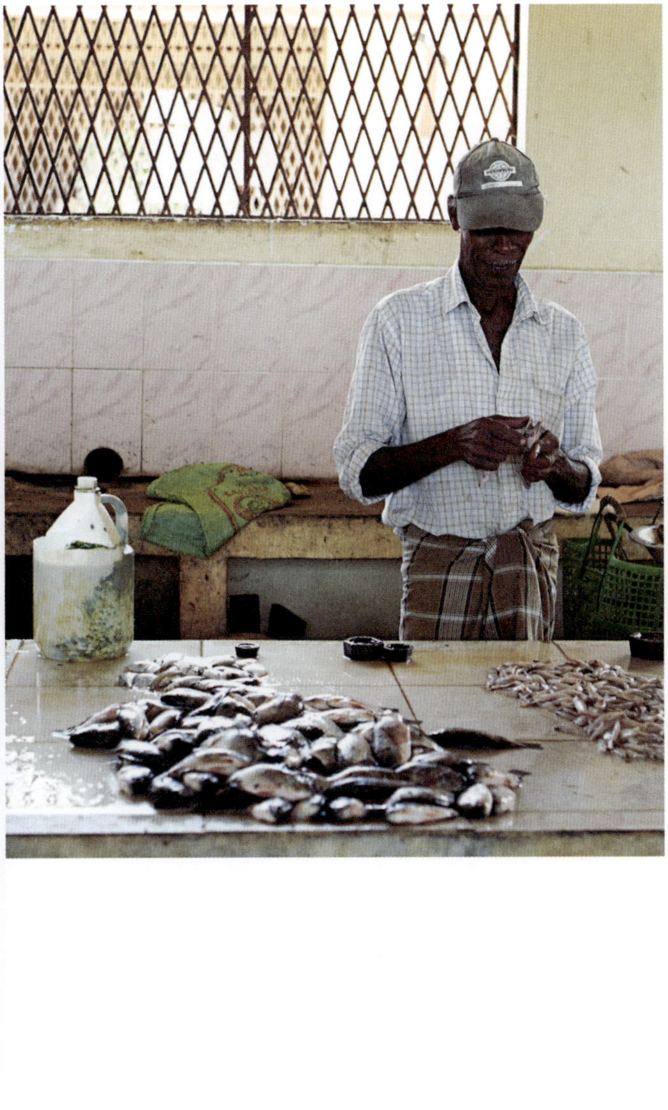

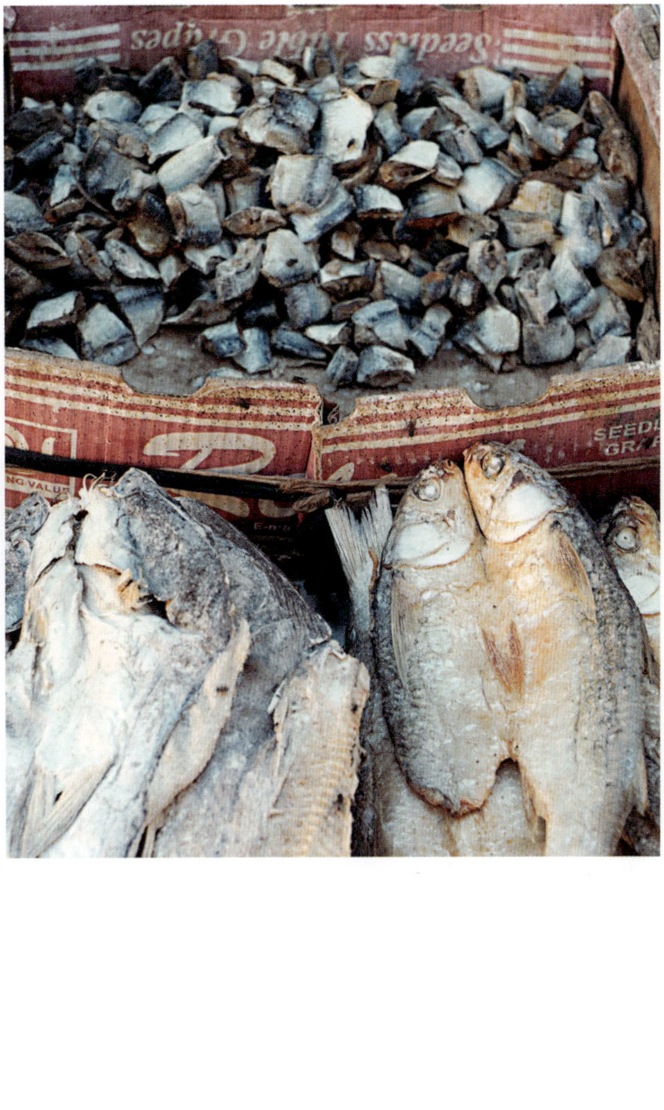

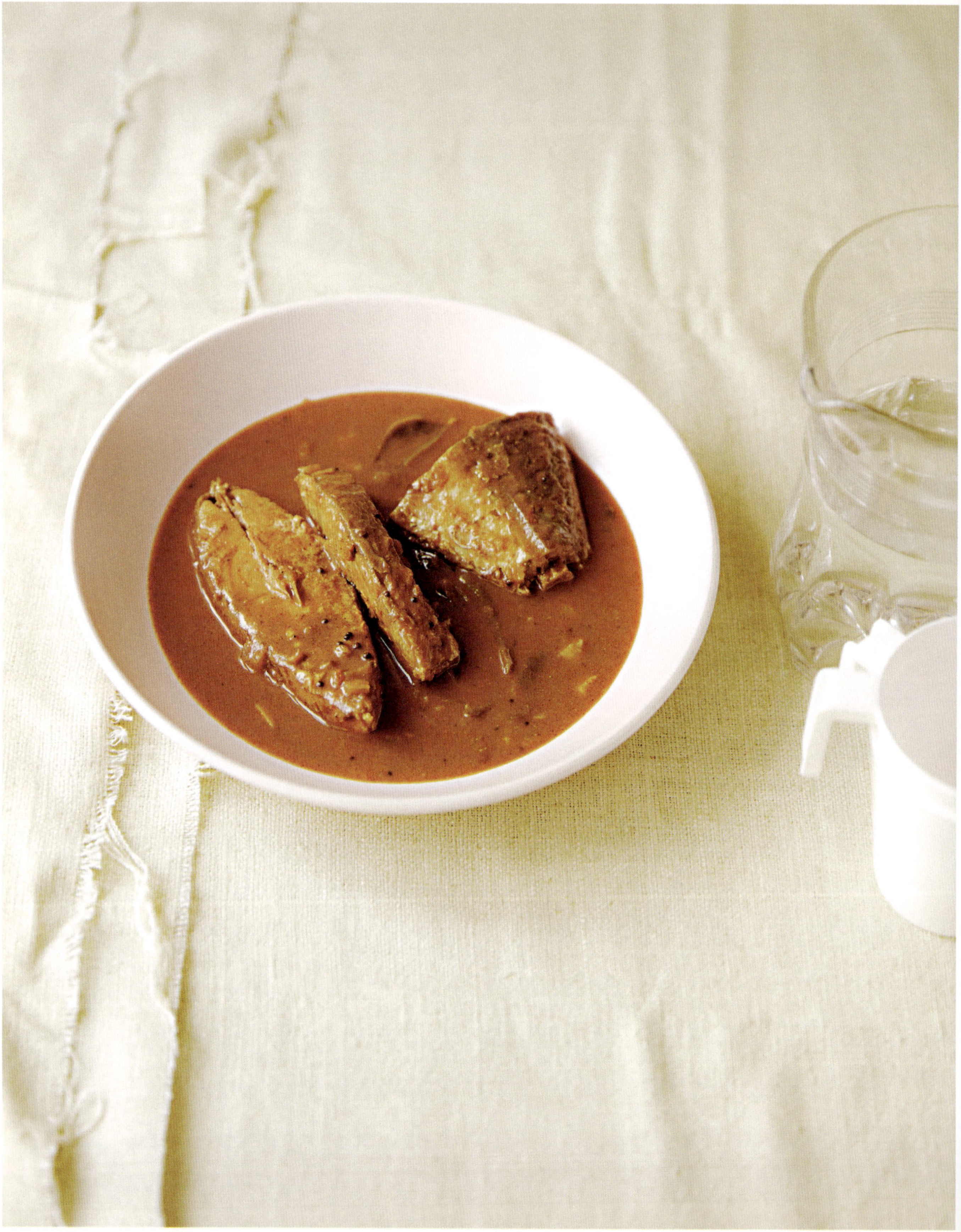

500g (1lb 2oz) firm fish, such as Atlantic mackerel, large trevally (jack fish) or tuna
2 tbsp oil
½ tsp mustard seeds
½ tsp fennel seeds
½ tsp cumin seeds
6 fresh curry leaves
½ tsp fenugreek seeds
2 green chillies, slit lengthways with seeds in
1 medium onion, medium diced
6 garlic cloves, cut into quarters
200ml (7 fl oz/generous ¾ cup) tamarind water
200ml (10½ fl oz/1¼ cups) water
½ tsp ground turmeric
1 tsp ground cumin
1 tsp ground coriander
½ tsp salt
1 tbsp Thool (curry powder on p16)
100ml (3½ fl oz/7 tbsp) coconut milk

Tamarind fish curry

Being an island surrounded by warm waters, Sri Lanka has a bountiful supply of fish. This classic Tamil curry shows off the trio of tamarind, coconut and curry leaves found in so many of our recipes.

Wash the fish well and cut it into small steaks or chunky pieces depending on the type of fish. Wash the pieces once or twice more and set aside.

Heat the oil in a medium, lidded saucepan over a low heat, then add the mustard seeds. Let them cook for a few seconds until they pop, then add the fennel and cumin seeds and give it a stir or two. Next, add the curry leaves and fenugreek seeds and stir-fry for a minute or so. Then, add the green chillies and give it another stir, then the onions and stir-fry for 30 seconds. Finally add the garlic and sauté until the onions are soft and turning golden.

Add the tamarind water and the water, all the ground spices, the curry powder and the salt. Mix well and bring to the boil. Reduce the heat and simmer for about 15 minutes, until the curry begins to thicken.

Add the coconut milk and a little extra water if it's too dry. Bring it to the boil, then slide the fish pieces in one by one, trying to keep the temperature of the curry at boiling point.

Once all the fish pieces are in and the curry has returned to the boil, reduce the heat, cover and simmer the fish for about 10 minutes until cooked and the sauce is medium thick. Gently move the fish around a little as it cooks, being careful not to break it. You could use a long spoon or slowly move the pan sideways while the base is still resting on the stove.

When the fish is ready, taste for salt and remove from the heat. Let it rest for about 5 minutes before serving.

Tip: Although white fish is not typically Sri Lankan, halibut works very well as an alternative in this dish.

Serves 4

MEEN KULAMBU

MAALU MIRISATA

Spicy fish curry

A wide range of well-balanced spices give this curry a complex, involved taste. There's a fair amount of chilli here – it's one of the dishes that gives Sri Lankan cooking its reputation for being fiery – but it's not overbearing.

500g (1lb 2oz) firm fish, such as kingfish, Atlantic mackerel or tuna
juice of ½ lime
½ tsp salt
1 tsp ground turmeric
½ tbsp ground cumin
½ tbsp ground coriander
1 tbsp chilli powder
3 tbsp oil
½ tsp mustard seeds
1 tsp cumin seeds
½ tsp fenugreek seeds
1 green chilli, slit lengthways and deseeded
8 fresh curry leaves
2.5cm (1-inch) piece of rampe (pandan) leaf
2.5cm (1-inch) cinnamon stick, broken into two
1 large onion, finely chopped
4 garlic cloves, finely chopped
2.5cm (1-inch) piece of ginger, peeled and finely chopped
1 medium tomato, medium diced
200ml (7 fl oz/generous ¾ cup) water
1 goraka clove (Malabar tamarind) (or juice of ½ lime at the end)
200ml (7 fl oz/generous ¾ cup) coconut milk
1 tbsp Bathapu Thuna Paha (curry powder on p17)

Serves 4

Wash the fish well, and cut it into small steaks or chunky pieces depending on the type of fish. Wash the pieces once more and put them in a bowl with the lime juice, salt, turmeric, cumin, coriander and chilli powder and leave to marinate for 15–20 minutes.

Heat the oil in a medium, lidded saucepan over a low heat, then add the mustard seeds. Let them cook for a few seconds until they pop, then add the cumin seeds, fenugreek seeds, green chilli, curry leaves, rampe and cinnamon and give it a stir or two.

Next, add the onion and give it another stir, then the garlic and ginger, and sauté until the onions are soft and turning golden. Add the tomato and sauté until it is soft.

Pour the water into the saucepan, add the goraka and bring to the boil. Reduce the heat, half-cover with the lid and cook on a medium heat for about 10 minutes. Add the coconut milk and simmer for a further 5 minutes or so until the sauce has thickened.

Bring it to the boil, then slide the fish pieces in one by one, trying to keep the temperature of the curry at boiling point.

Once all the fish pieces are in and the curry has returned to the boil, reduce the heat, cover and simmer for 5 minutes. Gently move the fish around a little as it cooks, being careful not to break it. Add the curry powder and cook for another 3–5 minutes until the fish is cooked and the sauce thick, then remove from the heat.

If not using goraka, add the lime juice, stir well and taste for salt. If you wish, you can sauté a dried red chilli for a minute or two, and use it to garnish the dish.

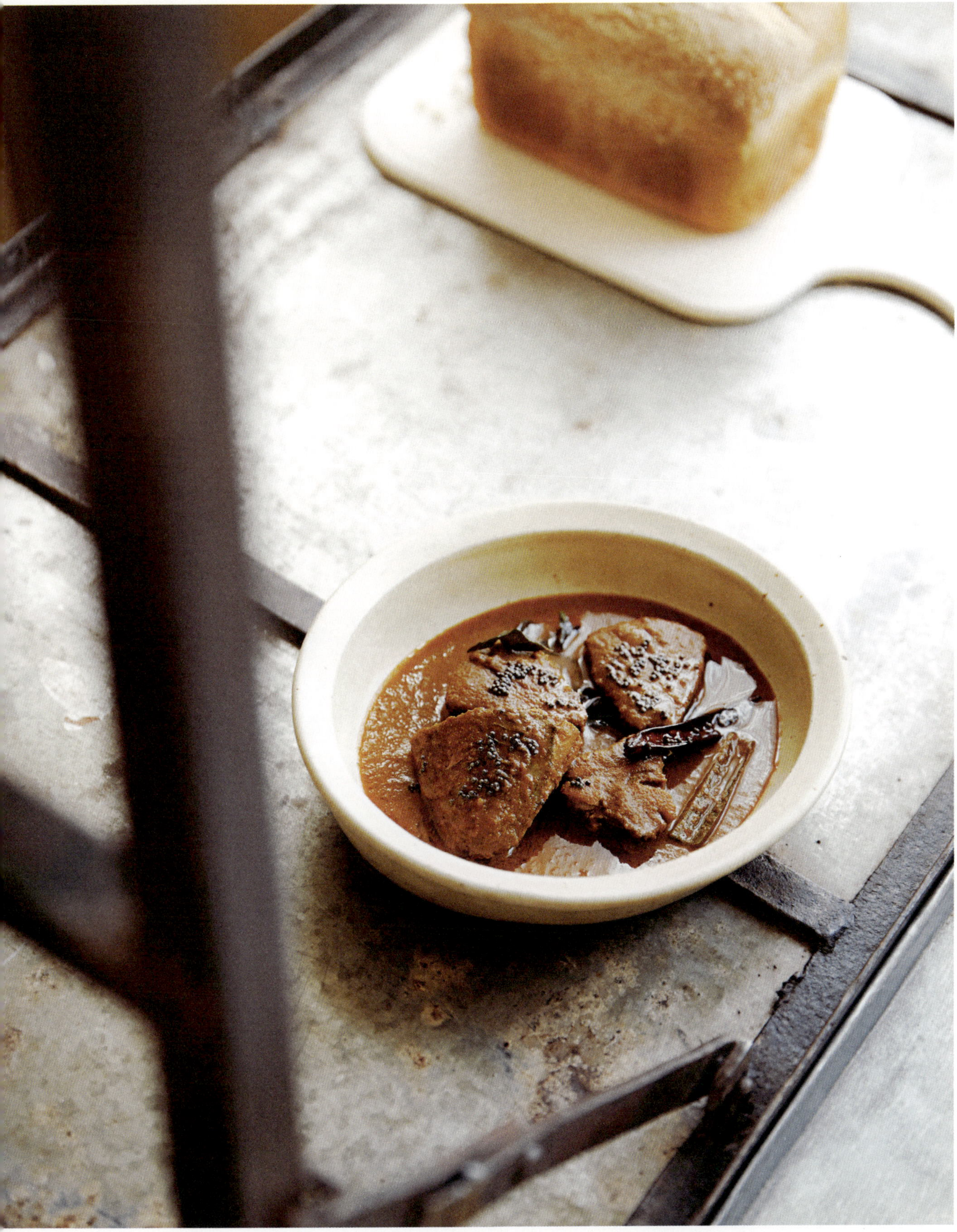

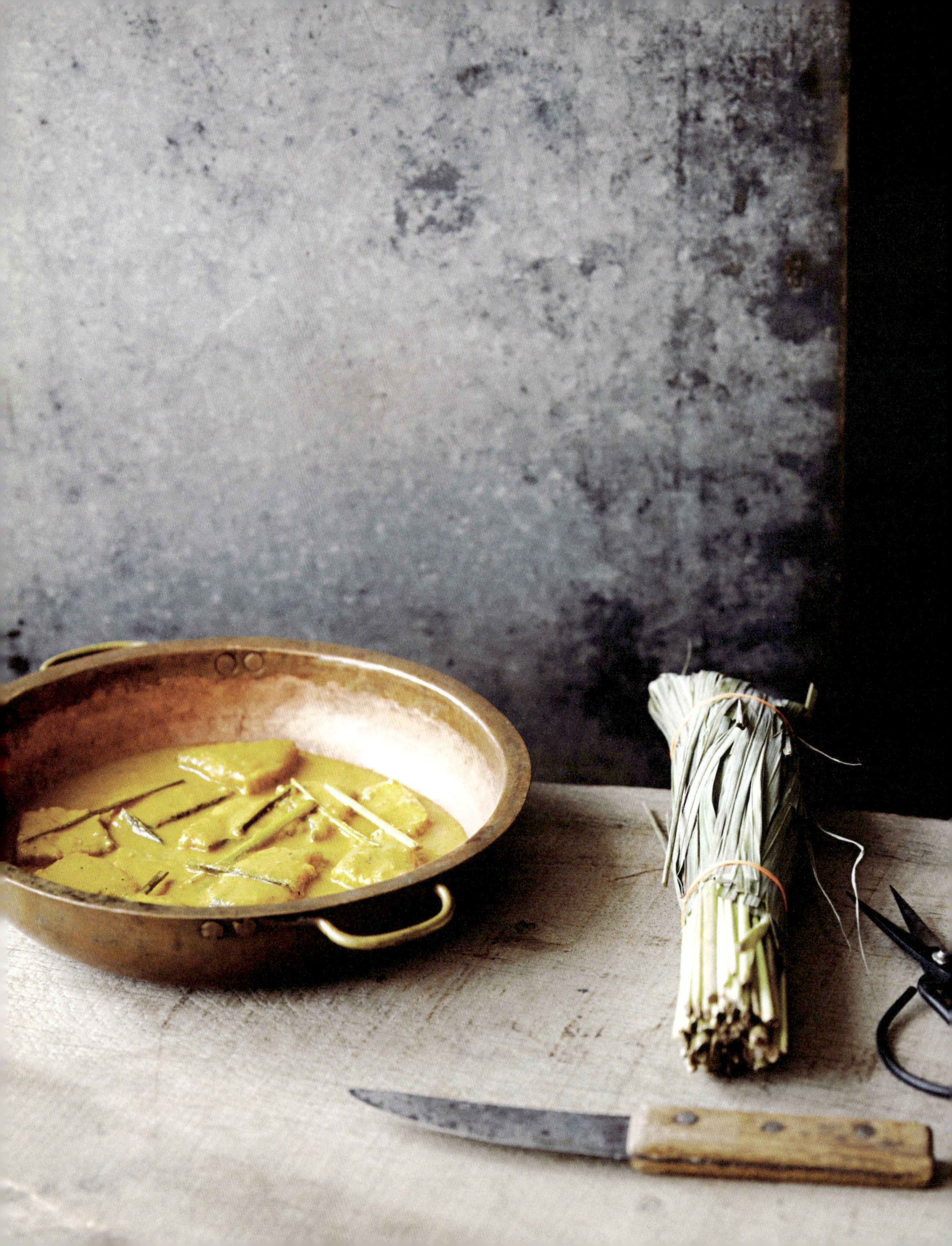

MAALU KIRATA

Coconut fish curry

Fish curries are most successful when made with firm-fleshed varieties like tuna, halibut, cod or mackerel (which works especially well in this recipe). Be sure to leave the pieces large enough that they don't break up. Serve it with a spicy sambol, steamed rice and dal.

Serves 4

500g (1lb 2oz) firm fish, such as kingfish, Atlantic mackerel or tuna
1 tbsp oil
7 fresh curry leaves
½ tsp cumin seeds
½ tsp fenugreek seeds
2.5cm (1-inch) rampe (pandan) leaf
5 lemongrass stalks
2.5cm (1-inch) cinnamon stick, broken into two
3 cardamom pods, crushed
1 green chilli, slit lengthways and deseeded
1 onion, finely chopped
3 garlic cloves, finely chopped
300ml (10½ fl oz/1¼ cups) water
1 goraka clove (Malabar tamarind) (or juice of ½ lime at the end)
1 tsp ground turmeric
½ tsp ground cumin
½ tsp ground coriander
¼ tsp ground black pepper
300ml (10½ fl oz/1¼ cups) coconut milk
1 tsp salt
juice of ½ lime

Wash the fish well, and cut it into small steaks or chunky pieces depending on the type of fish. Wash the pieces once more and set aside.

Heat the oil in a medium, lidded saucepan over a low heat. Add the curry leaves, cumin and fenugreek seeds, rampe leaf, lemongrass, cinnamon, cardamom and green chilli, and sauté for about 2 minutes. Add the onion, give it a stir, and then add the garlic and sauté until the onions are soft and turning golden.

Add the water, goraka, turmeric, cumin, coriander and black pepper, and bring to the boil. Cover the pan and cook for about 10 minutes.

Add the coconut milk, reduce the heat to medium and cook uncovered for a further 5 minutes, stirring now and then, until the sauce begins to thicken.

Bring it to the boil, then slide the fish pieces in one by one, trying to keep the temperature of the curry at boiling point.

Once all the fish pieces are in and the curry has returned to the boil, reduce the heat, and simmer for 15 minutes without covering, until the fish is cooked and you have a medium thick sauce. Gently move the fish as it cooks, being careful not to break it.

Remove from the heat. Add salt and lime to taste, and serve.

MAALU ABA HODI

Fish in mustard sauce

A healthy dose of mustard gives this curry an extra kick alongside the fresh and powdered chilli. The Sinhalese people can trace their historical roots back to Bengal, and fish with mustard is a very common combination in that eastern Indian region too.

- 500g (1lb 2oz) firm fish, such as kingfish, Atlantic mackerel or tuna
- 1 tsp chilli powder
- 1 tsp ground turmeric
- 1 medium red onion, finely chopped
- 3 garlic cloves, finely chopped
- ½ tsp salt
- ¼ tsp fenugreek seeds
- 8 fresh curry leaves
- 1 green chilli, deseeded and sliced
- 2.5cm (1-inch) piece of rampe (pandan) leaf
- 250ml (9 fl oz/generous 1 cup) water
- 1 tbsp ground mustard seeds
- 200ml (7 fl oz/generous ¾ cup) coconut milk
- juice of ½ lime

Wash the fish well, and cut it into small steaks or chunky pieces depending on the type of fish. Wash the pieces once more and set aside.

Put the chilli powder, turmeric, chopped onions, garlic, salt, fenugreek seeds, curry leaves, green chilli, rampe leaf and water in a medium, lidded saucepan. Cover, bring to the boil, then reduce the heat and simmer for 10 minutes.

Add the ground mustard seeds and cook for 5 minutes, without the lid to release the bitterness of the mustard.

Pour in the coconut milk in and cook for 5 minutes, stirring often so it doesn't curdle.

Bring to the boil, then slide the fish pieces in one by one, trying to keep the temperature of the curry at boiling point.

Once all the fish pieces are in and the curry has returned to the boil, reduce the heat, and simmer for 10–12 minutes without covering, until the fish is cooked and you have a thick sauce. Gently move the fish around a little as it cooks, being careful not to break it.

When the fish is done, remove from the heat and add the lime juice. Taste for salt before serving.

Serves 4

AMBUL THIAL

Hot and sour fish curry

This dish has plenty of chilli heat, plus a satisfyingly tart smack from the goraka, which is also known as black tamarind, kudampuli or cambodge. It is a small fruit similar to a tamarind, which after sun drying turns black and provides an amazing sour smokiness. Ask for it in Indian grocery stores, particularly those specialising in ingredients from the south of the country.

500g (1lb 2oz) firm fish, such as kingfish, Atlantic mackerel or tuna
375ml (13 fl oz/1½ cups) water
20 fresh curry leaves
2.5cm (1-inch) piece of rampe (pandan) leaf

For the paste
125ml (4 fl oz/½ cup) water
1 tsp ground turmeric
1 small onion, roughly chopped
3 garlic cloves
2.5cm (1-inch) piece of ginger, peeled
2 green chillies, deseeded
2 tbsp black peppercorns
75g goraka paste (or tamarind paste)
1.5cm (½-inch) cinnamon stick
½ tsp fenugreek seeds
1 tbsp coconut oil
1½ tsp salt

Serves 4

First make the paste. Put all of the past ingredients into a blender. Blitz until you have a coarse paste and set aside in a medium bowl.

Wash the fish well, and cut it into small steaks or chunky pieces. Arrange the fish in the bottom of a large, lidded saucepan.

Pour the 375ml of water into the bowl with the paste, add the curry leaves and the rampe leaf and pour it over the fish.

Cover with the lid and bring to the boil. Reduce the heat to medium and cook for 10 minutes. Then, turn the fish over gently with a spoon and cook for a further 10 minutes.

Note: If you can't find goraka paste, you can use tamarind paste as a substitute.

SURA VARAI

Coconut dogfish

I arrived in London many years ago as an exchange student, and on my second day in the city tried the strange-sounding 'rock and chips', which I thoroughly enjoyed. I was served rock salmon, or dogfish, actually a species of shark; here it's given a bolder treatment with plenty of fiery chilli, garlic and fresh coconut.

200g (7oz) dogfish (or canned tuna chunks)
300ml (10½ fl oz/ 1¼ cups) water
½ tsp salt
¾ tsp ground turmeric
4 black peppercorns
1 tbsp oil
½ tsp mustard seeds
¼ tbsp cumin seeds
¼ tsp fennel seeds
9 fresh curry leaves
4 dried red chillies, broken
2 green chillies, slit lengthways with seeds in
1 medium onion, finely chopped
7 garlic cloves, finely chopped
1 tsp ground cumin
200g (7oz/2½ cups) freshly grated or deciccated (shredded) coconut

Serves 4

Remove the skin from the fish, cut it into about 1.5cm (½-inch) chunks and wash well. Put it into a medium, lidded saucepan and pour on the water so that it half-covers the fish. Add the salt, the black peppercorns and half the turmeric, and partly cover with the lid. Bring to the boil and cook for about 15 minutes, stirring occasionally until the fish is cooked and all the water is absorbed. Remove from the heat, mash the fish a little so it breaks up a bit, then remove the meat from the cartilage and bones, set aside.

Heat the oil in a medium, lidded frying pan (skillet) over a low heat, then add the mustard seeds. Let them cook for a few seconds until they pop, then add the cumin and fennel seeds, followed by the curry leaves, and give it a stir or two. Next, add the dried red chillies and green chillies and give it another stir, then the onions and stir-fry for a few seconds. Finally, add the garlic and sauté until the onions are soft and turning golden. Keep an eye on the pan and do not let any of the seeds burn.

Add the remaining turmeric and give it a quick stir, then add the fish, followed by the cumin, and mix well. Finally, add the coconut and mix together well. Cover with the lid and cook for 2 minutes, stirring well. Taste for salt, remove from the heat and serve.

Variation: If using canned tuna for this recipe, you do not need to pre-cook the fish. Just start by frying the mustard seeds.

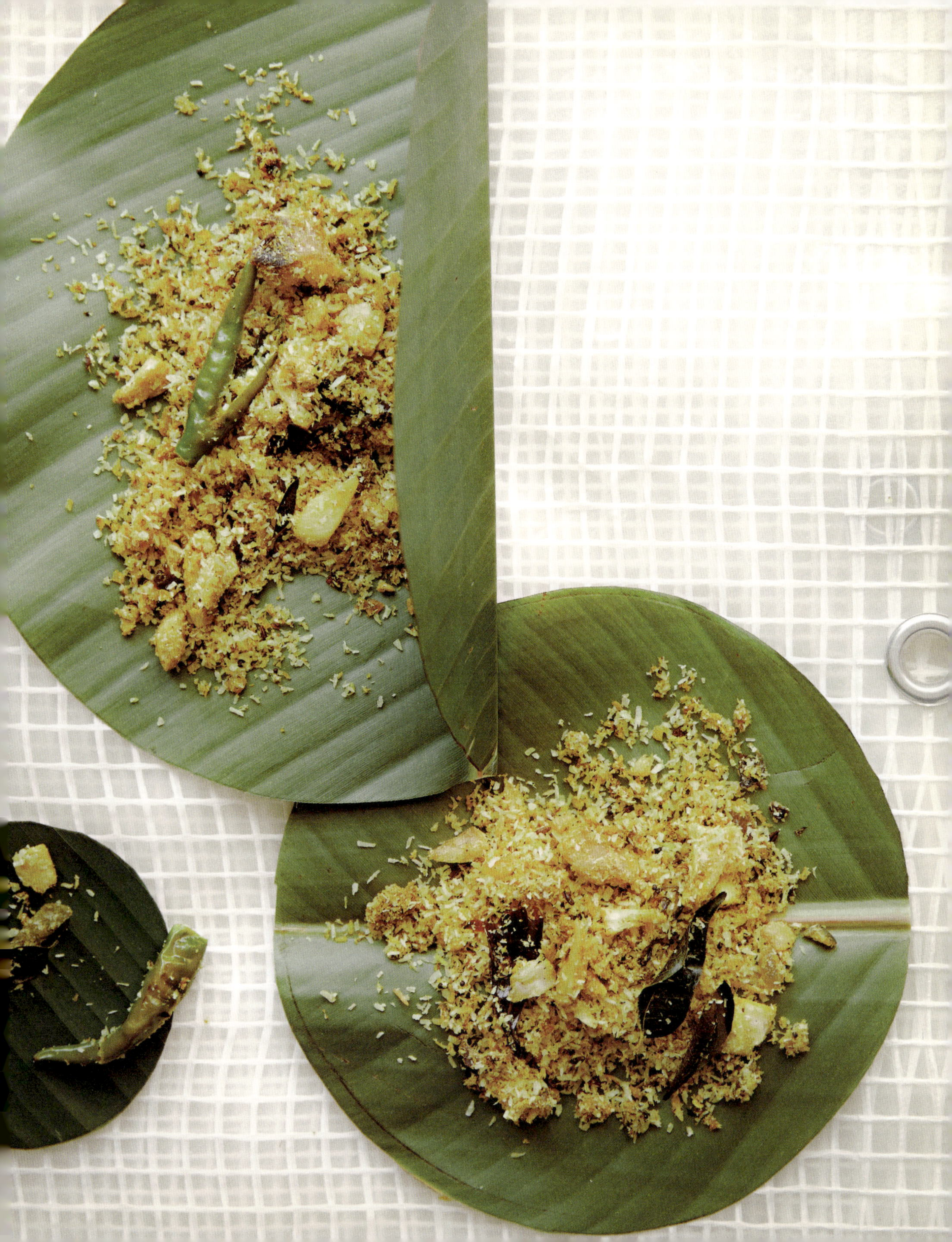

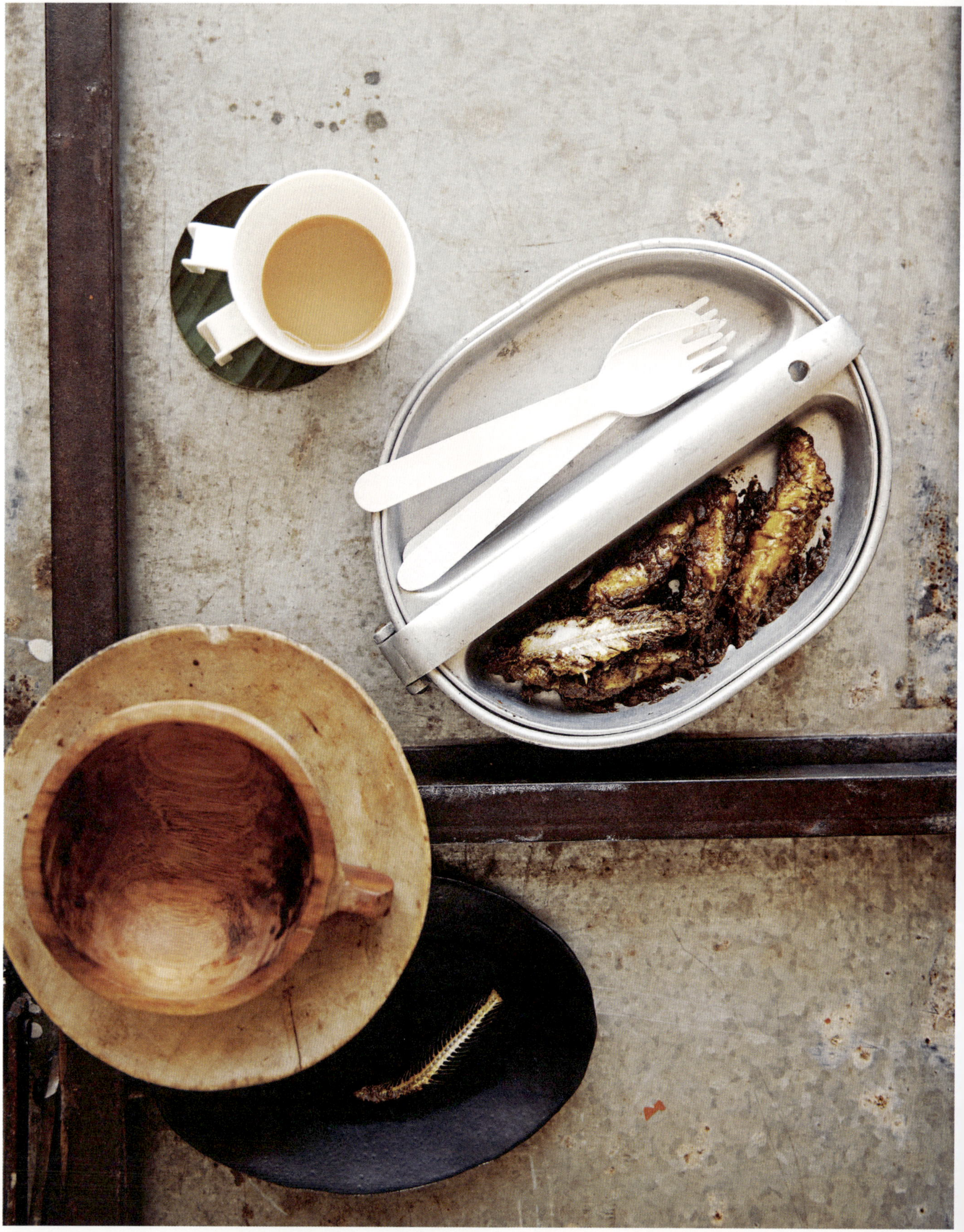

400g (14oz) whole fresh anchovies
1 tbsp red chilli flakes
1 tsp ground turmeric
½ tsp salt
4 tbsp oil
1 tsp cumin seeds
2 garlic cloves, finely chopped
2 medium onions, finely chopped
2.5cm (1-inch) piece of rampe (pandan) leaf
8 fresh curry leaves
juice of ½ lime

Stir-fried anchovies

Anchovies (or sprats) are landed in great numbers in Sri Lanka, and they only need brief preparation with a few choice spices then a quick fry to bring out the best in them. A fantastic dish to serve with Bamboo Pittu (p38).

Remove the heads from the anchovies and pull out the guts, discard both. Wash the anchovies well, at least two or three times in a medium bowl, then drain the water.

Mix the chilli flakes, turmeric and salt together in a medium bowl. Add the fish and leave to marinate for about 10 minutes.

Heat the oil in a medium, lidded frying pan (skillet) over a low heat. Tip in the anchovies, cover and fry for about 5–6 minutes on each side until they are crispy.

Gently remove the fried fish with a slotted spoon, being careful not to break them, and set aside.

Pour a little oil into the same pan if it looks dry, then add the cumin seeds, garlic, onions, rampe leaf and curry leaves, and sauté until the onions are brown. Take care not to let it burn.

Tip the anchovies back into the frying pan and mix it altogether gently. Squeeze over the lime juice, remove from the heat and serve.

Serves 4

HALMASSO BADUMA

MEEN PORIYAL

Chilli-fried fish steaks, anchovies and onions

Simple flavours, golden-brown fish, crispy onions and curry leaves: this no-fuss recipe is a celebration of great seafood. As a child it was the first dish on the table that my siblings and I would dive into, and I still love it today.

Serves 4

Wash the fish steaks well. Remove the heads from the anchovies and pull out the guts, and discard both. Wash the anchovies well.

Put both types of fish in a large bowl. Add all the other ingredients except the oil and leave to marinate for about 15 minutes, stirring well two or three times.

Bring the oil to boiling point in a deep saucepan, then reduce the heat to medium. Remove the fish steaks from the marinade one at a time, shaking off the excess, and carefully slide them into the oil, using a long spatula. Deep-fry for about 12 minutes until golden brown, turning them gently as they cook. Remove with a slotted spoon and lay them on a plate lined with kitchen towel to absorb the excess oil.

Next, remove the anchovies from the marinade, shaking off the excess, and carefully slide them into the oil. Deep-fry for about 5 minutes until golden brown, turning them gently as they cook. Remove with a slotted spoon.

Finally, remove the onion and curry leaves from the marinade, shaking off the excess, and deep-fry them until crispy, about 2 minutes. Serve as a garnish with the fried fish.

250g (9oz) firm fish steaks, such as Atlantic mackerel, large trevally (jack fish) or tuna
250g (9oz) fresh sprats or anchovies
1 medium onion, finely sliced
8 fresh curry leaves
½ tsp chilli powder
½ tsp salt
500ml (17 fl oz/generous 2 cups) oil, for deep-frying

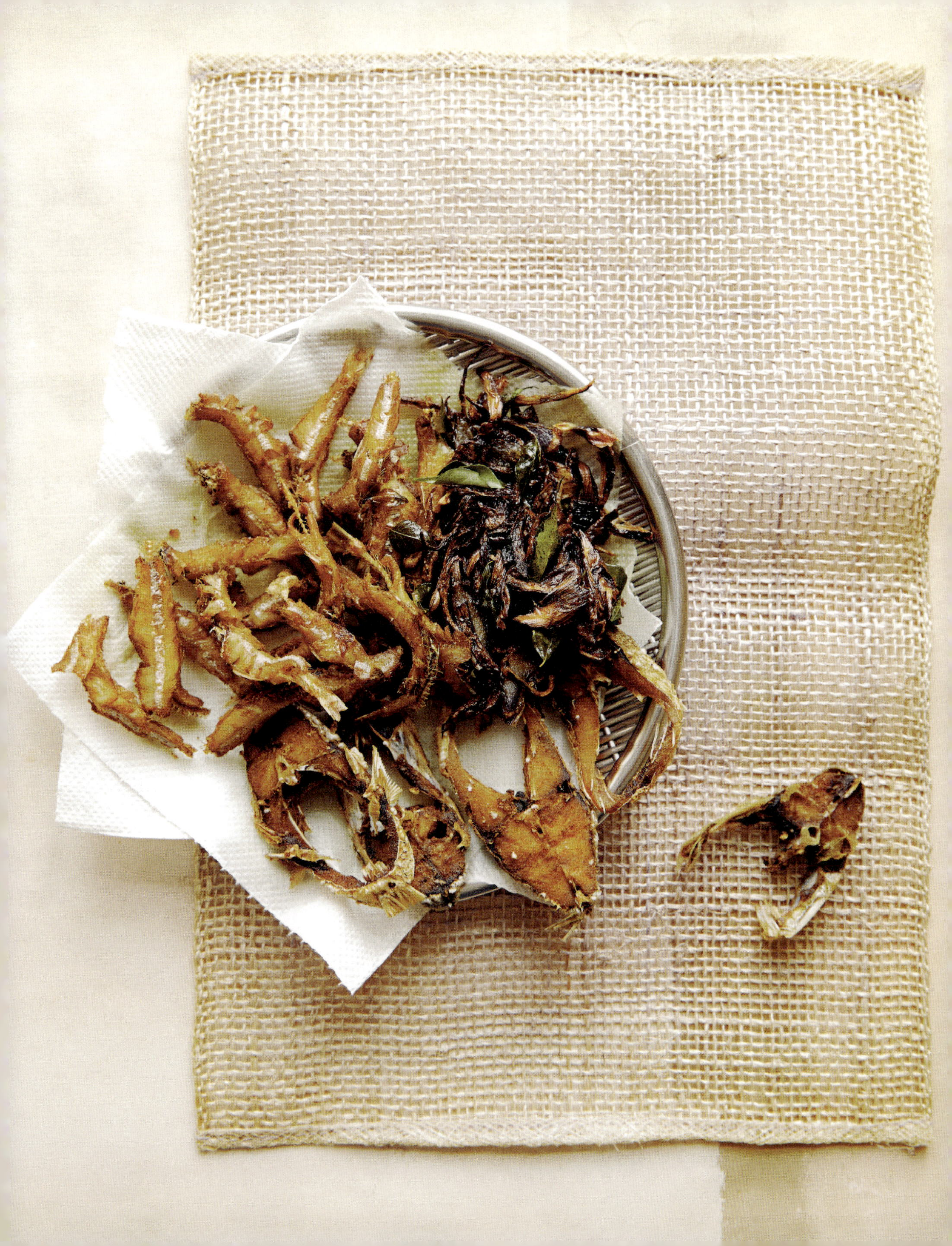

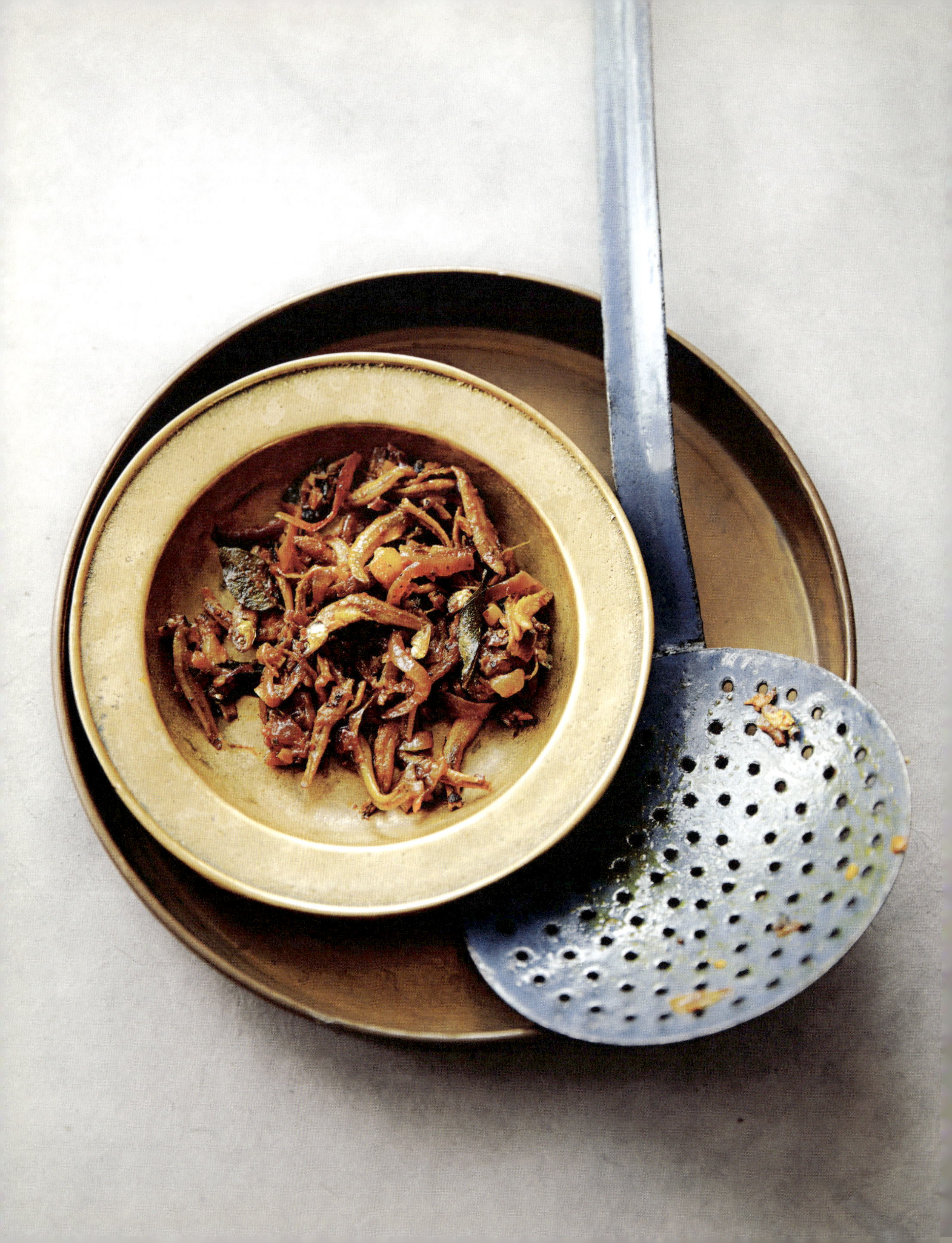

NETHALLY KARUVAATU PORIYAL

200g (7oz) dried anchovies
1 medium onion, sliced
8 fresh curry leaves
½ tsp chilli powder
2 tbsp oil

Chilli-fried anchovies
Unlike the fresh anchovies stir-fried in the Sinhalese dish on p165, this recipes uses dried and salted anchovies, which get an extra kick from the chillies.

Put the dried anchovies in a medium bowl and cover with water. Leave to soak for about 10 minutes to soften a little. Remove the heads and wash them well at least three times.

Put the anchovies in a medium bowl. Add all the other ingredients except the oil and leave to marinate for about 10 minutes, stirring well two or three times.

Remove the anchovies from the marinade, shaking off the excess. Heat the oil in a medium frying pan (skillet) over a medium heat, and shallow-fry the anchovies for about 8–10 minutes until golden brown, turning them as they cook.

Remove the onions and curry leaves from the marinade, shaking off the excess, and stir-fry for about 3 minutes until golden brown.

Mix together and serve.

Note: The dried anchovies are already salted so there is no need for salt in this recipe.

Serves 4

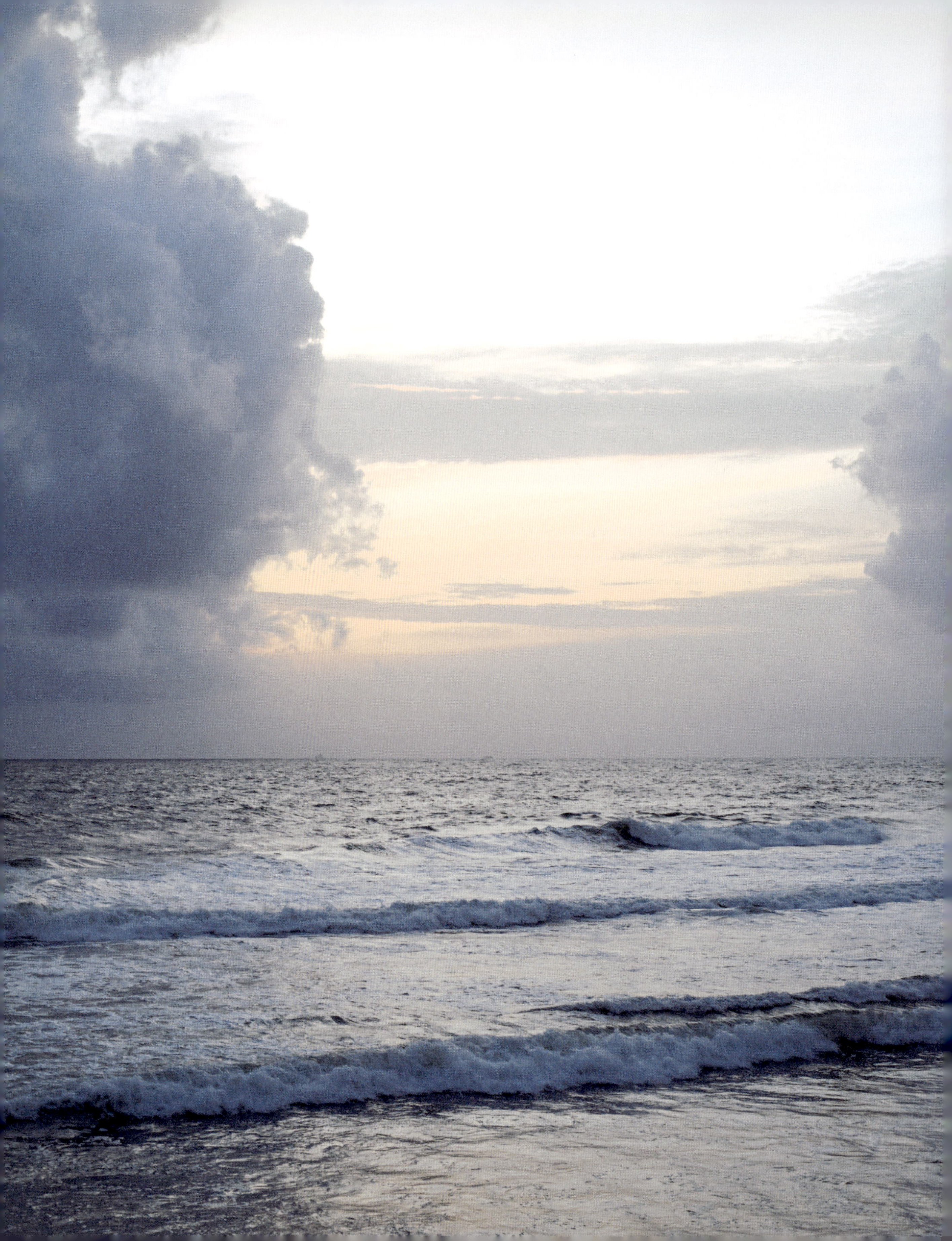

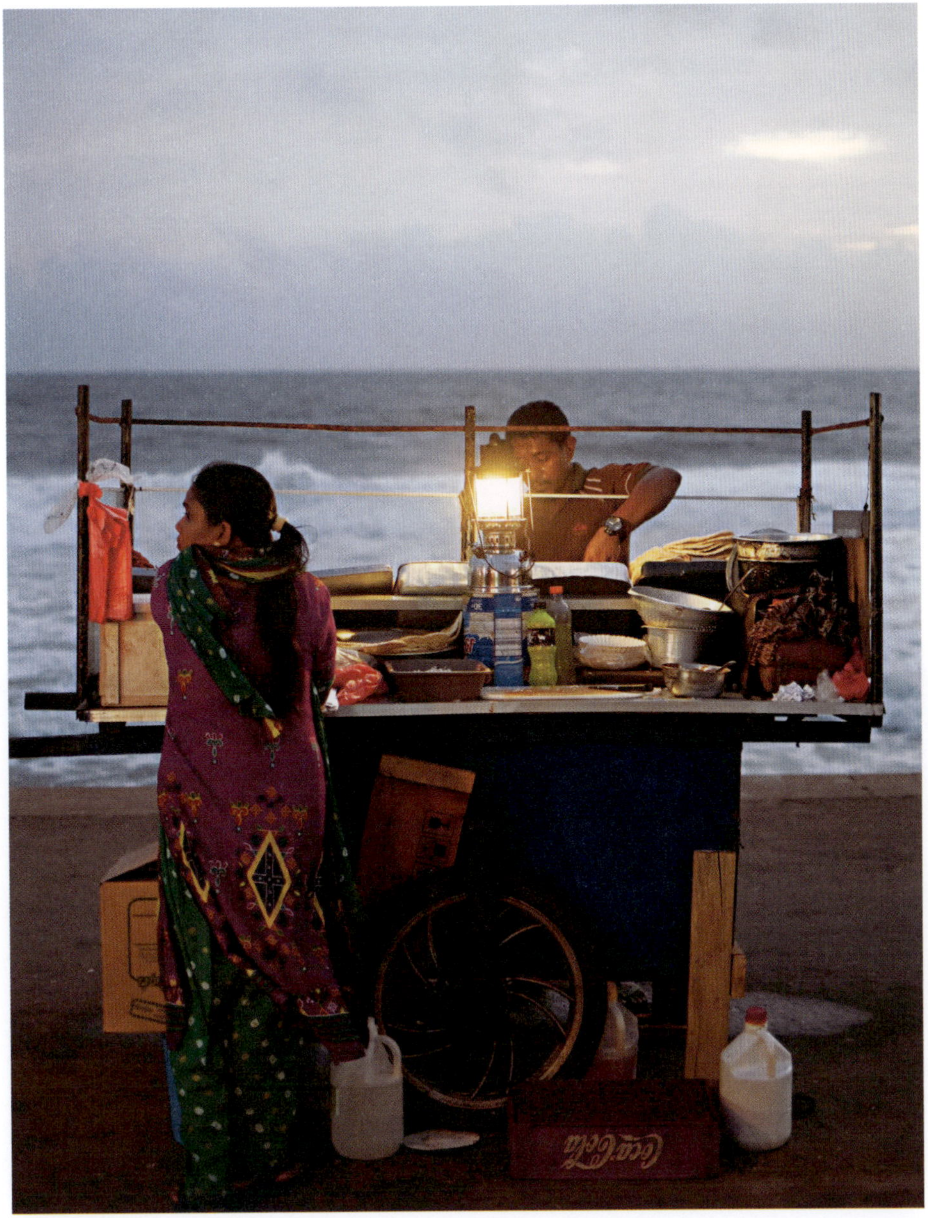

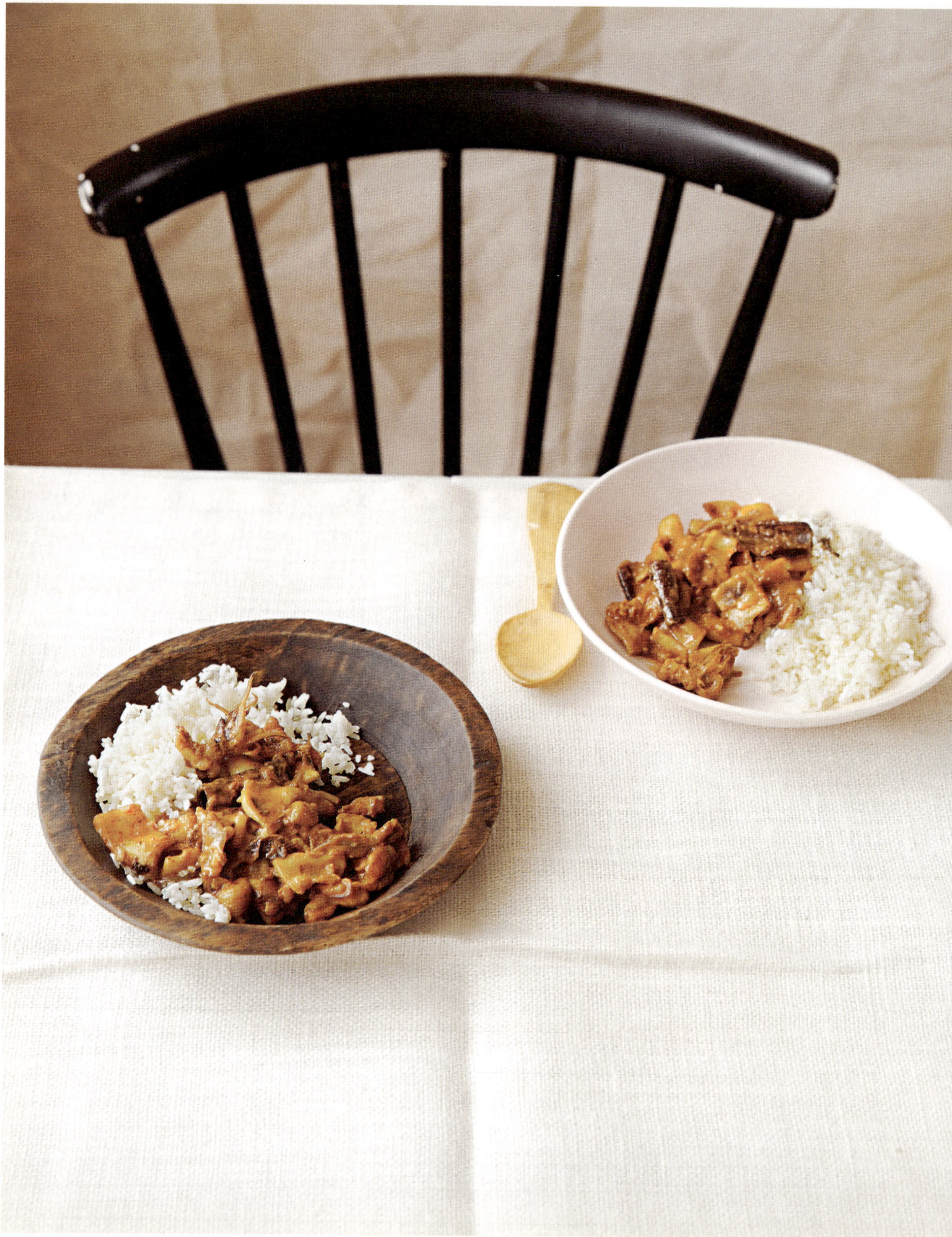

500g (1lb 2oz) squid
   or cuttlefish
½ medium onion,
   finely chopped
6 garlic cloves, cut into
   quarters
2 tsp finely chopped ginger
2 green chillies, slit
   lengthways and deseeded
4 fresh curry leaves
¼ tsp fenugreek seeds
½ tsp salt
600ml (21 fl oz/
   2½ cups) water
400ml (14 fl oz/
   1⅔ cups) coconut
   milk
1 tbsp Thool
   (curry powder on p16)

Squid curry
This Tamil dish from the north and east of the island can be made using squid or cuttlefish. It's got a subtle heat and makes a comforting lunch paired with plain boiled rice.

Ask your fishmonger to clean and prepare your squid. If you're doing it yourself, you need to extract all the insides and carefully remove the ink bag.

Wash the squid throughly, inside and out, and the tentacles. Then cut it into 2.5cm (1-inch) chunks and put it in a medium, lidded saucepan.

Add all the other ingredients, except the coconut milk and curry powder. The water should just cover the squid. Half-cover the pan with the lid and bring to the boil. Reduce the heat and simmer for 10–15 minutes, until the water evaporates and the squid is cooked through and soft.

Add the coconut milk and curry powder and stir well. Half-cover the pan with the lid and simmer for a further 10 minutes. Taste for salt, then remove from the heat and let it rest for at least 5 minutes before serving.

Tip: For a curry with a little more sauce, add another 200ml (7 fl oz/generous ¾ cup) coconut milk.

Serves 4

KANAVAI KARI

NANDU KARI

Crab curry

Crab in Sri Lanka is a delicacy and a special treat. You can use any type for this recipe, but blue swimmer crab is the most common around the island. Mangrove crabs (which are two to three times larger) are also popular in the north-west of the island.

Serves 6

1kg (2lbs 4oz) crabs
½ medium onion, finely chopped
6 garlic cloves, cut into quarters
2 green chillies, slit lengthways and deseeded
6 fresh curry leaves
½ tsp fenugreek seeds
1 tbsp Thool (curry powder on p16)
400ml (14 fl oz/1⅔ cups) tamarind water
400ml (14 fl oz/1⅔ cups) coconut milk
400ml (14 fl oz/1⅔ cups) water
¾ tsp salt
2 tbsp fragrant curry powder (see below)

For the fragrant curry powder

2 tbsp freshly grated or desiccated (shredded) coconut
1 tsp urid dal (split black gram)
1 tsp uncooked white rice (basmati or patna)
½ tsp fennel seeds
5 fresh curry leaves

Wash the crabs well. Pull off the top shell and clean the insides with your fingers. Cut the crabs in half and then twist off the pincer claws. Break the pincer claws at the joint and gently tap them with something hard, like the handle of a knife. The aim is to crack the shell, but leave it intact. Remove any small pieces of broken shell.

Place the crabs and the claws in a large, lidded saucepan set over a medium heat. Then add all the other ingredients, except the fragrant curry powder. The water should just cover the crabs. Bring to the boil, then reduce the heat, cover with the lid and let it simmer for about 20–25 minutes, stirring occasionally. While it is cooking, there always needs to be some liquid in the pan, so add a little water if it becomes too dry.

Meanwhile, make the fragrant curry powder. Dry-roast each of the ingredients separately in a dry frying pan (skillet) on a low heat, until golden brown. Leave to cool, then mix them together and grind into a fine powder in a spice grinder.

After about 20 minutes, when the liquid is nearly all absorbed and the crab cooked, sprinkle on the fragrant curry powder and give it a good stir, then cook for another minute before taking it off the heat. Allow the curry to rest for about 5 minutes before serving.

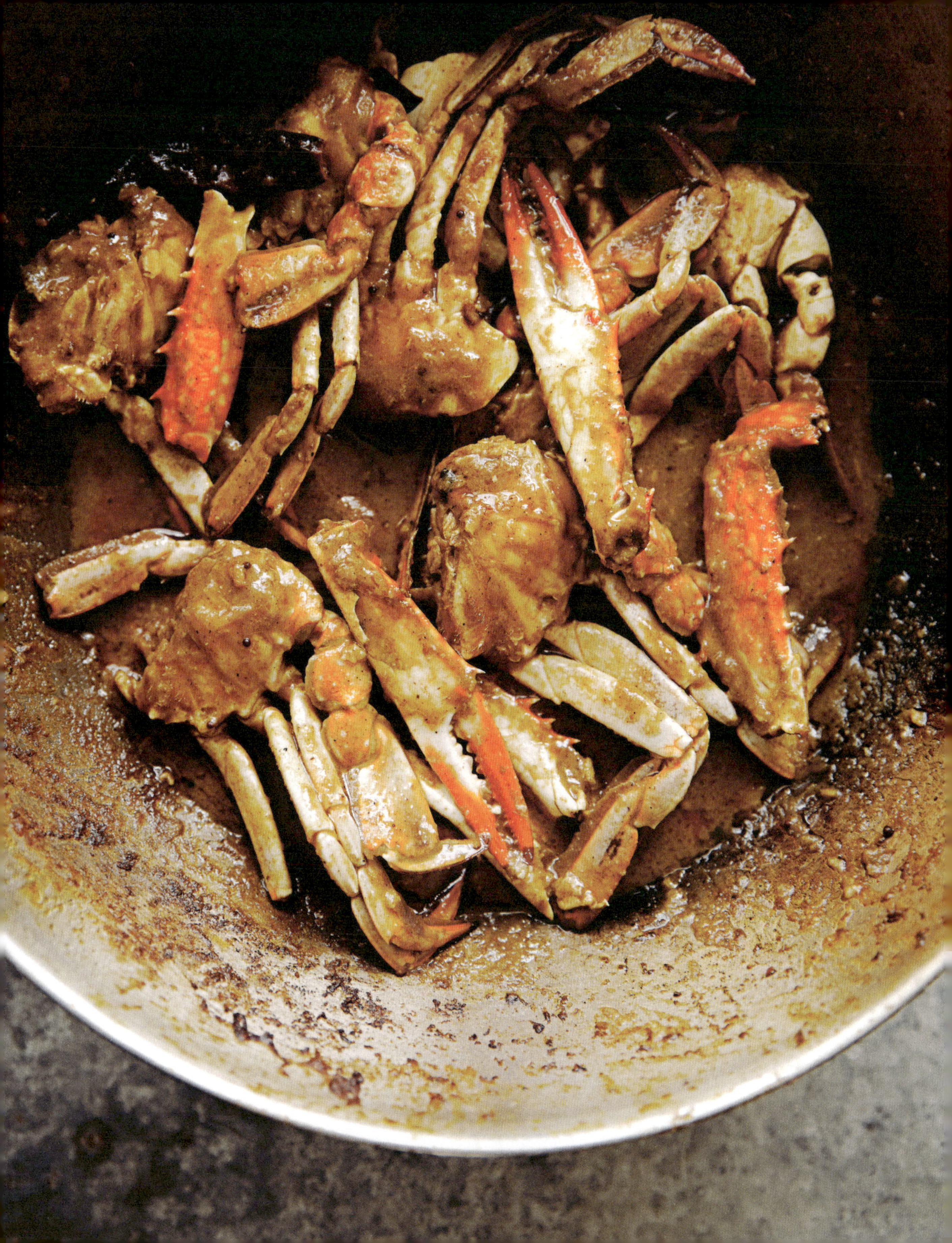

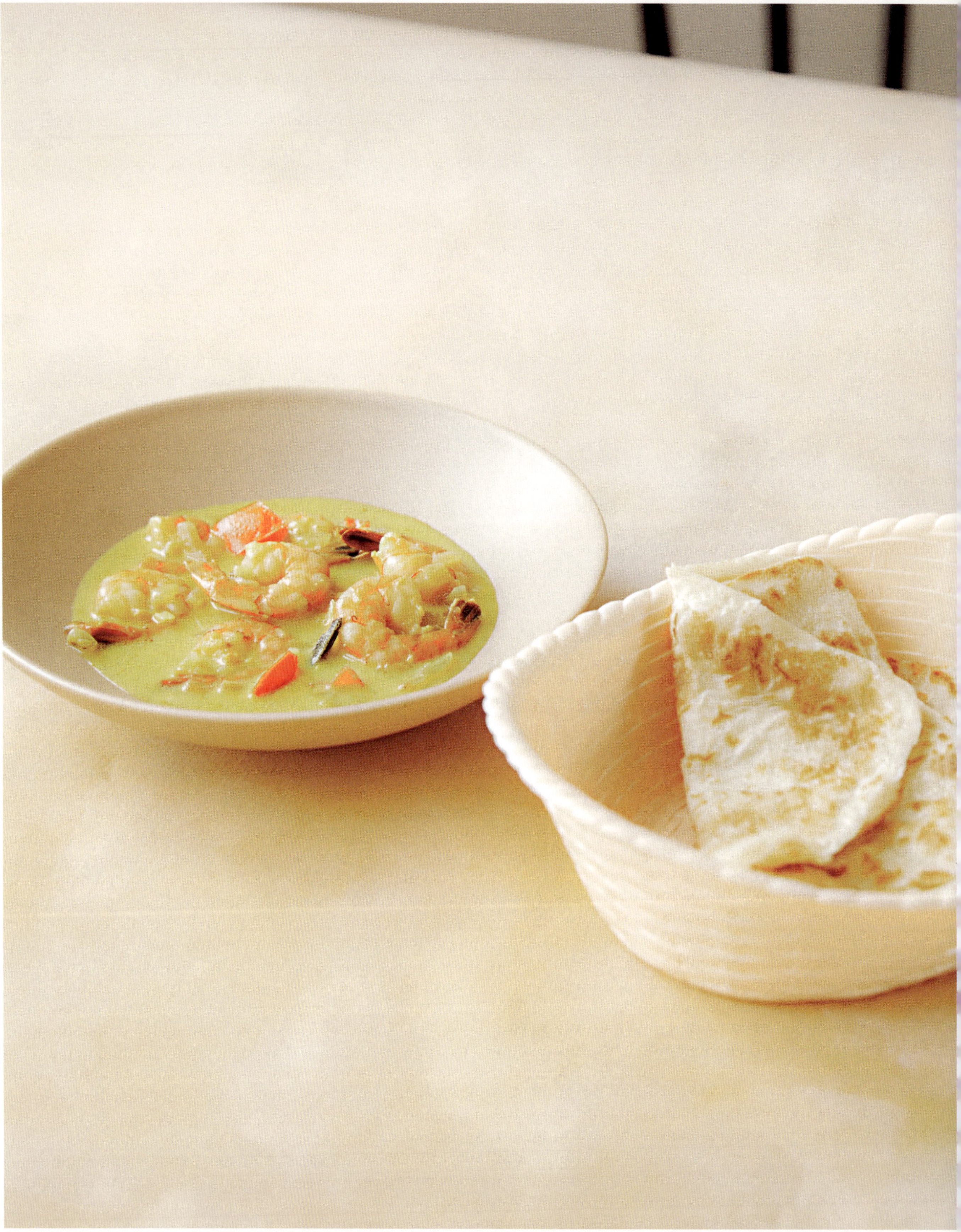

500g (1lb 2oz) raw prawns
  (shrimp), shell on
1 tbsp oil
5 fresh curry leaves
1 green chilli,
  slit lengthways
  and deseeded
2 garlic cloves,
  finely chopped
½ large onion,
  finely chopped
½ tomato,
  medium diced
½ tsp ground turmeric
½ tsp chilli powder
½ tsp roasted
  chilli powder
½ tsp cumin seeds,
  freshly ground
½ tsp salt
2.5cm (1-inch)
  cinnamon stick
1 tsp red wine vinegar
200ml (7 fl oz/generous
  ¾ cup) coconut milk

For the tempering
1 tbsp oil
½ tsp fenugreek seeds
5 fresh curry leaves
½ large onion,
  finely chopped

Prawn and coconut curry
Prawns in Sri Lanka are always wild, never farmed, and so are healthily large with delightful sweetness. White prawns and tiger prawns are the most common there, and this is a quick, super-tasty and satisfying way to cook them.

Wash and clean the prawns (shrimp). Remove the head and most of the shell, leaving it just on the tail. Wash them again, drain and put in a medium saucepan.

Heat the oil in a medium, lidded saucepan set over a low heat. Add the curry leaves, green chillies, garlic and onion, and sauté until the onions are soft and turning golden. Add the tomato, and stir-fry for a few more minutes until it is soft.

Tip in the prawns, and give it a quick stir. Then add the turmeric, two chilli powders, ground cumin seeds, salt, cinnamon and vinegar, and stir-fry for 1 minute.

Add the coconut milk, cover with the lid, and simmer for 10 minutes until the prawns are cooked and the sauce has thickened.

Now, temper the spices and onion. Heat the oil in a medium frying pan (skillet) over a low heat. Add the fenugreek seeds, curry leaves and onions, and sauté until the onions are soft and turning golden.

Once the curry has thickened, take it off the heat and pour in the tempered mix. Give it a good stir. Taste for salt, then let it rest for 2–3 minutes before serving.

Serves 4

ISSO KIRI HODI

400g (14oz) raw prawns
    (shrimp), shell on
1 green (bell) pepper
1 red (bell) pepper
1 medium onion,
    cut into quarters
2 tsp oil
2 tbsp tomato sauce
    (ketchup)
1 tbsp medium soya
    (soy) sauce (not dark)
2 tsp chilli powder
2 tsp sesame oil

Devilled prawns

This is a bar food originally served in drinking clubs during the era of the British Raj, and it has found its way into the homes and hearts of Sri Lankans. As a nation we're also fond of devilling squid, cuttlefish, pork, potato… you name it.

Wash and clean the prawns (shrimp). Remove the head and most of the shell, leaving it just on the tail. Wash them again, drain and set aside.

Remove the stems from the (bell) peppers, quarter and remove the seeds. Halve each quarter and cut them into about 1cm (½-inch) chunks and set aside. Loosen the layers of the onion quarters and set aside.

Put the oil in a large frying pan (skillet) or wok over a very high heat, and immediately add the onion. Stir-fry for 30 seconds, then add the peppers and stir-fry for a minute.

Tip in the prawns and stir-fry for just over a minute, then add the rest of the ingredients and stir-fry for another minute. Serve immediately.

Note: When making other devilled dishes, the main ingredient will need pre-cooking with a pinch or two of salt, before adding into the peppers and onions. You can use this method with prawns, but they do not need to be cooked for long.

Serves 4

ISSO BADUMA

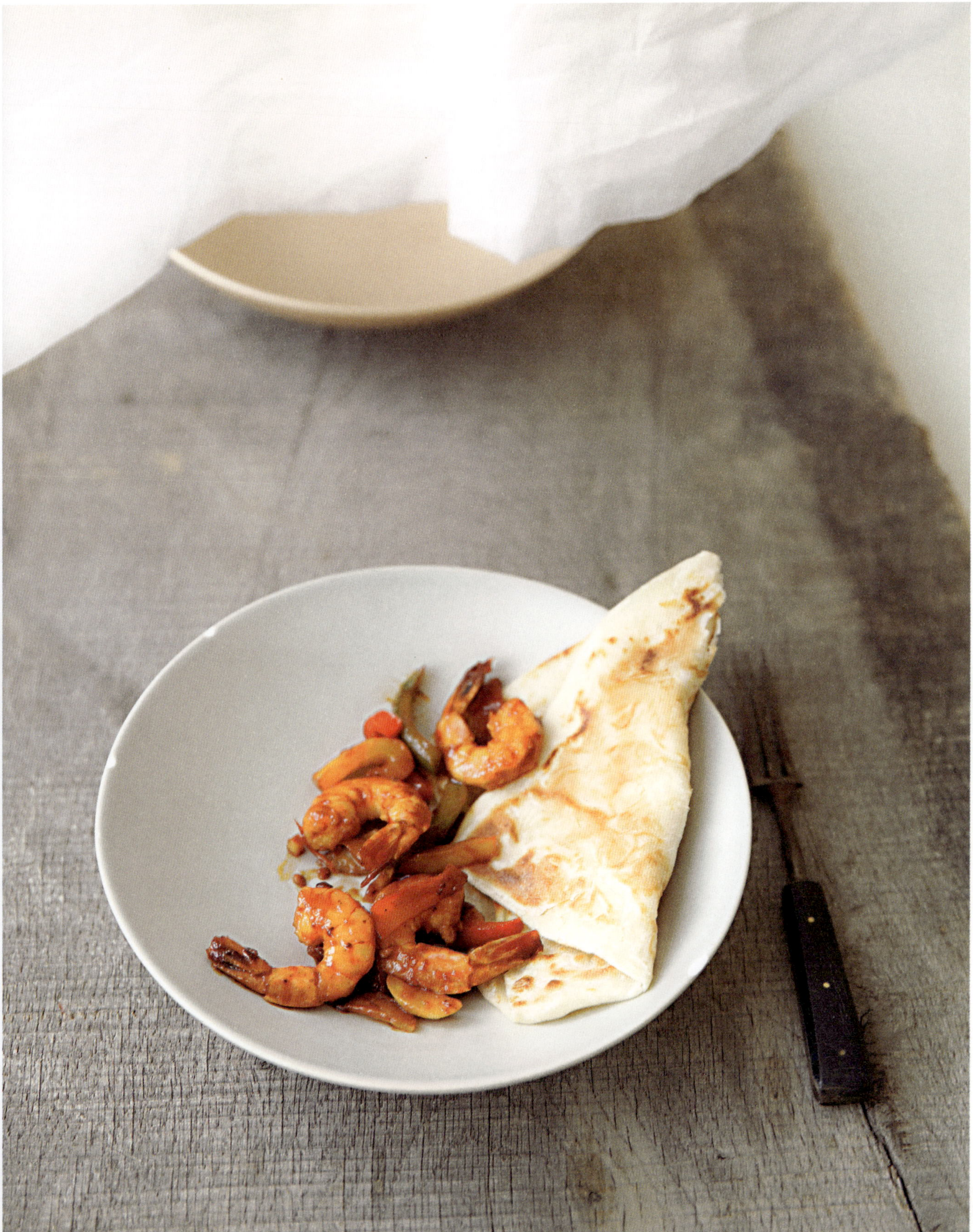

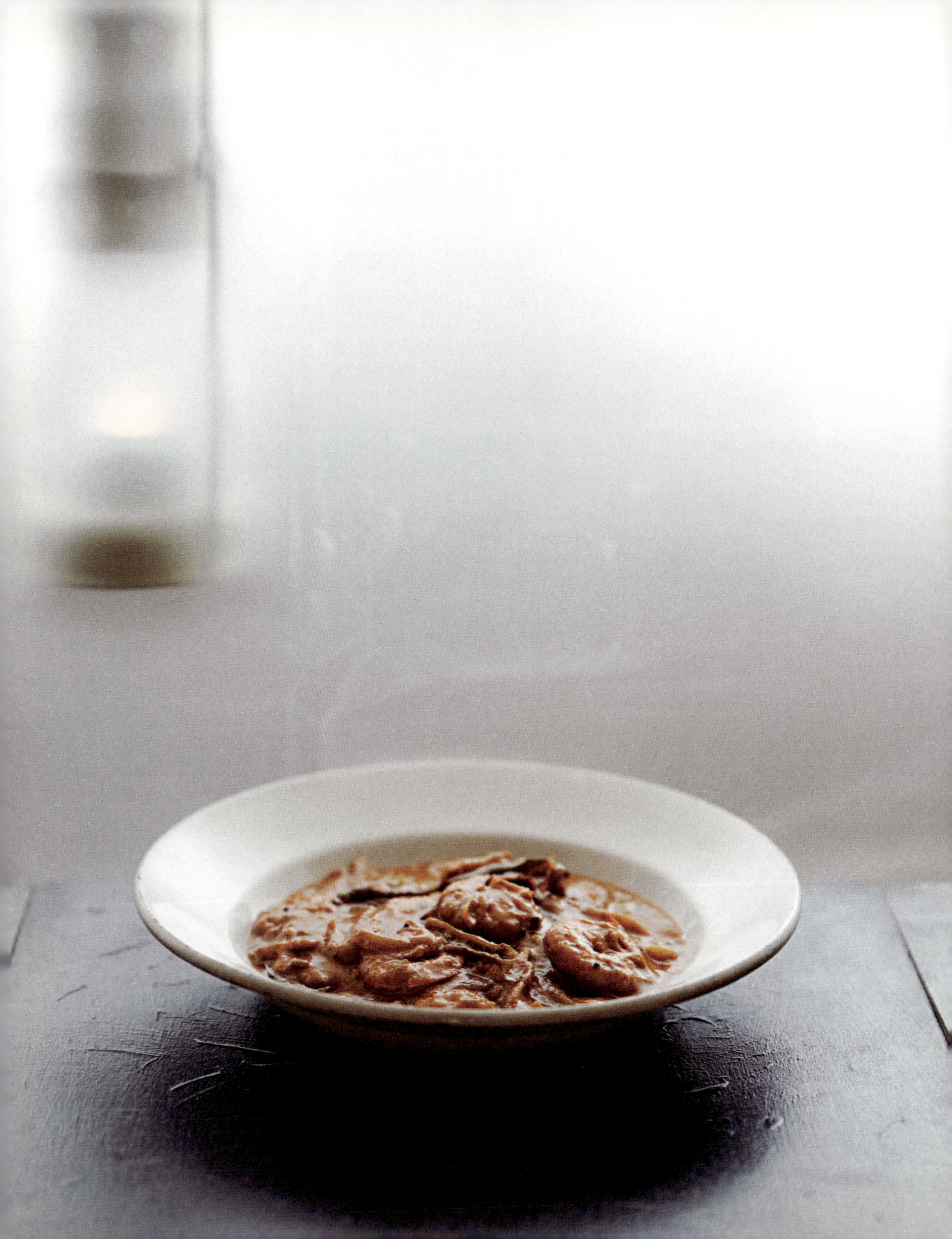

IRAL KULAMBU

*Prawn and tamarind curry
Traditional fishing methods in Sri Lanka are sustainable and respect the environment. On the east coast of the island women would wade knee-deep into estuaries and lagoons at night with lanterns to attract prawns, which they would trap in bamboo cages.*

400g (14oz) raw prawns (shrimp), shell on
1 tbsp oil
¼ tsp fennel seeds
9 fresh curry leaves
2 green chillies, slit lengthways with seeds in
¼ tsp fenugreek seeds
1 medium onion, finely chopped
5 garlic cloves, cut into quarters
¼ tsp ground turmeric
200ml (7 fl oz/generous ¾ cup) coconut cream
200ml (7 fl oz/generous ¾ cup) tamarind water
200ml (7 fl oz/generous ¾ cup) water
1 tsp Thool (curry powder on p16)
½ tsp salt

Serves 4

Wash and clean the prawns (shrimp). Remove the head and the shell, wash again and set aside.

Heat the oil in a medium saucepan over a low heat. Add the fennel seeds followed by the curry leaves and green chillies, stirring as you go. Add the fenugreek seeds and sauté for a few seconds, taking care not to burn any of the seeds. Next, add the onion and stir-fry for 30 seconds, then add the garlic and sauté until the onions are soft and turning golden.

Add the turmeric, coconut milk, tamarind water, water, curry powder and salt and give it all a good stir. Bring to the boil, then reduce the heat and simmer for 15–20 minutes, stirring occasionally, until the sauce begins to thicken.

Tip in the prawns, mix well and cook for a further 7–8 minutes until just cooked through. If the gravy is getting too thick, add a little extra water. It is important not to overcook the prawns as they will become tough. Taste for salt, remove from the heat and let it rest for at least 5 minutes before serving.

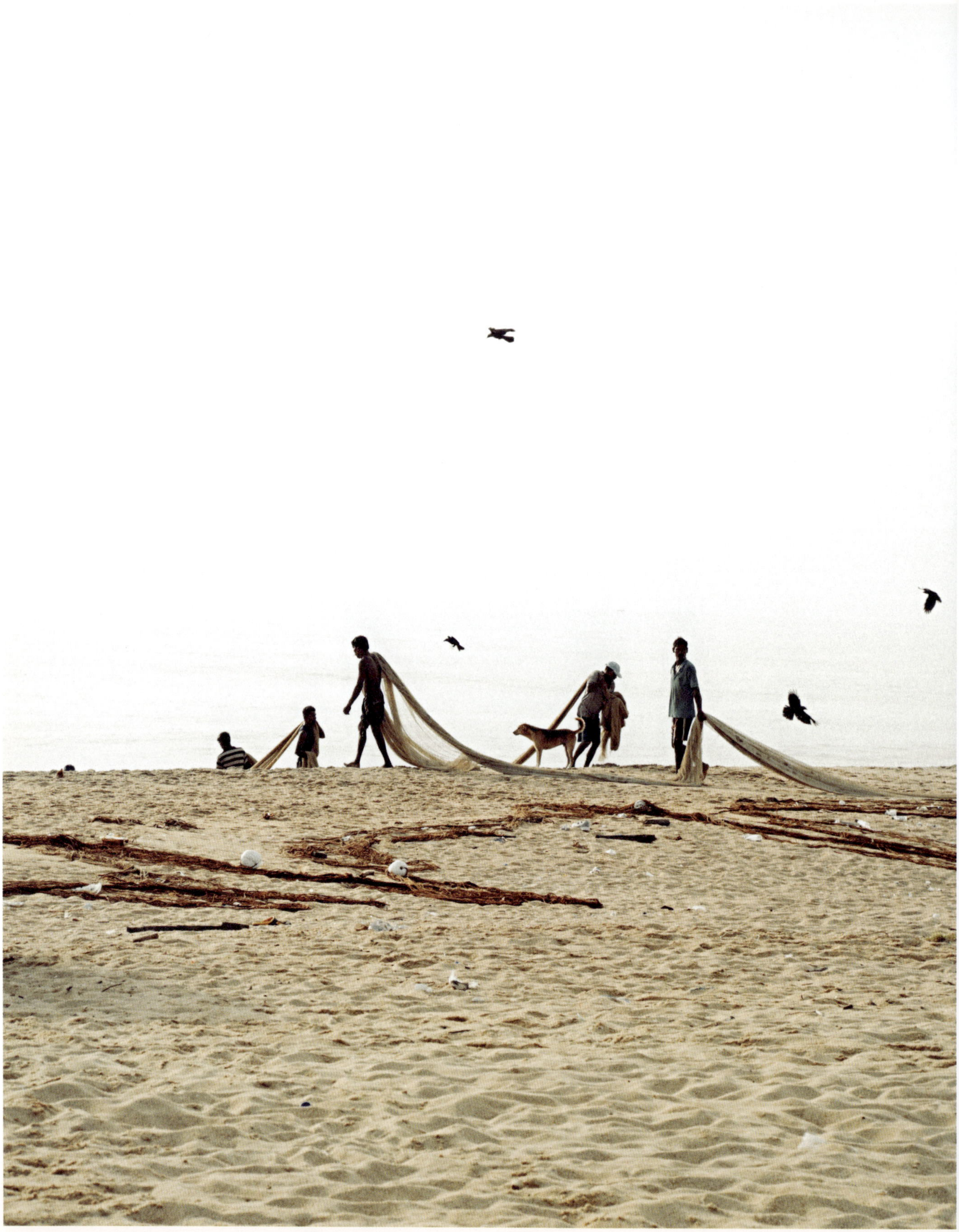

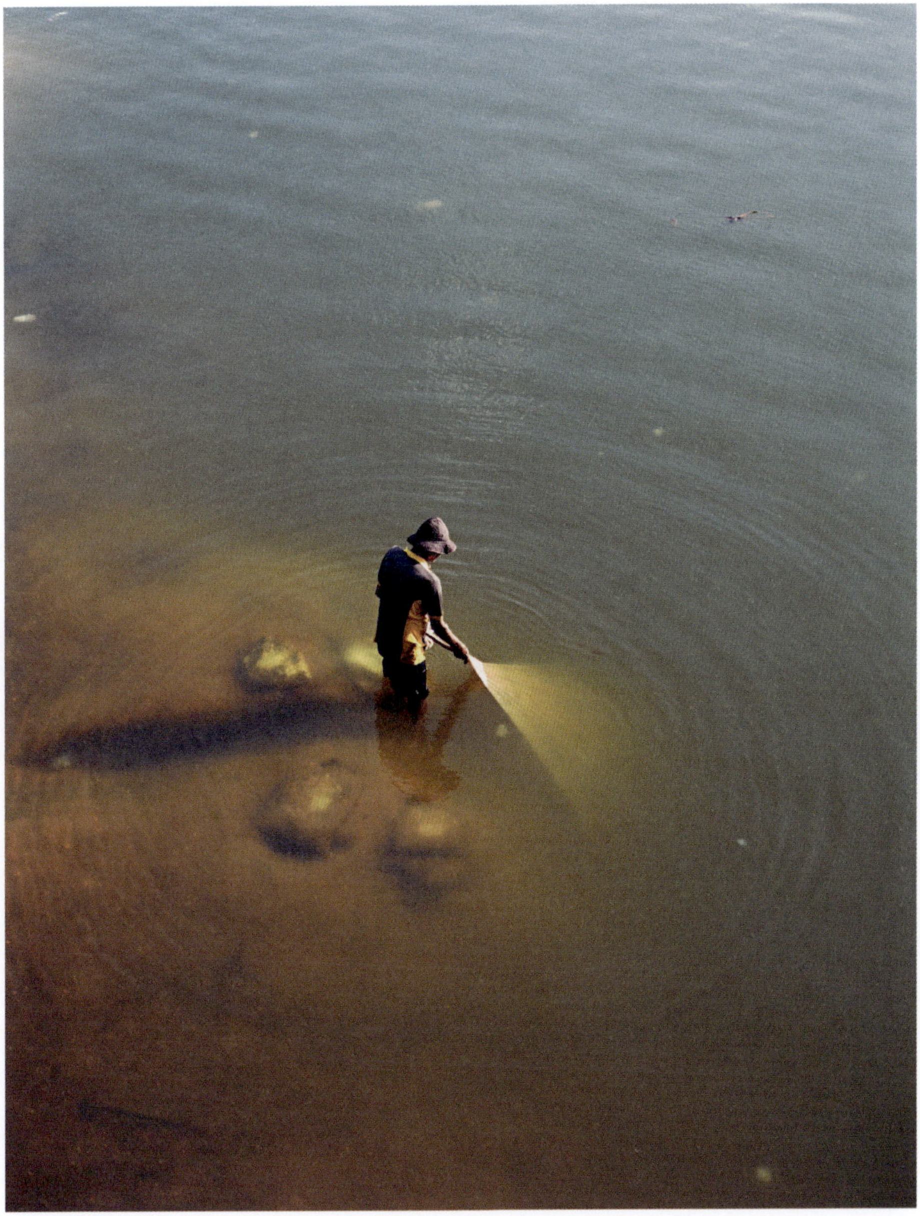

MAALU MOJU

Pickled fish

A pickle is an essential element of most Sri Lankan meals, not just an afterthought to be dolloped on the side of a plate. This is a lightly pickled accompaniment from the southern part of the island.

400g (14oz) tuna or kingfish steaks
¾ tsp salt
1 tsp ground black pepper
½ tsp ground turmeric
500ml (17 fl oz/generous 2 cups) oil for deep-frying, plus 2 tbsp for shallow frying
1 medium red (bell) pepper, cut into rings
5cm (2-inch) piece of ginger, peeled
3 garlic cloves
250ml (9 fl oz/generous 1 cup) red wine vinegar
2 tbsp ground mustard seeds
1 tbsp chilli flakes
1 tbsp sugar (white or brown)
8 fresh curry leaves
2 large onions, finely sliced
2 medium tomatoes, medium diced (optional)

Serves 4

Wash the fish well and put it in a medium bowl with ½ teaspoon of the salt, the pepper and turmeric and leave to marinate for about 15 minutes.

Heat the 500ml of oil in a deep saucepan, and deep-fry the fish steaks for 6–7 minutes until golden brown, turning them over as they cook. Remove with a slotted spoon and lay them on kitchen towel to absorb the excess oil.

In the same pan, deep-fry the (bell) pepper for 2 minutes and set it aside on kitchen towel.

Put the ginger and garlic in a spice grinder and blitz into a thick paste.

Mix ¼ teaspoon of salt, the vinegar, ground mustard seeds, chilli flakes, sugar and ginger and garlic paste together in a medium bowl.

Heat the remaining oil in a medium saucepan over a very low heat. Add the curry leaves, the vinegar mixture and the onions, and cook for a minute or two until it warms up.

Add the tomatoes (if using) and cook for another minute or two. Add the fried fish and peppers, mix together gently and remove from the heat. Taste for salt, and serve.

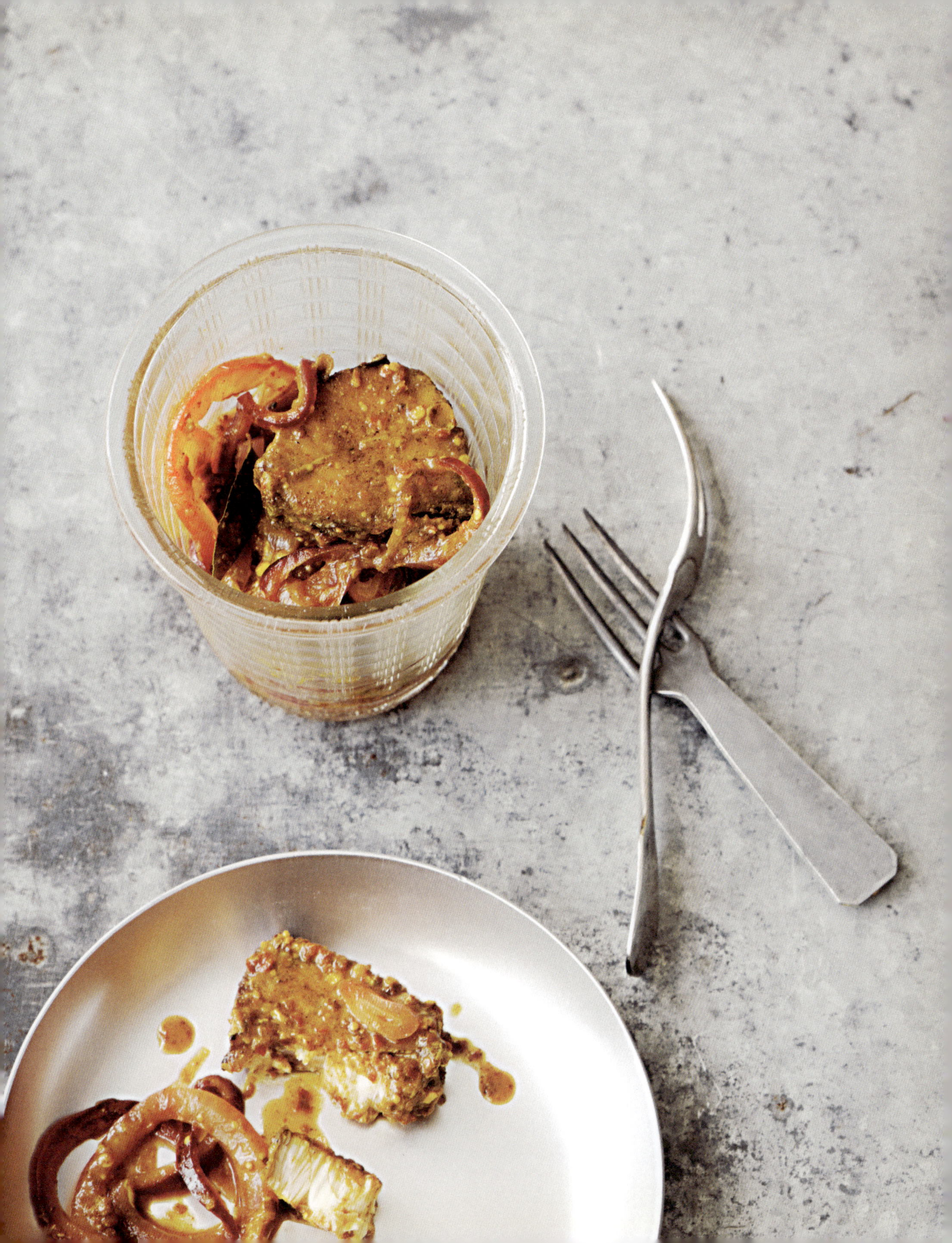

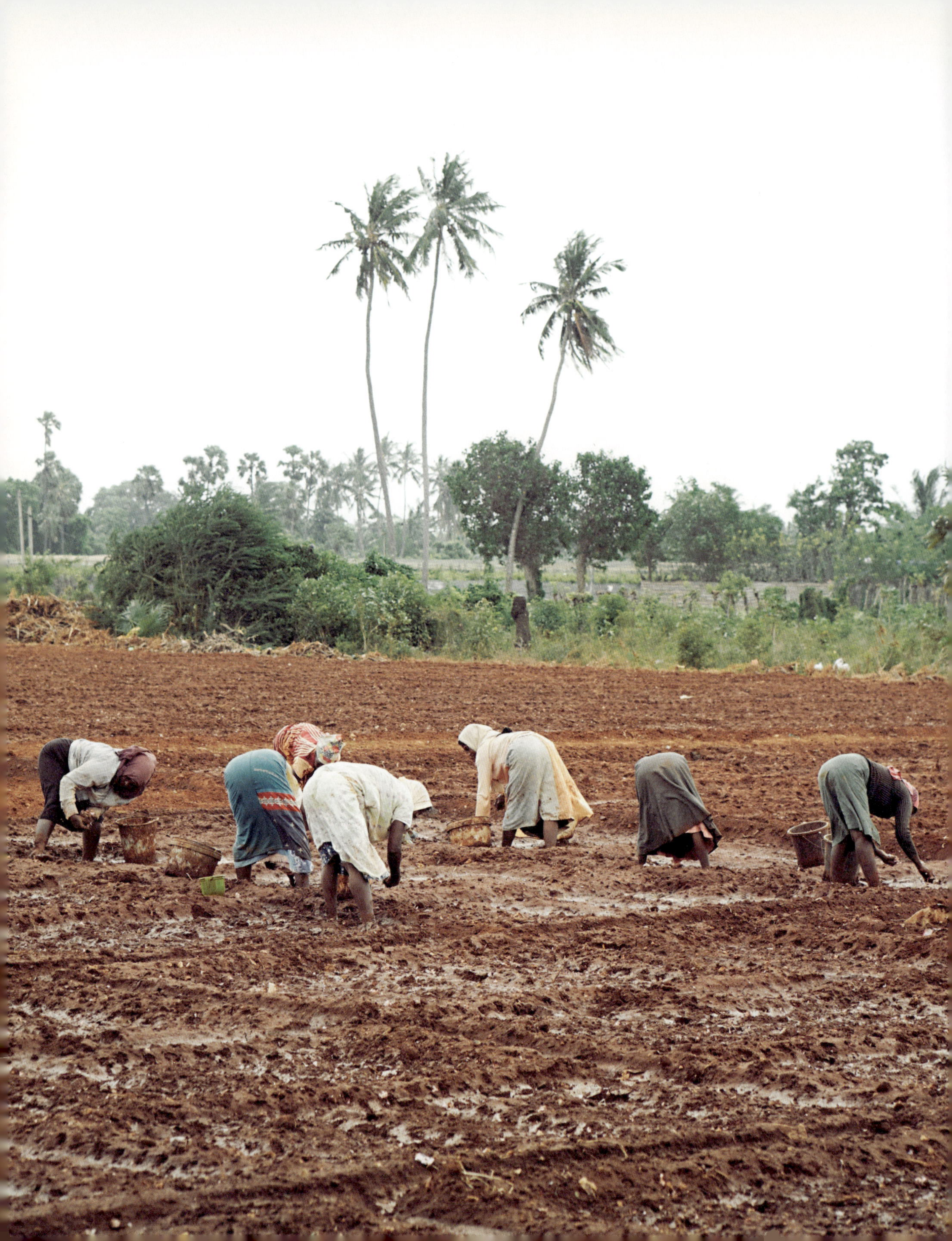

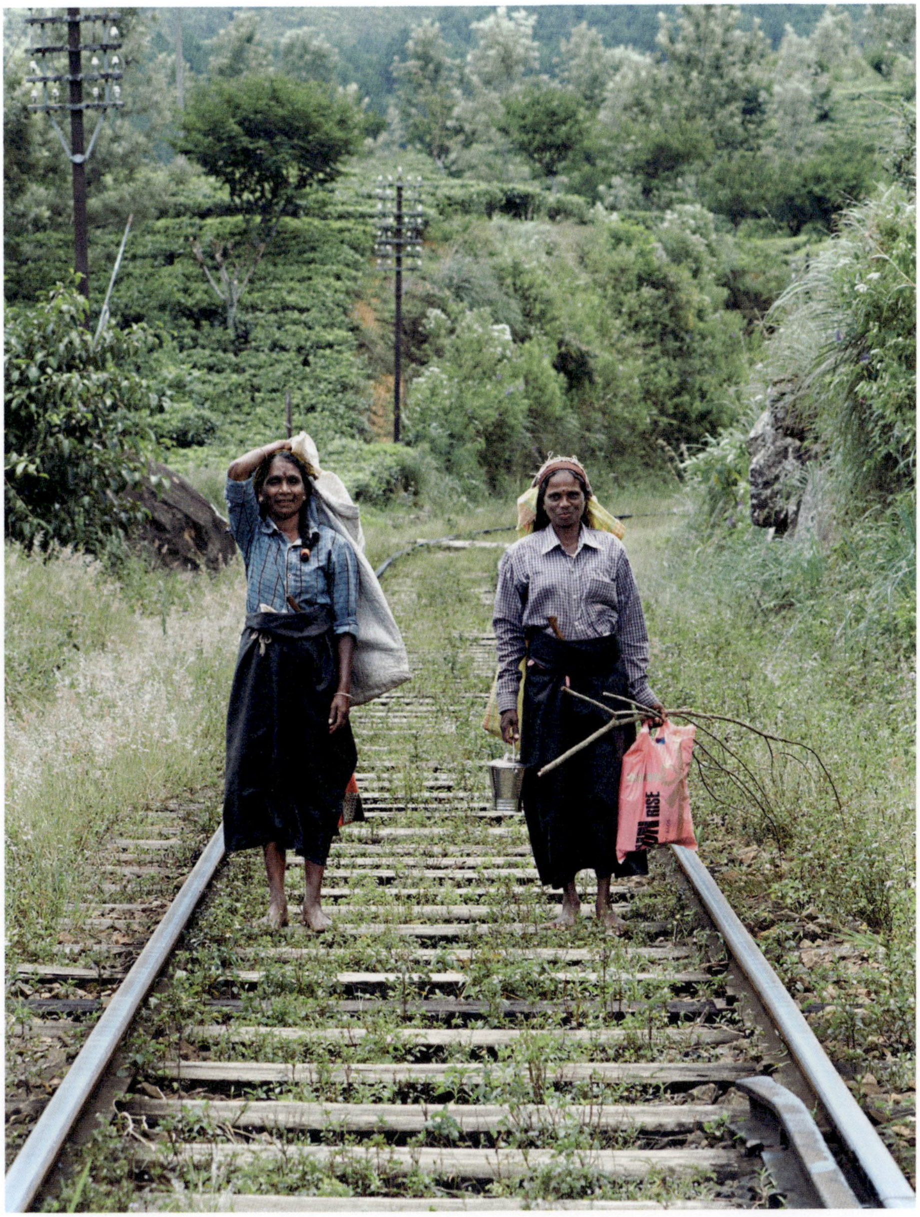

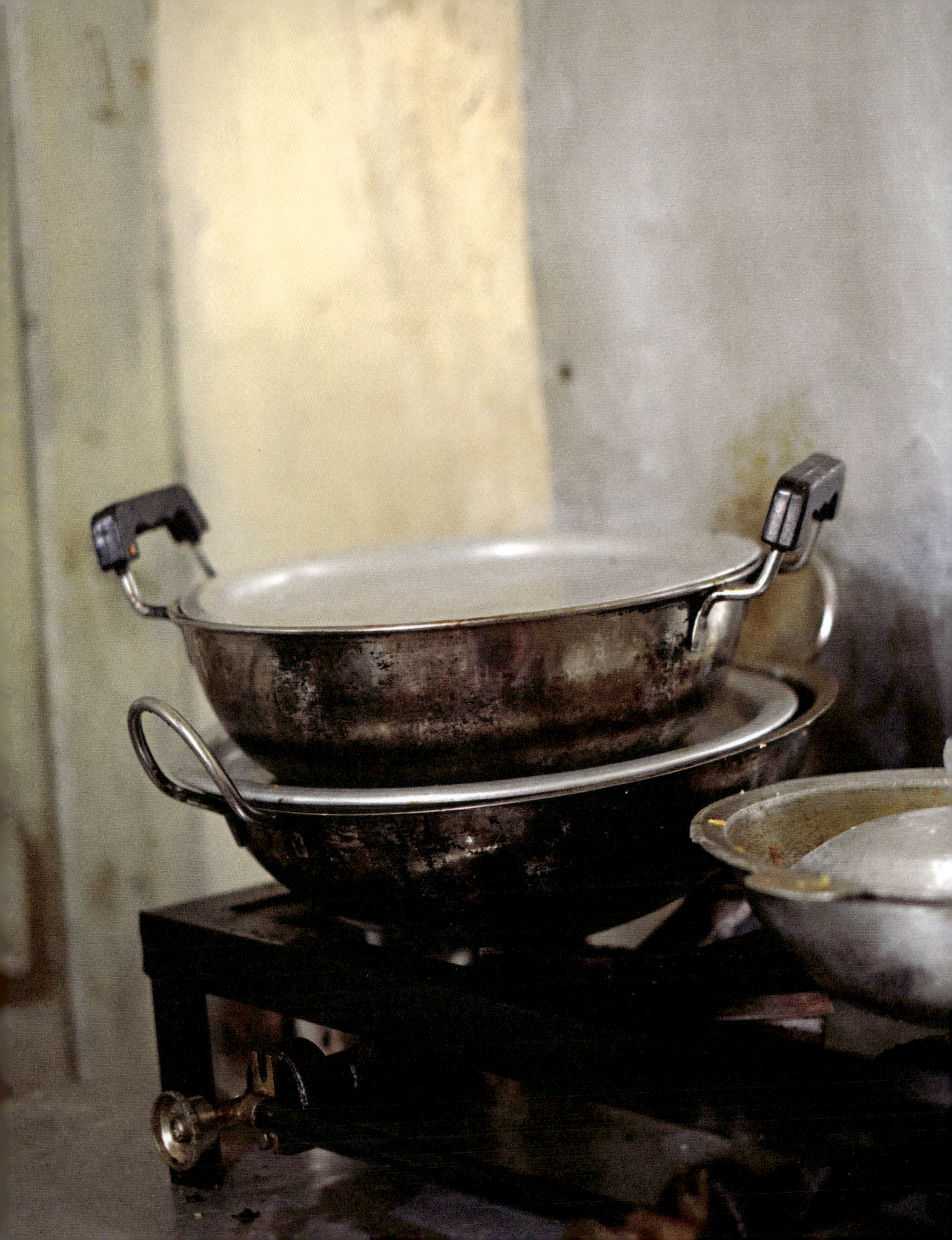

CHICKEN BIRYANI

The word 'biriyani' originates in Persia, and this exquisite meal must have found its way to Sri Lanka through Arab traders. I had my first taste of it during my senior school days, in the Maradana district of the capital Colombo. A whole team of us descended on a restaurant for dinner after a big cricket match. The match was memorable but the biriyani and the company of my classmates were even more so. What's so special about biryani? The rice and chicken are prepared separately then mixed and cooked together with a tight lid. This process is called 'dumming', and the fragrances and spices are infused into the rice to give an excellent lift of flavour. Versions of biryani exist across Asia from Iran to India; here is ours, uniquely Sri Lankan.

CHICKEN BIRYANI

600g (1lb 5oz/2¾ cups) white rice (samba or basmati)
750g (1lb 10oz) boneless chicken
2 tbsp oil
2.5cm (1-inch) cinnamon stick, broken into two
4 cardamom pods, slightly crushed
4 cloves
8 fresh curry leaves
4 green chillies, finely chopped with seeds in
1 medium onion, finely chopped
6 garlic cloves, finely chopped
2.5cm (1-inch) piece of ginger, peeled and finely chopped
2 tbsp biryani curry powder (see recipe below)
100g (3½oz/½ cup) plain yogurt
¾ tsp salt
100ml (3½ fl oz/ 7 tbsp) water
50g (1¾oz/⅓ cup) cashew nuts, halved
50g (1¾oz/⅓ cup) raisins
2 tsp ghee or butter
2 tsp rosewater
6 saffron strands, soaked in 1 tbsp warm water

For the biryani curry powder
50g (1¾oz/¾ cup) coriander seeds
25g (1oz/⅔ cup) dried red chillies
2 tsp cumin seeds
2 tsp black peppercorns
1 tsp cloves
1 tsp cardamom pods
1 tsp caraway seeds

Serves 6

Make the biryani curry powder
In two batches in a hot frying pan (skillet), dry-roast all the ingredients until fragrant: first, coriander and chillies, and second, all the other ingredients. Leave to cool, then mix them together and grind into a fine powder in a spice grinder.

Make the rice and chicken
Put the rice into a bowl and cover with water. Swirl the rice around to wash it, drain and repeat at least three times until the water is clear. Then, fill a medium, lidded saucepan three-quarters full with water and bring it to the boil. Tip in the washed rice and leave to cook. Strain the rice when it is 80 per cent cooked: it should still be firm to the bite.

Wash the chicken, cut it into 2.5cm (1-inch) chunks and wash it again just once.

Heat the oil in a large saucepan over a low heat. Add the cinnamon, cardamom and cloves, and give it a stir or two. Next, add the curry leaves and stir-fry for a minute or so. Add the green chillies and give it another stir, then the onion and stir-fry for 30 seconds. Finally, add the garlic and ginger, and sauté until the onions are soft and turning golden.

Add half the meat and mix well, then increase the heat to maximum and add the remaining meat and stir well again. Add the biryani curry powder, yogurt and salt, and sauté for 2 minutes.

Add the water and give it a good stir, cover with the lid and let it simmer on a low heat until the meat is cooked and there is a little bit of gravy left. If the curry dries out, add a little hot water to keep it moist and with some gravy (about 200ml/7 fl oz) left in the pan. Taste for salt and take the pan off the heat.

Put the cashew nuts and raisins into a dry frying pan (skillet) over a low heat and dry-roast until the nuts are golden. Set aside.

'Dumb' the biryani
Preheat the oven to 150°C (300°F/Gas Mark 2).

Take a heavy-bottomed casserole dish (with lid) and grease the bottom with ghee. Arrange a layer of rice in the bottom and put a drop or two of the rosewater and saffron water and 2 saffron strands on the rice. Arrange some chicken pieces and a little sauce evenly on top of the rice. Repeat until you end up with a final layer of rice. Pour a little sauce and the remaining saffron water evenly over the top.

Cover the top of the dish with a clean damp cloth and close tightly with the lid. Bake for about 30 minutes, or cook gently on a griddle, without direct heat being applied to the pan.

Take it off the heat, spread on a serving plate and garnish with roasted cashews and raisins, and serve.

Variation: Mutton Biryani
Follow the recipe above, using mutton instead of chicken, making sure the meat is cooked through. About 5 minutes before you take the mutton off the heat, add five torn mint leaves. Then, when it is time to remove it from the heat, add the juice of half a lime and mix it well.

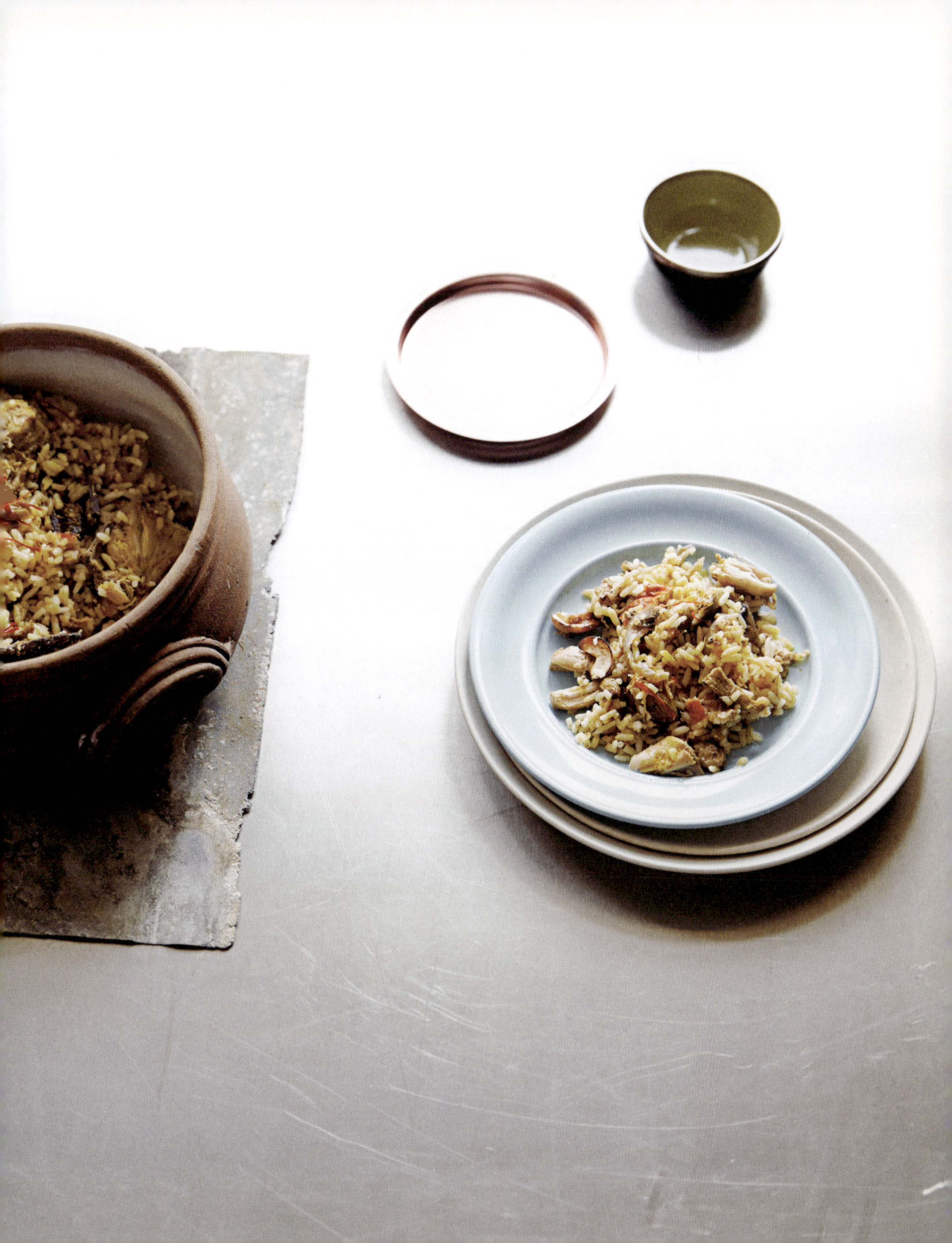

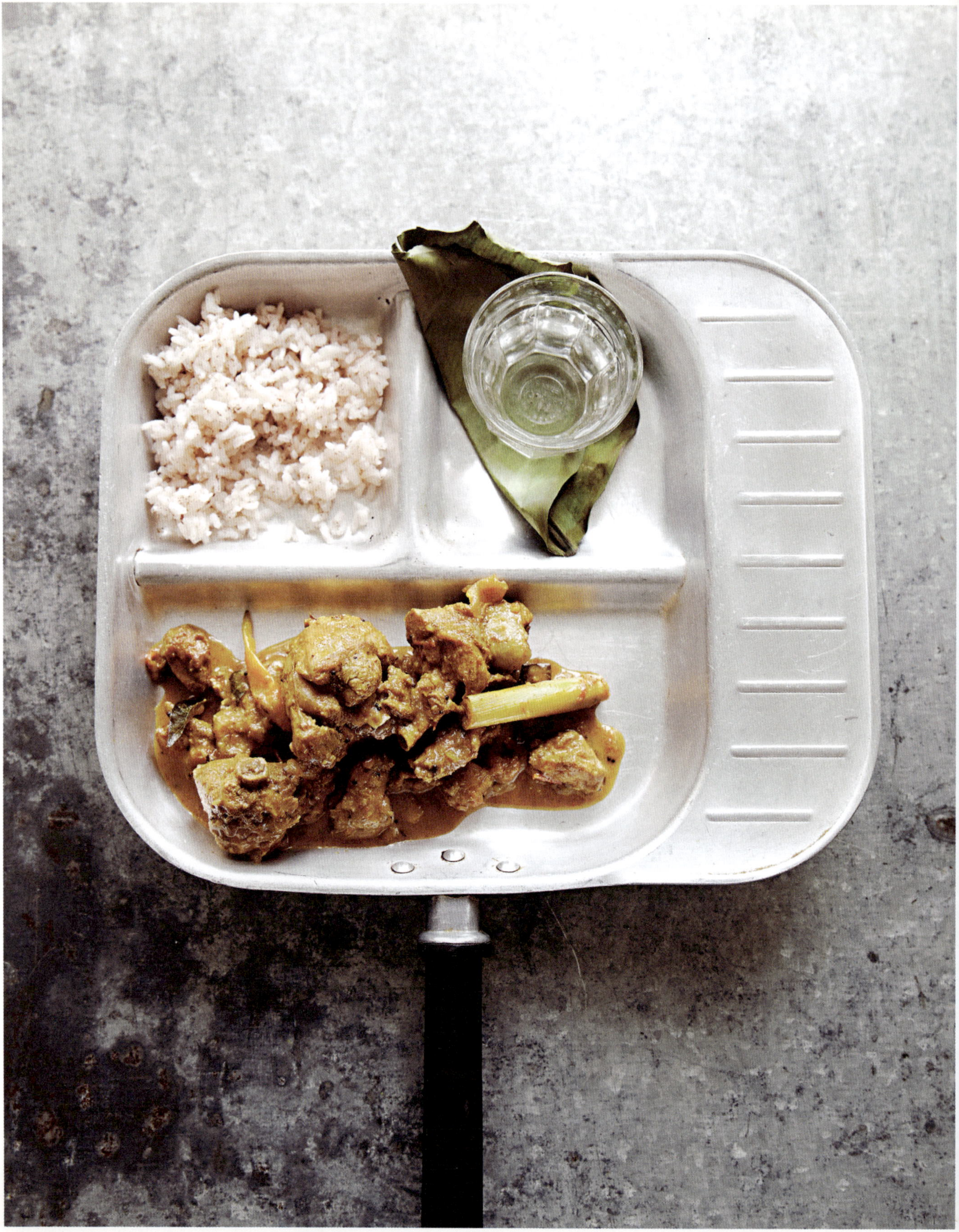

1kg (2lbs 4oz)
  whole chicken
3 tbsp oil
2.5cm (1-inch)
  cinnamon stick,
  broken into two
1 tsp cumin seeds
½ tsp mustard seeds
½ tsp fenugreek seeds
10 fresh curry leaves
2 x 2.5cm (1-inch)
  pieces of rampe
  (pandan) leaf
3 cloves
4 cardamom pods,
  crushed
1 large onion,
  finely chopped
5cm (2-inch) piece of
  ginger, peeled and
  finely chopped
1 tomato, finely chopped
150ml (5 fl oz/scant
  ⅔ cup) water
100ml (3½ fl oz/
  7 tbsp) coconut milk
juice of ½ lime
salt

For the marinade
1 tbsp chilli powder
1 tbsp Thuna Paha
  (curry powder on p17)
2 tsp ground cumin
1 tsp ground coriander
1 tsp ground turmeric
1 tsp salt
juice of ½ lime

Spicy chicken curry
Everyone loves chicken curry, and this dish will convert even those who have never tried Sri Lankan food before. It's spicy, warming, fragrant, hot and soothing all at once – the perfect meal.

Wash the chicken well and remove the skin Joint the chicken into breasts, thighs, legs and wings. Then cut these into 2.5cm (1-inch) pieces, cutting through the bone so many of the chunks of meat are on the bone. Wash the pieces once.

Place the meat in a bowl and add all the ingredients for the marinade. Mix it all together by hand, rubbing it into the chicken, and leave to marinate for 15 minutes.

Heat the oil in a medium saucepan over a low heat. Add the cinnamon, cumin seeds, mustard seeds, fenugreek seeds, curry leaves, rampe leaf, cloves and cardamom. Stir-fry for 2 minutes or so, making sure it doesn't burn.

Add the onions and sauté until they are soft and turning golden. Add the ginger and chopped tomatoes and sauté until soft.

Tip the chicken pieces and marinade into the pan and mix together well. Cover with the lid and cook for about 15 minutes on a low to medium heat, stirring every now and then, until the meat is brown.

Add the water, give it a stir, cover the pan and cook for 10 minutes. Pour in the coconut milk and cook for a further 10 minutes, uncovered, until the curry thickens and the oil begins to separate. Remove from the heat. Taste for lime and salt before serving.

Serves 4

KUKUL MAS MIRISATA

SPICY BAKED CHICKEN

The method here couldn't be simpler: whizz together all the ingredients, marinate the chicken, then bake. It's ideal for a midweek dinner, served with a punchy pickle and plain rice. Ovens are actually a relatively recent addition to Sri Lankan homes. All cooking used to be done over heat, so this is a fairly new idea – a Westernisation of a traditional dish.

Serves 4

Remove the skin from the chicken thighs, wash them well and put them in a shallow ovenproof dish.

Put all the other ingredients in a food processor and blitz until you have a very coarse paste. If there is not enough liquid, you can add a little water.

Add the paste in with the chicken, mixing it together by hand, and leave to marinate for 30 minutes.

Preheat the oven to 180°C (350°F/Gas Mark 4). Cover the dish with perforated foil and bake for 60 minutes. Serve hot.

8 chicken thighs
½ medium onion, cut into quarters
5 garlic cloves
1.5cm (½-inch) piece of ginger, peeled
4 tbsp tomato sauce (ketchup)
1 tbsp chilli powder
2 bay leaves
½ tbsp ground cumin
½ tsp ground coriander
1 tsp ground turmeric
5 black peppercorns
2 tbsp soy sauce
1 tbsp sugar (white or brown)
6 tbsp oil
juice of ½ lime
1 tsp salt

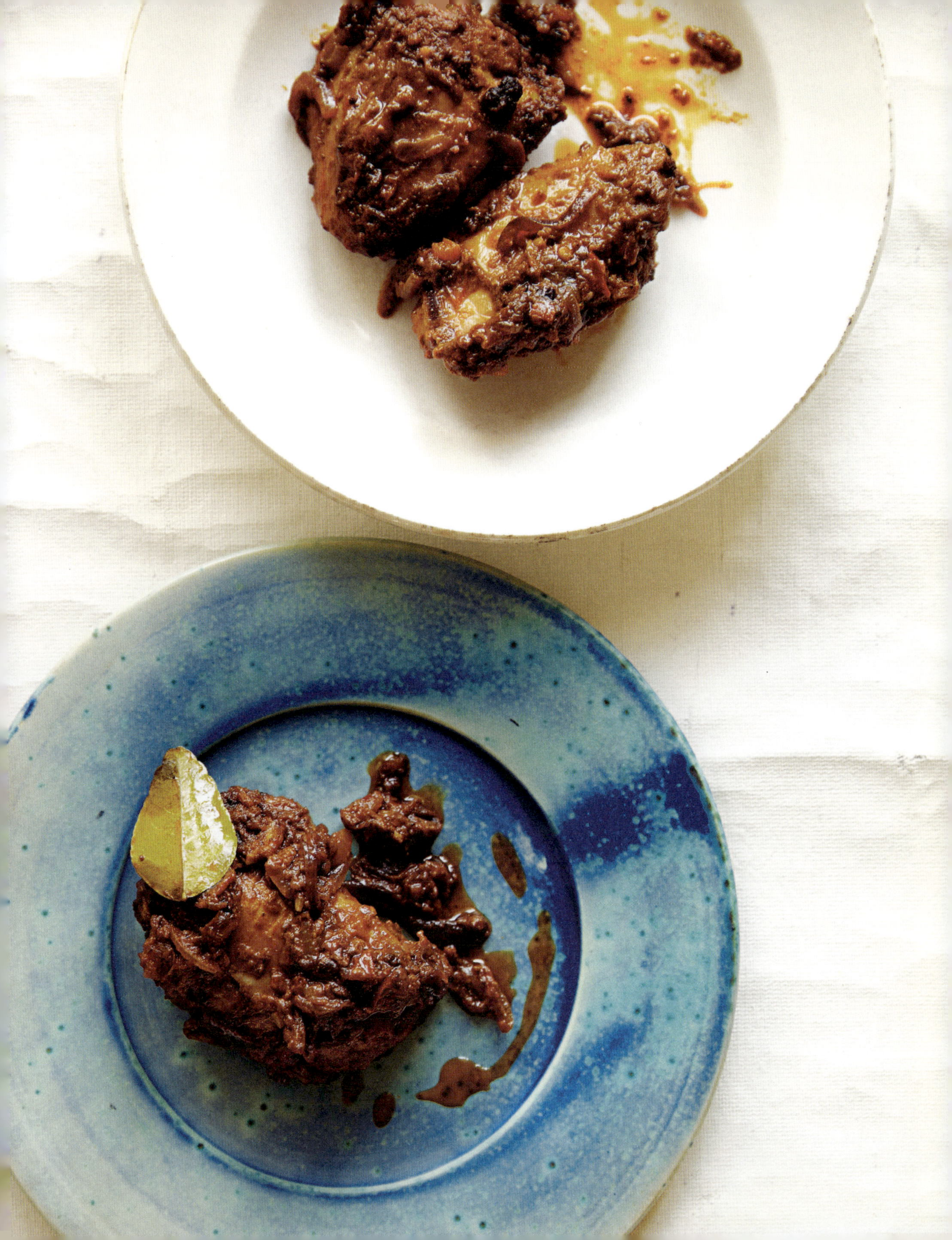

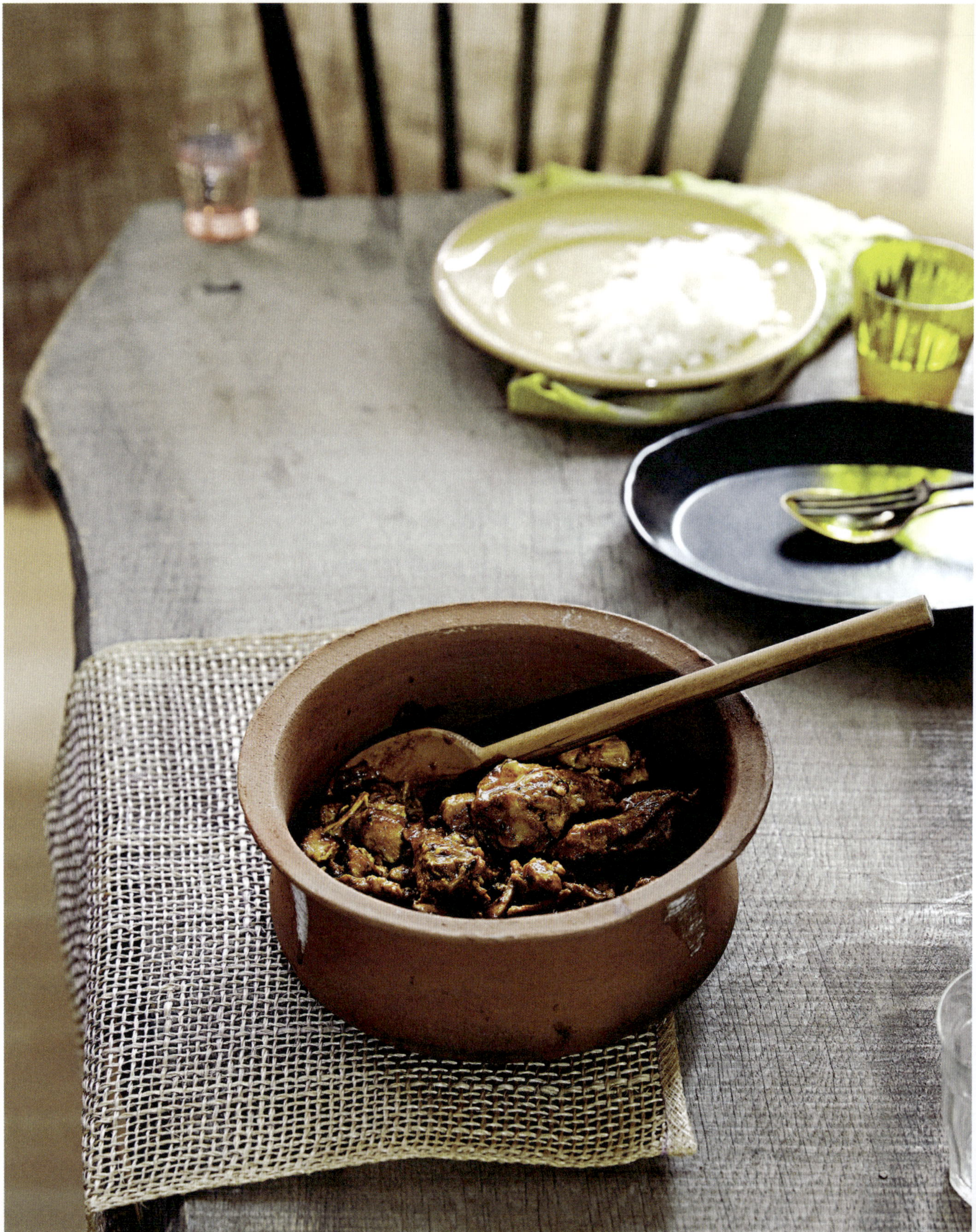

1kg (2lbs 4oz) whole chicken
2 tbsp oil
½ tsp mustard seeds
½ tsp fennel seeds
½ tsp cumin seeds
8 fresh curry leaves
½ tsp fenugreek seeds
2 green chillies, slit lengthways with seeds in
1 medium onion, finely chopped
6 garlic cloves, finely chopped
5cm (2-inch) piece of ginger, peeled and finely chopped
½ tsp ground turmeric
1 tsp ground cumin
1 tsp ground coriander
1 tbsp Thool (curry powder on p16)
¾ tsp salt
300ml (10½ fl oz/ 1¼ cups) water
100ml (3½ fl oz/ 7 tbsp) coconut milk
juice of ½ lime

Tamil chicken curry
In Sri Lanka, chicken is the most widely eaten meat and is always cooked on the bone. Try it – you'll find it adds a lot more flavour to the finished dish.

KOLI KARI

Wash the chicken well and remove the skin Joint the chicken into breasts, thighs, legs and wings. Then cut these into 2.5cm (1-inch) pieces, cutting through the bone so many of the chunks of meat are on the bone. Wash the pieces once.

Heat the oil in a medium, lidded saucepan over a low heat, then add the mustard seeds. Let them cook for a few seconds until they begin to pop, then add the fennel seeds and cumin seeds and give it a stir or two. Add the curry leaves and fenugreek seeds and stir-fry for a minute. Next, add the green chillies and give it another stir, then the onions and stir-fry for 30 seconds. Finally, add the garlic and ginger and sauté until the onions are soft and turning golden.

Add the turmeric and give it a quick stir, then add half the chicken and mix well. Increase the heat, add the rest of the meat and give it a good stir. Cover with the lid and cook for 6–7 minutes, stirring occasionally.

When the moisture starts to come out of the meat, reduce the heat, add the other spice powders, the salt and the water and give it a good stir. Cover and cook for about 20 minutes, stirring once or twice.

Pour in the coconut milk and mix well, adding a little water if you would like more sauce, then cook for another 10 minutes with the lid on. Taste for salt, remove from the heat and let it rest for a minute or so. Squeeze in the lime juice, give it a good stir. Taste for lime and salt, then rest for another 3 minutes or so before serving.

Serves 4

KOLI EERAL

Stir-fried chicken livers
None of the chicken is wasted in Sri Lankan cooking (in the south, the birds are usually cooked with the skin on too). Liver is the most popular offal, although some Muslim recipes use tripe from goats too.

400g (14oz) chicken livers
3 tbsp oil
2.5cm (1-inch) cinnamon stick, broken into two
4 cloves
4 cardamom pods, crushed
8 fresh curry leaves
2 green chillies, slit lengthways with seeds in
1 medium red onion, finely sliced
2 garlic cloves, finely chopped
1 tsp ground turmeric
½ tsp salt
2 tsp ground cumin
½ tsp chilli powder
100ml (3½ fl oz/ 7 tbsp) water
juice of ½ lime

Serves 4

Wash the livers well, cut them into 2.5cm (1-inch) chunks and set aside.

Heat the oil in a medium, lidded frying pan (skillet) over a low heat. Add the cinnamon, cloves and cardamom pods and stir-fry for 2 minutes. Next, add the curry leaves and green chillies and give it a stir or two. Add the onion and give it a stir, then add the garlic and sauté until the onions are soft and turning golden.

Add the turmeric and give it a quick stir, then tip in the liver and mix well. Increase the heat, cover with the lid and cook for 2–3 minutes. Give it another stir and cook for another 2–3 minutes.

Sprinkle in the salt, cumin and chilli powder and mix well. Pour the water in around the edge of the pan to stop it burning. Cover and cook for another 5 minutes, then take the pan off the heat.

Squeeze the lime juice in, mix well and serve.

Variation: Stir-fried lamb's liver
Use lamb's liver instead of chicken livers, and cook for 3–4 minutes longer.

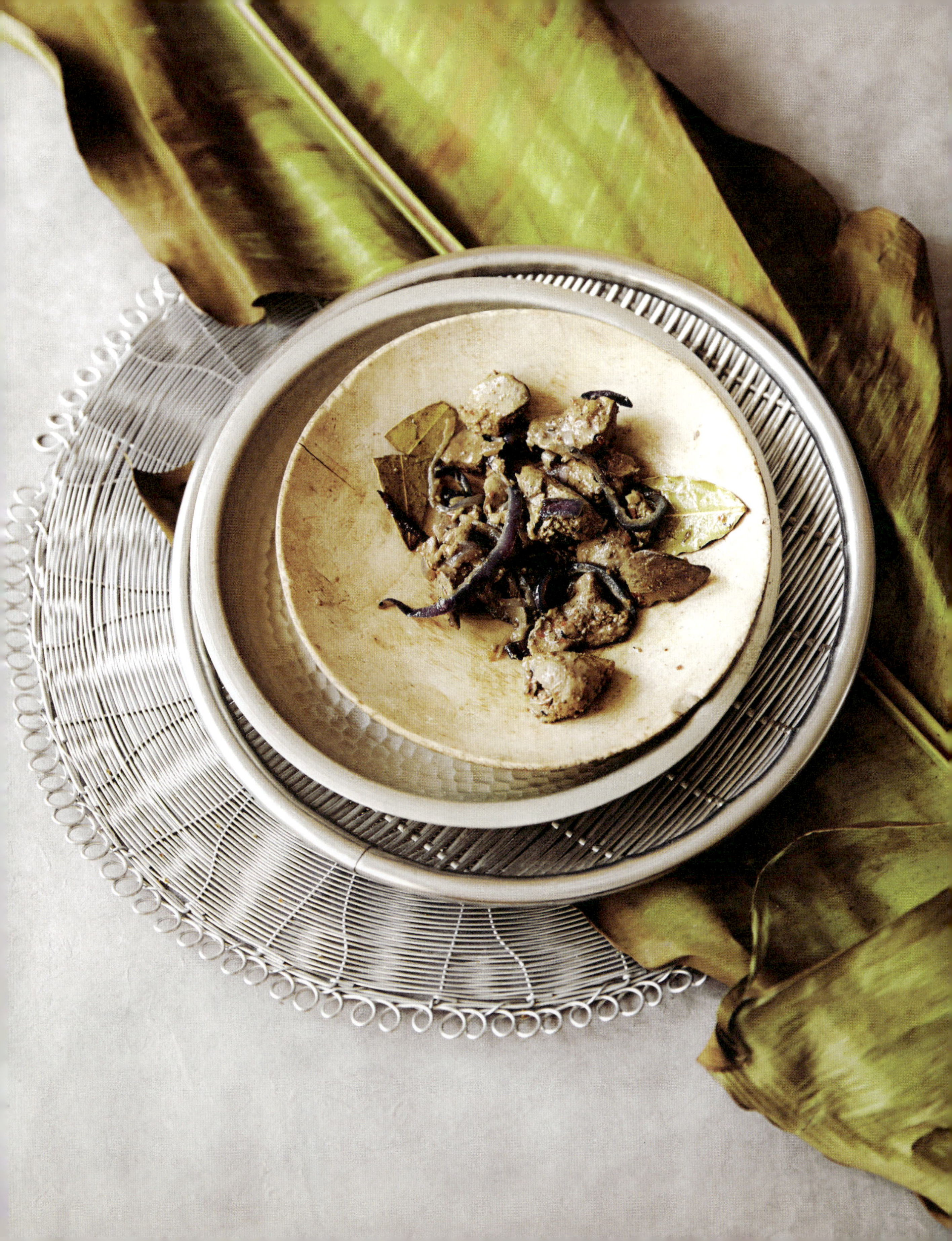

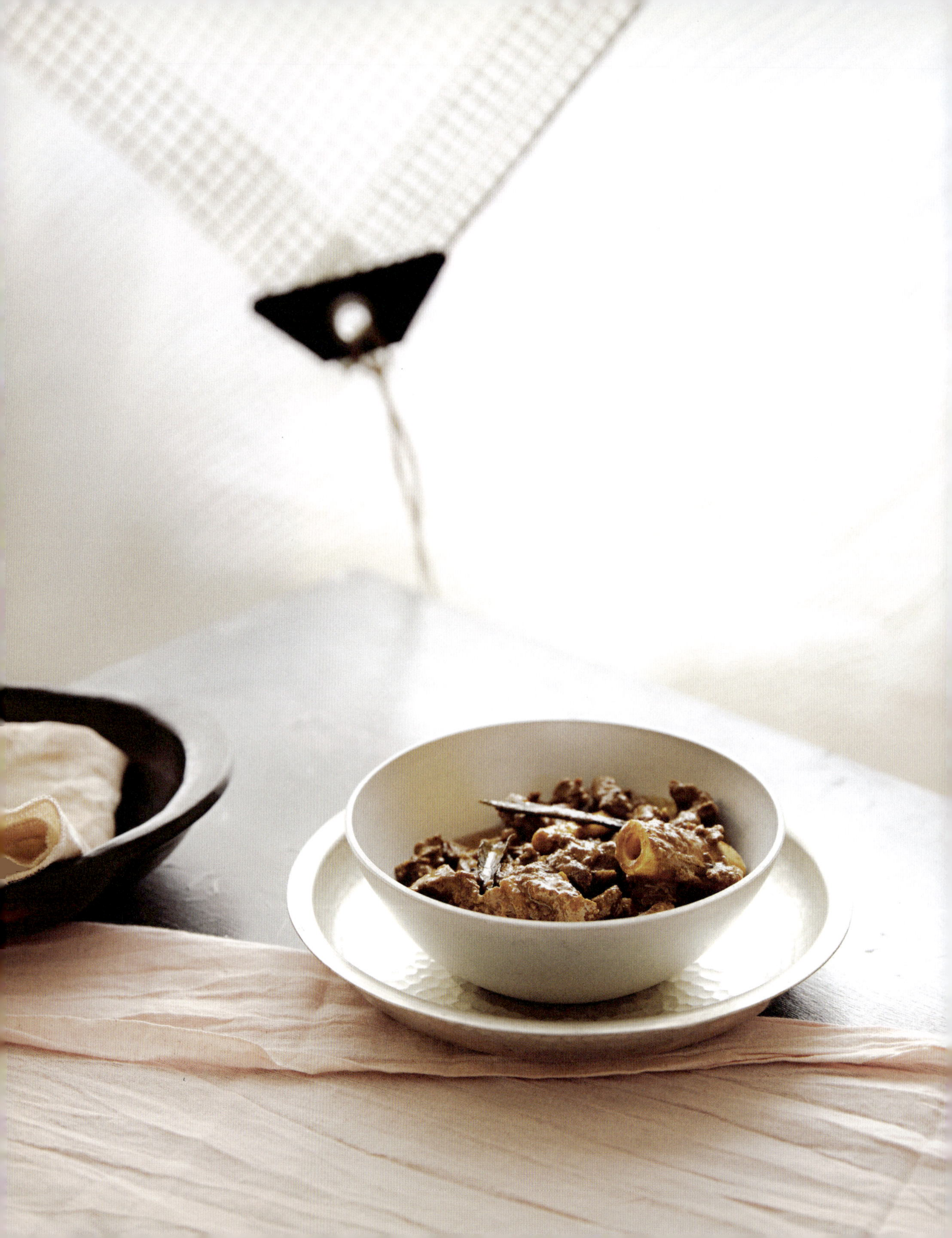

ELUMAS

Sinhalese lamb curry

'Elumas' means goat meat in Sinhalese, and in Sri Lanka we actually use the term 'mutton' to mean goat's meat. Goat (and indeed mutton) are becoming more popular and readily available in the UK, but this curry works equally well with lamb, cooked slow to tenderise and absorb all the spices.

Serves 4

600g (1lb 5oz) lamb
4 tbsp oil
½ tsp cumin seeds (optional)
½ tsp fenugreek seeds
1 tsp mustard seeds
2 x 2.5cm (1-inch) cinnamon sticks
3 cardamom pods
3 cloves
2 x 2.5cm (1-inch) pieces of rampe (pandan) leaf
10 fresh curry leaves
1 lemongrass stalk (optional)
2 green chillies, slit lengthways and deseeded
1 large onion, finely chopped
500ml (17 fl oz/generous 2 cups) water
200ml (7 fl oz/generous ¾ cup) coconut cream
½ tsp Bathapu Thuna Paha (curry powder on p17)
juice of ½ lime
salt

For the marinade
4 garlic cloves, finely chopped
5cm (2-inch) piece of ginger, peeled and finely chopped
1 tbsp Thuna Paha (curry powder on p17)
1 tbsp Bathapu Thuna Paha (curry powder on p17)
1 tbsp chilli powder
1 tsp ground turmeric
4 tbsp red wine vinegar
2 tsp salt

Wash the meat, cut it into 2.5cm (1-inch) chunks and put it in a large bowl. Add all the ingredients for the marinade and mix it all together by hand, rubbing it into the meat. Leave to marinate for 30 minutes.

Heat the oil in a large, lidded saucepan over a low heat. Add the cumin seeds (if using), fenugreek seeds, mustard seeds, cinnamon, cardamom pods, cloves, rampe leaf, curry leaves, lemongrass (if using), green chillies and onion, and sauté until the onions are soft and turning golden.

Add the marinated meat and mix well. Add the water (to cover the meat), and bring to the boil. Put the lid on and cook on a medium heat for about 45 minutes, until the water has evaporated and the meat is cooked through.

Add the coconut cream, mix well and simmer for another 10–15 minutes until the sauce is thick.

Remove from the heat and sprinkle in the curry powder and squeeze in the lime juice. Stir, taste for salt, and serve.

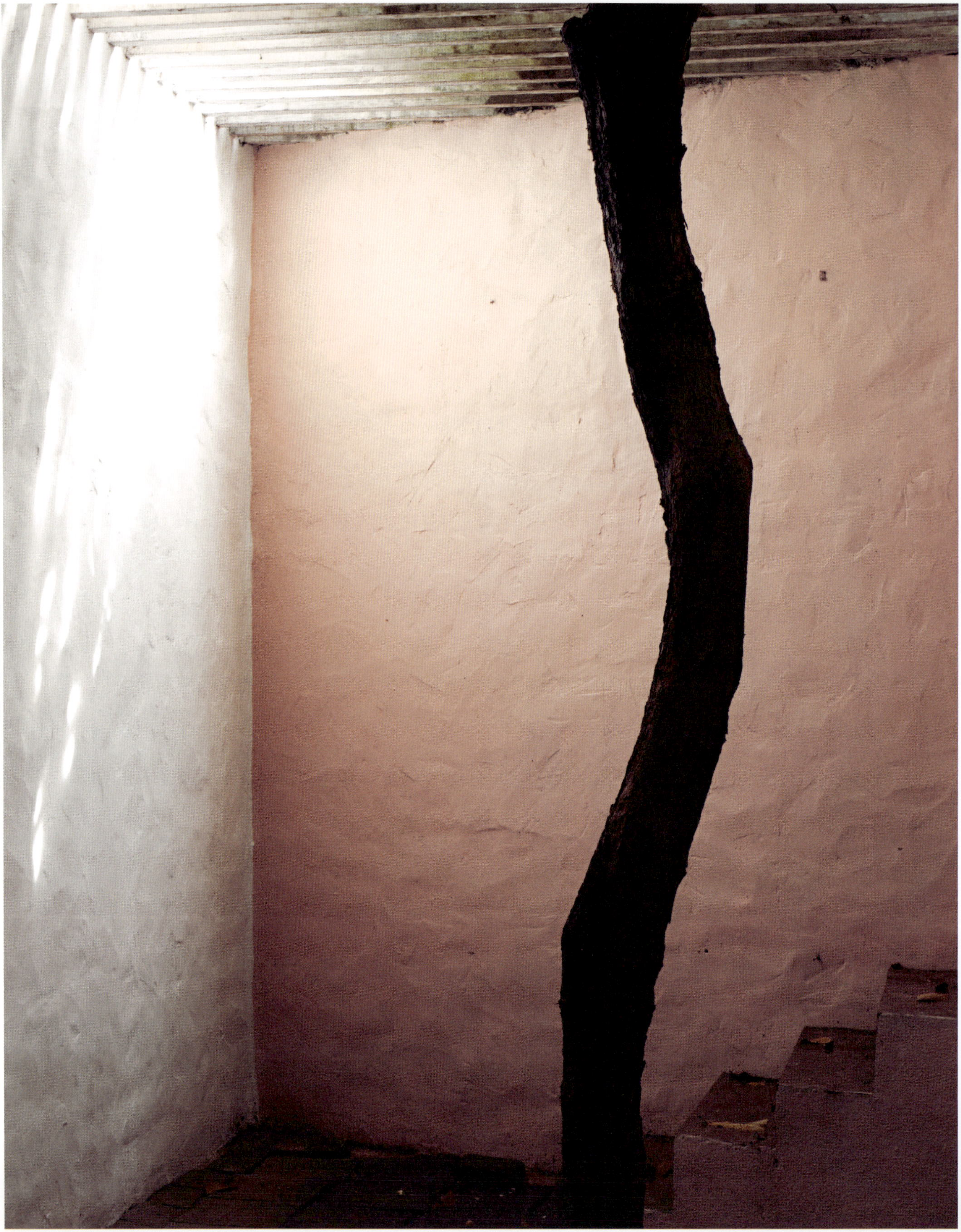

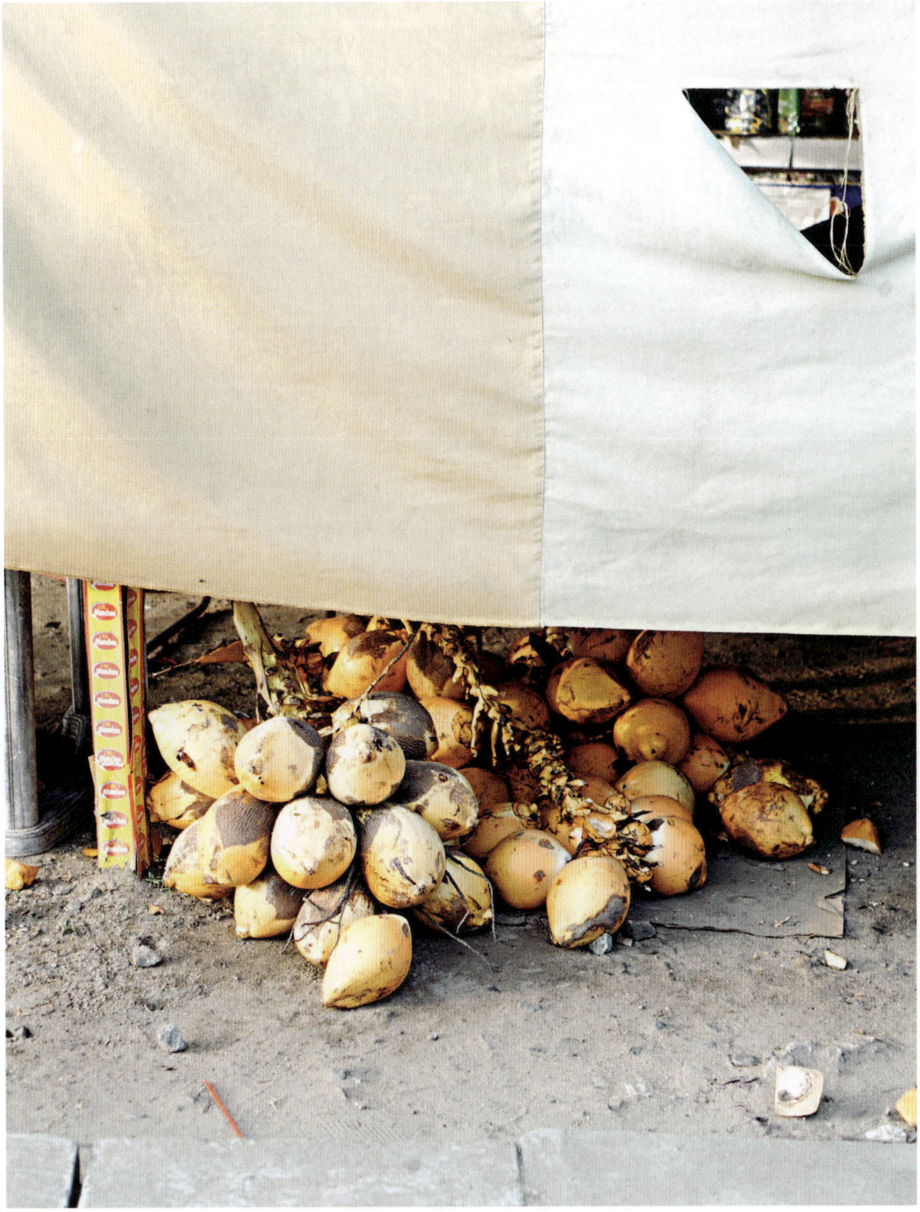

250g (9oz) lamb or mutton bones (about 5cm/2 inches long, with a little meat on them)
1 medium tomato, cut into quarters
3 cloves
4 cardamom pods, crushed
4 black peppercorns
4 garlic cloves,
8 fresh curry leaves
3 green chillies, slit lengthways with seeds in
½ medium onion, sliced
½ tsp ground turmeric
400ml (14 fl oz/ 1⅔ cups) water
½ tsp salt
100ml (3½ fl oz/ 7 tbsp) coconut milk
juice of ½ lime

Bone broth

The cooking of necessity brings the best out of humble ingredients and can yield very special results. What could be more simple than a bone broth? Here bones are simmered gently with spices and coconut milk to create a bowlful of nourishing goodness. It's great on its own, even better served with steamed rice or String Hoppers (p34).

Wash the bones well and put them in a medium, lidded saucepan. Add all the ingredients except the coconut milk and lime juice. Bring to the boil, then reduce the heat, half-cover the pan with the lid and simmer for 35–40 minutes.

When the water is reduced almost by half, increase the heat, add the coconut milk and bring to the boil. Reduce the heat and simmer for a further 5 minutes until you have a thin broth.

Taste for salt and remove from the heat. Add the lime juice, to taste, mix well and serve.

Serves 4

AATTUKAL SOTHI

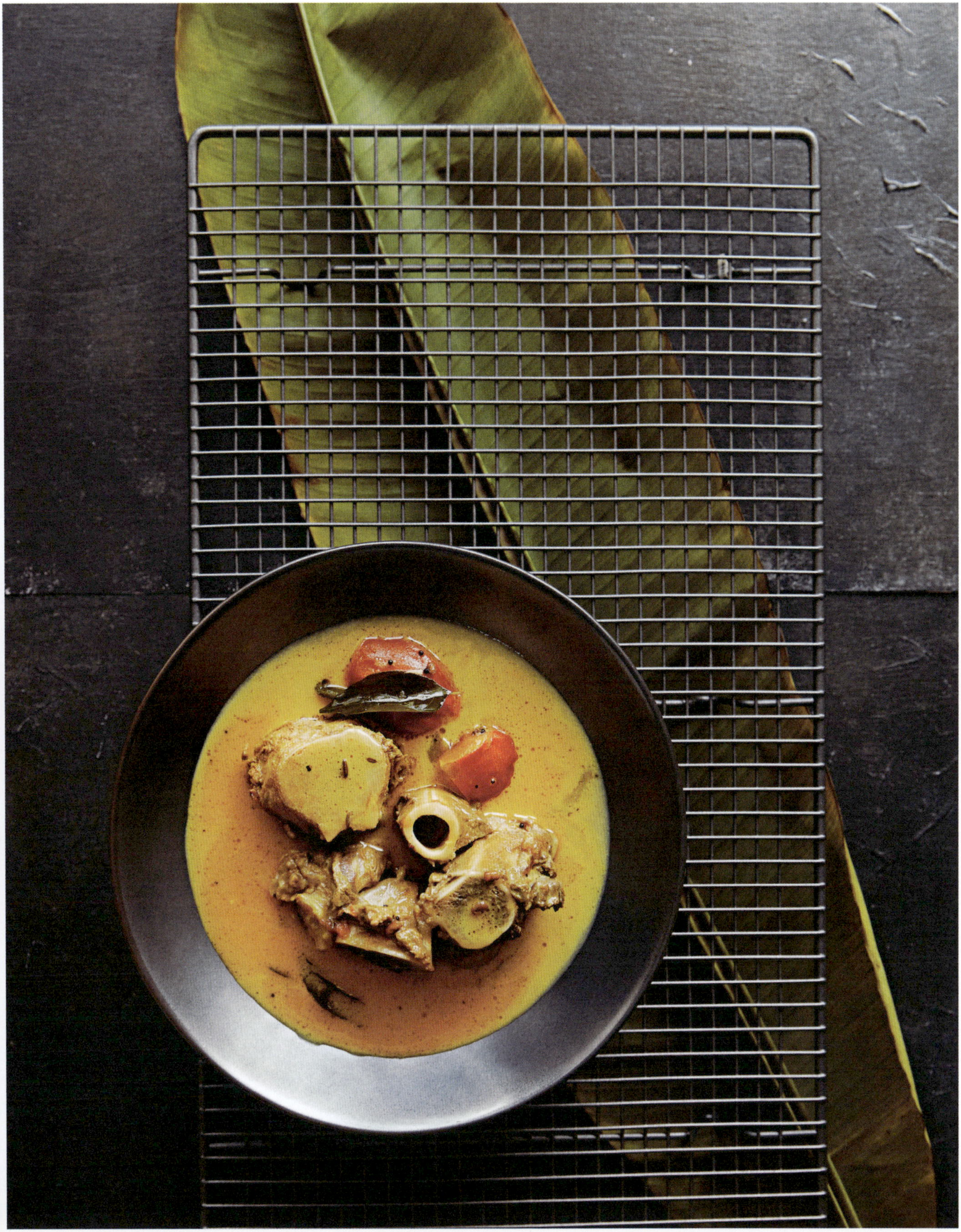

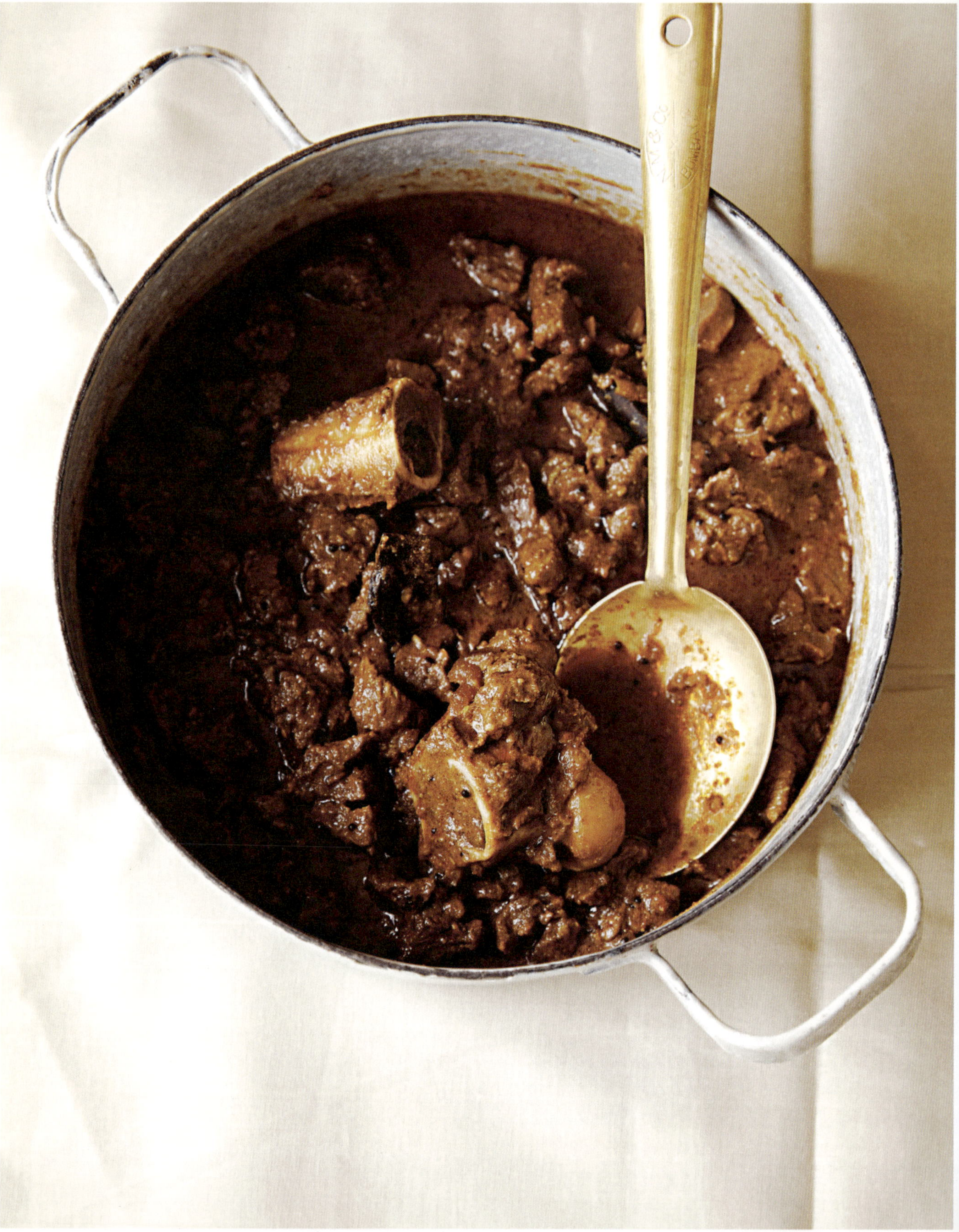

AATTURATCHI KARI

Tamil mutton curry

Aadu means 'goat' in Tamil and gives its name to this lusciously flavourful curry. Here we've made it with mutton, which is a more than suitable substitute, but it would be delicious with lamb or beef, although that meat is only really eaten by the Christian or Muslim communities in Sri Lanka.

- 600g (1lb 5oz) boneless mutton or lamb
- 2 marrow bones
- 2 tbsp oil
- 2 x 2.5cm (1-inch) cinnamon sticks
- 4 cloves
- 4 cardamom pods, crushed
- 8 fresh curry leaves
- ¼ tsp fennel seeds
- ½ tsp cumin seeds
- 2 green chillies, slit lengthways with seeds in
- 1 medium onion, medium diced
- 6 garlic cloves, cut into quarters
- 5cm (2-inch) piece of ginger, finely chopped
- ½ tsp ground turmeric
- 1 tsp ground cumin
- 1 tsp ground coriander
- 1 tbsp Thool (curry powder on p16)
- ¾ tsp salt
- 300ml (10½ fl oz/ 1¼ cups) water
- 100ml (3½ fl oz/ 7 tbsp) coconut milk
- juice of ½ lime

Wash the mutton, cut it into 2.5cm (1-inch) chunks and set aside in a large bowl with the marrow bones.

Heat the oil in a medium, lidded saucepan over a low heat. Add the cinnamon sticks, cloves and cardamom pods and stir-fry for about a minute. Add the curry leaves, fennel seeds and cumin seeds, one by one, stirring as you go. It is important not to burn the spices.

Next, add the green chillies and give it another stir, then the onions and stir-fry for 30 seconds. Finally, add the garlic and ginger and sauté until the onions are soft and turning golden.

Add the turmeric and give it a quick stir, then add half the meat and mix well. Increase the heat, add the rest of the meat and give it a good stir. Cover with the lid and cook for 6–7 minutes, stirring occasionally.

When the moisture starts to come out of the meat, reduce the heat, add the other spice powders, the salt and the water and give it a good stir. Cover and cook for about 30 minutes, stirring every 10 minutes or so.

Pour in the coconut milk and mix well, adding a little water if you would like more sauce, then cook for another 15 minutes with the lid on. Taste for salt, remove from the heat and let it rest for a minute or so. Squeeze in the lime juice, give it a good stir. Taste for lime and salt, then rest for another 3 minutes or so before serving.

Serves 4

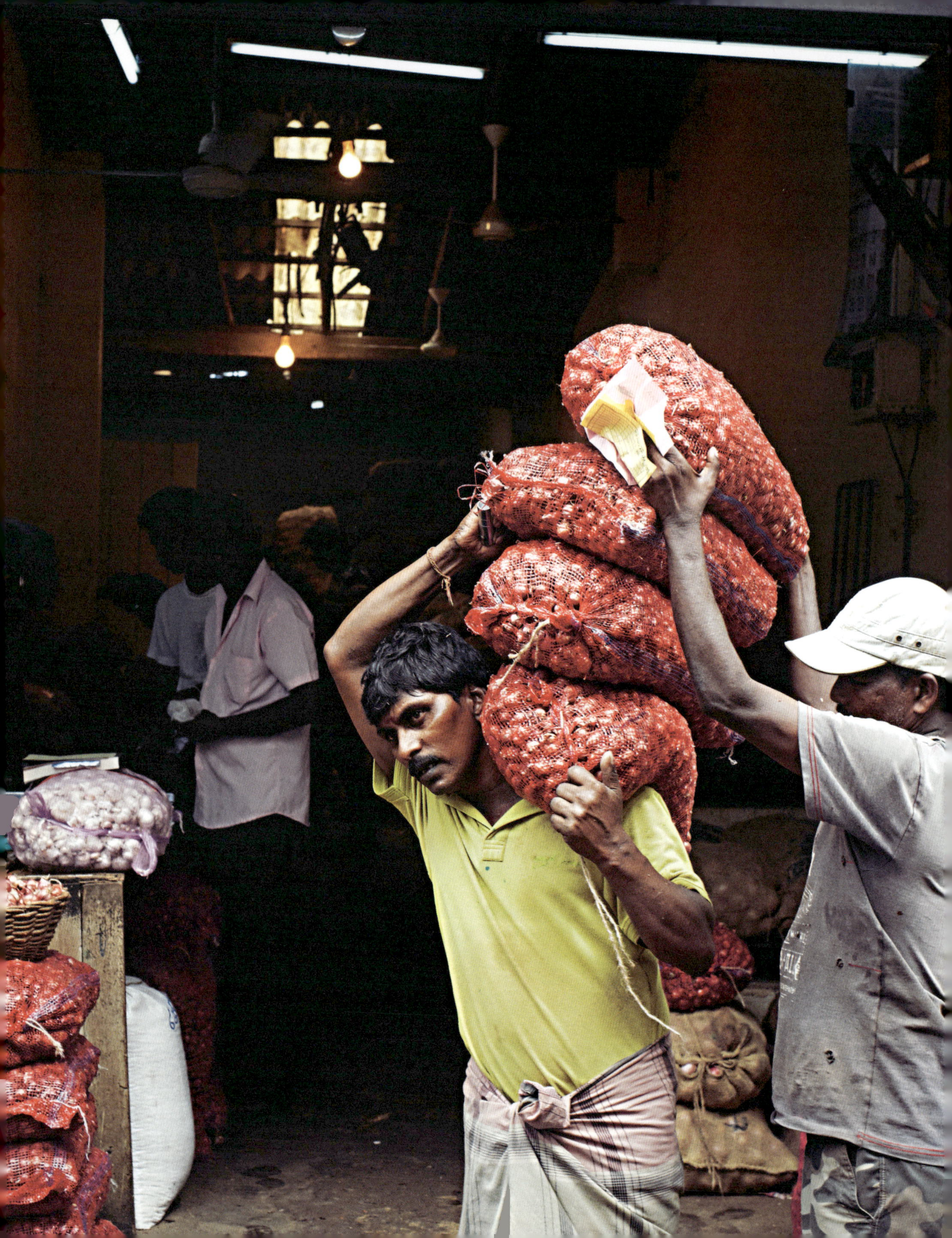

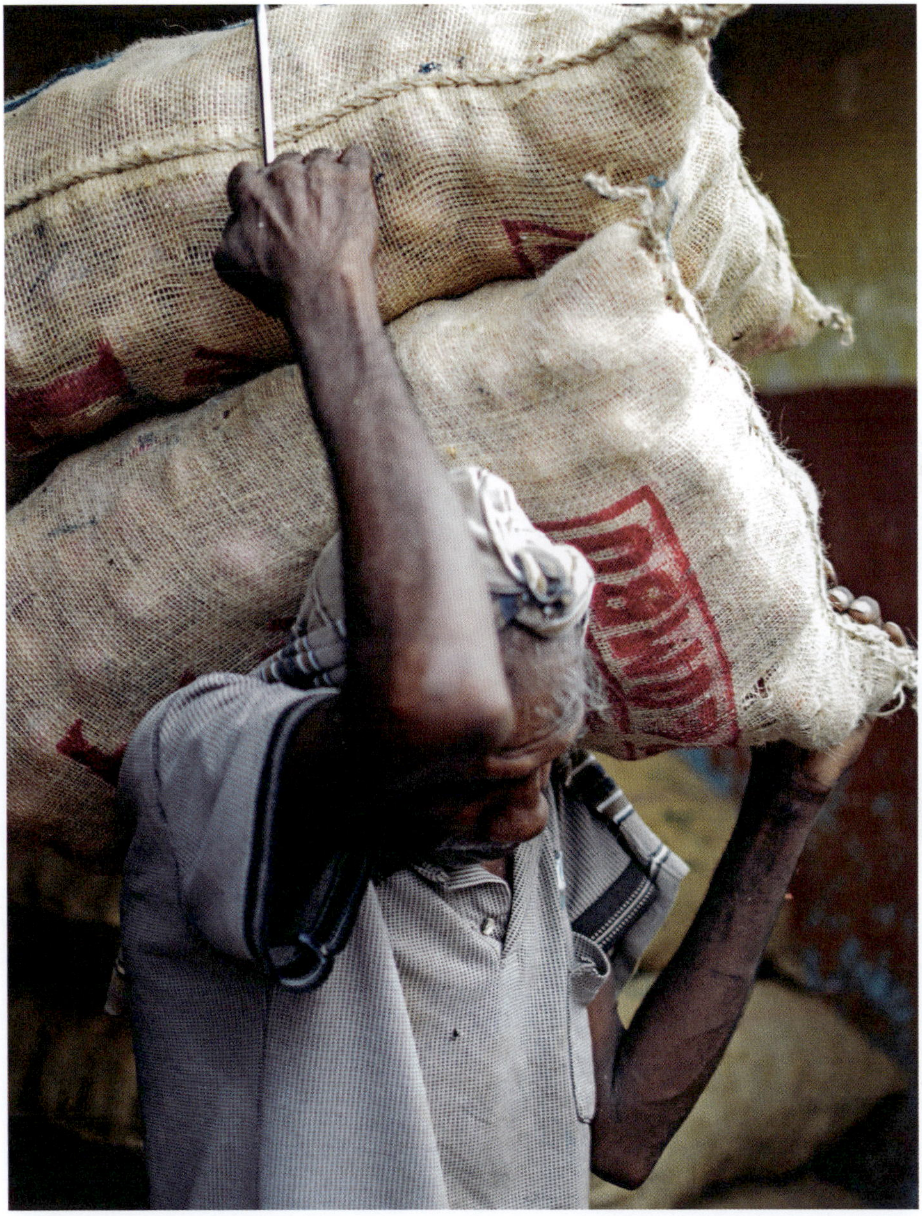

KAATU PANDY RATCHI KARI

Wild boar curry

Wild boar is a delicacy in Sri Lanka and only cooked once in a while due to availability. The animals are found in number around the jungles, tea plantations and farmlands of the island, where they root for vegetables. However, pork as an alternative also makes an excellent curry.

Serves 4

500g (1lb 2oz) boneless wild boar or pork
2 tsp ground turmeric
1 tbsp Thool (curry powder on p16)
¾ tsp salt
2 tbsp oil
2 x 2.5cm (1-inch) cinnamon sticks
4 cardamom pods, crushed
1 medium onion, medium diced
8 fresh curry leaves
½ tsp fenugreek seeds
¼ tsp fennel seeds
6 garlic cloves, cut into quarters
2 green chillies, slit lengthways with seeds in
5cm (2-inch) piece of ginger, peeled and finely chopped
200ml (7 fl oz/generous ¾ cup) tamarind water
300ml (10½ fl oz/ 1¼ cups) water

Wash the meat, cut it into 2.5cm (1-inch) chunks and put it in a large bowl. Sprinkle the turmeric over the meat and mix well with your hands to coat the meat. Repeat with the curry powder and the salt, mixing well both times. Leave to marinate for about 20 minutes.

Heat the oil in a medium, lidded saucepan over a low heat. Add the cinnamon sticks and cardamom pods and stir-fry for about a minute. Add the onion and sauté for about 20 seconds. Add the curry leaves and give it a stir or two, then add all the seeds, the garlic, green chillies and ginger, and sauté until the onions are soft and turning golden.

Increase the heat, tip in the meat and stir well to coat it with the oil and the other ingredients in the pan. Stir-fry for 4–5 minutes, cover with the lid and cook on a medium heat for 15 minutes until brown.

Add the tamarind water and bring it to the boil, then add the water, mix well and bring it to the boil again. Reduce the heat, cover and cook until the meat is tender, stirring occasionally. It should take another 30–40 minutes.

Taste for salt, remove from the heat and let it rest for at least 5 minutes before serving.

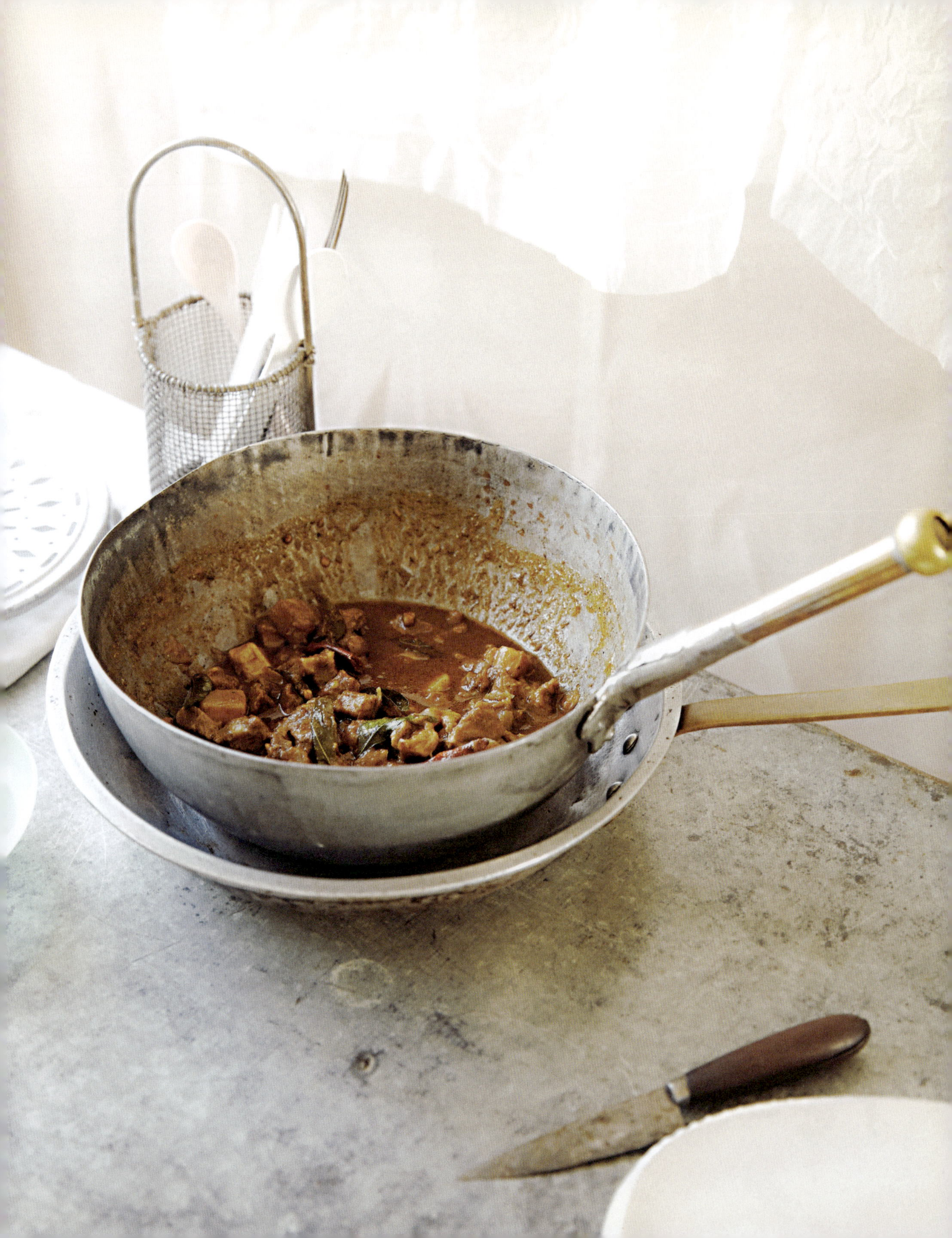

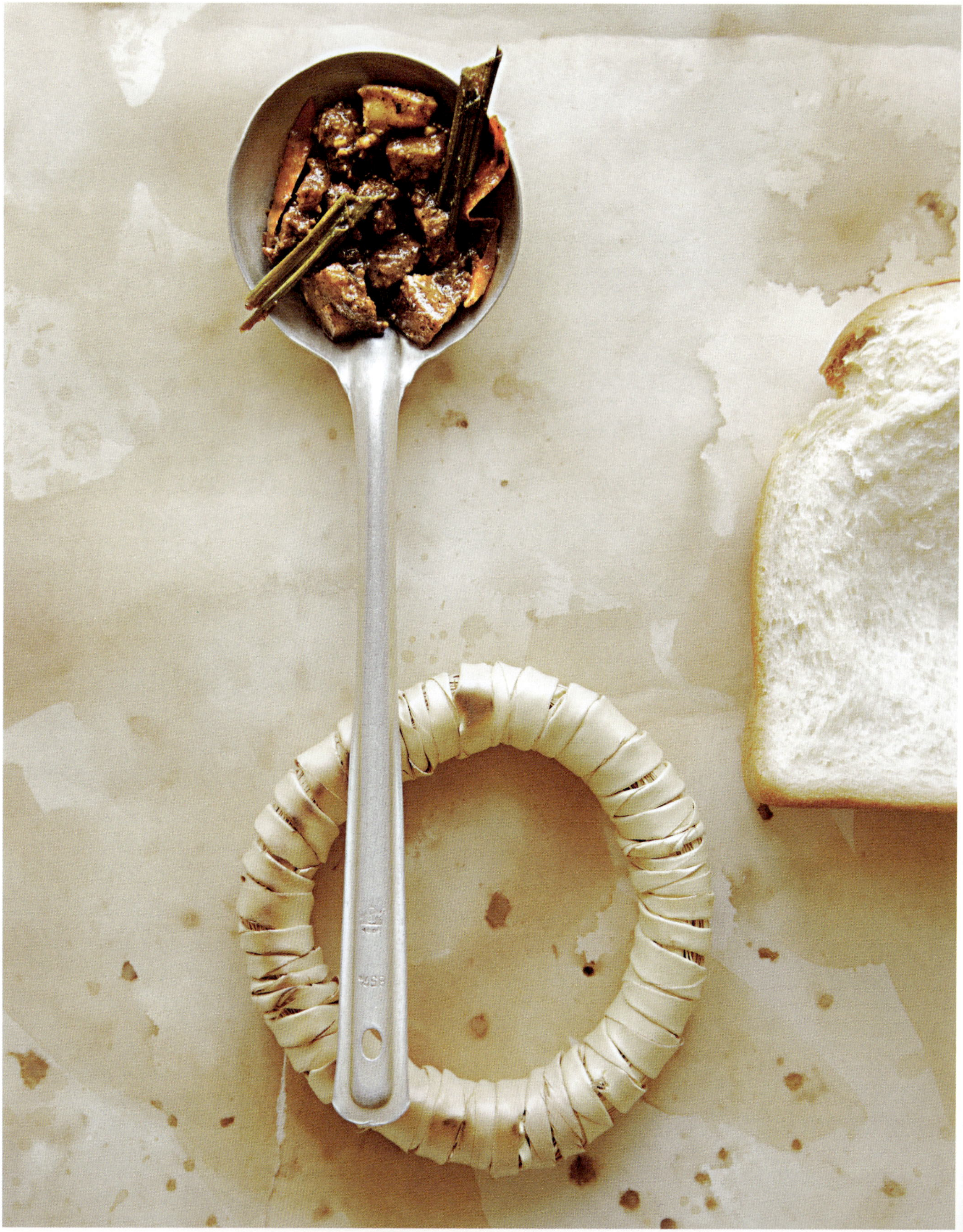

- 600g (1lb 5oz) boneless pork
- 2 tbsp oil
- 2 x 2.5cm (1-inch) cinnamon sticks
- 3 cloves
- 2 x 2.5cm (1-inch) pieces of rampe (pandan) leaf
- 1 lemongrass stalk (optional)
- 1 green chilli, slit lengthways with seeds in
- 5cm (2-inch) piece of ginger, peeled and finely chopped
- 6 garlic cloves, finely chopped
- 1 medium onion, finely chopped
- 1 tsp ground turmeric
- 500ml (17 fl oz/generous 2 cups) water
- ½ tsp Bathapu Thuna Paha (curry powder on p17)

For the marinade
- 2 tbsp ground black pepper
- 2 tbsp Bathapu Thuna Paha (curry powder on p17)
- 1 tsp ground cardamom
- ½ tsp ground cinnamon
- 100ml (3½ fl oz/7 tbsp) red wine vinegar
- 100ml (3½ fl oz/7 tbsp) tamarind water
- 1 tsp salt
- ½ tsp sugar (white or brown)

Dark pork 'padre' curry
This dish was introduced by the Portuguese during their time (1505-1658) in Ceylon, as it was then known. The word 'padre' means priest, and this was a favourite of the Portuguese Catholic clergymen who followed their army to the island.

Wash the pork well, cut it into 2.5cm (1-inch) chunks and place in a large bowl. Add all the ingredients for the marinade and mix it all together well. Leave to marinate for at least 6 hours, ideally overnight in a fridge.

Heat the oil in a large, lidded saucepan over a low heat. Add the cinnamon sticks, cloves, rampe leaf and lemongrass (if using), and stir-fry for a minute or so. Next, add the green chillies, ginger and garlic and give it a stir or two. Finally, add the onions and sauté until they are soft and turning golden.

Add the turmeric and give it a quick stir, then tip in the pork and its marinade and mix well. Increase the heat.

Pour in the water (to cover the meat by about 5cm/2 inches) and bring it to the boil. Reduce the heat to medium, cover with the lid and cook for 40–45 minutes until the meat is soft and tender. Make sure there is always enough water in the pan to keep the meat well covered. If it dries out, just add some water and give it a stir.

When the meat is cooked, drain the liquid out into a bowl and fry the cooked meat with the lid on for 15 minutes until it turns brown. There is no need to add oil as there is fat in the meat.

Pour the liquid back into the pan and simmer for about 5 minutes until the curry has thickened. Sprinkle with the curry powder, stir and remove from the heat. Let it rest for 5 minutes, then taste for salt and serve.

Serves 4

URU MAS

RASAM

Spiced drink

In Ayurveda, rasam is prescribed to aid digestion – but it's far too good to be considered just medicine. On its own it makes a flavoursome drink to round off a meal, or it's sometimes served with rice. Here's a speedy and straightforward rasam recipe, as well as another more complex version made with Rasam Podi spice blend on p216.

3 tbsp corriander seeds
1 tsp cumin seeds
1 tsp black peppercorns
1 dried red chilli
2 garlic cloves
2 fresh curry leaves (optional)
100ml (3½ fl oz/7 tbsp) tamarind water
¼ tsp salt
300ml (10½ fl oz/ 1¼ cups) water
½ tomato, roughly chopped

In a pestle and mortar, pound the coriander and cumin seeds, peppercorns, chilli and garlic until crushed.

Put the mix into a small saucepan on a high heat. Add the curry leaves (if using), tamarind water, salt, water and tomato, and bring to the boil. When it reaches boiling point, remove from the heat. Serve hot.

Serves 4

RASAM PODI

Rasam powder spice blend

200g (7oz/3 cups) coriander seeds
2 tbsp chana dal (split chick peas)
1 tbsp toor dal (split pigeon peas, optional)
1 tsp cumin seeds
4 fresh curry leaves (optional)
1 tbsp black peppercorns
3 dried red chillies

In a small dry frying pan (skillet) set over a low heat, dry-roast the coriander seeds until they turn golden. Tip into a dry bowl. Then, dry-roast the chana dal and toor dal (if using) until they turn golden, taking care not to burn them. Add them to the bowl.

Next, dry-roast the cumin seeds and curry leaves (if using) together and add to the bowl. Then, dry-roast the peppercorns separately, and finally the dried chillies.

Mix all the roasted ingredients together. When cool, grind them to a fine powder in a spice grinder. The powder will keep well in an airtight container for about 6 weeks. To make rasam with rasam podi, see p216.

Makes 300g

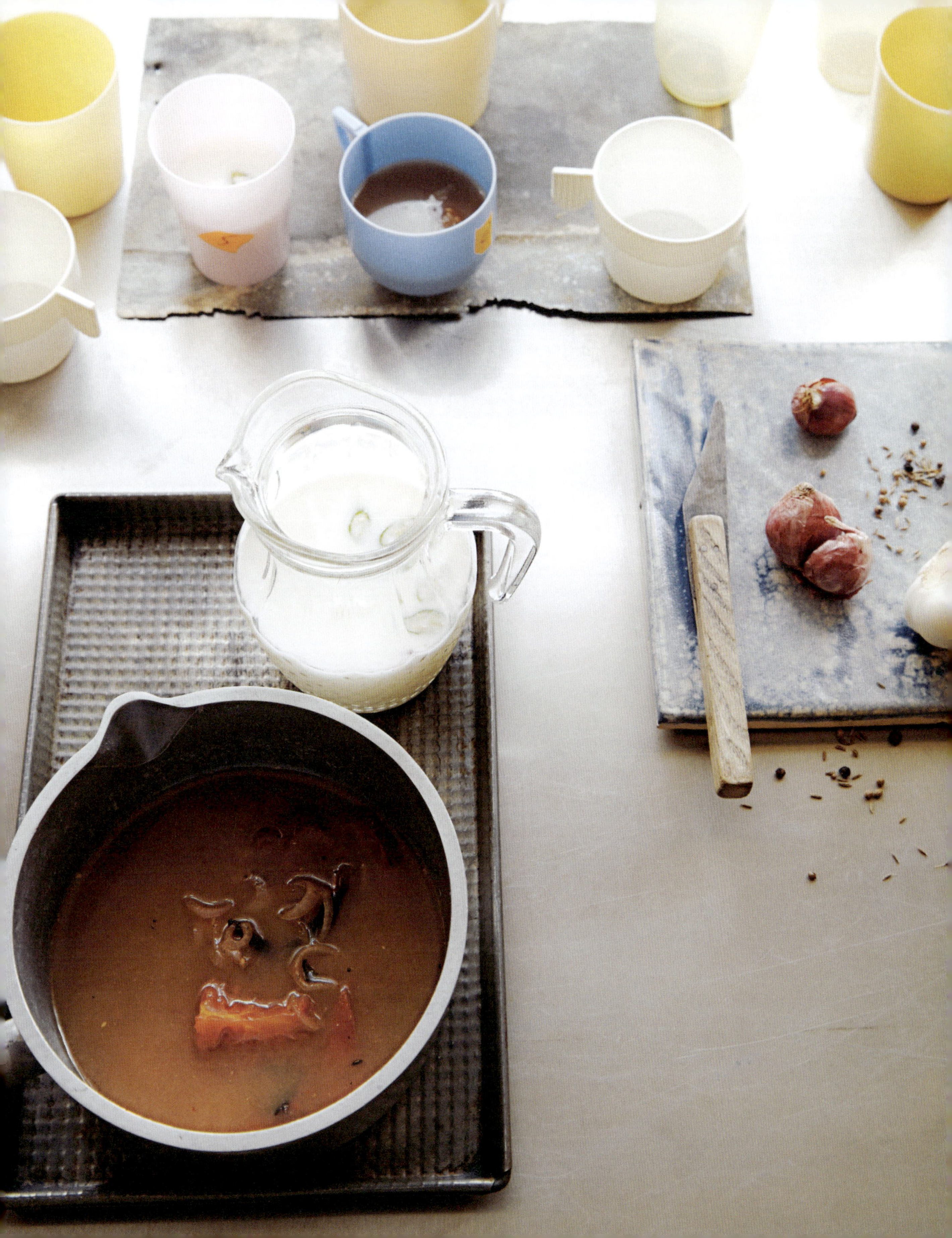

RASAM WITH RASAM PODI

2 tsp oil
4 fresh curry leaves (optional)
1 dried red chilli, broken
½ small onion, finely chopped
3 garlic cloves, crushed
100ml (3½ fl oz/ 7 tbsp) tamarind water
300ml (10½ fl oz/ 1¼ cups) water
¼ tsp salt
1 tomato, roughly chopped
1 tbsp Rasam Podi (recipe on p214)

Heat the oil in a medium saucepan over a low heat. Add the curry leaves (if using) and red chillies and give it a stir. Then, add the onion and give it another stir. Finally, add the garlic and sauté until the onions are soft and turning golden.

Add the tamarind water, water, salt and tomato, and bring to the boil. Add the Rasam Podi and give it a stir. Once it reaches boiling point again, take it off the heat. Serve hot.

Serves 4

MORR

Spiced yogurt drink

A lightly spiced yogurt drink to be taken on its own as a mid-morning refresher on a hot day, or as an accompaniment to a vegetarian rice and curry meal. It's a little like a salted Indian lassi.

500g (1lb 2oz/2 cups) plain yogurt or curd
800ml (28 fl oz/ 3⅓ cups) water
½ small onion, finely chopped
1 green chilli, very finely chopped with seeds in
1 tbsp lime juice
salt

Put the yogurt and water into a blender and liquidize well. You may have to liquidise the ingredients in smaller quantities, depending on the size of your blender.

Pour the mixture into a big jug. Add the onions, green chilli and lime juice. Season with salt and give it a good stir using a long spoon. It is ready to serve.

Serves 4

விலைப்பட்டியல்

ரூ-ச

தேநீர் ....
பால் தேநீர் ....
மைலோ பால் ...
பசும்பால் .....
பி.கோப்பி ....
பால் கோப்பி ..
மல்லி ....
பால் மல்லி ...
இடியப்பம் ...
தோசை ......
இட்லி ....
பிட்டு ....
ரொட்டி .....
அப்பம்..சோடி
உ. வடை .....
க. வடை .....
சுசியம்
போளி

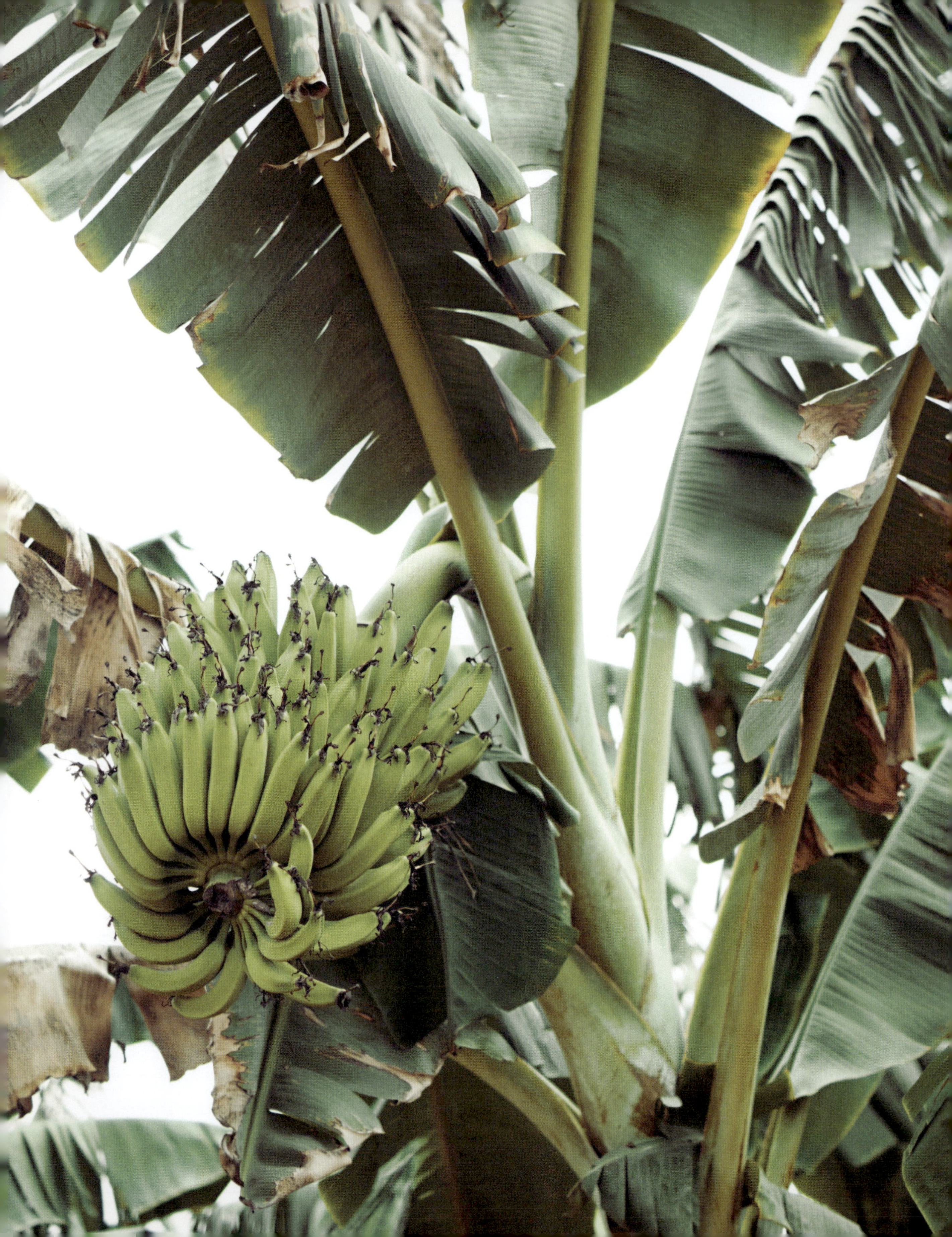

LAMPRAIS

Another dish showcasing the influence of colonisers on Sri Lankan cuisine, lamprais was popularised during the Dutch occupation (1658-1796) and comes from their 'lomprijst', meaning 'lump of rice'. It's well loved among expat Sri Lankans as well as the Burgher diaspora, a group descended from the unions between locals and European colonisers. As a dish it has enjoyed a resurgence in popularity recently, and has found its way into top restaurants in Colombo. Chefs will agree that lamprais is a little painstaking to make, but it's a real labour of love with a rich reward at the end. It consists of rice, meat curry, frikkadels (breaded Dutch meatballs), wambatu pahi (pickled aubergine), blachan (spicy shrimp paste balls), fried plantain and a fried boiled egg, all wrapped in a banana leaf and baked. I've provided the recipes and methods separately on the following pages; for a real special-occasion meal to serve four. believe me, it's worth it!

Serves 4

1. MEAT CURRY

150g (5½oz) boneless chicken
150g (5½oz) boneless mutton
150g (5½oz) boneless beef
150g (5½oz) boneless pork
meat bones
1 litre (35 fl oz/4¼ cups) water
2 tbsp ghee
4 garlic cloves, finely chopped
2.5cm (1-inch) piece of ginger, peeled and finely chopped
½ tsp fenugreek seeds
7 fresh curry leaves
2 x 2.5cm (1-inch) pieces of rampe (pandan) leaf
½ lemongrass stalk
5cm (2-inch) cinnamon stick, broken into two
5 cloves
½ medium onion, finely chopped
400ml (14 fl oz/1⅔ cups) water
200ml (7 fl oz/generous ¾ cup) coconut milk
100g (3½oz) dried prawns (shrimp), dry-roasted and powdered
1 tsp ground cardamom
juice of ½ lime

For the marinade
1 tsp ground coriander, lightly roasted
1 tsp ground cumin
½ tsp fennel powder
1 tsp ground turmeric
1 tsp chilli powder
1 tsp salt

Wash the meat, cut it into 2.5cm (1-inch) chunks and put it in a large bowl as you go. Reserve two pieces of each meat for the stock. Add all the marinade ingredients into the bowl, and leave to marinate for at least 20 minutes.

To prepare the stock, put the reserved pieces of meat and the bones into a medium, lidded saucepan, add the water and bring to the boil. Reduce the heat, cover with the lid and simmer until the liquid has reduced by about a third and you have about 300ml of stock left in the pan. It will take about 40 minutes.

Remove the meat from the stock with a slotted spoon and add it to the marinating meat. Reserve the stock for cooking the Lamprais rice (p225).

Heat the ghee in a large saucepan over a low heat. Add the garlic, ginger, fenugreek seeds, curry leaves, rampe leaf, lemongrass, cinnamon stick, cloves and onion, and sauté until the onions are soft and turning golden.

Add the meat and the marinade, and stir-fry for a few minutes, then add the water and bring to the boil. Reduce the heat, cover and simmer for 40 minutes. Then, add the coconut milk, cover and simmer for another 10 minutes until the meat is tender. Add the dried prawns (shrimp) and cardamom, mix well, cover and cook for another 5 minutes or so until the sauce is thick. Remove from the heat, add the lime and set aside to serve in the Lamprais parcel.

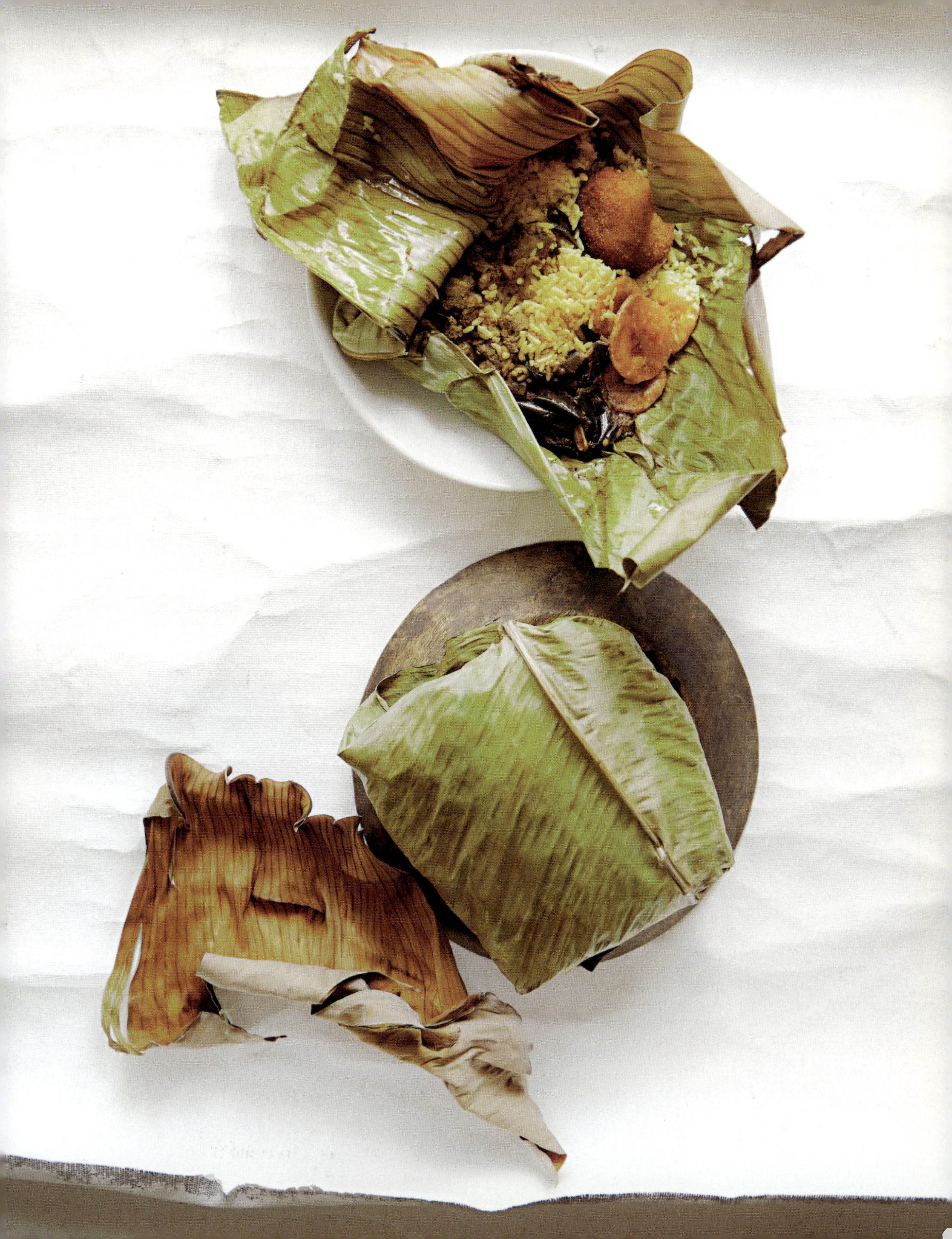

2. WAMBATU PAHI

300g (10½oz) aubergine (eggplant) (about 1 medium)
1 tsp salt
½ tsp ground turmeric
500ml (17 fl oz/generous 2 cups) oil, for deep frying, plus 1 tbsp for frying
5cm (2-inch) piece of rampe (pandan) leaf
4 fresh curry leaves
2 green chillies, slit lengthways with seeds in
3 garlic cloves, finely chopped
1.5cm (½-inch) piece of ginger, peeled and finely chopped
½ medium onion, sliced
1 tbsp Maldive fish, crushed
½ tsp ground cinnamon
1 tsp ground coriander
1 tsp ground cumin
¼ tsp fennel powder
1 tsp chilli powder
100ml (3½ fl oz/7 tbsp) tamarind water (thin concentrate)
1 tsp ground mustard seeds
1 tsp sugar (white or brown)
100ml (3½ fl oz/7 tbsp) coconut cream

Pickled aubergine

Wash the aubergine (eggplant) and cut it into 1cm (½-inch) chunks. Put it in a medium bowl, sprinkle with ½ teaspoon of the salt and the turmeric and set aside for 5 minutes.

Bring the 500ml of oil to boiling point in a deep saucepan, then reduce the heat to medium. Squeeze the aubergine and slide it into the pan. Deep-fry for several minutes until golden brown. Remove with a slotted spoon and lay it on kitchen towel. Remove the pan from the heat.

Heat the remaining oil in a medium saucepan over a low heat. Add the rampe leaf, curry leaves and green chillies, and give it a stir or two. Next, add the garlic and ginger and stir a couple more times. Finally, add the onions and sauté until they are soft and turning golden.

Add the Maldive fish and give it a stir or two, then add all the spice powders and give it a quick stir. Add the tamarind water, vinegar, ground mustard seeds, the rest of the salt, sugar and coconut milk, and bring to the boil. Reduce the heat to low and simmer for another 5–6 minutes.

Tip in the fried aubergine and mix together well. Cook for another 2–3 minutes, take the pan off the heat and set aside to serve in the Lamprais parcel.

For the filling
200g (7oz) minced (ground) chicken or mutton
½ tsp ground black pepper
½ tsp salt
½ tsp ground cloves
½ tsp ground cinnamon
1 tsp fennel powder
1 slice bread, chopped
juice of ½ lime
1 tbsp oil
7 fresh curry leaves, chopped
2.5cm (1-inch) piece of ginger, peeled and chopped
2 garlic cloves, chopped
1 large onion, chopped
500ml (17 fl oz/generous 2 cups) oil, for deep-frying

For the coating
3 egg whites
200g (7oz/1½ cups) plain (all-purpose) flour
200g (7oz/3⅓ cups) breadcrumbs

3. FRIKKADELS

Breaded Dutch meatballs

Mix the meat with the pepper, salt, cloves, cinnamon, fennel, chopped bread and lime juice.

Heat the oil in a large, lidded frying pan (skillet) or wok (with a lid) over a low heat. Add the curry leaves, ginger, garlic and onion and stir-fry for a few minutes.

Add the meat mixture into the fried onions, cover with the lid and cook for about 15 minutes for chicken and 30 minutes for mutton until brown. Remove from the heat and let it cool.

Once cool, make 8 lime-sized meatballs and set aside.

For the coating, beat the egg whites in a medium bowl until frothy. Lay out the flour and breadcrumbs in separate dishes.

One by one, roll the meatballs in the flour, dip them into the egg whites and then coat them in breadcrumbs. Place them in a shallow dish and chill for at least 10 minutes in the fridge.

Heat the oil in a deep saucepan and deep-fry the meatballs for 10 minutes until golden. Set aside to serve in the Lamprais parcel.

For blachan
100g (3½oz) dried prawns (shrimp)
1 tbsp oil
1 medium onion, roughly chopped
2 garlic cloves
1.5cm (½-inch) piece of ginger, peeled and sliced
2 tsp Bathapu Thuna Paha (curry powder on p17)
1 tsp lime juice
400ml (14 fl oz/1⅔ cups) oil, for deep-frying

For fried plantain
1 plantain
½ tsp chilli powder
¼ tsp ground turmeric
¼ tsp salt
400ml (14 fl oz/1⅔ cups) oil, for deep-frying

4. BLACHAN

Spicy shrimp paste balls

Wash the dried prawns (shrimp) well.

Heat the oil in a small frying pan (skillet) over a medium heat. Fry the dried prawns for about 2 minutes, turning as they cook, and set aside.

Once the prawns are cool, put them in a food processor with the rest of the ingredients and blitz into a coarse paste.

Shape the paste into 4 balls, half the size of a lime, and set aside to serve in the Lamprais parcel.

5. FRIED PLANTAIN

Peel the plantain, cut it into thin slices and put them in a small bowl.

Sprinkle in the chilli, turmeric and salt, stir and leave for 5 minutes.

Heat the oil in a deep saucepan over a medium heat. When it reaches boiling point, tip in the drained plantain and deep-fry for 10 minutes until golden brown. Remove with a slotted spoon and set aside to serve in the Lamprais parcel.

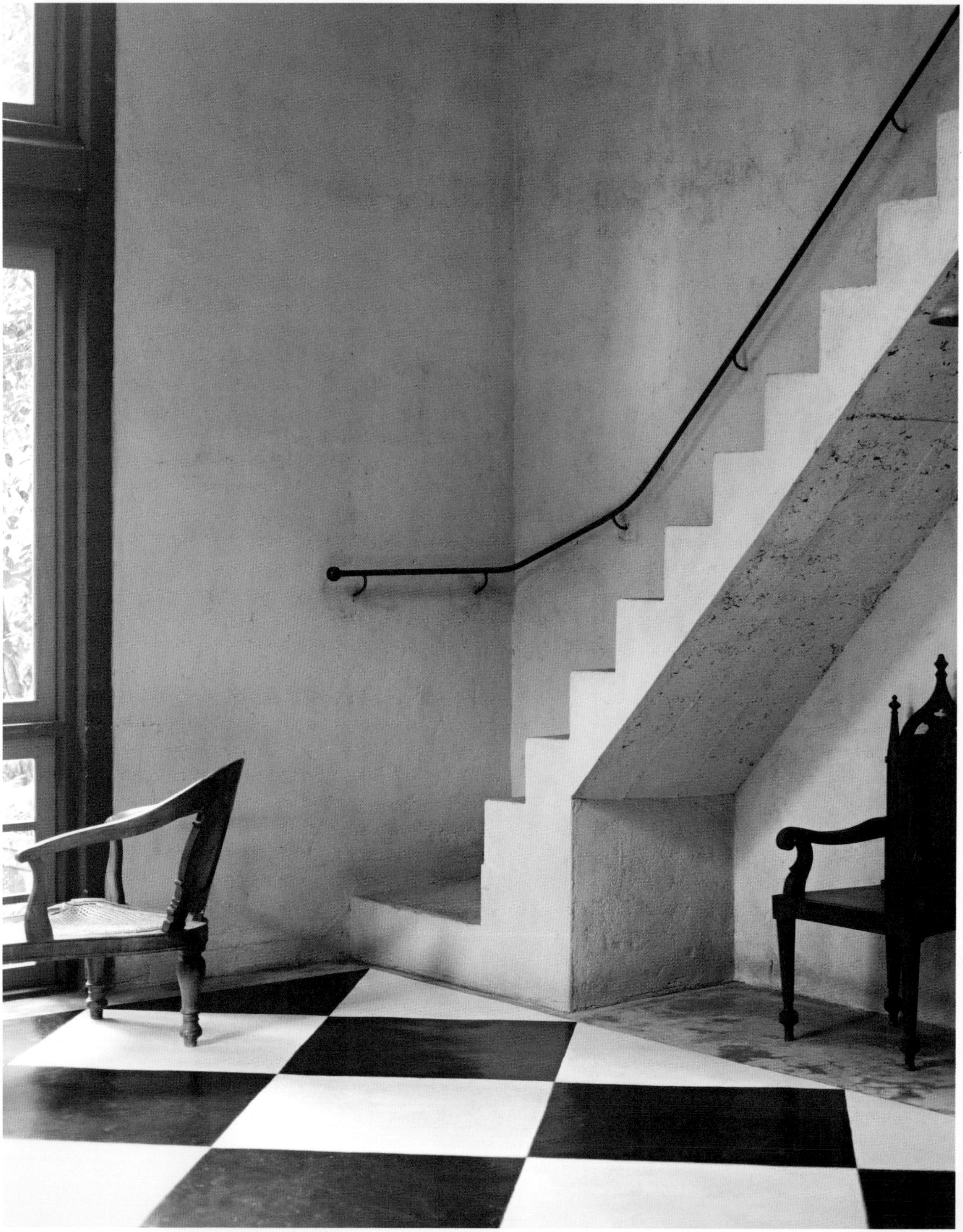

For fried boiled egg
4 eggs
½ tsp ground turmeric
¼ tsp salt
1 tbsp oil

For the rice
400g (14oz/1¾ cups) white rice (samba or basmati)
4 tbsp ghee
½ small onion, finely chopped
3 x 2.5cm (1-inch) pieces of rampe (pandan) leaf
1 lemongrass stalk, cut into two
300ml (10½ fl oz/ 1¼ cups) stock from Meat Curry recipe (p220)
10 black peppercorns
5 cloves
200ml (7 fl oz/generous ¾ cup) water
2 tsp ground cardamom

6. FRIED BOILED EGG

In a small saucepan, cover the eggs with water, bring to the boil and cook until hard-boiled, about 7 minutes. Once cooled, remove the shell and prick each egg with a skewer.

Sprinkle the salt and turmeric in a shallow dish and stir to combine. Roll the boiled eggs in the dish to coat.

Heat the oil in a small frying pan (skillet) over a medium heat. Shallow-fry the boiled eggs, turning occasionally, until they are golden, about 6 minutes. Remove from the heat and set aside to serve in the Lamprais parcel.

7. RICE

Swirl the rice around in a saucepan of water to wash it, drain and repeat at least three times until the water is clear. Set aside.

Heat the ghee in a large, lidded saucepan over a low heat, or in a rice cooker. Add the onion, rampe leaf and lemongrass, and sauté until the onions are soft and turning golden. Tip in the rice and stir-fry for about 5 minutes.

Add the stock, peppercorns and cloves, and give it a good stir. Add the water to cover the rice by about 2.5cm (1 inch). Bring to the boil, then simmer for 12 minutes. Add the cardamom and give it a gentle stir with the handle of a long spoon, then cover with the lid. Avoid lifting the lid too often, but when the rice is cooked and the water is absorbed, turn off the heat but leave the lid on. Set aside to serve in the Lamprais parcel.

---

4 large banana leaves (or baking/parchment paper)
Rice (see above)
Meat Curry (p220)
8 x Frikkadels (p223)
4 x Blachan (p223)
Wambatu Pahi (p222)
Fried Plantain (p223)
4 x Fried Boiled Eggs (see above)

8. HOW TO PARCEL

The authentic way to parcel up the Lamprais is with a banana leaf, but if you haven't got access to any banana leaves, baking (parchment) paper would also work.

First, preheat the oven to 180°C (350°F/Gas Mark 4).

Cut the leaf into a 30cm x 30cm (12 inch x 12 inch) square. Hold it over a gas or electric hob and lightly heat it until it begins to colour. Then lay it on a work surface in a diamond shape.

Put 5 or 6 tablespoons of rice in the middle of the leaf, and place about 3 tablespoons of the meat curry on top, towards the edge of the rice. Add 2 teaspoons of the pickled aubergine (eggplant) on the side, plus two frikkadel, one blachan and four or five plantain. Finally, almost bury one egg in the rice.

Fold the top corner of the leaf over the rice and almost tuck it underneath. Now, fold up the bottom corner and tuck it over the top and underneath. Finally, fold the right side over the parcel, followed by the left side.

Use a toothpick or two to secure the leaf and hold the parcel together. Repeat with all four parcels.

Lay the parcels on a baking sheet and bake for about 20 minutes. Serve immediately.

ODIYAL KOOL

Spicy seafood soup

We've kept this apart from the other seafood recipes (p155–185) as it's such a special, celebratory dish, much like the Lamprais (p219–225). A traditional thick soup made using odiyal flour and a variety of seafood combined with jackfruit seeds, long beans and tamarind. An exquisite treat indeed, best enjoyed with friends and family around the table.

200g (7oz) large fish such as grouper (with head)
150g (5½oz) small fish such as anchovies
150g (5½oz) crab
150g (5½oz) squid or cuttlefish
150g (5½oz) raw prawns (shrimp), shell on
150g (5½oz) long beans or green beans
100g (3½oz/½ cup) jackfruit seeds or butter (lima) beans
100g (3½oz) cassava (manioc) root
3 tbsp rice (red or white)
2 tsp salt
3 litres water (2½ litres for soup + ½ litre to soak the flour)
250g (9oz/1½ cups odiyal (palmyra) flour
200ml (7 fl oz/generous ¾ cup) tamarind water
1 tbsp red chilli flakes
½ tsp ground turmeric
50g (1¾oz) spinach, chopped

Serves 6

Clean the fish thoroughly. Cut the head off the large fish and remove the gills and blood traces. Chop the rest of the large fish into chunky pieces. Chop the heads off the small fish and pull out the guts.

Wash the crabs well. Pull off the top shell and clean the insides with your fingers. Cut the crabs in half and then twist off the pincer claws. Break the pincer claws at the joint and gently tap them with something hard, like the handle of a knife. The aim is to crack the shell, but leave it intact. Remove any small pieces of broken shell.

Clean the squid well and cut it into about 1cm (½-inch) pieces. Cut the tentacles into three or four pieces. Shell the prawns (shrimp), leaving the shell on the tail, and wash well.

Cut the top off the beans, pulling the fibre down one side, then cut the bottom off and pull the fibre off the other side. Chop into 1cm (½-inch) lengths. Wash and roughly chop the spinach. Halve the jackfruit seeds and peel off the hard outer skin. Peel and chop the cassava into 1cm (½-inch) chunks.

Now, make the soup. Put all the ingredients up to and including the salt into a very large saucepan, pour in the 2½ litres of water and bring to the boil. Simmer for about 40 minutes, giving it a gentle stir every now and then.

Meanwhile, soak the odiyal flour in ½ litre of water for about 10 minutes. Strain the water, removing any fibres with it.

Place the flour, tamarind water, chilli flakes and turmeric into a large bowl and stir until you have a thick paste.

After the soup has been cooking for 40 minutes, add the flour paste and the spinach and gently stir. Taste for salt, then simmer for about 12 minutes until it thickens. Remove from the heat and serve.

O 10-16-18-41
4 - 9 - 6 - 6 - 3
12-15-29-50
Z 01-09-10-22
A 7-6-5-6-1-2
08-20-25
31-33-41-70
27-50-59-61

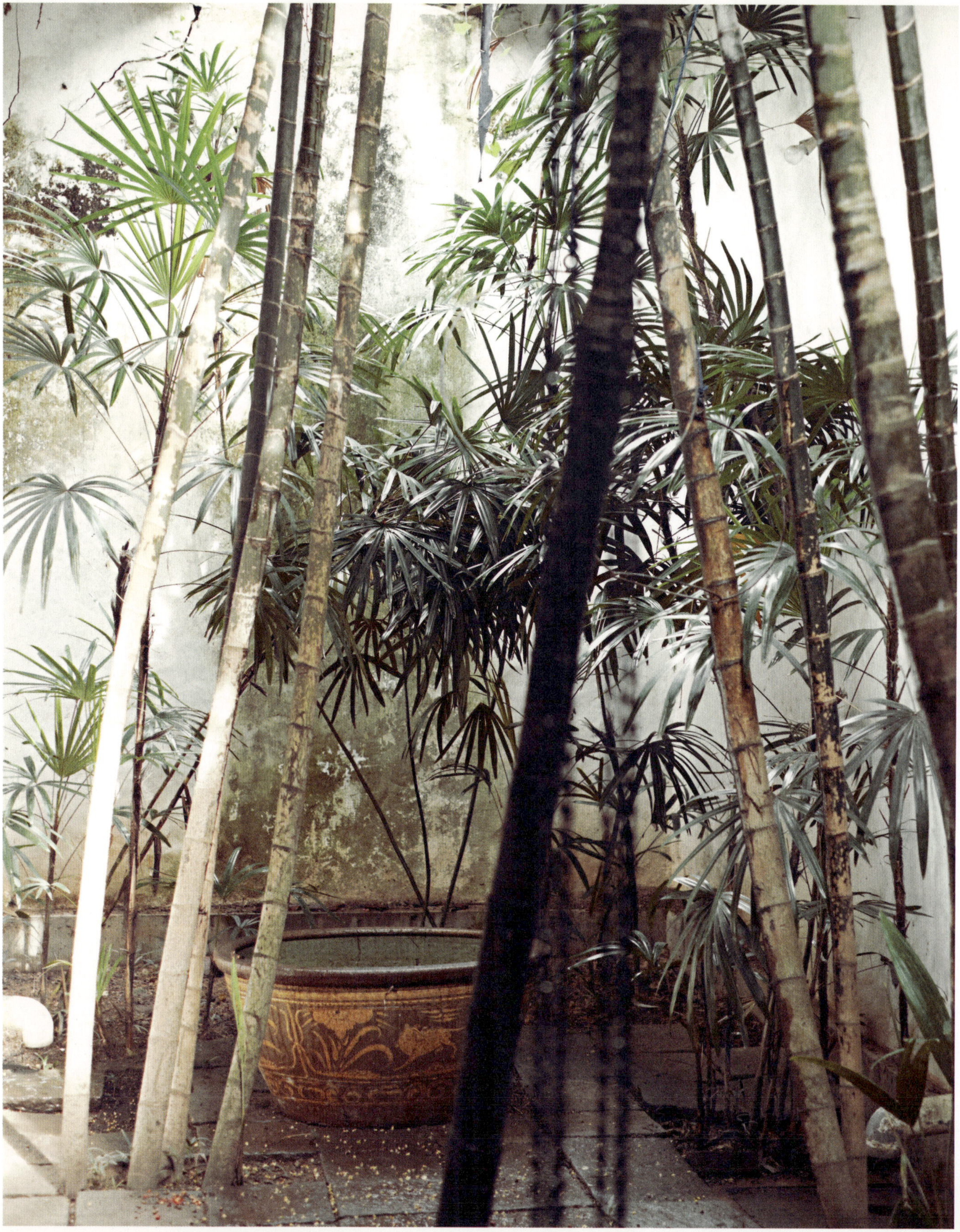

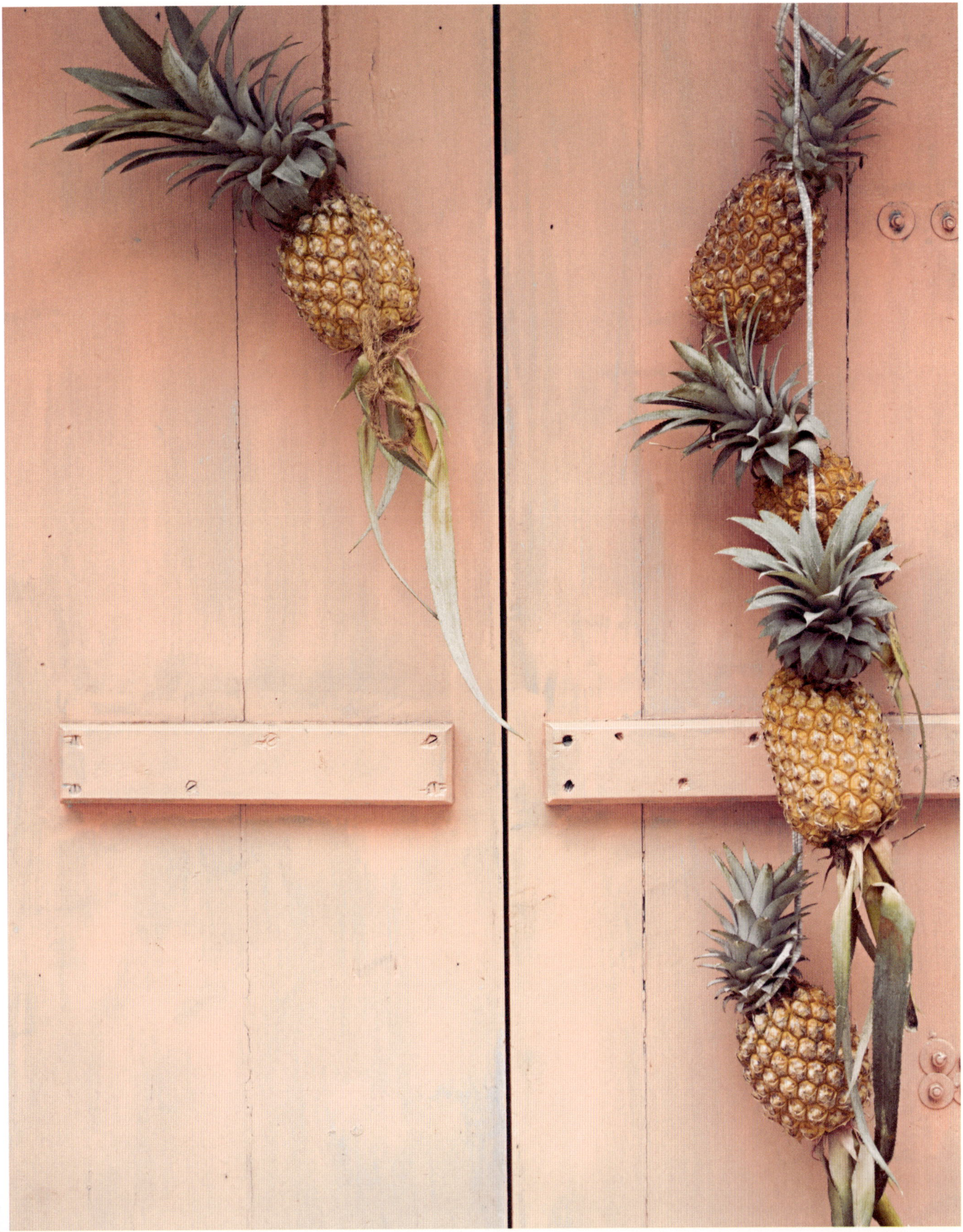

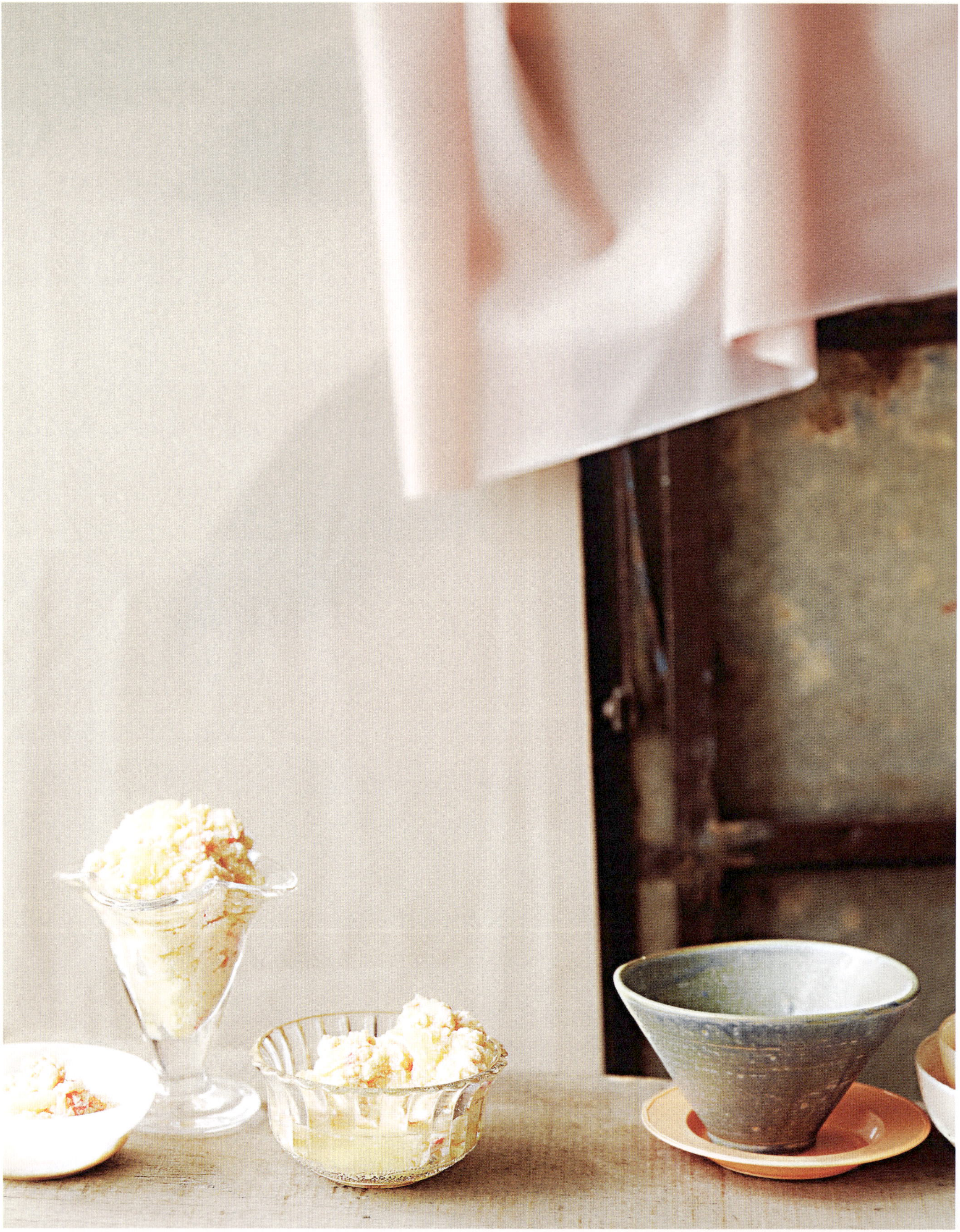

PINEAPPLE FLUFF

1 x 12g (½oz) sachet of gelatine powder
100ml (3½ fl oz/ 7 tbsp) warm water
400g (14oz/1¾ cups) evaporated milk
200g (7oz/1 cup) caster (superfine) sugar
250g (9oz) pineapple (fresh or canned)
1 tsp vanilla essence

A 'retro' Sri Lankan pudding with a clear British influence – but our delectable pineapples make this favourite more than just a nostalgic throwback!

In a small jug, mix the gelatine with the warm water and set aside.

Put the evaporated milk and sugar in a medium saucepan on a low heat and gently warm it until the sugar dissolves. Set aside to cool.

Roughly chop the pineapple using a food processor. In a large bowl, combine the prepared ingredients and the vanilla essence, and mix well.

Pour into a serving dish and chill in the fridge for 3–4 hours to set.

Variation: If you like colourful desserts, add a few drops of red food colouring into the final mixture. Stir with a fork for a ripple effect, then chill in the fridge as above.

Serves 6

---

butter, for greasing
1 tsp sweet cumin seeds
110g (4oz/½ cup) semolina (medium coarse)
125ml (4 fl oz/½ cup) water
150g (5½oz/1 cup) kithul jaggery, broken into small pieces
200g freshly grated or desiccated (shredded) coconut
¼ tsp salt
110g (4oz/¾ cup) raisins
110g (4oz/generous ¾ cup) plain (all-purpose) flour
110g (4oz/¾ cup) cashew nuts, roughly chopped
125g (8oz) dates, finely chopped
110g (4oz/½ cup) pumpkin preserve (optional)
85ml (2¾ fl oz/⅓ cup) vegetable oil
315ml (10½ fl oz/1⅓ cups) coconut milk
1 tbsp vanilla essence
1 tsp ground cardamom
½ tsp ground cinnamon
1 tsp baking powder

BIBIKKAN

Coconut cake

Preheat the oven to 180°C (350°F/Gas Mark 4) and grease a baking tray or shallow cake tin (pan) about 25cm x 20cm (10 x 8 inches) with butter.

Dry-roast the sweet cumin seeds in a dry frying pan (skillet) over a low heat, until golden. When cool, put the seeds in a spice grinder and blitz to a fine powder. Next, dry-roast the semolina until it starts to turn golden. Set aside.

Put the water and jaggery into a large saucepan set over a low heat and simmer until the jaggery melts. Add the coconut and salt and stir well over a very low heat until they bind together. Remove from the heat and leave to cool for 5 minutes. Once cool, add all the remaining ingredients and mix well. Pour the mixture evenly into the prepared cake tin. Bake for about 30 minutes until firm. Remove from the oven and let it cool.

Serves 15

WATTALAPPAN

Coconut caramel custard

As with most inhabitants of the subcontinent, Sri Lankans have a sweet tooth. This gently spiced custard has a lot of flavour from the kithul jaggery, a fudgy sugar made from the sap of a local blossoming palm tree.

150g (5½oz/1 cup) kithul jaggery
200ml (7 fl oz/generous ¾ cup) coconut cream
50ml (1¾ fl oz/scant ¼ cup) water
5 eggs
1 tbsp ground cardamom
¼ tsp ground nutmeg
1 tbsp vanilla essence
50g (1¾oz/⅓ cup) cashew nut halves, dry-roasted and crushed

Serves 12

Preheat the oven to 160°C (310°F/Gas Mark 2½). Break the jaggery into chunks.

Put the jaggery, coconut milk and water into a medium saucepan set over a low heat, and simmer until the jaggery melts. Set aside to cool.

Put the eggs, cardamom, nutmeg and vanilla essence into a blender and liquidize until smooth.

Strain the cooled jaggery into a bowl, add the blended egg mixture and whisk until everything is combined.

Pour the mixture into twelve 5cm (2-inch) ramekins or similar moulds, or a shallow ovenproof baking dish about 25cm x 20cm (10 x 8 inches). Cover the top with foil.

Place the ramekin moulds or the baking dish into a roasting tin half-full with water, which helps to stop the watalappan drying out.

Bake in the oven for 30-40 minutes until it looks like caramel pudding texture.

Remove from the oven and set aside to cool. Sprinkle on the cashew nuts (if using) just before serving. It can be stored in the fridge for 2-3 days.

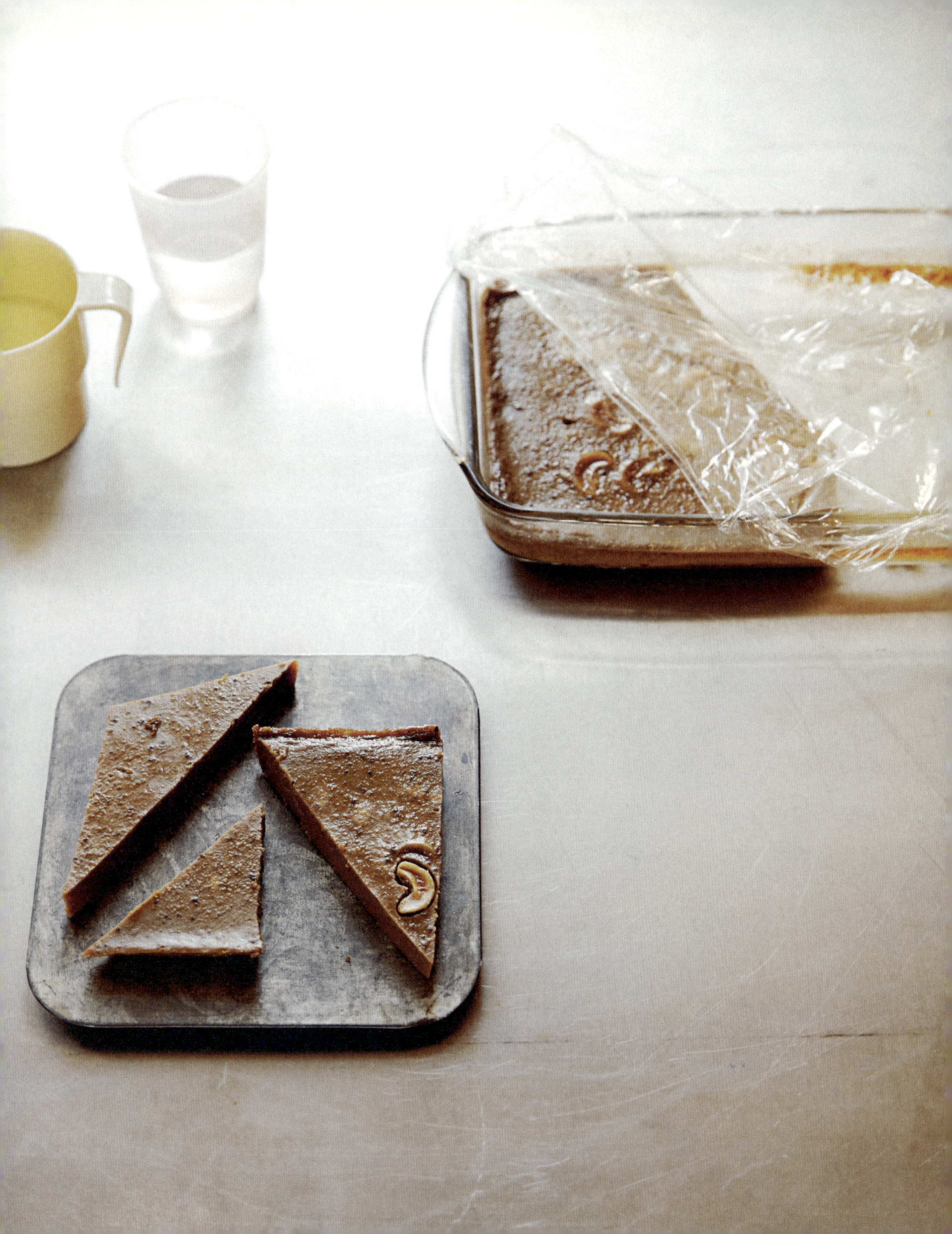

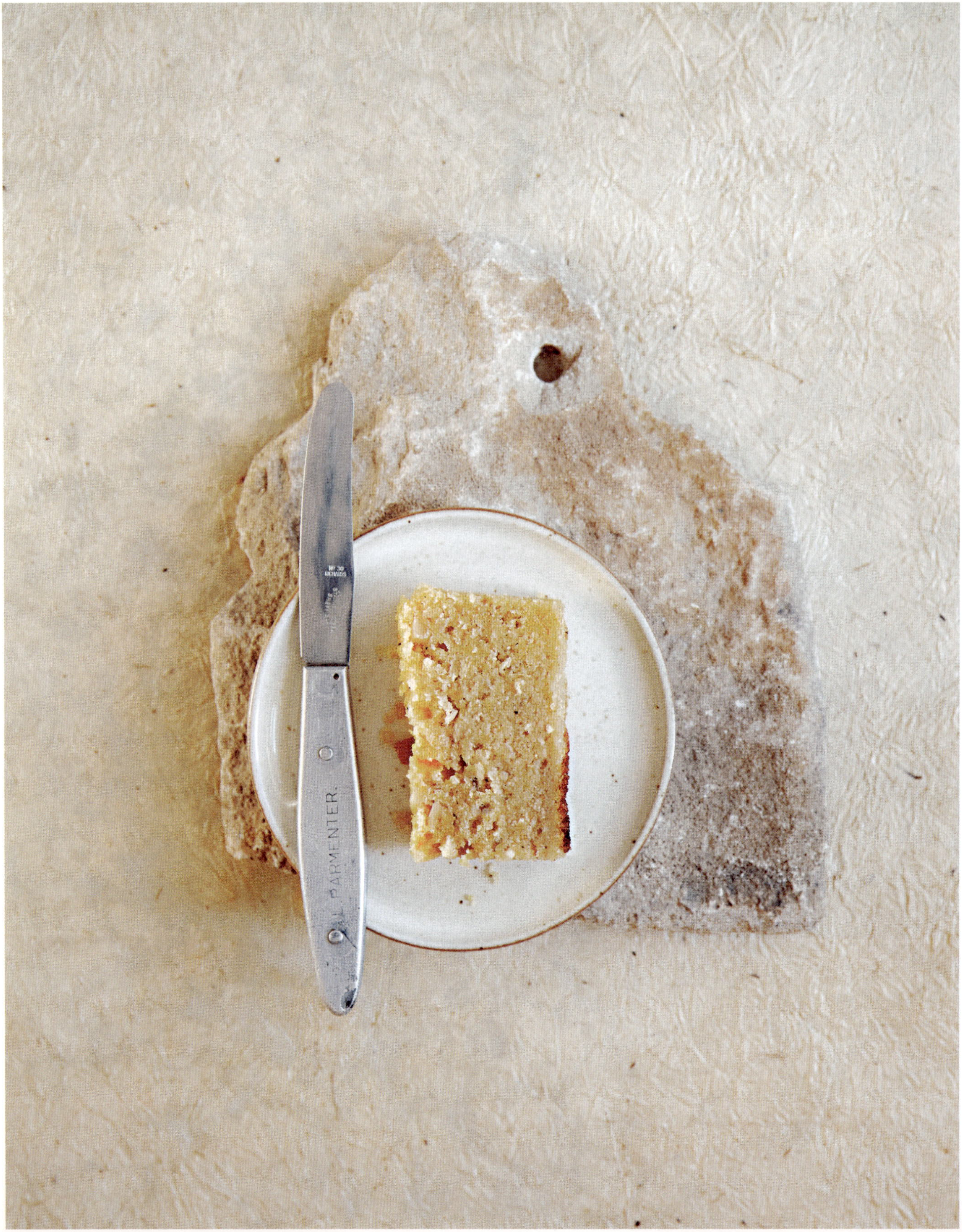

250g (9oz/1¼ cups) semolina (medium coarse)
200g (7oz) unsalted butter
1 tsp ground cardamom
½ tsp ground nutmeg
¼ tsp ground cinnamon
2 tsp lemon zest
375g (13¼oz/2¾ cups) pumpkin preserve, finely chopped
375g (13¼oz/2¾ cups) cashew nuts, chopped
2 tsp rosewater
3 tsp almond essence
3 tsp vanilla essence
315g (11oz/1½ cups) caster (superfine) sugar
9 egg yolks
5 egg whites
80ml (2¾ fl oz/⅓ cup) honey

This is a sweet treat of national importance, perfumed with exotic spices, and probably originates from the era of Portuguese colonisation. Its natural place is next to a cup of fine Ceylon tea in the afternoon, and then you'll discover how apt its name is.

In a medium, lidded, dry frying pan (skillet) set over a very low heat, dry-roast the semolina until golden.

Put the roasted semolina in a bowl and, while it is still warm, mix in the butter. Add all the spices and the lemon zest and mix well, then cover with the lid and set aside for about 5 hours.

In a separate medium bowl, tip in the pumpkin preserve, cashew nuts, rosewater, almond and vanilla essences, and mix well. Set aside for about 5 hours.

When you are ready to make the cake, preheat the oven to 180°C (350°F/Gas Mark 4) and line a baking tray or shallow cake tin (pan) about 25cm x 20cm (10 x 8 inches) with baking (parchment) paper.

Beat the sugar and egg yolks in a large bowl, until thick, creamy and very pale. In a separate bowl, whisk the egg whites until stiff.

Take the bowl with the pumpkin preserve and cashew mixture, add the honey and beat well. Add the semolina mixture and give it a good stir. Then, pour in the egg yolk mixture little by little, stirring as you go. Finally, fold the egg whites into the mixture.

Pour the cake mixture evenly into the prepared tin. Cover the tray with perforated foil. Bake the cake for 60 minutes until firm.

Serves 15

LOVE CAKE

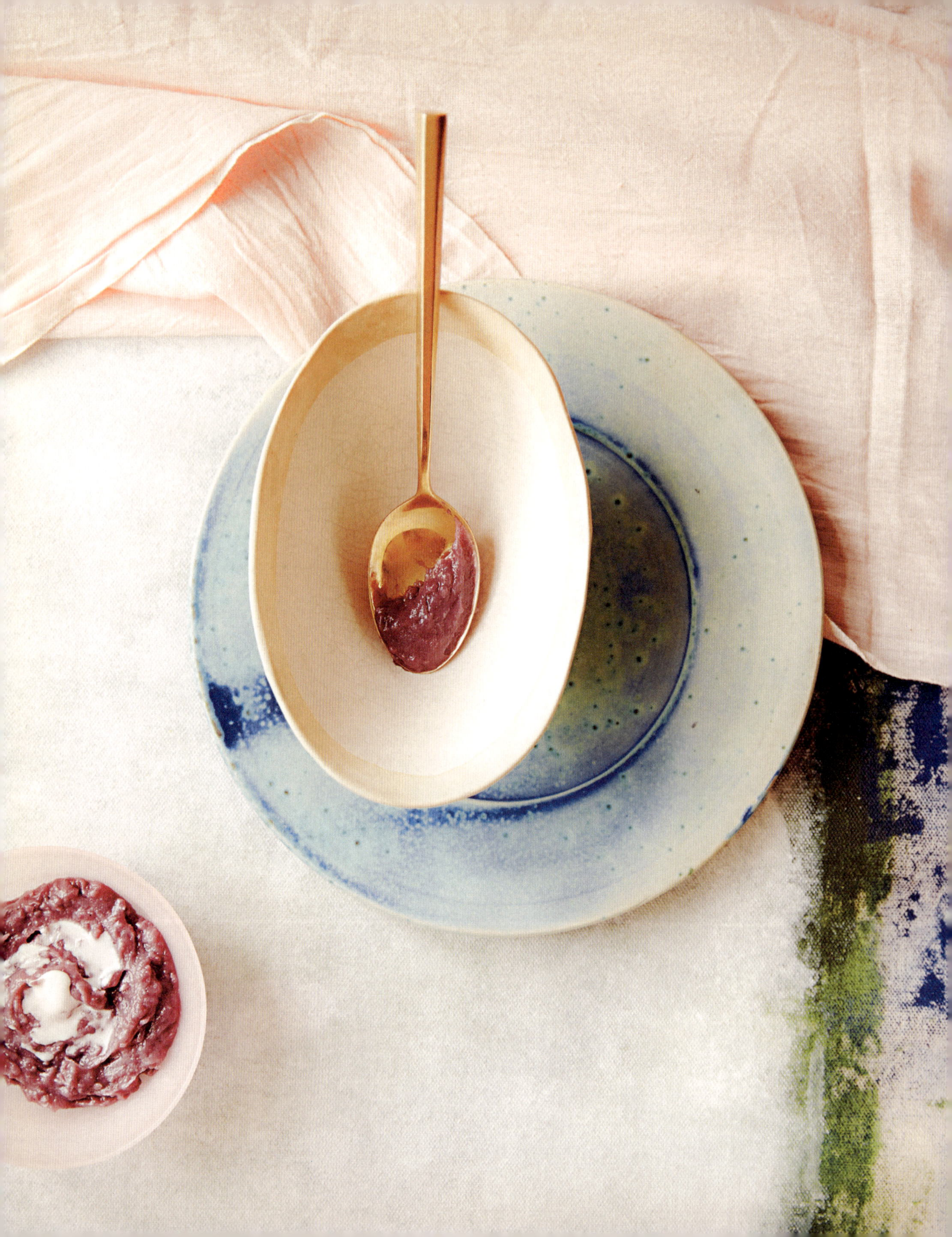

400g (14oz) raasavalli yam (purple yam)
300ml (10½ fl oz/1¼ cups) coconut cream
300ml (10½ fl oz/1¼ cups) water
100g (3½oz/½ cup) sugar (white or brown)
¼ tsp salt

Purple king yam pudding
The word 'raasa' in Tamil means king, and the raasavalli yam used in this recipe is truly the finest of all yams. This sweet, creamy pudding is enjoyed during late afternoon tea or as a dessert after a meal.

First, grease your fingers and palms with oil to avoid any irritation from the skin of the yam. Peel the skin and cut the flesh into thin slices. Wash the slices well and put them in a medium, lidded saucepan, cover with half the coconut milk and enough of the water to cover the yam. Bring to the boil, then reduce the heat, half-cover with the lid and simmer until soft, about 20–25 minutes.

Remove from the heat and mash the yam until it is smooth with a few small chunks. Add the remaining coconut milk, the sugar and salt, mix well and put the pan on a low heat. Cook for another 2–3 minutes, making sure that the bottom does not burn.

Remove from the heat, and serve either warm or cool.

Serves 6

RAASAVALLI KILANGU

KESARI

Semolina pudding

Tea is the national drink of Sri Lanka and the country is the one of the largest exporters of tea leaves in the world. People drink it first thing in the morning and in the afternoon, when it is often enjoyed with a sweetmeat like this kesari.

Serves 15

1 tbsp cashew nut halves
1 tbsp raisins or sultanas (golden raisins)
250g (9oz/1¼ cups) semolina (medium coarse)
400ml (14 fl oz/1⅔ cups) boiling water
¼ tsp kesari powder (or saffron powder)
150g (5½oz/¾ cup) caster (superfine) sugar
1 tsp ghee
¼ tsp ground cardamom
butter, for greasing

Dry-roast the cashew nuts in a medium frying pan (skillet) over a low heat until golden brown. Set aside. In the same pan, dry-roast the raisins until they start to turn golden and plump. Put them together with the roasted cashews.

In the same pan, dry-roast the semolina until just beginning to turn golden. Then, add the boiling water and kesari powder and cook for 10–12 minutes, stirring continuously, until the semolina is soft and most of the water is absorbed.

Add the sugar, mix well and cook for 4–5 minutes, stirring continuously. Then, add the ghee and cook for a further 3–4 minutes, stirring continuously. Add the cardamom, cashews and raisins and give it a good stir.

Grease a round cake tin (about 23cm/9 inches) with some butter, pour the kesari in and spread it to a thickness of about 1.5–2cm (½–¾ inch). Cut into diamonds or squares, and serve either warm or cold.

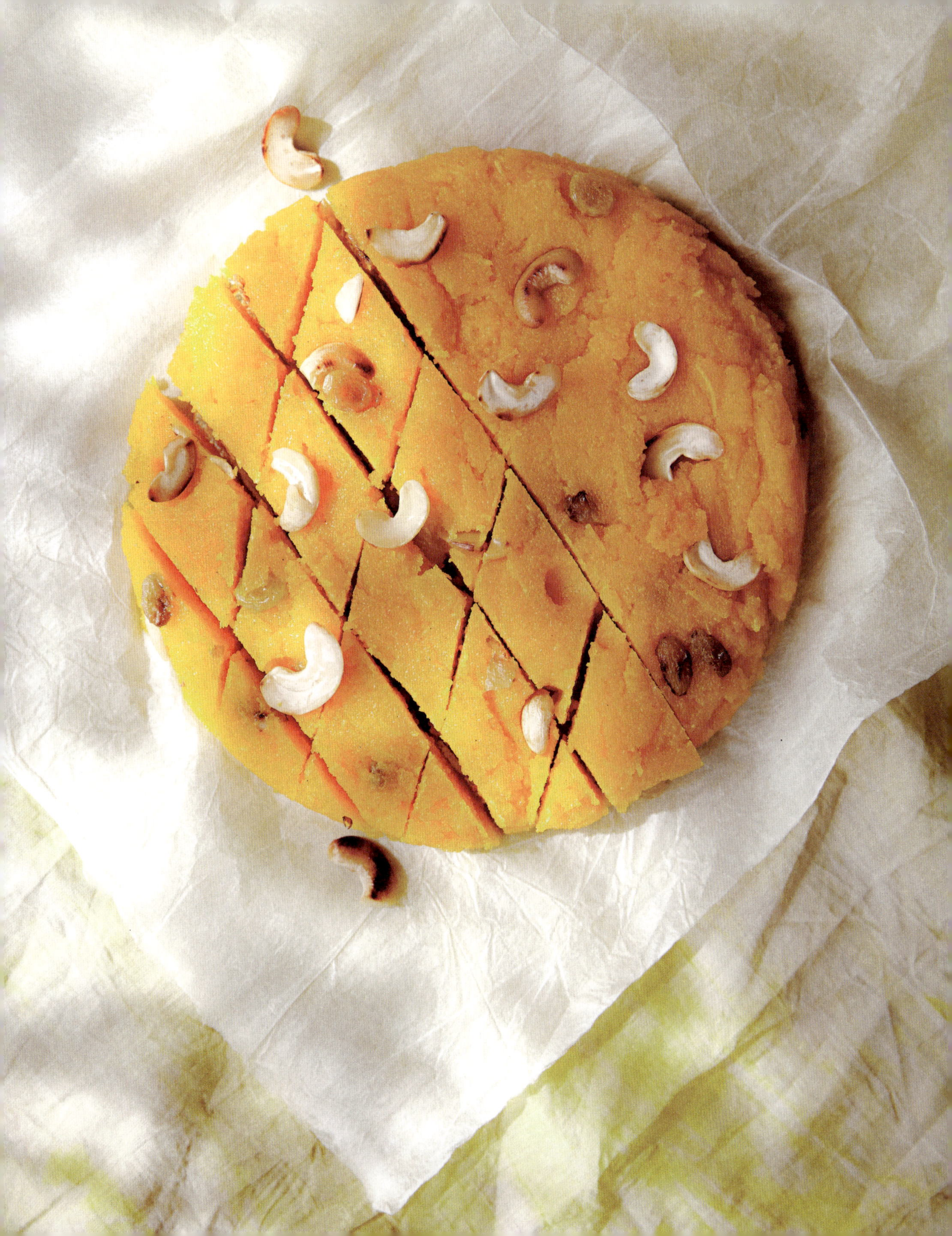

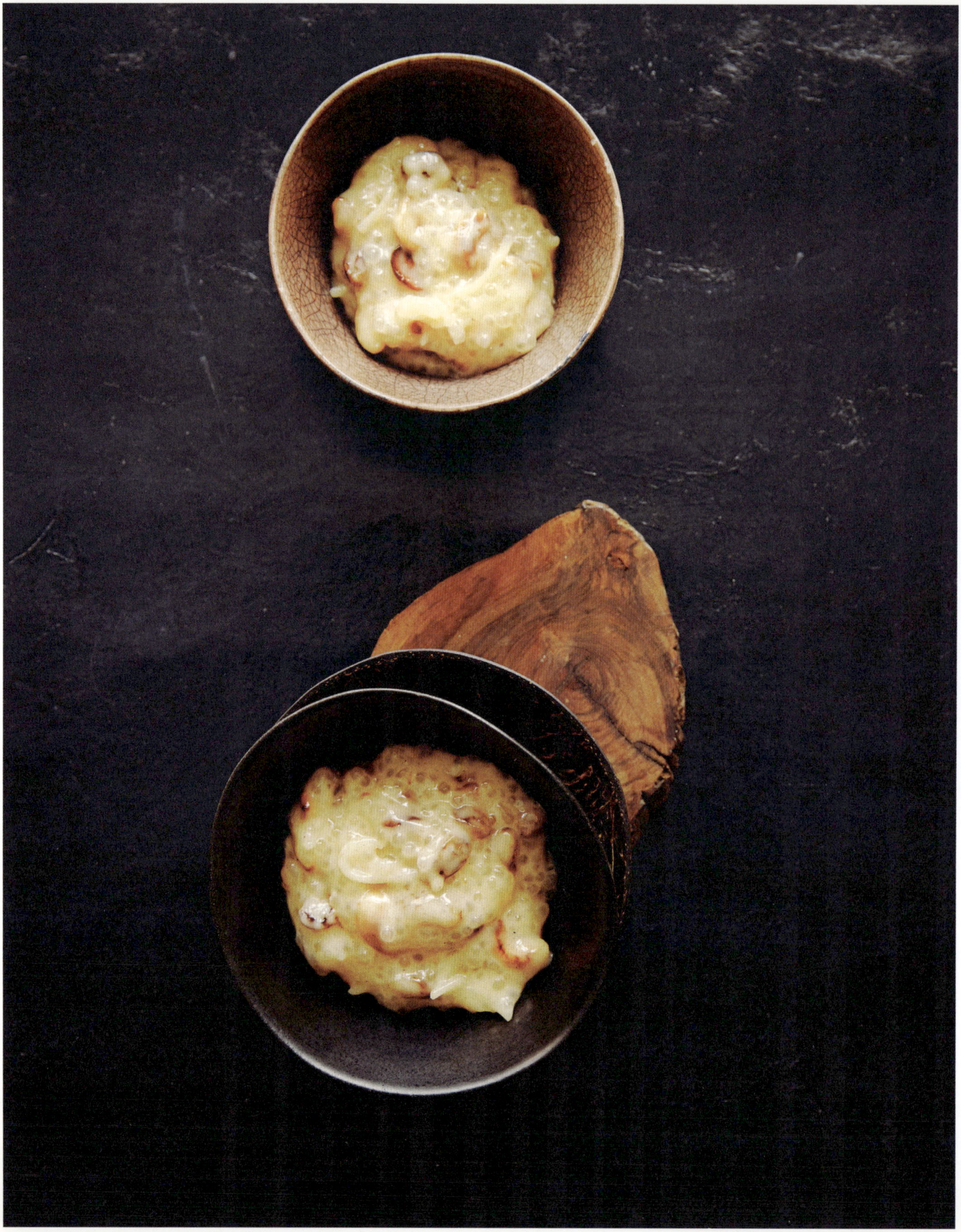

200g (7oz/1⅓ cups) tapioca pearls
10g (¼oz/2 tsp) semiya (seviyan or vermicelli)
1 tbsp cashew nuts
1 tbsp raisins or sultanas (golden raisins)
400ml (14 fl oz/1⅔ cups) water
200ml (7 fl oz/generous ¾ cup) coconut milk
3 tbsp sweetened condensed milk
50g (1¾oz/¼ cup) sugar (white or brown)
1 tbsp ghee or butter
½ tsp ground cardamom

Tapioca pudding

Made with the root vegetable manioc, or cassava (maravalli kilangu in Tamil, maiyokka in Sinhalese), this pearl-like dessert is a must at Hindu weddings and other auspicious functions. It also contains semiya, or vermicelli as it's known in the West.

In a dry medium frying pan (skillet) over a low heat, dry-roast the tapioca pearls until golden brown and set aside. Break the semiya into short pieces if it is not already, then dry-roast until just beginning to colour, and set it aside in a separate dish. Separately, dry-roast the cashew nuts until golden, and the raisins until turning brown. Set them both aside.

Put the roasted tapioca into a medium saucepan set over a medium heat, add the water and bring to the boil. Reduce the heat and simmer gently for about 8 minutes, until the tapioca is transparent.

Add the coconut milk, condensed milk and semiya and cook for a further 2–3 minutes until the tapioca begins to thicken slightly. Do not let it get too thick, and add water if necessary to keep it slightly runny.

Add the sugar, ghee and cardamom and cook for about 5 minutes. Take it off the heat, tip in the roasted cashews and raisins and stir them in. Alternatively, you could garnish the dish with these when serving.

Serves 4

PAYASAM

BANANA FRITTERS

A simple, sweet and nutty dessert to soothe the tongue after a spicy meal. More than twenty-five varieties of banana grow in Sri Lanka, including the beautifully sweet ambul, the small, slightly rounder seeni and the highly prized kolikuttu.

Serves 4

First, in a dry medium frying pan (skillet) over a low heat, dry-roast the cashew nuts until golden brown. Roughly crush them and set aside.

Peel the bananas and slice them in half widthways and again lengthways.

Heat the butter in a medium frying pan over a low heat, and as it sizzles spread it around the bottom of the pan. Add the bananna and sprinkle half the sugar on top.

When the banana slices begin to go brown on the bottom, turn them over. Sprinkle the remaining sugar on top, and when the other side begins to brown, remove from the heat.

Sprinkle the cashew nuts evenly on top of the bananas, squeeze over the lime juice and serve.

100g (3½oz/1⅓ cups) cashew nuts
4 ripe medium bananas
½ tbsp butter
2 tsp brown sugar
juice of ½ lime

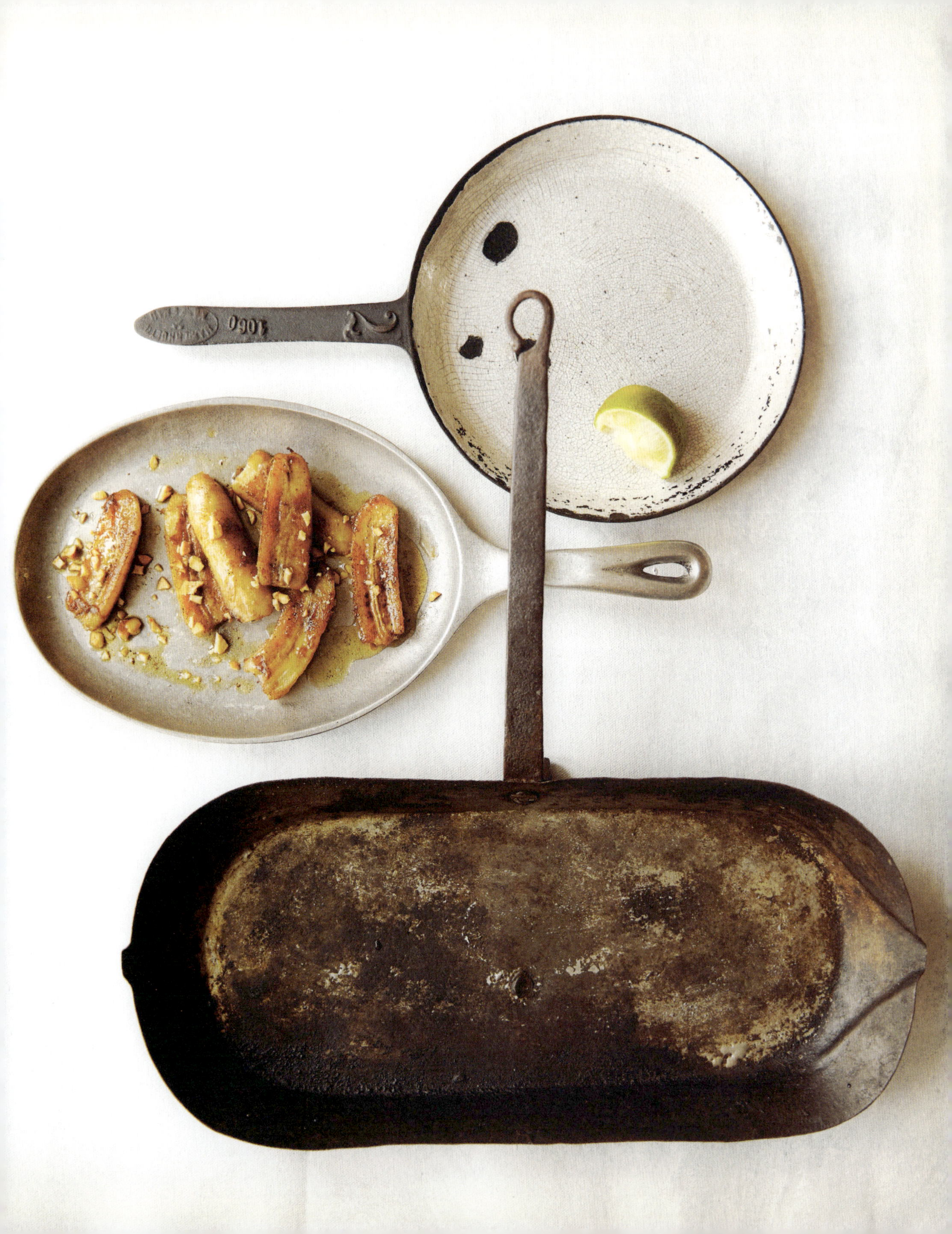

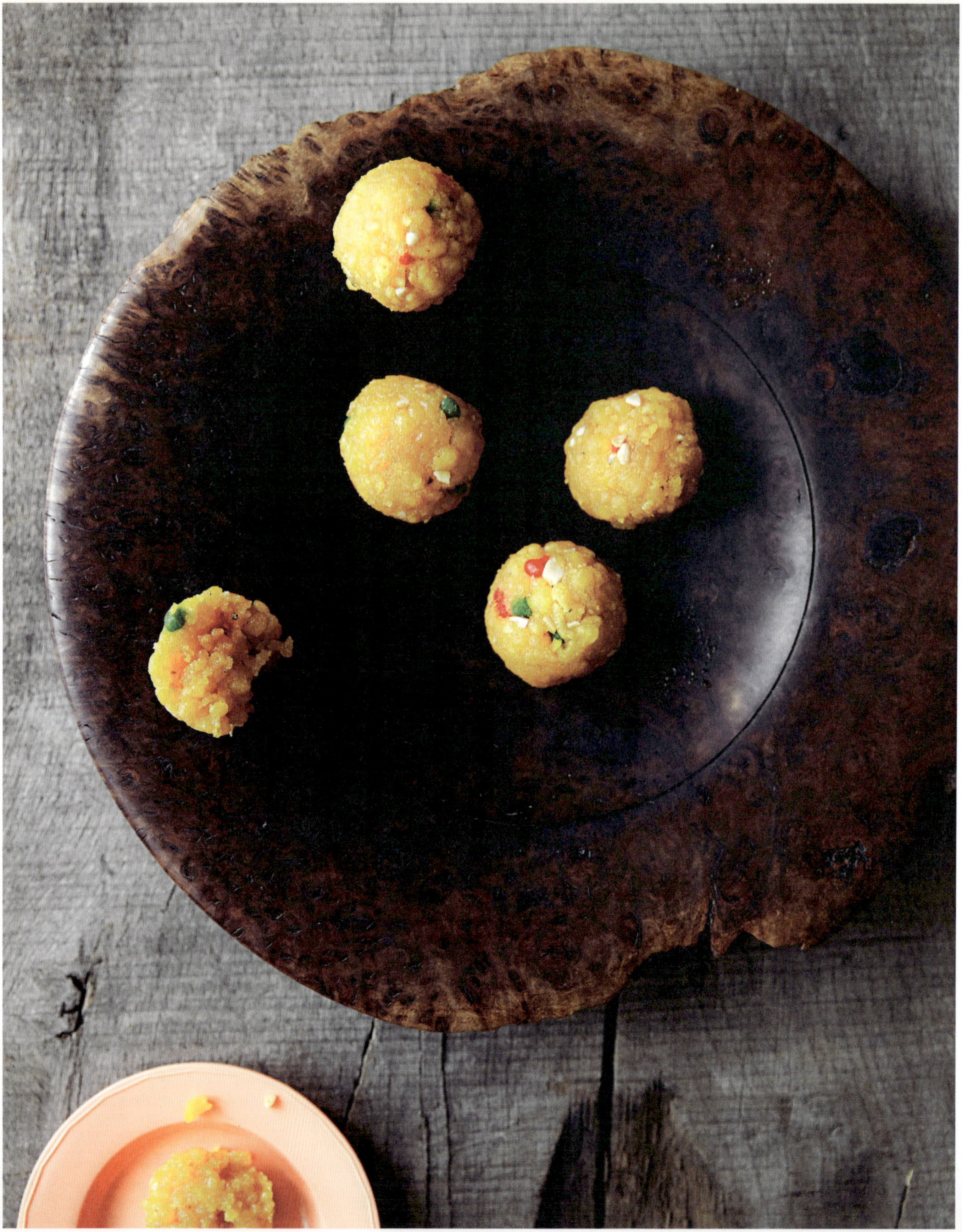

BOONDI LADDU

Sweet chick pea balls
In Sri Lanka these sweets are prepared for weddings and birthdays. They make thoughtful gifts when visiting friends.

8 saffron strands
420ml (7½ fl oz/scant 1 cup) water (20ml/½ fl oz for the saffron and 200ml/7 fl oz/generous ¾ cup each for the batter and sugar syrup)
50g (1¾oz/⅓ cup) cashew nuts
200g (7oz/1½ cups) gram flour (chick pea flour)
1 tbsp ghee
red and green food colouring
200g (7oz/1 cup) white granulated sugar
500ml (17 fl oz/generous 2 cups) oil
1 tsp ground cardamom

Serves 4

Put the saffron and the 20ml of water into a small bowl and leave to soak for at least 5 minutes.

In a dry medium frying pan (skillet) over a low heat, dry-roast the cashew nuts until golden brown. Roughly crush them and set aside.

Put the flour and ghee in a medium bowl. Drain the saffron water into the bowl, reserving the strands. Add 200ml of water a little at a time, stirring continuously, until you have a thick but slightly runny batter, with a dropping consistency. Spoon 1 tablespoon of the batter into a separate small bowl and add a drop of red food colouring. Spoon another tablespoon into another small bowl and add a drop of green food colouring. Set all the batter aside.

In a medium saucepan, mix the sugar and 200ml of water and bring to the boil. Reduce the heat and stir continuously. Check the consistency of the sugar syrup by lifting it up with your spoon every now and then. Once the syrup reaches a continuous thread-like consistency, remove from the heat and set aside.

Heat the oil in a deep frying pan until it reaches boiling point. Holding the large slotted spoon above the oil, take a ladleful of batter and pour it onto the large slotted spoon. Give it a little shake so the batter drops through the holes into the oil. Reduce the heat a little.

Use a tablespoon to gently push the batter through the holes, moving the slotted spoon around so that the boondi don't fall on top of each other and form heaps.

Using a long spoon, gently move the frying balls around in the oil so they don't stick to each other. When they turn a golden colour, which takes about 8 minutes, remove them from the oil using a clean slotted spoon and lay them on kitchen towel to absorb the excess oil.

Repeat the process with another batch or two of batter until all the plain batter is used up. Repeat with the green and red batters to make green and red boondi.

When the fried boondi has cooled down, tip them into the sugar syrup. Sprinkle in the cardamom and cashew nuts and gently mix it all together well, until all the boondi are covered in syrup.

Using your palms, make 25 lemon-sized balls and set them on a serving platter as you go. Keep a bowl of water handy when you are making the balls, so that you can clean your sticky palms in it now and then.

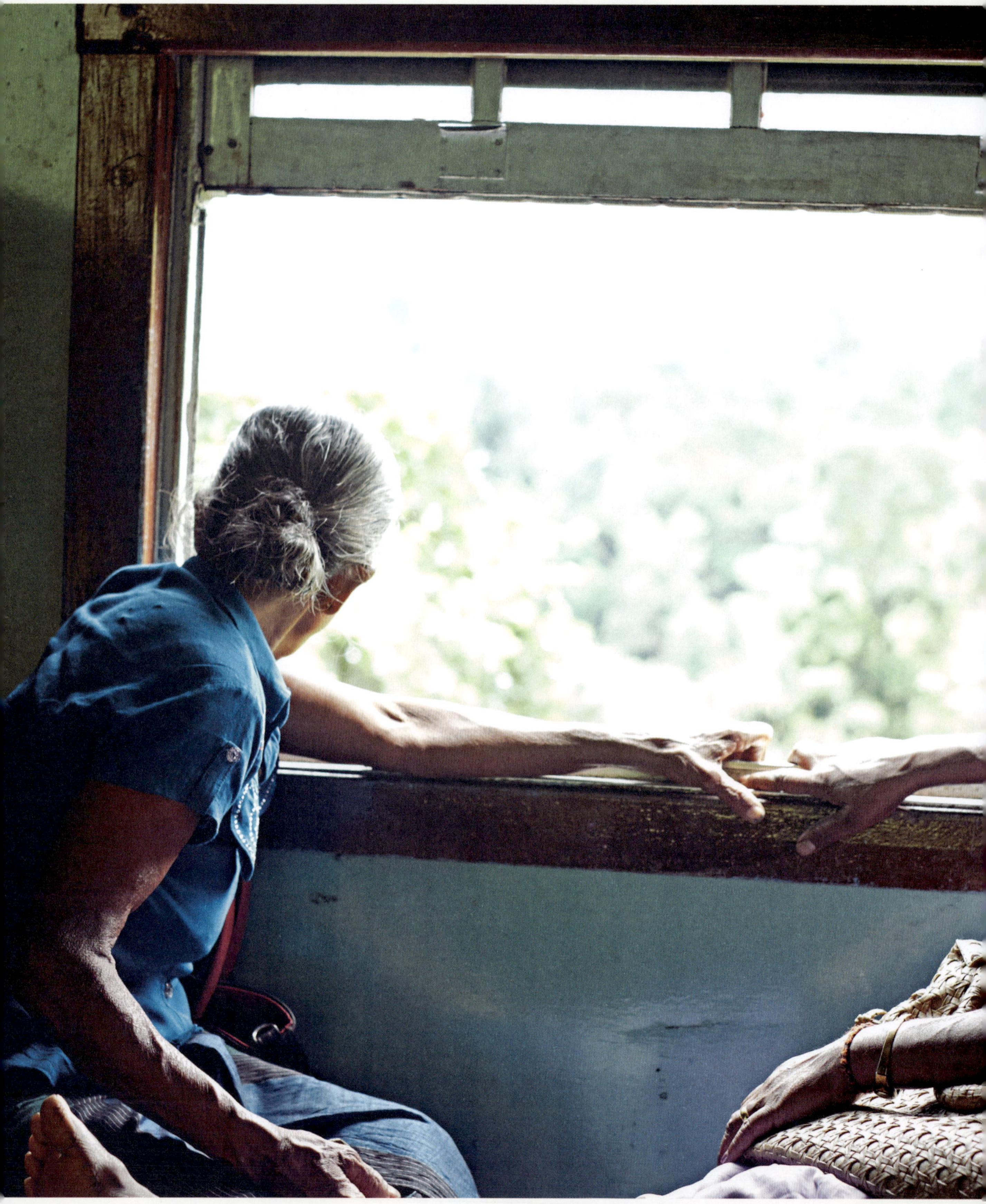

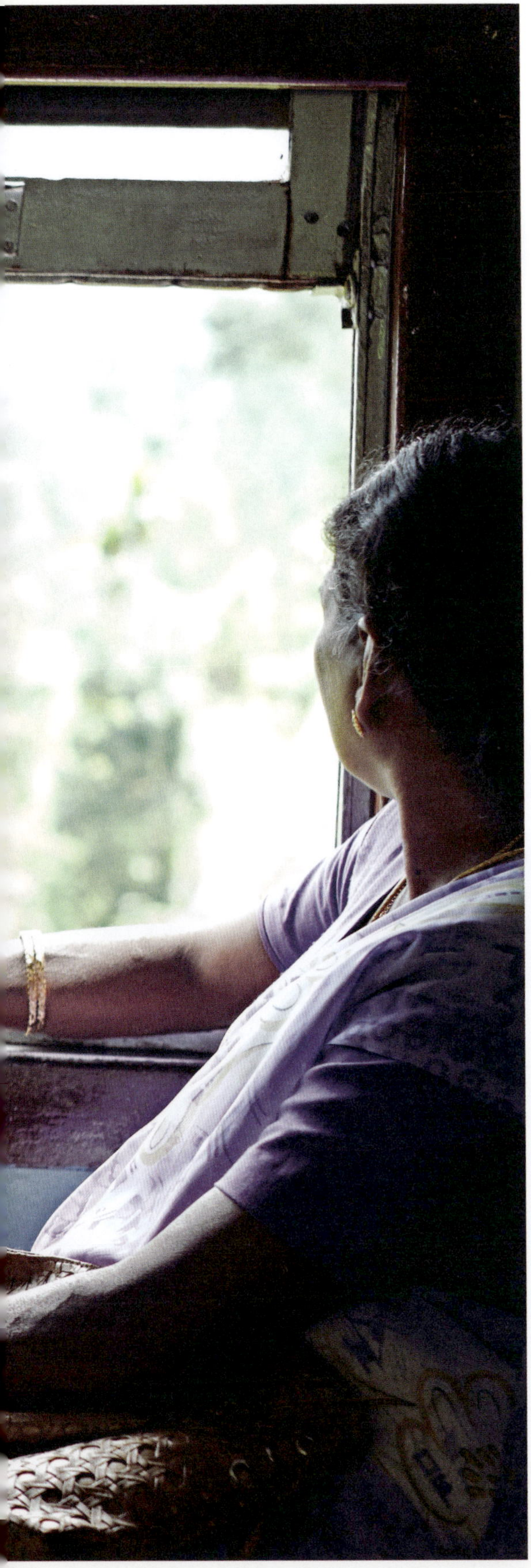

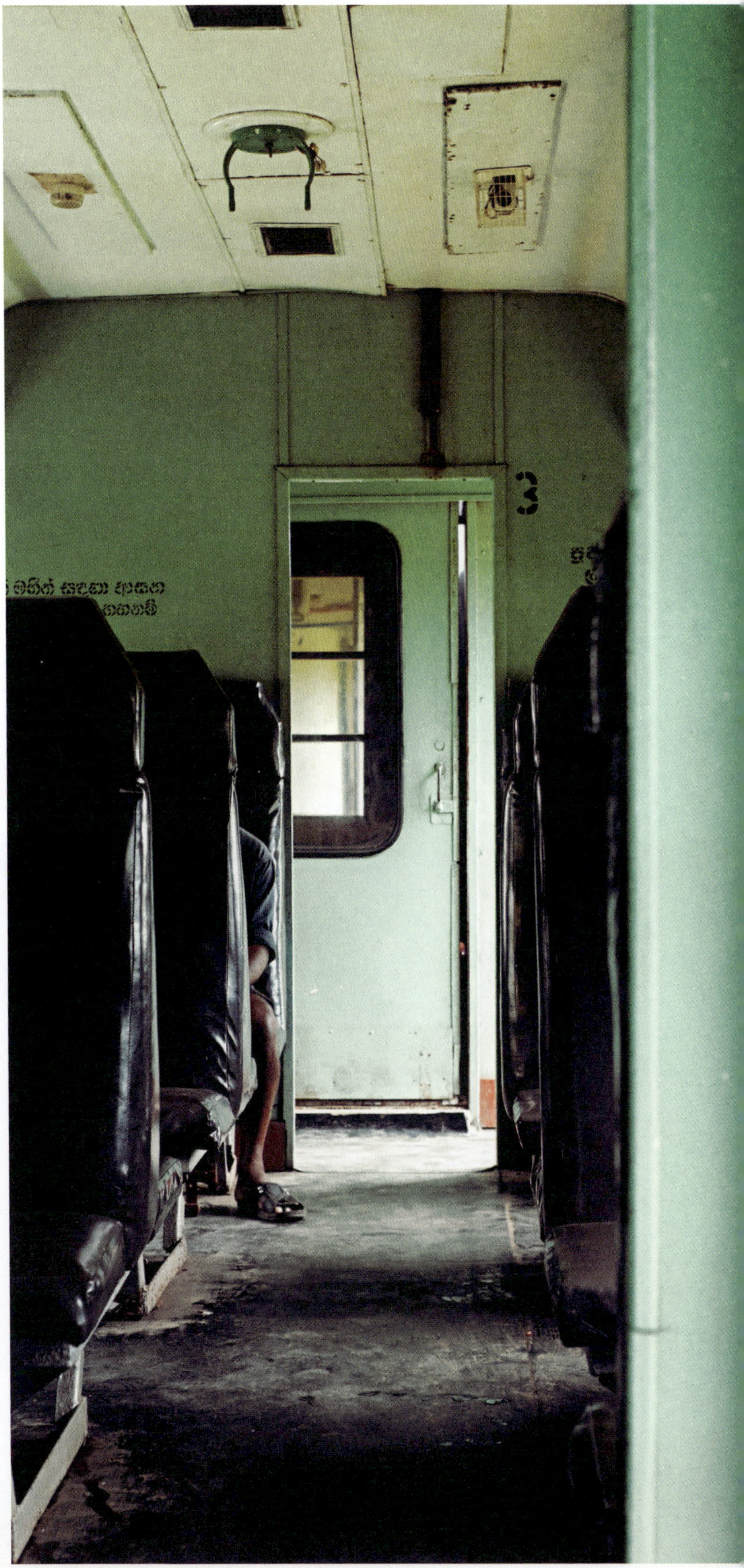
3

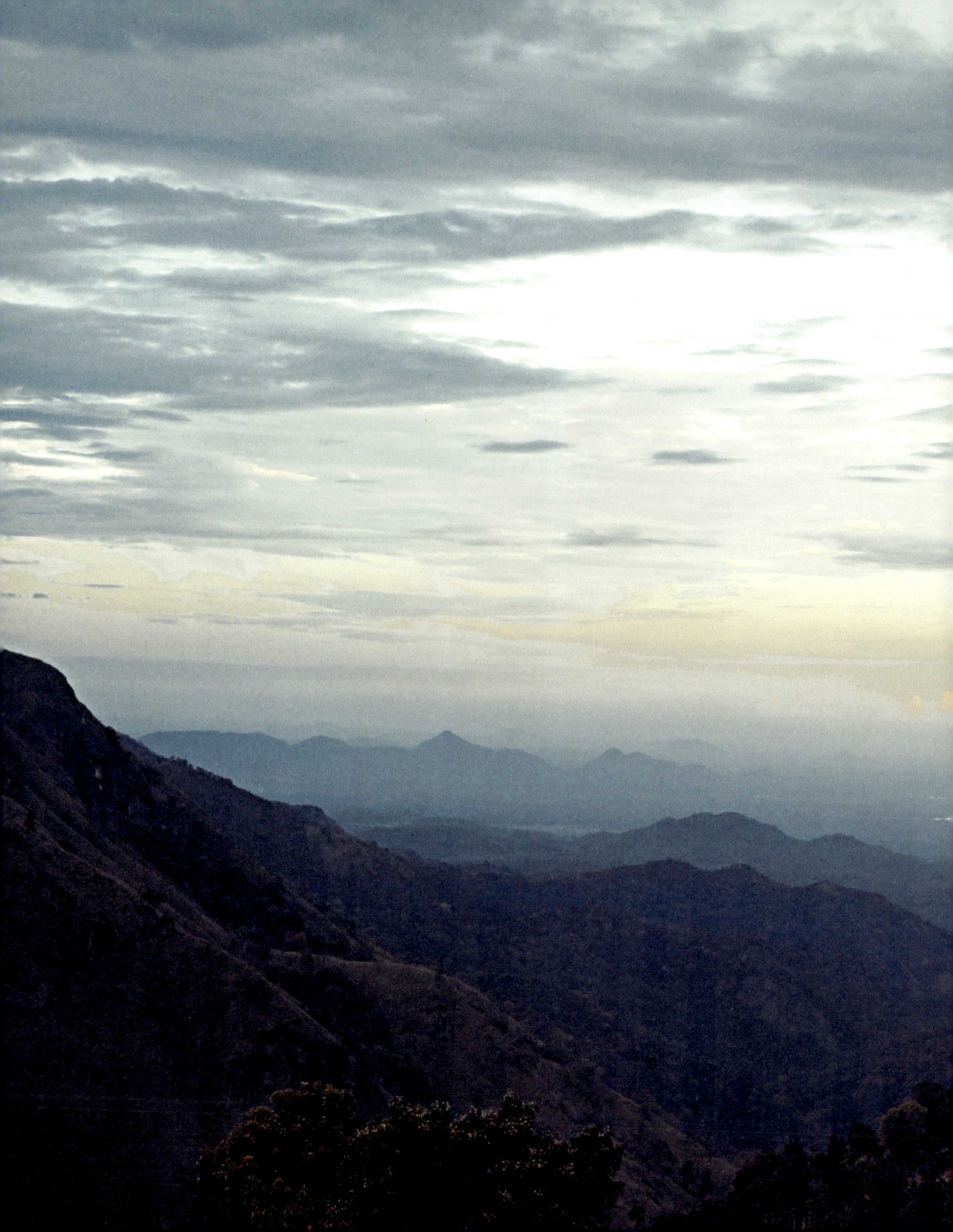

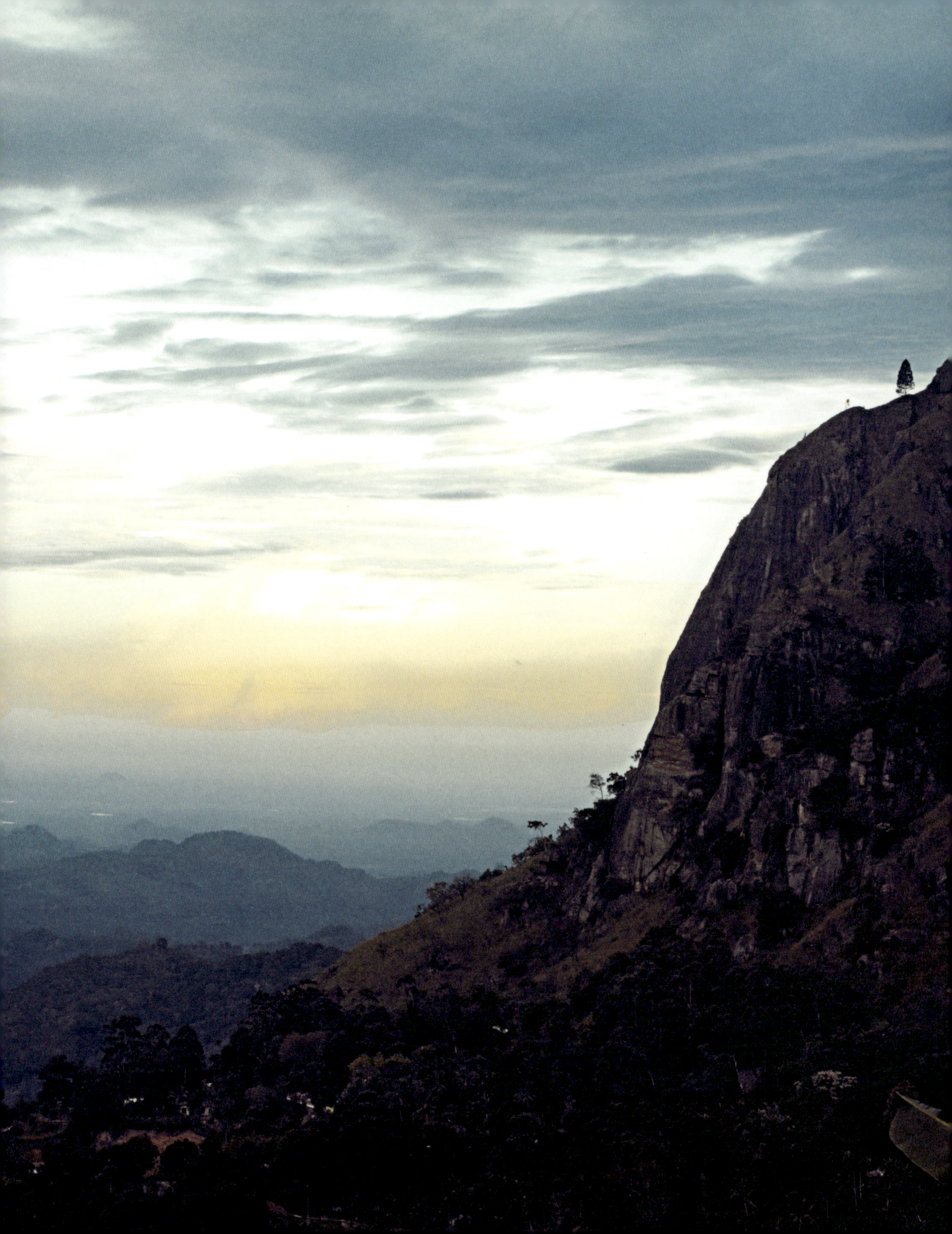

INDEX

Aatthukal Sothi (bone broth) 204
Aatturatchi Kari (Tamil mutton curry) 207
Achcharu (date and shallot pickle) 86
Agati (vegetable hummingbird) 13
   Kathurumurunga Mallung (stir-fried greens) 98
Ala Thel Dala (devilled potatoes) 119
Alu Kesel Baduma (stir-fried plantain) 113
Ambul (banana)
   Banana Fritters 242
Ambul Thial (hot and sour fish curry) 161
Anchovies
   Halmasso Baduma (stir-fried anchovies) 165
   Meen Poriyal (chilli-fried fish steaks, anchovies and onions) 166
   Nethally Karuvaatu Poriyal (chilli-fried anchovies) 169
   Odiyal Kool (spicy seafood soup) 226
Appa (plain hoppers: savoury rice pancakes) 30
Appalam (papadums) 89
Aubergine (eggplant)
   Kathirikai Pirattal (aubergine and tamarind curry) 131
   Sambar (lentil and vegetable side) 81
   Thalana Battu (round aubergine curry) 132
   Wambatu Moju (pickled aubergine and shallots) 82
   Wambatu Pahi (pickled aubergine) 222

Bamboo Pittu (steamed coconut and red rice flour rolls) 38
Bananas
   Banana Fritters 242
   Valakkai Paal Kari (plantain and coconut milk curry) 110
Banana Fritters 242
Banana leaves
   Lamprais (how to parcel) 225
Bandakka Kari (spiced okra curry) 109
Bathala (sweet potato) 102
Bathapu Thuna Paha (roasted Sinhalese curry powder) 17
   Bithara Miris Hodi (omelette curry) 151
   Blachan (spicy shrimp paste balls) 223
   Dhel (breadfruit curry) 147
   Elumas (Sinhalese lamb curry) 201
   Isso Kiri Hodi (prawn and coconut curry) 177
   Kiri Kos (jackfruit curry) 127
   Maalu Mirisata (spicy fish curry) 156
   Sudu Lunu Kari (garlic curry) 103
   Uru Mas (dark pork 'padre' curry) 213
Batter
   Appa (plain hoppers) 30
   Boondi Laddu (sweet chick pea balls) 245
   Mutton Rolls 46
   Thosai (savoury pancakes) 41
   Tuna Cutlets 49
Beans, broad
   Paithangai Pirattal (long bean curry) 139
Beans, green
   Odiyal Kool (spicy seafood soup) 226
Beans, long 13
   Odiyal Kool (spicy seafood soup) 226
   Paithangai Pirattal (long bean curry) 139
Beans, mung, see Mung beans
Beans, runner
   Paithangai Pirattal (long bean curry) 139
Beans, snake 13
   Odiyal Kool (spicy seafood soup) 226
Beef
   Aatturatchi Kari (Tamil mutton curry) 207
   Meat Curry (Lamprais) 220
Bibikkan (coconut cake) 231
Bithara Miris Hodi (omelette curry) 151
Bitter gourd 12
   Karawila Sambol (warm bitter gourd relish) 79
   Pavakkai Kari (bitter gourd curry) 136
Bitter melon, see bitter gourd
Blachan (spicy shrimp paste balls)
   Lamprais 223
Boar, wild
   Kaatu Pandy Ratchi Kari (wild boar curry) 210
Bread
   Kothu Rotti (flatbread stir-fry) 64
   Maalu Pang (fish buns) 53
   Pol Rotti (coconut flatbread) 60
   Veechu Rotti (thin flatbread) 63, 64
Breadfruit 12
   Dhel (breadfruit curry) 147
Breakfast
   Bamboo Pittu 38
   Gotu Kola Kanda (gotu kola congee) 23
   Idli (rice cakes) 27
   Indiappa Kothu (string hopper stir-fry) 37
   Uppuma (roasted semolina) 24

Cabbage
   Indiappa Kothu (string hopper stir-fry) 37
   Kathurumurunga Mallung (stir-fried greens) 98
   Kothu Rotti (flatbread stir-fry) 64
   Uppuma (roasted semolina) 24

Carrot
   Achcharu (date and shallot pickle) 86
   Carrot Sambol (spicy carrot relish) 72
   Indiappa Kothu (string hopper stir-fry) 37
   Kothu Rotti (flatbread stir-fry) 64
   Sambar (lentil and vegetable side) 81
   Uppuma (roasted semolina) 24

Carrot Sambol (spicy carrot relish) 72

Cashew nuts
   Banana Fritters 242
   Bibikkan (coconut cake) 231
   Boondi Laddu (sweet chick pea balls) 245
   Cauliflower Mallung 97
   Chicken Biryani 190
   Kaju Kari (cashew nut curry) 123
   Kesari (semolina pudding) 238
   Love Cake 235
   Payasam (tapioca pudding) 241
   Wattalappan (coconut caramel custard) 232

Cassava (manioc root)
   Odiyal Kool (spicy seafood soup) 226
   Payasam (tapioca pudding) 241

Cauliflower 97
Cauliflower Mallung 97

Chana dal (split chick peas) 12
   Masala Thosai (potato masala pancakes) 45
   Parippu Vadai (deep-fried chana dal) 56
   Rasam Podi (rasam powder spice blend) 214
   Sambar (lentil and vegetable side) 81

Chick peas, see Chana Dal

Chicken
   Chicken Biryani 189, 190
   Frikkadels (breaded Dutch meatballs) 223
   Indiappa Kothu (string hopper stir-fry) 37
   Koli Kari (Tamil chicken curry) 197
   Kothu Rotti (flatbread stir-fry) 64
   Kukul Mas Mirisata (spicy chicken curry) 193
   Meat Curry (Lamprais) 220
   Spicy Baked Chicken 194

Chicken Biryani 189, 190

Chicken livers
   Koli Eeral (stir-fried chicken livers) 198

Coconut 12
   Bamboo Pittu 38
   Bathala (sweet potato) 102
   Bibikkan (coconut cake) 231
   Nandu Kari (crab curry) 174
   Pachai Sambal (chilli coconut relish) 80
   Parippu Mallung (lentil mallung) 94
   Pol Mallung (spiced coconut salad) 94
   Pol Rotti (coconut flatbread) 60
   Pol Sambol (coconut relish) 71
   Pudalangai Varai (stir-fried snake gourd) 116
   Sura Varai (coconut dogfish) 162

Coconut cream 12, see also coconut milk
   Elumas (Sinhalese lamb curry) 201
   Iral Kulambu (prawn and tamarind curry) 181
   Raasavalli Kilangu (purple king yam pudding) 237
   Thalana Battu (round aubergine curry) 132
   Wambatu Pahi (pickled aubergine) 222
   Wattalappan (coconut caramel custard) 232

Coconut milk 13
   Aatthukal Sothi (bone broth) 204
   Aatturatchi Kari (Tamil mutton curry) 207
   Appa (plain hoppers) 30
   Bibikkan (coconut cake) 231
   Bithara Miris Hodi (omelette curry) 151
   Pol Kiri Kanda (coconut milk congee) 20
   Dhel (breadfruit curry) 147
   Gotu Kola Kanda (gotu kola congee) 23
   Isso Kiri Hodi (prawn and coconut curry) 177
   Kaju Kari (cashew nut curry) 123
   Kanavai Kari (squid curry) 173
   Kathirikai Pirattal
     (aubergine and tamarind curry) 131
   Kiri Hodi (coconut milk broth) 144
   Kiri Kos (jackfruit curry) 127
   Kiribath (coconut milk rice) 68
   Koli Kari (Tamil chicken curry) 197
   Kukul Mas Mirisata (spicy chicken curry) 193
   Maalu Aba Hodi (fish in a mustard sauce) 160
   Maalu Kirata (coconut fish curry) 159
   Maalu Mirisata (spicy fish curry) 156
   Malu Miris (stuffed bell peppers) 124
   Meat Curry (Lamprais) 220
   Meen Kulambu (tamarind fish curry) 155
   Murunga Hodi (drumstick tree curry) 143
   Muttai Kulambu (egg curry) 148
   Nandu Kari (crab curry) 174
   Paithangai Pirattal (long bean curry) 139

   Pathola Maluwa (snake gourd curry) 120
   Pavakkai Kari (bitter gourd curry) 136
   Payasam (tapioca pudding) 241
   Pol Kiri Kanda (coconut milk congee) 20
   Poosanikai Kari (pumpkin curry) 105
   Seeni Sambol (sweet and sour onion relish) 76
   Sudu Lunu Kari (garlic curry) 103
   Thalana Battu (round aubergine curry) 132
   Valakkai Paal Kari (plantain and coconut
     milk curry) 110
   Vendaya Kulambu (fenugreek sauce) 110
   Vendikai Paal Kari
     (okra and coconut milk curry) 106
   Wattakka Kalu Pol (pumpkin and
     coconut milk curry) 100

Coconut oil 14

Cod
   Maalu Kirata (coconut fish curry) 159

Coriander seeds
   Bathapu Thuna Paha (roasted Sinhalese
     curry powder) 17
   Thool (roasted Tamil curry powder) 16
   Thuna Paha (Sinhalese curry powder) 17

Crab
   Nandu Kari (crab curry) 174
   Odiyal Kool (spicy seafood soup) 226

Croquettes
   Tuna Cutlets 49

Curry leaves 13

Curry/spice mixes
   Bathapu Thuna Paha (roasted Sinhalese
     curry powder) 17
   Biryani curry powder 190
   Rasam Podi (rasam powder spice blend) 214
   Sambar Podi (spice blend) 81
   Thool (roasted Tamil curry powder) 16
   Thuna Paha (Sinhalese curry powder) 17

Cuttlefish
   Kanavai Kari (squid curry) 173
   Odiyal Kool (spicy seafood soup) 226

Dal, see Mung dal; Toor dal; Urid dal

Dates
   Achcharu (date and shallot pickle) 86
   Bibikkan (coconut cake) 231

Dhel (breadfruit) 12
   Dhel (breadfruit curry) 147

Dogfish
  Sura Varai (coconut dogfish) 162
Drinks
  Morr (spiced yogurt drink) 216
  Rasam (spiced drink) 214
Drumsticks (murunga) 13
  Murunga Hodi (drumstick tree curry) 143
  Sambar (lentil and vegetable side) 81

Eggplant, see Aubergine
Eggs
  Bithara Miris Hodi (omelette curry) 151
  Egg Hoppers (rice pancakes) 31
  Fried Boiled Egg (Lamprais) 225
  Indiappa Kothu (string hopper stir-fry) 37
  Kothu Rotti (flatbread stir-fry) 64
  Muttai Kulambu (egg curry) 148
Elumas (Sinhalese lamb curry) 201

Fenugreek seeds
  Vendaya Kulambu (fenugreek sauce) 110
Fish
  Ambul Thial (hot and sour fish curry) 161
  Blachan (spicy shrimp paste balls) 223
  Fish Patties 50
  Halmasso Baduma
    (stir-fried anchovies) 165
  Isso Kiri Hodi
    (prawn and coconut curry) 177
  Isso Baduma (devilled prawns) 178
  Iral Kulambu
    (prawn and tamarind curry) 181
  Kanavai Kari (squid curry) 173
  Maalu Aba Hodi
    (fish in a mustard sauce) 160
  Maalu Kirata (coconut fish curry) 159
  Maalu Mirisata (spicy fish curry) 156
  Maalu Moju (pickled fish) 184
  Maalu Pang (fish buns) 53
  Meen Kulambu (tamarind fish curry) 155
  Meen Poriyal (chilli-fried fish steaks,
    anchovies and onions) 166
  Nandu Kari (crab curry) 174
  Nethally Karuvaatu Poriyal
    (chilli-fried anchovies) 169
  Odiyal Kool (spicy seafood soup) 226

  Sura Varai (coconut dogfish) 162
  Tuna Cutlets 49
Fish Patties 50
Flatbread
  Kothu Rotti (flatbread stir-fry) 64
  Pol Rotti (coconut flatbread) 60
  Veechu Rotti (thin flatbread) 63
Flour, odiyal 14
  Odiyal Kool (spicy seafood soup) 226
Flour, palmyra 14
  Odiyal Kool (spicy seafood soup) 226
Flour, udad 14
  Appalam (papadums) 89
Flour, urid 14
  Appalam (papadums) 89
Fried Plantain
  Lamprais 223
Frikkadels (breaded Dutch meatballs)
  Lamprais 223

Goat
  Elumas (Sinhalese lamb curry) 201
Goraka (Malabar tamarind) 13
  Kiri Hodi (coconut milk broth) 144
  Maalu Mirisata (spicy fish curry) 156
  Maalu Kirata (coconut fish curry) 159
  Ambul Thial (hot and sour fish curry) 161
Gotu kola (pennywort) 13
Gotu Kola Kanda (gotu kola congee) 23
Gotu Kola Sambol (green herb salad) 75
Gram flour 14
  Boondi Laddu (sweet chick pea balls) 245
Gram, black 13, 14
  Appalam (papadums) 89
  Idli (rice cakes) 27
  Sambar Podi (spice blend) 81
  Thosai (savoury pancakes) 41
  Ulundu Vadai (black gram doughnuts) 55
Gram, green 13, 14
Greens
  Kathurumurunga Mallung (stir-fried greens) 98
Grouper fish
  Odiyal Kool (spicy seafood soup) 226

Haddock
  Maalu Pang (fish buns) 53

Halibut
  Maalu Kirata (coconut fish curry) 159
  Meen Kulambu (tamarind fish curry) 155
Halmasso Baduma (stir-fried anchovies) 165
Hoppers (rice pancakes) 30
  Egg hoppers 31
  Jaggery hoppers 31
  Milk hoppers 31
  String hoppers: Indiappa 34, 37

Idli (rice cakes) 27
Indiappa (string hoppers) 34
Indiappa Kothu (string hopper stir-fry) 37
Iral Kulambu (prawn and tamarind curry) 181
Isso Baduma (devilled prawns) 178
Isso Kiri Hodi (prawn and coconut curry) 177

Jack fish
  Meen Kulambu (tamarind fish curry) 155
  Meen Poriyal (chilli-fried fish steaks,
    anchovies and onions) 166
Jackfruit 13
  Kiri Kos (jackfruit curry) 127
Jaggery 13
  Bibikkan (coconut cake) 231
  Jaggery hoppers (rice pancakes) 31
  Wattalappan (coconut caramel custard) 232

Kaatu Pandy Ratchi Kari (wild boar curry) 210
Kaju Kari (cashew nut curry) 123
Kale
  Kale Mallung 97
  Kathurumurunga Mallung (stir-fried greens) 98
Kale Mallung 97
Kanavai Kari (squid curry) 173
Karawila 12, see also Bitter gourd
Karawila Sambol (warm bitter gourd relish) 79
Kathirikai Pirattal
  (aubergine and tamarind curry) 131
Kathurumurunga
  (agati, vegetable hummingbird) 13
Kathurumurunga Mallung (stir-fried greens) 98
Katta Sambol (hot and sour fish relish) 72
Kesari (semolina pudding) 238

Kingfish
    Ambul Thial (hot and sour fish curry) 161
    Maalu Aba Hodi (fish in a mustard sauce) 160
    Maalu Kirata (coconut fish curry) 159
    Maalu Mirisata (spicy fish curry) 156
    Maalu Moju (pickled fish) 184
Kiri Hodi (coconut milk broth) 144
Kiri Kos (jackfruit curry) 127
Kiribath (coconut milk rice) 68
Kithul jaggery 13
    Bibikkan (coconut cake) 231
    Wattalappan (coconut caramel custard) 232
Koli Eeral (stir-fried chicken livers) 198
Koli Kari (Tamil chicken curry) 197
Kothu Rotti (flatbread stir-fry) 64
Kukul Mas Mirisata (spicy chicken curry) 193

Lamb
    Aatthukal Sothi (bone broth) 204
    Aatturatchi Kari (Tamil mutton curry) 207
    Elumas (Sinhalese lamb curry) 201
    Mutton Rolls 46
Lamb's liver
    Koli Eeral (stir-fried chicken livers) 198
Lamprais 219-225
    Blachan (spicy shrimp paste balls) 223
    Fried Boiled Egg 225
    Fried Plantain 223
    Frikkadels (breaded Dutch meatballs) 223
    Meat Curry 220
    Rice 225
    Wambatu Pahi (pickled aubergine) 222
Leeks
    Indiappa Kothu (string hopper stir-fry) 37
    Kothu Rotti (flatbread stir-fry) 64
    Uppuma (roasted semolina) 24
Lemons
    Pulli Chatham (lemon rice) 71
Lentils, see mung dal; urid dal
Lentils, red
    Parippu Mallung (lentil mallung) 94
    Sambar (lentil and vegetable side) 81
Lime
    Lunu Dehi Sambola
        (pickled lime with coconut milk) 80
    Oorukai (lime pickle) 85

Liver
    Koli Eeral (stir-fried chicken livers) 198
Love Cake 235
Lunu Dehi Sambola
    (pickled lime with coconut milk) 80
Lunu Sambol (onion relish) 75
Maalu Aba Hodi (fish in a mustard sauce) 160
Maalu Kirata (coconut fish curry) 159
Maalu Mirisata (spicy fish curry) 156
Maalu Moju (pickled fish) 184
Maalu Pang (fish buns) 53
Mackerel, Atlantic
    Ambul Thial (hot and sour fish curry) 161
    Maalu Aba Hodi (fish in a mustard sauce) 160
    Maalu Kirata (coconut fish curry) 159
    Maalu Mirisata (spicy fish curry) 156
    Meen Kulambu (tamarind fish curry) 155
    Meen Poriyal (chilli-fried fish steaks,
        anchovies and onions) 166
Malabar tamarind (goraka) 13
    Kiri Hodi (coconut milk broth) 144
    Maalu Mirisata (spicy fish curry) 156
    Maalu Kirata (coconut fish curry) 159
    Ambul Thial (hot and sour fish curry) 161
Maldive fish (smoked dried tuna) 13
Mallung 94-8
Malu Miris (stuffed bell peppers) 124
Manioc root (cassava)
    Odiyal Kool (spicy seafood soup) 226
    Payasam (tapioca pudding) 241
    Masala Thosai (potato masala pancakes) 45
Meat, see also Beef; Chicken; Goat; Lamb;
Mutton; Pork
    Aatthukal Sothi (bone broth) 204
    Meat Curry: Lamprais 220
Meat Curry
    Lamprais 220
Meen Kulambu (tamarind fish curry) 155
Meen Poriyal (chilli-fried fish steaks,
    anchovies and onions) 166
Morr (spiced yogurt drink) 216
Morr Milagai (curd chillies) 90
Mung beans, black 14, see also mung dal
Mung dal 13
    Payaru Keerai (dal and spinach curry) 135
    Pudalangai Varai (stir-fried snake gourd) 116
Murunga (drumsticks) 14
    Murunga Hodi (drumstick tree curry) 143

Muttai Kulambu (egg curry) 148
Mutton
    Aatthukal Sothi (bone broth) 204
    Aatturatchi Kari (Tamil mutton curry) 207
    Elumas (Sinhalese lamb curry) 201
    Frikkadels (breaded Dutch meatballs) 223
    Indiappa Kothu (string hopper stir-fry) 37
    Kothu Rotti (flatbread stir-fry) 64
    Meat Curry (Lamprais) 220
    Mutton Biryani 190
    Mutton Rolls 46
Mutton Biryani 190
Mutton Rolls 46

Nandu Kari (crab curry) 174
Nethally Karuvaatu Poriyal
    (chilli-fried anchovies) 169
Noodles 34

Odiyal Kool (spicy seafood soup) 226
Oil, coconut 14
Okra
    Bandakka Kari (spiced okra curry) 109
    Vendikai Paal Kari (okra and coconut
        milk curry) 106
Omelette
    Muttai Kulambu (egg curry) 148,
    Bithara Miris Hodi (omelette curry) 151
Onion
    chilli-fried fish steaks, anchovies and onions
        166
    Lunu Sambol (onion relish) 75
    Seeni Sambol (sweet and sour onion relish)
        76
Oorukai (lime pickle) 85

Pachai Sambal (chilli coconut relish) 80
Paithangai Pirattal (long bean curry) 139
Palmyra flour 14
    Odiyal Kool (spicy seafood soup) 226
Pancakes, see also Hoppers
    Thosai (savoury pancakes) 41
    Masala Thosai (potato masala pancakes) 45
Pandan leaf (rampe) 14
Papadum (Appalam) 89

Parippu Mallung (lentil mallung) 94
Parippu Vadai (deep-fried chana dal) 56
Pathola Maluwa (snake gourd curry) 120
Pavakkai 12, see also Bitter gourd
Pavakkai Kari (bitter gourd curry) 136
Payaru Keerai (dal and spinach curry) 135
Payasam (tapioca pudding) 241
Pennywort 13, see also gotu kola
Peppers, red
   Isso Baduma (devilled prawns) 178
Peppers, green (bell)
   Isso Baduma (devilled prawns) 178
   Malu Miris (stuffed bell peppers) 124
Pickle
   Achcharu (date and shallot pickle) 86
   Lunu Dehi Sambola (pickled lime with coconut milk) 80
   Maalu Moju (pickled fish) 184
   Oorukai (lime pickle) 85
   Wambatu Moju (pickled aubergine and shallots) 82
   Wambatu Pahi (pickled aubergine) 222
Pigeon peas (toor dal)
   Rasam Podi (rasam powder spice blend) 214
Pineapple Fluff (pudding) 231
Plantain 14
   Alu Kesel Baduma (stir-fried plantain) 113
   Fried Plantain 223
   Valakkai Paal Kari (plantain and coconut milk curry) 110
Pol Kiri Kanda (coconut milk congee) 20
Pol Mallung (spiced coconut salad) 94
Pol Rotti (coconut flatbread) 60
Pol Sambol (coconut relish) 71
Poosanikai Kari (pumpkin curry) 105
Pork
   Kaatu Pandy Ratchi Kari (wild boar curry) 210
   Meat Curry (Lamprais) 220
   Uru Mas (dark pork 'padre' curry) 213
Potatoes
   Ala Thel Dala (devilled potatoes) 119
   Fish Patties 50
   Malu Miris (stuffed bell peppers) 124
   Maalu Pang (fish buns) 53
   Masala Thosai (potato masala pancakes) 45
   Murunga Hodi (drumstick tree curry) 143
   Mutton Rolls 46
   Tuna Cutlets 49

Prawns 13
   Blachan (spicy shrimp paste balls) 223
   Iral Kulambu (prawn and tamarind curry) 181
   Isso Baduma (devilled prawns) 178
   Isso Kiri Hodi (prawn and coconut curry) 177
   Meat Curry (Lamprais) 220
   Odiyal Kool (spicy seafood soup) 226
Pudalangai Varai (stir-fried snake gourd) 116
Pulli Chatham (lemon rice) 71
Pumpkin
   Poosanikai Kari (pumpkin curry) 105
   Sambar (lentil and vegetable side) 81
   Wattakka Kalu Pol (pumpkin and coconut milk curry) 100

Raasavalli Kilangu (purple king yam pudding) 237
Raisins
   Bibikkan (coconut cake) 231
   Chicken Biryani 190
   Kesari (semolina pudding) 238
   Payasam (tapioca pudding) 241
Rampe leaf (pandan) 14
Rasam (spiced drink) 214
Rasam Podi (rasam powder spice blend) 214
Rasam with Rasam Podi 216
Relishes
   Carrot Sambol (spicy carrot relish) 72
   Karawila Sambol (warm bitter gourd relish) 79
   Katta Sambol (hot and sour fish relish) 72
   Lunu Dehi Sambola (pickled lime with coconut milk) 80
   Lunu Sambol (onion relish) 75
   Pachai Sambal (chilli coconut relish) 80
   Pol Sambol (coconut relish) 71
   Seeni Sambol (sweet and sour onion relish) 76
Rice dishes
   Lamprais 225
   Kiribath (coconut milk rice) 68
   Pol Kiri Kanda (coconut milk congee) 20
   Pulli Chatham (lemon rice) 71
Rice flour 14

Sambar (lentil and vegetable side) 81
Sambar Podi (spice blend) 81

Sambols (relishes)
   Carrot Sambol (spicy carrot relish) 72
   Karawila Sambol (warm bitter gourd relish) 79
   Katta Sambol (hot and sour fish relish) 72
   Lunu Dehi Sambola (pickled lime with coconut milk) 80
   Lunu Sambol (onion relish) 75
   Pachai Sambal (chilli coconut relish) 80
   Pol Sambol (coconut relish) 71
   Seeni Sambol (sweet and sour onion relish) 76
Seeni Sambol (sweet and sour onion relish) 76
Semolina
   Bibikkan (coconut cake) 231
   Kesari (semolina pudding) 238
   Love Cake 235
   Uppuma (roasted semolina) 24
Shallots
   Achcharu (date and shallot pickle) 86
   Wambatu Moju (pickled aubergine and shallots) 82
Shrimps, see also prawns
   Blachan (spicy shrimp paste balls) 223
Snake gourd (pathola, pudalangai) 14
   Pathola Maluwa (snake gourd curry) 120
   Pudalangai Varai (stir-fried snake gourd) 116
Soup
   Odiyal Kool (spicy seafood soup) 226
Spicy Baked Chicken 194
Spinach
   Payaru Keerai (dal and spinach curry) 135
Sprats
   Halmasso Baduma (stir-fried anchovies) 165
   Meen Poriyal (chilli-fried fish steaks, anchovies and onions) 166
Squid
   Kanavai Kari (squid curry) 173
   Odiyal Kool (spicy seafood soup) 226
Sudu Lunu Kari (garlic curry) 103
Sura Varai (coconut dogfish) 162
Sweet dishes
   Banana Fritters 242
   Bibikkan (coconut cake) 231
   Boondi Laddu (sweet chick pea balls) 245
   Kesari (semolina pudding) 238
   Love Cake 235
   Payasam (tapioca pudding) 241
   Pineapple Fluff 231
   Raasavalli Kilangu (purple yam pudding) 237

Wattalappan (coconut caramel custard) 232
Sweet potato
  Bathala (sweet potato) 102

Tamarind 14
  Sambar (lentil and vegetable side) 81
Tamarind water
  Iral Kulambu (prawn and tamarind curry) 181
  Kaatu Pandy Ratchi Kari (wild boar curry) 210
  Kathirikai Pirattal (aubergine and tamarind curry) 131
  Meen Kulambu (tamarind fish curry) 155
  Nandu Kari (crab curry) 174
  Odiyal Kool (spicy seafood soup) 226
  Paithangai Pirattal (long bean curry) 139
  Rasam (spiced drink) 214
  Rasam with Rasam Podi 216
  Uru Mas (dark pork 'padre' curry) 213
  Vendaya Kulambu (fenugreek sauce) 110
  Wambatu Pahi (pickled aubergine) 222
Tapioca
  Odiyal Kool (spicy seafood soup) 226
  Payasam (tapioca pudding) 241
Thalana Battu (round aubergine curry) 132
Thool (roasted Tamil curry powder) 16
  Aatturatchi Kari (Tamil mutton curry) 207
  Iral Kulambu (prawn and tamarind curry) 181
  Kaatu Pandy Ratchi Kari (wild boar curry) 210
  Kanavai Kari (squid curry) 173
  Koli Kari (Tamil chicken curry) 197
  Meen Kulambu (tamarind fish curry) 155
  Muttai Kulambu (egg curry) 148
  Nandu Kari (crab curry) 174
Thosai (savoury pancakes) 41
Thuna Paha (Sinhalese curry powder) 17
  Kukul Mas Mirisata (spicy chicken curry) 193
Toor dal (pigeon peas)
  Rasam Podi (rasam powder spice blend) 214
Trevally
  Meen Kulambu (tamarind fish curry) 155
  Meen Poriyal (chilli-fried fish steaks, anchovies and onions) 166
Tuna
  Ambul Thial (hot and sour fish curry) 161
  Fish Patties 50
  Maalu Aba Hodi (fish in a mustard sauce) 160
  Maalu Kirata (coconut fish curry) 159

Maalu Mirisata (spicy fish curry) 156
Maalu Moju (pickled fish) 184
Maalu Pang (fish buns) 53
Meen Kulambu (tamarind fish curry) 155
Meen Poriyal (chilli-fried fish steaks, anchovies and onions) 166
Sura Varai (coconut dogfish) 162
Tuna Cutlets 49
Ulundu (urid dal) 14, see also Urid dal
Ulundu Vadai (black gram doughnuts) 55
Uppuma (roasted semolina) 24
Urid dal (ulundu) 14
  Idli (rice cakes) 27
  Sambar (lentil and vegetable side) 81
  Thosai (savoury pancakes) 41
  Ulundu Vadai (black gram doughnuts) 55
Uru Mas (dark pork 'padre' curry) 213

Valakkai Paal Kari (plantain and coconut milk curry) 110
Veechu Rotti (thin flatbread) 63
Vegetable hummingbird (agati) 13
  Mallung (stir-fried greens) 98
Vegetable dishes, see also vegetable sides
  Ala Thel Dala (devilled potatoes) 119
  Alu Kesel Baduma (stir-fried plantain) 113
  Bandakka Kari (spiced okra curry) 109
  Dhel (breadfruit curry) 147
  Kaju Kari (cashew nut curry) 123
  Kathirikai Pirattal (aubergine and tamarind curry) 131
  Kiri Hodi (coconut milk broth) 144
  Kiri Kos (jackfruit curry) 127
  Malu Miris (stuffed bell peppers) 124
  Murunga Hodi (drumstick tree curry) 143
  Paithangai Pirattal (long bean curry) 139
  Pathola Maluwa (snake gourd curry) 120
  Pavakkai Kari (bitter gourd curry) 136
  Payaru Keerai (dal and spinach curry) 135
  Poosanikai Kari (pumpkin curry) 105
  Pudalangai Varai (stir-fried snake gourd) 116
  Sudu Lunu Kari (garlic curry) 103
  Thalana Battu (round aubergine curry) 132
  Valakkai Paal Kari (plantain and coconut milk curry) 110
  Vendaya Kulambu (fenugreek sauce) 110

Vendikai Paal Kari (okra and coconut milk curry) 106
Wambatu Pahi (pickled aubergine): Lamprais 222
Wattakka Kalu Pol (pumpkin and coconut milk curry) 100
Vegetable sides, see also vegetable dishes
  Bathala (sweet potato) 102
  Cauliflower Mallung 97
  Fried Plantain 223
  Kale Mallung 97
  Kathurumurunga Mallung (stir-fried greens) 98
  Morr Milagai (curd chillies) 90
  Pol Mallung (spiced coconut salad) 94
  Parippu Mallung (lentil mallung) 94
  Wambatu Moju (pickled aubergine and shallots) 82
Vendaya Kulambu (fenugreek sauce) 110
Vendikai Paal Kari (okra and coconut milk curry) 106

Wambatu Moju (pickled aubergine and shallots) 82
Wambatu Pahi (pickled aubergine) Lamprais 222
Wattakka Kalu Pol (pumpkin and coconut milk curry) 100
Wattalappan (coconut caramel custard) 232

Yam, purple
  Raasavalli Kilangu (purple king yam pudding) 237
Yogurt
  Morr (spiced yogurt drink) 216

This book is lovingly dedicated to our mothers who guided us in life.

We would like to thank…

Our commissioning editor Zena Alkayat for steering us in the right direction, Kim Lightbody for taking brilliant photographs, Alexander Breeze for his imaginative styling, Glenn Howard for the book design, and Sarah Chatwin and Euan Ferguson for their excellent editing.

We would also like to thank our close friends and family for their support throughout our culinary journey to this point. Our uncles Bala Mama and Dr. Tharmaseelan, old school friends Dr. Mohana Ruban and Dr. Velayuthapillai, and family friends Nial Fernando and Manoj Develamunige. In addition, our sisters Visaka, Vanaja, Girija and our daughters Ramyya and Kosalaa and son-in-law Vino for their unwavering support.

For more about what we do now please visit:
www.coconutkitchens.com

Frances Lincoln Limited
A subsidiary of Quarto Publishing Group UK
74–77 White Lion Street
London N1 9PF

Sri Lanka: The Cookbook
© Frances Lincoln Limited 2017
Text © Prakash K Sivanathan and Niranjala M Ellawala 2017
Photographs © Kim Lightbody 2017
Design: Glenn Howard
Commissioning editor: Zena Alkayat

First Frances Lincoln edition 2017

All rights reserved.
No part of this publication may be reproduced, stored in a retrieval system, or transmitted, in any form, or by any means, electronic, mechanical, photocopying, recording or otherwise without the prior written permission of the publisher or a licence permitting restricted copying. In the United Kingdom such licences are issued by the Copyright Licensing Agency, Barnard's Inn, 86 Fetter Lane, London, EC4A 1EN.

A catalogue record for this book is available from the British Library.

ISBN 978-0-7112-3858-9

Printed and bound in China

1 2 3 4 5 6 7 8 9

FSC® MIX Paper from responsible sources FSC® C008047

Quarto Knows

Quarto is the authority on a wide range of topics.
Quarto educates, entertains and enriches the lives of our readers – enthusiasts and lovers of hands-on living.
www.QuartoKnows.com